# ADULT LEARNING METHODS

# ADULT LEARNING METHODS:

## A Guide
## for Effective Instruction

Edited by
**Michael W. Galbraith**
Temple University

Foreword by
**Malcolm S. Knowles**

ROBERT E. KRIEGER PUBLISHING COMPANY
MALABAR, FLORIDA
1990

Original Edition 1990


Printed and Published by
ROBERT E. KRIEGER PUBLISHING CO., INC.
KRIEGER DRIVE
MALABAR, FLORIDA 32950


Copyright © 1990 by Robert E. Krieger Publishing Co., Inc.

**Library of Congress Cataloging-in-Publication Data**


Adult learning methods: a guide for effective instruction/edited by
    Michael W. Galbraith.
        p. cm.
    Includes index.
    ISBN 0-89464-285-5 (alk.paper)
    1.Adult education—Study and teaching. I. Galbraith, Michael W.
    LC5215.A349 1990
374—dc19
                                                                88-13950
                                                                    CIP




    10   9   8   7   6   5   4   3   2

This book is caringly dedicated
to my graduate students.

# CONTENTS

Foreword ix

Preface xiii

The Authors xvii

## PART ONE

### UNDERSTANDING AND FACILITATING ADULT LEARNING 1

1. Attributes and Skills of an Adult Educator 3
   Michael W. Galbraith

2. Understanding Adult Learners 23
   Huey B. Long

3. Identifying Your Philosophical Orientation 39
   Lorraine M. Zinn

4. Identifying Your Teaching Style 79
   Gary J. Conti

5. Strategies to Enhance Adult Motivation to Learn 97
   Raymond J. Wlodkowski

6. The Art of Questioning 119
   Ray E. Sanders

PART TWO

## METHODS AND TECHNIQUES                          131

7. Learning Contracts                                                    133
   Judith M. O'Donnell and Rosemary S. Caffarella

8. Lecture                                                               161
   Shirley J. Farrah

9. Discussion                                                            187
   Stephen D. Brookfield

10. Mentorship                                                           205
    Laurent A. Parks Daloz

11. Case Study                                                           225
    Victoria J. Marsick

12. Nominal Group Technique                                             247
    Lloyd J. Korhonen

13. Demonstration and Simulation                                        261
    Jerry W. Gilley

14. Forum, Panel, and Symposium                                         283
    Burton R. Sisco

15. Computer-Enriched Instruction                                       303
    Linda H. Lewis

16. Internship                                                          329
    Susan B. Premont

17. Correspondence Study                                                345
    Michael G. Moore

18. Communications Technology in Adult Education                        367
    and Learning
    Barbara M. Florini

# PART THREE

## A FUTURE PERSPECTIVE 391

19. Perspectives on the Future 393
    Susan Imel

Index 409

# FOREWORD

The past half century has been an era of prolific—indeed, one might say explosive—developments in the methodology of adult education. One strong impetus for this phenomenon occurring at this time was the publication of Lindeman's *The Meaning of Adult Education* in 1926, Thorndike's *Adult Learning* in 1928 and *Adult Interests* in 1935, Bryson's *Adult Education* in 1936, and Sorenson's *Adult Abilities* in 1938. These early contributions to the literature of our field began raising the consciousness of practitioners to the fact that adults were different from children and youth as learners in many respects and that therefore different methods from those of tradicional pedagogy would be likely to be more effective with them. A second impetus, largely an outgrowth of the first, was a shift in focus by adult educators away from methods of teaching to methods of facilitating learning. These two "paradigm shifts" released a growing surge of energy for experimentation and innovation in adult education methodology.

It was not uncommon for new methods and techniques to be considered as "fads" when they were introduced—and therefore viewed with some skepticism by some people. For example, when I entered the field in 1935 the hot new method was group discussion, stimulated largely by the enthusiastic writings of Eduard Lindeman and Alfred Sheffield and reinforced subsequently by such "classics" of the time as Frank Walser's *Art of Conference* (1933), Leroy Bowman's *How to Lead Discussion* (1934), Grace Coyle's *Studies in Group Behavior* (1937), S.R. Slavson's *Creative Group Education* (1937), and Thomas Fansler's *Creative Power Through Discussion* (1950). Group discussion was the "in" technique; it was touted as the best way to help people learn almost anything.

During the early 1940s popular enthusiasm shifted to a new fad—audio-visual aids and presentations. What had happened was that the need for rapid conversion of civilians into soldiers, and of rural and female populations into war-industry workers, had forced the military services and industry to invent more speedy training methods. I jumped aboard this bandwagon, as I had that of group discussion, and read avidly (Edgar Dale's *Audio-Visual Methods in Teaching* (1946) was my favorite), took courses, and attended workshops to become an expert on the use of audio-visual aids. For a while I wouldn't think of making a presentation without overhead transparencies, filmstrips or slides, and the like. But I began running into trouble. Learners were getting overloaded with information and much of what they got they didn't know how to apply. So I started experimenting with a combination of audio-visual aids and group discussion and found that things went much better.

In the early 1950s three new fads made their appearance and gained momentum that carried them into the next decade: human relations training, programmed instruction, and community development. I identified primarily with the human relations training fad, attended several summer sessions at the National Training Laboratories in Bethel, Maine, and introducing "T-groups" into my programs in the Chicago YMCA and, in 1960, at Boston University. My wife and I wrote a little book, *Introduction to Group Dynamics*, in 1959 that became a best seller of sorts. I didn't directly join the programmed instruction and community development fads, but became well enough informed about them to adapt some valuable elements from them into my practice.

In the 1960s there was a veritable explosion of fads; business games and other simulation exercises, change theory and organizational development, transactional analysis, management by objectives, behavioral objectives, systems theory, values clarification, and others I probably don't know about. The explosion of fads continued in the 1970s with computer-assisted instruction, competency-based education, multimedia learning modules, behavior modification, behavior modeling, individualized instruction, self-directed learning, learner-controlled instruction, contract learning, dial-access resource systems, educational brokering, networking, and others. I chose a few fads to get into deeply: during the sixties it was change theory, organizational development, and systems theory, and during the seventies it was competency-based education, self-directed learning, and contract learning. But I tried to find out all I could about the others and borrow from them what made sense.

During the 1980s the trend was not so much in the invention of new fads as in the refinement, extension, and combination of existing methods—interactive television and computer-based learning, videodiscs, questioning techniques, motivational techniques, mentorship, nominal group techniques, and distance-learning strategies—and in the laying of theoretical foundations for selecting the most effective methods and techniques for accomplishing particular purposes.

This book represents a landmark in this latter effort. It is not only a how-to-do-it manual, but a what-to-do-and-why guide book. It presents a state-of-the-art picture of adult education methodology as it has evolved to date, and in the last chapter, provides hopes and challenges for a continuation of this dynamic process into the next century. It is an important contribution to our literature.

MALCOLM S. KNOWLES

# Preface

Helping adults learn is an exciting, challenging, exhilarating, and rewarding process. Each year millions of adult learners engage in educational programs provided by adult, continuing, and vocational education agencies and institutions, as well as by business and industry who provide human resource development opportunities for them through various training formats. In most cases the instructors in these programs are content experts who have little formal preparation in the process of instructing adult learners.

*Adult Learning Methods* provides an overview of the various aspects of understanding and facilitating adult learning and the numerous methods and techniques that can be utilized to enhance the instructional and learning process in a plethora of educational settings. It aims at strengthening and broadening the knowledge base and skills of those who help adults learn. This book is designed for the practitioner and is written from a practical "how-to" perspective. Each chapter focuses on a particular aspect of understanding and facilitating adult learning or a specific methodology that can be used in the instructional and learning process. Because of the book's organizational structure, you can select chapters according to your specific needs and interests. In addition, at the end of each chapter is a list of references for you to investigate if you wish to pursue any of the topics in greater detail.

Any educational activity should promote and encourage development; that is, it should provide for growth and evolution of change. The premise of this book is that by acquiring a greater understanding of the process of helping adults learn and the methodologies that can enhance this process, instructors and their adult learners will share in a positive, meaningful, and developing educational experience.

Adult Learning Methods is divided into three parts. Part One, "Understanding and Facilitating Adult Learning," contains six chapters. Chapter 1 describes the attributes and skills essential for the adult educator to possess if an effective teaching and learning transaction is to occur. A framework for understanding adult learners is presented in Chapter 2. Every instructor has a philosophical orientation and a preferred teaching style, although at times it is difficult to identify, when working with adult learners. Chapter 3 discusses the topic and the importance of having an educational philosophy and provides a self-administering and self-scoring instrument that will help you identify your philosophical orientation to instruction. Being aware of your teaching style is also essential, therefore in Chapter 4 an informative discussion on the topic is provided along with a self-administering and self-scoring instrument that will assist you in identifying your teaching style and what it means in terms of working with adult learners. Motivation is also an important element in a successful teaching and learning transaction. In Chapter 5 the author presents sixteen strategies that can be used to enhance adult learning motivation. Chapter 6 focuses on the art of questioning and provides practical and concise ways of how it can be used more effectively, regardless of the method that is employed.

Part Two, "Methods and Techniques," contains twelve chapters which describe in detail an array of methods and techniques that can be used with adult learners. A method can be defined as a way of organizing an educational activity with the purpose of promoting learning for all involved personnel. Following the "how-to" orientation, most of the method chapters are guided by a set of identical practical questions such as:

- How do you define the method?

- What audience is most appropriate for the specific method and why?

- What are the advantages and limitations of the method?

- What are the duties and responsibilities of the personnel involved when using the method?

- What are the lines of communication between the instructor and learner and how does it look pictorially?

- What does the layout of the room and facilities look like?

- How do you evaluate the method to determine if it was used effectively?

Several of the method chapters could not easily be guided by this framework of questions because of the nature of the specific method discussed.

No evidence has been generated that suggests that any one method is effective in achieving the educational goals of all learners. Each method described must be judged on its own merit according to purpose, audience, desired outcomes and proficiencies, and so forth. Some methods may seem to be structured around a more rigid and directive learning transactional process, while others may appear more interactional and collaborative in nature. The methods presented are not sequenced in any particular order of importance or effectiveness. You, as an instructor of adult learners, will recognize that at times several types of methods will be incorporated into one educational activity to bring about the most effective and meaningful learning experience.

Part Three, "A Future Perspective," consists of one chapter that describes some of the social, demographic, economic, and technological forces shaping the future of adult education. Critical issues for the future, which emerge from this context, are discussed along with a forecast of what methods will be used to deliver adult education. The author concludes the chapter by presenting some possible scenarios for adult education in the future.

*Adult Learning Methods* provides an overview of the major aspects of understanding and facilitating adult learning and an array of methodologies that can be employed to enhance in the process of helping adults learn. Whether you use this book as a textbook or as a resource book where you pick and choose specific chapters to read according to your immediate needs and interests, it is hoped that your perspective about and skills in working with adult learners will be enriched and strengthened. It is also hoped that the learners who are engaged in the various educational activities will experience an increase in satisfaction and achievement as a result of your initiative to improve the instructional and learning process.

One could not complete a project such as this without the help of so many to push the boulders from the pathway. To Mary Roberts, my editor at Krieger Publishing, who believed in the project and served as a supporting guide throughout it, I am deeply thankful. To my friends and colleagues who agreed to write chapters goes my sincere gratitude. It has been a pleasure working with each of you. I hope you found the journey worthwhile.

Many thanks to Pat Wehmeyer for the help provided at the various stages of this project. Your unselfish way and welcoming smile makes work such a delight. For the critical questioning and continuing support and encouragement from my friend and colleague Irving Epstein, many thanks too. I owe a special debt of gratitude to Bonnie Zelenak, a special kind of adult educator, who willingly listens to the stories of my journey.

A loving thank you to my Mom (who still wonders what I do) for the encouragement to journey geographically and intellectually. To T.J. Galbraith, thank you for holding the lantern high during the thunderstorms and dark times. You are a very special lady. And finally to Bo, my Old English Sheepdog and forever friend, for continuously reminding me over these many years together that I am still needed.

# The Authors

Stephen D. Brookfield, Professor of Adult Education, Department of Higher and Adult Education, Teachers College, Columbia University.

Rosemary S. Caffarella, Associate Professor, Virginia Commonwealth University.

Gary J. Conti, Kellogg Researcher and Associate Professor of Adult Education, Center for Adult Education Research, Montana State University.

Laurent A. Parks Daloz, Associate Professor, Adult Degree Option Program, Lesley College, Cambridge, Massachusetts.

Shirley J. Farrah, Director, Continuing Education Program, School of Nursing, University of Missouri-Columbia.

Barbara M. Florini, Associate Professor of Adult Education, School of Education, Syracuse University.

Michael W. Galbraith, Associate Professor of Adult Education and Coordinator of the Adult Education Program, Temple University.

Jerry W. Gilley, Director of Internal Professional Development, Mercer, Meidinger and Hansen, Deerfield, Illinois.

Susan Imel, Director, ERIC Clearinghouse on Adult, Career, and Vocational Education, The Ohio State University.

Lloyd J. Korhonen, Associate Professor of Adult Education, The University of Oklahoma.

Linda H. Lewis, Associate Professor of Adult and Human Resources Education, Department of Educational Leadership, University of Connecticut.

Huey B. Long, Professor and Director, Oklahoma Research Center for Continuing Professional and Higher Education, The University of Oklahoma.

Victoria J. Marsick, Assistant Professor of Adult and Continuing Education, Teachers College, Columbia University.

Michael G. Moore, Associate Professor of Adult Education, The Pennsylvania State University.

Judith M. O'Donnell, Vice President, O'Donnell and Associates, Inc., Midlothian, Virginia.

Susan B. Premont, Senior Education Specialist, Individual Training Branch, U.S. Army Engineer School, Fort Leonard Wood, Missouri.

Ray E. Sanders, Assistant Professor of Occupational and Adult Education, Oklahoma State University.

Burton R. Sisco, Assistant Professor of Adult Education, University of Wyoming.

Raymond J. Wlodkowski, Core Faculty, Graduate Programs in Education, Antioch University, Seattle, Washington.

Lorraine M. Zinn, Professor, Curtin University, Perth, Western Australia; formerly Director of Faculty and Curriculum, Regis College, Denver, Colorado.

# Part One

# Understanding and Facilitating Adult Learning

# CHAPTER 1

## Attributes And Skills Of An Adult Educator

MICHAEL W. GALBRAITH

A countless number of individuals help adults learn in a wide variety of formal and informal educational settings such as universities, community colleges, vocational/technical institutes, businesses and industries, correctional institutions, churches, museums, voluntary organizations, community action agencies, armed forces, and a plethora of other settings too numerous to list. Those helping adults learn carry such labels as facilitator, mentor, teacher, instructor, trainer, or adult educator. Simple categorization of the teaching and learning transaction is difficult because of the complex and multifaceted orientation of adult learners and the variety of settings in which the interaction occurs. It is this type of educational environment that makes helping adults learn a challenging, rewarding, and creative activity. Knox (1986) and Daloz (1986) suggest that picking a metaphor to describe your instructional role will assist you in understanding that the process of helping adults learn is continuously evolving and changing. They have metaphorically described the process of helping adults learn as a transformational journey, a spiral, or a mobius strip. Daloz metaphorically uses a journey to describe this process because it allows "both teachers and students to see their lives in motion: it provides an accessible and effective way of viewing educational change" (p.243). Helping adults learn is a transactional process in which the adult educator interacts with learners, content, other people, and material to plan and implement an educational program. The adult educator is in a sense a guide to learners who are involved in an educational journey.

3

A successful trip for the adult educator and for the learner depends on well-planned and carefully implemented educational programs. Knox (1986, p.xi) suggests however that "most instructors in adult education programs are expert in the content they teach, but they usually have little preparation in the process of helping adults learn."

This chapter will examine some of the attributes and skills needed by an adult educator to effectively help adults learn. The first part of the chapter will review some of the exemplary characteristics and teaching principles in relationship to being an adult educator. Personality characteristics and interpersonal skills will be examined in light of how they influence the teaching and learning interaction. A major portion of the chapter will be devoted to program planning skills that the adult educator should possess. Finally, how to provide challenging teaching and learning interactions and the skills necessary to make this occur will be examined.

## CHARACTERISTICS OF AN ADULT EDUCATOR

What characteristics should an adult educator possess that will enhance the teaching and learning interaction? Being technically proficient in the content area in which the instruction is being directed is paramount, as are the abilities to plan and administer educational programs. Being technically proficient is not enough, however; the adult educator must also possess personality characteristics and interpersonal skills that engender an image of caring, trust, and encouragement. Merge these desired characteristics together and an effective and meaningful educational experience can result, both for the adult educator and the learner.

In reviewing the literature, a list of general characteristics and exemplary principles for instruction and practice that an adult educator should have emerges. Knox (1980) suggests that an adult educator should possess three specific areas of knowledge: knowledge of content, knowledge of learners, and knowledge of methods. The personality characteristics of the adult educator should suggest a sense of self-confidence, informality, enthusiasm, responsiveness, and creativity. Apps (1981) found that the best adult educators were those that showed an interest in students, possessed a good personality, had an interest in the subject matter, had the ability to make the subject interesting, and were objective in presenting subject matter and in dealing with students. General characteristics of exemplary instructors included technical and interpersonal skills and attributes such as being more concerned about learners than about things and events, knew the subject matter, related theory to practice, were confident as instructors, were open to a variety of teaching approaches, showed themselves as human beings, encouraged learning outcomes that went beyond course objectives, and created a positive learning atmosphere. Draves (1984) echoes similar agreement by stating that an instructor of adults must have understanding, flexibility, patience, humor, practicality, creativity, and preparation. Acquisition and acceptance of these diverse and varied characteristics suggest that an effective adult educator plays many roles within the teaching and learning interaction including role model, counselor, content resource person, learning guide, program developer, and institutional representative (Apps, 1981; Brookfield, 1986; Daloz, 1986).

Principles of effective practice and their implementation should also characterize the adult educator. Knowles and Associates (1984) identified seven components of andragogical practice (the art and science of helping adults learn) that suggest the type of skills and abilities a good adult educator or facilitator should possess in the effort of helping adults learn. He proposes that a facilitator must:

* establish a physical and psychological climate conducive to learning;

* involve learners in mutual planning of methods and curricular directions;

* involve participants in diagnosing their own learning needs;

* encourage learners to formulate their own learning objectives;

* encourage learners to identify resources and to devise strategies for using such resources to accomplish their objectives;

* help learners to carry out their learning plans;

* involve learners in evaluating their learning.

The andragogical approach indicates that an adult educator must possess both technical and interpersonal skills to be an effective facilitator of learning. Central to the success of this approach are the personality characteristics and interpersonal and human relations skills of the adult educator in relationship to the adult learner.

Brookfield (1986) provides six principles of effective practice that indicate particular beliefs and characteristics associated with the facilitator of adult learning (pp. 9-11):

1. Participation is voluntary; adults engage in learning as a result of their own volition.

2. Effective practice is characterized by a respect among participants for each other's self-worth.

3. Facilitation is collaborative.

4. Praxis is placed at the heart of effective facilitation; "learners and facilitators are involved in a continual process of activity, reflection upon activity, collaborative analysis of activity, new activity, further reflection, and collaborative analysis, and so on" (p.10).

5. Facilitation aims to foster in adults a spirit of critical reflection.

6. The aim of facilitation is the nurturing of self-directed, empowered adults.

Implicit in this framework are general characteristics and guiding principles of an effective instructor. It suggests that adult educators should have an understanding of adult learners; provide a climate conducive to learning; provide a contextual setting for the exploration of new ideas, skills, and resolutions; provide a forum for critical reflection; and have the ability to assist adults in the process of learning "how to change our perspectives, shift our paradigms, and replacing one way of interpreting the world by another" (Brookfield, 1986, p. 19). Implementing these principles requires the adult educator to be technically proficient in content and program planning areas as well as highly competent in interpersonal and human relation skills.

In all of the above characterizations of the adult educator, caring and respect appear as major attributes. Adult educators' abilities to "work well with others in a peer or colleagial fashion is a significant dimension" in the process of constructing a conducive learning environment (Watkins & Croft, 1986, p.15). Daloz (1986, p.xvii) states that the "element of good teaching becomes the provision of care rather than use of teaching skills and transmission of knowledge." Tough (1979) suggests four characteristics of ideal helpers as being warm, loving, caring, and accepting of the learners; having a high regard for learner's self-planning competencies and not wishing to trespass on these; viewing themselves as participating in a dialogue between equals with learners; and being open to change and new experiences and seeking to learn from their helping activities. Brundage and Mackeracher (1980) propose that teachers should be sensitive to learners' self-concepts, past experiences, and be willing to share their experiences as well as being open to learners' suggestions. Recognizing that caring, listening, and passion are powerful elements and having the capacity to provide emotional support when it is needed are hallmarks of a good adult educator. One can envision the interpersonal relationship that exists between the instructor and adult learner as being connected by a gossamer thread that weaves itself throughout the various characteristics of each person involved in the learning experience. The thread is fragile and when poor interpersonal skills are exercised, it snaps apart. Adult educators need to wrap or coat this gossamer thread to strengthen and protect it so a positive teaching and learning relationship is not severed. Developing and maintaining good interpersonal and human relationship skills is therefore vital to the adult educator.

Acquiring technical proficiency in a content area is not enough, nor is just having a friendly personality and a wealth of interpersonal and human relation skills. The literature indicates that an adult educator must play many different roles, must have an understanding of adult learners, must be knowledgeable in the content area, must be technically proficient, must utilize a variety of instructional methods and formats, must understand principles of effective practice, and must possess interpersonal and human relation skills that enhance the teaching and learning transaction.

The adult educator needs to be technically proficient in the planning process of educational programs for adult learners. It is one of the most important tasks, as well as a major responsibility, of the adult educator in the process of helping adults learn. In the next section, the necessary skills will be examined.


## PROGRAM PLANNING SKILLS

Planning an educational program for adult learners is not a series of independent steps or processes, but is an interactive system. In this section, the program planning components of needs assessment, context analysis, objective setting, organizing learning activities, and program evaluation will be examined as well as the skills of the adult educator associated with each. As Knox (1986, p.10) states, "Most people who help adults learn have done so before. They start planning a program with a general idea (distilled from past experience) of how the major parts of the upcoming program are likely to fit together. So the planning process does not begin with a blank slate." Considering the multifaceted nature of adult learners as well as the instructional and organizational related factors, all components of the program planning process should be outlined in a preliminary way and then progressively refined as they begin to fit together.

*Needs Assessment*

A needs assessment should identify the gaps between the learners' current and desired proficiencies as perceived by the learner and others; that is, it should help define the "what is" and "what should be." Why should you be familiar with the needs assessment process? It can help you review your assumptions about the educational needs of potential participants; it can assist you in being responsive to the adult learner through the appropriate selection of topics and materials; it can increase the likelihood that potential participants will participate if program descriptions emphasize the responsiveness to the educational needs identified; and it can encourage adult learners to persist, learn, and apply what they learn if the program focuses on meeting their needs (Knox, 1986). The assessment of needs should be an ongoing process throughout the program planning activity in an effort to ensure that individual and program desired outcomes are congruent.

There are numerous methods for identifying learning needs,

but no consensus on the most appropriate method (Long, 1983). The selected method will generate different types of information depending who is involved in the assessment. If you as the adult educator, your supervisor, or other experts make the assessment, the current proficiency level will be identified and compared against the standards desired by you or others involved. If the learners themselves are the sources of identifying educational needs, the results will most likely reveal information about "their preferences for the topics they want to study and the proficiencies they want to enhance and about the choices they make when given opportunities to participate in educative activities" (Knox, 1986, p.57). The needs identified will help justify decisions made by you, by learners, supervisors, and experts as well (Brackhaus, 1984). Brookfield (1986) suggests that the needs identified by learners and by others can be distinguished as felt needs and prescribed needs. Felt needs are those wants, desires, and wishes of the learner while prescribed needs are "premised upon educators' belief concerning the skills, knowledge, behaviors and values that they feel adults should acquire" (Brookfield, 1986, p. 222). It is inappropriate to plan an educational program for adult learners on a felt needs approach and it is equally unacceptable to plan a program totally on needs prescribed by others. Combining felt needs and prescribed needs is a more rational approach. In this way a mutual collaborative teaching-learning environment can result that ensures greater participation and a desire to persist and achieve in the educational experience. Needs assessment methods used can range from highly informal and intuitive to highly formal and in-depth analysis techniques (Brackhaus, 1984; Cameron, 1988; Grotelueschen, 1980; Knowles, 1980; Knox, 1986; Zemke & Kramlinger, 1982). As an adult educator you can decide to use data-collection procedures such as individual interviews, questionnaires, tests, observation checklists, self-assessment diagnostic instruments, surveys, performance analysis, or marketing analysis techniques to assess the most appropriate educational needs. Each identified procedure has both strengths and weaknesses associated with it. The educational needs identified in terms of importance tend to be judged "in light of expectations of learners, yourself, and representatives of organizations" (Knox, 1986, p.62). If a new program is being developed, an in-depth needs assessment project may be required. A more informal needs assessment approach may be sufficient if you are working with a familiar program and clientele. In any case, conducting needs assessments is a vital component in the process of helping adults learn and educators must develop the skills required in analyzing and using the findings.

## Context Analysis

Another component in the program planning process is context analysis. Context analysis considers the societal trends and issues, the resources, and the mission of the provider organization and how it influences the process of helping adults learn (Knox, 1986). By combining the data of the various influences with information found through the needs assessment process, feasible learning objectives can be agreed upon by you and the learners. Brookfield (1986) and Long (1983) suggest that as adult educators it is imperative that we become more aware of the influences, both societal and organizational, and their impact on the instructional process, curricula, program formats, and evaluative standards.

Context analysis is concerned with the influences on the setting in which the learning occurs as well as where the learners are likely to apply what they learn. As an adult educator, it is important to understand the impact of these influences on the learner and on the instructional process. Adults have perceptions of standards, expectations, and opportunities that are directly related to their purpose for learning. Understanding these perceptions allows the learner and you to contribute to the decisions on "using learning activities to strengthen problem solving, specifying mastery levels, and helping learners use educational strategies that enable them to use or deflect influences that encourage or discourage them to learn and apply" (Knox, 1986, p.67). In short, analysis of current issues, trends, technologies, and so forth can suggest the affects they have on the personal and sociopolitical aspects of the learner's life. The contextual influences also affect you and the decisions that you can make. An understanding of the organizational mission, resources, priorities, trends, and constraints is essential when making decisions and arrangements for an educational program. Analyses of contextual influences related to a specific organizational setting can be found in professional books and journals (Knox, 1980). Recognition of the various contextual influences of the organization can lead to planning and implementation of programs that are more likely to be successful and lead to a more meaningful and rewarding educational experience for the participants and for you.

As an adult educator, you need to know the trends, issues, resources, purposes, and mission of the organization in which you work and be aware of how contextual influences affect adult learners in their participation and learning efforts in your program. With these understandings, appropriate program planning decisions can be made.

## Setting Educational Objectives

Selecting and setting educational objectives should draw heavily from the needs assessment and context analysis information; however, other sources can contribute to the objective setting process. Setting educational objectives is the joint responsibility of you and the learners who will participate, the coordinators and administrators of the program, and other resource and expert persons. It should be an ongoing and interactive process, not only during the program planning stages but throughout the implementation of the educational activity. It is impossible to identify through prespecified objectives all the unplanned and unanticipated learning needs of the adult learner; therefore opportunities to modify the educational objectives must be present as the program unfolds.

A learning objective is the intended or desired outcome and proficiency level that the learner should obtain as a result of participating in the educational experience. Learning objectives may focus on knowledge, skill, or attitude enhancement or a combination of the three to reach the desired outcomes. Knox (1986) suggests that clearly stated specific objectives are based on "understanding the learners, their current proficiencies, and the conditions under which they are expected to demonstrate the extent to which they achieved desired proficiencies" (p.72). It is therefore imperative that you, the adult educator, as well as the learners and other resource and expert persons agree that the learning objectives specified are productive, satisfying, and efficient. By this collaborative approach, adult learners can increase their understanding of and commitment to achieving the objectives, understand the relationship between current and desired proficiencies, reflect on questions that need addressing, and acquire a framework for learning how to learn beyond the present program (Knowles, 1980;

Knox, 1980; Smith, 1982). As an adult educator, you can use the
agreed upon learning objectives to help you in the process of selecting materials, outlining content, deciding on methods of teaching and learning, and preparing evaluations procedures (Knox,
1986).

How do you select high priority educational objectives from
the unmanageably long list that results from the needs assessment
process? Knowles (1980) suggests that each specified learning objective should be "filtered" through the purpose of the organization, the feasibility of what we know about the learners and
available resources, and the interests of the clientele. Normally,
because of limited time and resource allocations as well as other
factors, additional ways to achieve agreement on objectives should
be initiated. Knox (1980, 1986) proposes several useful procedures
including using planning committees composed of participants, resource persons, and program coordinators; having all participants
engage in a nominal group process; obtaining written and oral descriptions of successful practice to highlight intended outcomes;
using an existing group of adults who have specified goals and
develop an educational program with them; providing program
time and emphasis to agreement on learning objectives; and using
reaction forms to ask participants periodically to identify the objectives that are most important and least important to them. The
latter action can serve as a basis for modifying the program and
educational activities.

Learning objectives should not be considered unchanging and
unchallengeable. Brookfield (1986) suggests that:

> the most fundamental flaw with the predetermined objectives ap-
> proach, then, is its tendency to equate one form of adult learning—
> instrumental learning (how to perform technical or psychomotor
> operations more effectively)—with the sum total of adult learning.
> It neglects completely the domain of the most significant personal
> learning—the kind that results from reflection on experiences and
> from trying to make sense of one's life by exploring the meanings
> others have assigned to similar experiences. (p.213)

Adult learners develop differently and as a result reformulate their
goals and needs to correspond to their perceptions of the world.
The unplanned, incidental, and serendipitous learning that takes

place may not produce the specified outcomes suggested by the predetermined goal setting activities. You should not consider such outcomes as invalid or less valid, since it is impossible to prescribe for such a diverse group of learners the exact "range, form, and number of learning outcomes that will result from their participation in our program" (Brookfield, 1986, p.219).

This is not to suggest that the educational program developed should not have specified purposes, goals, or intentions in the form of learning objectives. Setting educational learning objectives should be an important component in the program planning process and acquisition of such skills is essential for the adult educator.

## Organizing Learning Activities

The information and decisions made from the needs assessment, context analysis, and objective setting activities result in the identification of the intended outcomes for the educational program. You, as the adult educator, must now have the skill to select and organize learning activities to meet the intended outcomes. This process must be rational and based on the program objectives, the adult learner characteristics, as well as on your own perspective and experience. Knox (1986, p.79) suggests that educational objectives that "include both the subject matter content to be learned and what participants should be able to do with the content provide a useful basis for selecting learning activities likely to enable learners to achieve those objectives". Selecting appropriate learning activities should depend upon the desired outcomes such as knowledge acquisition, practice, application, and so forth. Knowledge of the current proficiency level and the preferred learning styles of the learners will also aid in the selection of the most appropriate learning activities. You can develop a list of competencies that have been identified for the educational program and ask participants to check on a Likert-type scale the level at which they believe they are presently performing. Knowing something about the preferred way the adult learner wishes to process information is also important. Asking participants how they like to process information and what methods they like to use in that process is one easy and rather quick method for acquiring information (Galbraith, 1987). Analyzing the feedback from the participants can assist in the selection of the most appropriate learning activities whether you are working with learners individually or in large groups or small groups. Your own perspective and past experiences coupled with the understanding of the educational learning objectives and the learners' characteristics will guide you to successful planning.

The teaching and learning methods you select for the learning activities should be based upon the information gained in the above assessments—both formal and informal. A vast array of methods exist (Knox, 1986; Klevins, 1987; Lewis, 1986; Niemi & Gooler, 1987) and each one is influenced by the content that you are teaching, the program and learning objectives, the desired outcomes, the characteristics of the learners, the size of the group, and the availability of time, equipment, facilities, and budget. Part Two of this book will present specific methods that can be utilized in various learning activities; therefore they will not be discussed here. It is important to note, however, that if the methods used in the learning activity are satisfying to the learner, that person is more likely to persist until the learning objective has been obtained (Knox, 1986). In addition, the selection and organization of learning activities and methods will assist in the determination of how they will be sequenced, from simple to more complex, in the learning experience.

You also need skill in selecting and preparing educational and instructional materials for the learning activities. The primary criteria for selecting materials should be the educational purposes they serve in conjunction with the learners' needs and learning styles. Educational materials can be grouped into categories such as print (e.g., books, newspapers, programmed texts), audio (e.g., radio, audiotapes), visual (e.g., slides, charts, flip charts, photographs), audiovisual (e.g., slide tapes, television, videotapes, computer software), simulations (e.g., case studies, critical incident cases, discussion guides), and examples (e.g., equipment demonstrations, mock-ups) (Knox, 1986). In selecting from available materials, you should be concerned with how the materials help the learners meet the program objectives, and how appropriate and responsive the materials are considering the learners' background, current levels of proficiency, and motivation (Wilson, 1983). Instead of purchasing materials, you may find the need to develop new ones that better fit the educational purpose of your specific program and the learners' backgrounds and interests.

*Evaluation*

The evaluation process is the final component in the program planning process and in most cases is the one given the least attention. Program evaluation procedures can help determine if the participants in the learning activity reached their educational objectives and desired outcomes; they can be used in the planning process and for program improvement; and they can be used for program justification and accountability (Grotelueschen, 1980). In essence, program evaluation provides specific feedback to you, to the adult learners participating in the program, and to the others that help guide program decisions. One single evaluation procedure will not provide you with useful information about all aspects of the program (Deshler, 1984). Therefore, it is important to focus on specific components on which you want evaluative data, such as needs, objectives, learning activities, participants, materials, facilities, and so forth. The expected benefits of the specific component selected must exceed the cost of conducting the evaluation.

In conducting an evaluation, you may want to group it into summative evaluation and formative evaluation processes. Summative evaluation judges the program's worth and impact on outcomes and is used for justifying the program. Formative evaluation of process focuses on procedures of the program and is used for decision making in the improvement of the program (Knox, 1986). Depending upon the resources, time, money, audience, purpose, and desired information, the adult educator can select from various sources for the evaluative data, such as standardized tests, observation checklists, questionnaires, organizational records, interview guides, self-assessment inventories, and anonymous participant reaction forms. Knox (1986, p.186) provides a set of guidelines for conducting evaluations which include "building on existing understandings, focus on what you want to analyze, design a basic study, collect and analyze data, and involve people and report findings in ways that encourage use of the conclusions". Knowles (1980) and Brookfield (1986) suggest that the adult learners in the program must be actively involved in the evaluation process and that selecting participatory evaluation procedures "is grounded in, and derived from, some central features of adult learning" (Brookfield, 1986, p.276).

It is out of the scope of this chapter to provide a detailed critique of the various program evaluation models and procedures; however a review of such models is encouraged, since you are one of the main users of the evaluation findings.

## TEACHING AND LEARNING TRANSACTION SKILLS

The teaching and learning process is a transactional and collaborative adventure. It involves an understanding of adults as learners, program planning, and an awareness of our own content expertise. In essence, it is how we as adult educators influence our adult students and how they influence us in the process of helping them learn. In this final chapter section, skills needed to build supportive and active educational climates and abilities needed to provide challenging teaching and learning interactions will be examined.

### The Educational Climate

An educational climate consists of two major components, the physical environment and the psychological or emotional climate. These two components are always present, therefore close attention to them will help enhance achievement and satisfaction in the teaching and learning transaction.

The physical environment should encourage adults to participate. Facilities should be as attractive and comfortable as possible. Utilizing tables and chairs, with five or six chairs to a table, is preferred by most adult learners. The tables and chairs can be arranged into one large circle or, depending on the number of participants, into several small circles or a semicircular arrangement. Arranging rooms this way allows active face-to-face communication with the instructor and each learner, increases participation, and enhances the adult learning situation (Vosko, 1984). Knowles and Associates (1984) suggest that the

> typical classroom setup, with chairs in rows and a lectern in front, is probably the *least* conducive to learning that the fertile human brain could invent. It announces to anyone entering the room that the name of the game here is one-way transmission, that the proper role of the student is to sit and listen to transmissions from the lectern. (p.15)

Other physical factors affect learning as well. Each physical environment should have good lighting and ventilation, colorful decor, appropriate temperature settings (not too hot or not too cold), a public address system if in a large room, availability of refreshment canteens for breaks, designated smoking and nonsmoking areas, and an absence of distracting sounds from outside the classroom.

Another important aspect of the educational climate is the psychological climate. The first session of any educational program is vital, for here a climate for learning must be established that is supportive, challenging, friendly, informal, open, and spontaneous without being threatening and condescending (Knox, 1986). What is established in these early sessions will affect all of the remaining sessions in the program. The first action is to introduce yourself in a way that says "I'm human and I want to be an active participant and learner in this educational experience." Participants should feel that you are there to assist them in the learning process in an open, collaborative, and supportive manner. Setting a tone of informality and mutual respect helps encourage active participation. In the first session, you can help participants get acquainted by having them introduce themselves or by getting them into small groups where each person gathers some personal and professional information about another and introduces that person to the class. Encouraging participants to say something about why they are participating is also helpful, not only for the information that you can gain but also to help other participants realize that perhaps they are here for the same reason. This can lead to informal conversations between participants as well as collaboration in educational activities. Providing name cards and conducting various ice-breaker activities also helps participants get acquainted.

Adult learners want to know what is expected of them as they venture into an educational experience. It is important to review the goals and objectives of the program with the participants and to obtain feedback from them. As a result, modifications may be necessary. The extent of the modifications should depend upon the feasibility and desirability of them and the contextual influences of such revisions. Adult learners are very capable of being involved in the planning process and should be given the opportunity (Knowles and Associates, 1984). Building this climate of mutual respect, collaboration, mutual trust, support, and authenticity, or as Knowles suggests "a climate of humanness," is important. The effectiveness

of Brookfield's (1986) six principles of effective practice mentioned
previously relies heavily on a conducive learning environment.

*Providing Challenging Teaching and Learning Interactions*

The teaching and learning interaction suggests that you and
the adult learner are engaged in an active, challenging, and supportive encounter. It suggests that both are involved in the planning
and the learning process of the educational activity. Providing challenging interactions requires an understanding of the program planning process and how to implement each component of it to bring
about appropriate desired learning outcomes (Knox, 1986). Understanding adults as learners and how to respond to their diversity
and variability is also essential (see Chapter 2). One of the most
important aspects is to understand learning styles of adult learners
and the implications they have for improving educational practices
(Bonham, 1988; Claxton & Murrell, 1987; Dixon, 1985; Galbraith, 1987). A challenging teaching and learning interaction is
also predicated on understanding your philosophical orientation as
well as your teaching style and whether it is conducive to an educational activity that requires collaboration and challenge among
learners and yourself (see Chapters 3 and 4).

In addition to the acquisition of program planning skills, a
philosophical orientation, and understanding learning and teaching
styles, what are the major elements that are involved in a teaching
and learning interaction that make that interaction challenging and
meaningful? How do you bring about this challenge? First, you
need to care enough to maintain standards and have high expectations for the adult learner. Daloz (1986) suggests that teaching is
an act of caring and the promotion of development. He states:

> good teaching rests neither in accumulating a shelfful of knowledge
> nor in developing a repertoire of skills. In the end good teaching lies
> in a willingness to attend and care for what happens to our students,
> ourselves, and the space between us. Good teaching is a certain kind
> of stance. It is a stance of receptivity, of attunement, of listening.
> (p.244)

To build an effective teacher/learner interaction, you must be supportive. You must care enough about your learners to set up challenging tasks that call out for closure, while at the same time provide

insight to how this new knowledge can be applied to their lives. Providing realistic and varied practice opportunities will help the adult learner to persist and to apply what is learned. In a collaborative manner, you can carefully subdivide and sequence learning tasks from simple to more complex and establish a pace for the learning that allows for individualization. Throughout the entire activity you and the learner should be engaged in a continuous process of feedback (oral, written, or directed observation) about how the learning activity is progressing (Knox, 1986). Finally, you must provide reinforcement for satisfactory performance and accomplishments and make note of exemplary achievements. As Daloz (1986) suggests you should provide a "mirror" for your learners which allows them to see themselves in a different way; to see how they have changed and developed as a result of their accomplishments. Exposure to standards of good practice and excellence and having encounters with role models can serve as a reinforcement, challenge, and motivation for improvement.

Next, you need to organize educational settings which demand that learners act and think critically and reflectively (Brookfield, 1987; Meyers, 1986; Schon, 1987; Stice, 1987). Brookfield (1987, p.1) suggests that this activity entails much more "than the skills of logical analysis taught in so many college courses on critical thinking. It involves calling into question the assumptions underlying our customary, habitual ways of thinking and acting and then be ready to think and act differently on the basis of this critical questioning." Central to helping adult learners think critically is the element of challenge. As Brookfield (1987) states "the right to challenge someone must be earned . . . [and] . . . when helpers' actions contradict their declared beliefs and intentions, they have effectively forfeited their right to challenge" (p.91). Challenge, according to Egan (1986), is the last stage necessary before an individual can develop alternative ways of thinking and acting. To provide a challenging teaching and learning interaction, strategies for facilitating critical thinking must be embraced as a vital component of the process of helping adults learn. Strategies that could be used may include critical questioning, critical incident exercises, criteria analysis, role playing, and crisis-decision simulations. Questioning givens, examining the assumptions that form the foundation of thoughts and actions, and developing alternative ways of thinking are consequences for those who think critically (Brookfield, 1987).

A meaningful teaching and learning transaction suggests that it must promote development both for you and for the learner. Acquisition of various skills is essential for you as an adult educator if this is to be brought about:

- The ability to establish a conducive educational climate

- The knowledge of the program planning process and how to implement its various components

- An understanding of adults as learners and their diversity

- The ability to develop caring, supporting, and challenging teaching and learning interactions

Daloz (1986) summons up what seems to reflect the most desirable outcome of the teacher and learner interaction, "Like guides, we walk at times ahead of our students, at times beside them, and at times we follow their lead" (p.237).

## CONCLUSION

Helping adults learn can be a challenging, exciting, creative, passionate, and rewarding experience. A basic understanding of a variety of skills can enhance and help guide those involved in this journey. This chapter has provided, I hope, a partial map of those essential attributes and skills needed to be an effective adult educator.

## REFERENCES

Apps, J. W. (1981). *The adult learner on campus: A guide for instructors and administrators.* Chicago: Follett.

Bonham, L. A. (1988). Learning style use: In need of perspective. *Lifelong Learning: An Omnibus of Practice and Research, 11*(5), 14-17, 19.

Brackhaus, B. (1984). Needs assessment in adult education: Its problems and prospects. *Adult Education Quarterly, 34*(4), 223-239.

Brookfield, S. D. (1986). *Understanding and facilitating adult learning.* San Francisco: Jossey-Bass.

Brookfield, S. D. (1987). *Developing critical thinkers.* San Francisco: Jossey-Bass.

Brundage, D. H., & Mackeracher, D. (1980). *Adult learning principles and their applications to program planning.* Toronto: Ministry of Education, Ontario.

Cameron, C. (1988). Identifying learning needs: Six methods adult educators can use. *Lifelong Learning: An Omnibus of Practice and Research, 11*(4), 25-28.

Claxton, C., & Murrell, P. (1987). *Learning styles: Implications for improving educational practice* (ASHE-ERIC Higher Education Report 4). Washington, D.C.: ASHE-ERIC Clearinghouse on Higher Education.

Daloz, L. A. (1986). *Effective teaching and mentoring.* San Francisco: Jossey-Bass.

Deshler, D. (Ed.). (1984). *Evaluation for program improvement.* New Directions for Continuing Education, no.24. San Francisco: Jossey-Bass.

Dixon, N. M. (1985). The implementation of learning style information. *Lifelong Learning: An Omnibus of Practice and Research, 9*(3), 16-18, 26.

Draves, W. A. (1984). *How to teach adults.* Manhattan, KS: Learning Resources Network.

Egan, G. (1986). *The skilled helper: A systematic approach to effective helping* (3rd ed.). Monterey: Brooks/Cole.

Galbraith, M. W. (1987). Assessing perceptual learning styles. In C. Klevins (Ed.), *Materials and methods in adult and continuing education* (pp.263-269). Los Angeles: Klevens.

Grotelueschen, A. D. (1980). Program evaluation. In A. Knox and Associates, *Developing, administering, and evaluating adult education* (pp.75-123). San Francisco: Jossey-Bass.

Klevins, C. (Ed.). (1987). *Materials and methods in adult and continuing education.* Los Angeles: Klevens.

Knowles, M. S. (1980). *The modern practice of adult education: From pedaggy to andraggy* (revised and updated). New York: Cambridge.

Knowles, M. S. and Associates. (1984). *Andragogy in action: Applying modern principles of adult learning.* San Francisco: Jossey-Bass.

Knox, A. B. (Ed.). (1980). *Teaching adults effectively.* New Directions for Continuing Education, no. 6. San Francisco: Jossey-Bass.

Knox, A. B. (1986). *Helping adults learn: A guide to planning, implementing, and conducting programs.* San Francisco: Jossey-Bass.

Lewis, L. H. (Ed.). (1986). *Experiential and simulation techniques for teaching adults.* New Directions for Continuing Education, no.30. San Francisco: Jossey-Bass.

Long, H. B. (1983). *Adult learning.* New York: Cambridge.

Meyers, C. (1986). *Teaching students to think critically.* San Francisco: Jossey-Bass.

Niemi, J., & Gooler, D. (Eds.). (1987). *Technologies for learning outside the classroom.* New Directions for Continuing Education, no. 34. San Francisco: Jossey-Bass.

Schon, D. A. (1987). *Educating the reflective practitioner: Toward a new design for teaching and learning in the professions.* San Francisco: Jossey-Bass.

Smith, R. M. (1982). *Learning how to learn.* New York: Cambridge.

Stice, J. E. (1987). *Developing critical thinking and problem-solving abilities.* New Directions for Teaching and Learning, no. 30. San Francisco: Jossey-Bass.

Tough, A. M. (1979). *The adult's learning projects: A fresh approach to theory and practice in adult learning.* Toronto: Ontario Institute for Studies in Education.

Vosko, R. (1984). Shaping spaces for lifelong learning. *Lifelong Learning: An Omnibus of Practice and Research, 8*(2), 4-7, 28.

Watkins, K., & Croft, C. (1986). Assessing interpersonal skills of adult educators. *Lifelong Learning: An Omnibus of Practice and Research, 9*(6), 15-17, 28.

Wilson, J. (Ed.). (1983). *Materials for teaching adults: Selection, development, and use.* New Directions for Continuing Education, no. 17. San Francisco: Jossey-Bass.

Zemke, R., & Kramlinger, T. (1982). *Figuring things out: A trainer's guide to needs and task analysis.* Reading: Addison Wesley.

# CHAPTER 2

## Understanding Adult Learners

HUEY B. LONG

    Two conflicting views of adult learners are fairly widespread. The first is held by Main Street Americans: it represents adult learners as less capable than younger learners. Its essence is captured in the proverb "You can't teach an old dog new tricks." The second is held by many professional educators of adults; it represents adult learners as super learners. Its essence is captured in Malcolm Knowles's (1984) assumptions underlying his ideas of andragogy. The disparity between these views is important for two pragmatic reasons. First, beliefs affect action. Second, learning is of increasing importance to adults (Long, 1987).

    The truth about adult learners rests somewhere between the negative stereotype and the super learner idea encouraged by Knowles (1984). Specifically, he describes adult learners as being self-directing, as deriving only positive benefits from experience, as possessing great readiness to learn, as voluntarily entering an educational activity with a life-centered, task-centered, or problem-centered orientation to learning, and as being internally motivated.

    Adult learners are an increasingly important segment of the population of students in the United States (Cross & McCartan, 1984; Long, 1987). The incremental growth of this population has significant implications in a variety of areas: economic development, occupational trends, governmental policy, and educational programs and practice. Unfortunately adult learners often remain a mystery. Even experienced teachers of adults reveal inadequate awareness of adult learners. Reasons for shortcomings in our understanding of adult learners are not difficult to identify. Some of these reasons include an unimaginative traditional view of the adult

23

learner, a focus on only one aspect of adulthood such as physical health and related physiological variables, and the assumption that only limited variability exists among adult learners. A few additional observations will clarify the nature of the above sources for awareness of adult learner characteristics.

The unimaginative traditional view of the adult learner represents the adult as a big child. In other words, proponents of this perception equate the adult learner with the child learner. The only difference, according to this view, is a physical one, e.g., most adults are larger than children. In response, teacher behavior and institutional policies are quite limited. Some educational provisions do not even recognize this distinction. Not many years ago the author visited an adult education class in an elementary school where the adult learners, some weighing over two hundred pounds, were required to squeeze into the tiny desks used during the day by seven year old second graders.

Another unsatisfactory view is based on a tendency to focus on only one aspect of adulthood. This perception is more sophisticated than the first one, as it recognizes there are more significant changes that occur across the human life span than physical growth. Adherents to this position tend to emphasize more complex ideas, but the concepts are generally limited to one area such as physiological changes, cognitive development, or sociological variables.

A third view may be more sophisticated in some ways, but in another way it is even more simplistic. For example, individuals may be well informed about adult physiology, adult psychology, and adult sociology. Yet, their understanding is weakened by focusing on "central tendencies." As a result, adults are blandly described in terms of means, medians, and modes. For example, a research report may state the mean income level of a particular population segment as being $15,333. In reality it is possible that *no* individual actually has such an income. The mean fails to communicate either the modal, or most frequent income, or the income range in the population. For example, given a sample of six individuals whose incomes are as follows: $25,00, $24,000, $21,000, $10,000, $6,000, $6,000. The total income of the six individuals is $92,000. The range is from $6,000 to $25,000. The mean is $15,333 and the model income is $6,000. This reveals how the $15,333 mean income is rather low when compared with the three highest incomes and is equally high compared with the three lowest incomes. Therefore, anyone who casually accepts the mean income of $15,333 as anything other than an arithmetical representation should do so with great caution. Even the income ranges can be misleading.

In summary, it is obvious that the three perceptions discussed above are invalid representations of adult learners. In essence, individually or collectively they yield a caricature rather than a complete view. If this is the case, how do we face the issue and develop a more realistic understanding of adult learners? Important keys to this understanding which will be developed in the rest of this chapter are (a) adult variability, (b) motives for learning (c) physiological variables, and (d) psychosocial variables.

## ADULT VARIABILITY

Physiologically, psychologically, and sociologically adults are more diverse than children. Variability across the life span generally may be represented by a V. Younger individuals are more likely to share more critical common variables than older adults, at least through the latter decades. Another way of expressing this idea is to say that given three cohorts of 10, 30, and 50 years of age one would expect greater variability within the 50 year old cohort than either of the other two; similarly the 30 year cohort should be more heterogeneous than the 10 year old cohort. A number of studies illustrate this point (Long, 1971).

Therefore, it is erroneous to speak of "*the* adult learner" as if there is a generic adult that can represent all adults. On the other hand, it is awkward to continually qualify comments about adult learners by pointing out the problems of variability and diversity discussed here. Perhaps the best we can do is to observe that exceptions to the rule, as represented by statistical central tendencies, are rather commonplace when speaking about adult learners. Teachers of adults as well as program planners and educational administrators are of necessity more concerned with the majority of adult learners who cluster around the statistical means than with those who fall into the extreme ends of the curve. The 5 to 10 percent of adults who fall into the latter categories are interesting subjects and should not be completely forgotten. Yet, it is impossible to be aware of each and every individual difference that may exist among a group of adult learners. The goal is to arrive at a realistic balance between recognition of individual idiosyncratic characteristics and identification of those normative characteristics that allow us to consider adult learners as a group.

## MOTIVES FOR LEARNING

Educators have a long term interest in trying to understand the motives adults express for learning. The research and philosophical results of inquiry into this issue may be expressed in a variety of ways. First, we might consider the question: Is motivation for learning, as a human activity, intrinsic or extrinsic? Stated another way, do adults learn because of some innate characteristic or because of external circumstances? There is support for the position that learning and learning-directed behavior is a basic or fundamental human characteristic (Long, 1985). According to this premise, the adult's learning behavior originates at the genetic level. The *focus* of learning, however, is frequently based on some external circumstance (Spear & Mocker, 1981) or some social condition to which the individual responds. It is appropriate to observe that learning and schooling are not the same. Schooling is a social response that society has made in recognition of the innate human drive to learn as well as of society's need to reproduce itself in order to survive. All learning is not the consequence of schooling, neither does all schooling result in the learning goals for which it was designed. Thus, discussions of adult learning must clearly specify if the topic is (a) limited learning activity that occurs in some sponsored group activity as often provided by educational and other institutions, if it is (b) restricted to nonsponsored group activity, e.g., personally planned and pursued learning, or if it is (c) inclusive of both (a) and (b).

Discussions of specific motives for adults' learning usually are limited to the formal learning activities and the key term for communicating this framework is *participation*. Participation studies are generally of interest to administrators, program specialists, and others affiliated with institutions or agencies that have some educative mission, because they are seeking information to help make their programs successful. Success is often defined in terms of the number of people served, income generated, or social outcomes.

The diversity among adults, as discussed in the previous section, is aptly illustrated by participation studies. The simplest typology is derived from the work of Houle (1961). Houle's study of adults who were involved in learning at a high degree identifies three kinds of learning motives: activity oriented, goal oriented, and learning oriented. Houle suggests that one of the three orientations is usually primary in adults' learning activity. He also implies that often two or three of the orientations may interact. In other words the individual who is primarily goal oriented may reflect an activity or learning for learning sake orientation also. It is entirely possible that only a very few adults would represent any one of the pure orientations identified by Houle.

Following Houle a number of other investigators such as Aslanian and Brickell (1980), Boshier (1971), Burgess (1971), Sheffield (1962), and others expanded the list of motives. Elsewhere (Long, 1983a) these studies are described as identifying either global motives or specific studies. Motives identified in Aslanian and Brickell's (1980) research are an example of global motives. They identify such general categories as career, family, leisure, art, health, religion, and citizenship. Examples of specific motives are found in the work of Johnstone and Rivera (1965): to become a better informed person; to prepare for a new job or occupation; to become better qualified for the job currently held; to spend spare time more enjoyably; to meet new and interesting people; to better carry out everyday tasks and household duties; to get away from the daily routine; and so forth.

Botsman's (1975) study of blue collar workers discovered motives differed according to the age and sex of the subjects. For example younger workers (under 29 years of age) identified motives to help get a new job and meet new people more often than workers between 30 and 44 years of age. In addition they cited such reasons as: to help get a new job, to work toward licensure/certification, to work toward a degree, and to earn more money more often than workers in the over 45 age group. In contrast the older workers (45 or older) more often cited the motive "to be better able to serve their church" than the youngest group and the 30-44 age group. Women and men also gave different reasons for learning. The motives of males more frequently were employment related. In contrast women more often gave social, personal improvement, and religious reasons.

Given the above range of motives it is difficult to know, without any doubt, the motives any one adult would give for learning. Some adult educators might be tempted to assume that they can predict the motive by the nature or content of the learning activity. Yet, Sheffield's (1962) work indicates that learners with the same primary orientations are often found in diverse kinds of learning activities. For example, an individual with a personal goal orientation, as defined by Sheffield, may participate in learning activities identified as being liberal, occupational, functional, or recreational. To confuse things further, adults with a learning orientation were also found in the above range of activities. In fact the percentage of learners with the above learning orientations found in the four kinds of activities identified by Sheffield are not greatly different.

Despite the apparent difficulty in disentangling the results produced by the various studies of adult motives for learning, one general agreement seems to unite most educators of adults. The most common bond among adult learners is their "problem" orientation. A learning problem may be defined in a number of ways, but preference is given to Dewey's (1933) idea. He suggested we extend the meaning of the word *problem* to whatever " . . . perplexes and challenges the mind so that it makes belief at all uncertain . . . " (Dewey, 1933, p.13). It is this perplexity, according to Dewey, that leads to reflective thinking. We might extend his language to suggest that it is this kind of "problem" that so often leads to adults' learning.

In contrast to childhood schooling, and even university education, much of adult learning is focused on some immediate perplexing conditions or circumstance. Application, in the above sense, rather than scholasticism is important. Thus, the challenge to the adult educator is to discover the problematic element that will arouse and maintain the interest of adult learners regardless of their global or specific motives for learning.

## PHYSIOLOGICAL VARIABLES

Many of the physical characteristics of adult learners are easy to identify. Unfortunately the highly visible ones are not always the most significant where learning is concerned. For example, the adult appearance, e.g., mature facial configuration, body size, and other evidence of increasing age such as gray hair, wrinkles, crow's feet and so forth may not have very important consequences for learning. Yet, some of the less apparent characteristics such as diminished auditory and visual acuity, reduced energy levels, and increasing frequency of health problems are more substantive considerations.

## Vision

The teacher of adults can safely assume that most of the individuals will have some kind of vision problem. In most instances, problems associated with loss of visual acuity will be corrected to some degree by glasses or contact lenses. A percentage of the individuals over 40, however, may be involved in the bifocal battle. That is, their prescription is out-of-date, they resist trying bi-focals, or they are having some adjustment problems. These problems can be real if there is a use of print and projected media where the learner is frequently required to shift fields of vision from 18 inches to 20 feet and back to 18 inches.

## Hearing

A more subtle and less conspicuous problem is associated with loss of hearing. Unlike corrected vision, relatively few Americans seriously consider a prosthesis to overcome hearing problems. The difficulties for learning posed by diminished auditory ability may be more significant than changes in eyesight. This is true, first, because hearing problems are seldom corrected; second, because the learner may not be fully conscious of the problem; third, because others in the group may ignore the possibility; and fourth, because so much instruction is based on auditory methods. Elsewhere (Long, 1983b) it is noted that older learners expressed greater concern about the effects of reduced hearing ability than they did about problems with vision.

## Energy

Reduction in overall energy levels in adult learners also presents a problem for adult learners and teachers. Teacher insensitivity to the reality of diminished energy can have negative consequences. At best the learner's attention levels diminish as fatigue increases. At worst, the adult learner physically withdraws from the learning situation.

*Health*

Another consideration is increased frequency of poor health. Health problems can affect the adult learner in a variety of ways. First, they may interfere with attendance at instructional sessions. Second, they may interfere with study. Third, they divert attention. Unfortunately for the teacher of adults the diversion of interest may occur in several ways. Medication taken before class can significantly affect cognition. Pain experienced during the learning activity robs the learner of energy and attention. Certainly the consideration of new information, creative problem solving, and reflective thinking can be reduced by medication despite the learner's heroic efforts. In some situations the learner's attention may be diverted to different considerations.


## PSYCHOSOCIAL VARIABLES

A number of significant psychosocial variables are important when we seek to understand adult learners: cognitive characteristics, personality characteristics, experiential characteristics, and role characteristics.

*Cognitive Characteristics*

Following Piaget (1971) and folk wisdom it became easy for educators and others to assume that all adults operated at what Piaget identified as the formal operations stage of cognition. According to Piaget, humans go through four cognitive stages: sensory-motor stage (to about 2 years), pre-operational stage (2 to 6 years), operational stage (7 to 11 years), and formal stage (12-15 years). The formal operations stage, also referred to as the abstract level, is reached by all children by about age 12 to 15 years. Later Piaget (1972) raised the upper age of attainment to about 20 years. People in the formal stage are believed to be able to think in the abstract and work with hypothetical knowledge. Immediately preceding this stage is the concrete level where the individual's manipulation of ideas is limited to the concrete rather than the abstract. Ability to reason in terms of hypotheses before knowing they are true or false is not possible.

Beginning about 1975 (Arlin, 1975) researchers began to question Piaget's theory concerning attainment of the formal operations stage. Several investigators, (see Long 1983b for a brief review) discovered that a sizable proportion of their subjects failed to meet formal operations criteria. Chiappetta (1975) found that 53 percent of her sample of female schoolteachers failed to operate at the formal operations level.

The implications of the above research provide significant support for the premise that age alone does not guarantee attainment of formal stage operational abilities. Thus, educators of adults should be wary of educational practices that are heavily biased toward formal operations.

Similar cautions emerge from researchers and theorists involved in the study of meta-cognition. Gagne (1985) implies that interventions designed to increase the use of meta-cognition are apt to prove less effective than anticipated by some. He bases his opinion on the belief that sufficient mental maturity is critical to meta-cognition. Such maturity cannot be obtained as a result of interventions. This position is related to experiential characteristics discussed in another section of this chapter.

All of this brings us close to the debate about the nature of adult learning. Often the debate is stated in terms such as "adults do/do not learn differently than children." The wording of the premise is faulty. It begs the questions as it fails to recognize the global nature of learning. A preferred definition of learning is that it is a cognitive *process* that is influenced by a variety of other elements: (a) existing or prior knowledge that the learner has; (b) attitudes and beliefs, held by the learner, toward the source, content, topic, and mode of presentation; and (c) the state of the learner, e.g., whether the learner is rested, tired, well, sick, angry, anxious, and so forth.

Assuming the learning process as a cognitive activity is generally the same for most human beings, it is obvious that children and adults' learning process should be similar. Yet, it is equally apparent that adults and children differ in some important ways. For example, adults are normally expected to have more prior knowledge. Adult trait characteristics are not as plastic as in children. Variables are likely to be differentially distributed among adults. If one believes that individuals respond to information as if it were a sterile phenomenon and believes the learning process is not influenced by nonrational and noncognitive elements, the issue of learning differences among different age groups is not important. Yet, these considerations are important if one believes that the relationships learners form with bodies of knowledge, events, and circumstances are influenced by phenomena that lie beyond the event or topic. Ample evidence exists from a variety of investigations to support the latter view. Hollander and Hunt (1963) established that an individual's impressions of a situation, including another person, result from three major elements: the situation, other people, and the perceiver. Shibutani (1963) observes that judgments rest upon perspective; people with different outlooks define more or less identical situations differently. Sherif (1935) demonstrated that individuals interpret the written expression of an individual according to their perception of the writer.

*Personality Characteristics*

If one rejects the proposition that learning is impacted by variables such as personality, this section is meaningless. In contrast, if the contention of interaction between the cognitive process and trait and state variables is accepted, these comments extend the previous section.

Personality is defined as a consistent way of behaving. It is a multidimensional construct composed of at least eight properties: (1) physique; (2) temperament, (3) intellectual and other abilities; (4) interests and values; (5) social attitudes; (6) motivational dispositions; (7) expressive and stylistic traits; and (8) pathological trends (Hilgard & Atkinson, 1967).

Travers (1967) is quite clear in his assessment of the importance of personality in learning. He reports research that supports the proposition that what is observed or attended to in the environment is at least partly a product of personality structure. He also says "research in the specific area of attitudes indicates that personality structure may determine, to some extent, what is learned" (Travers, 1967 p. 403).

The complexity of the process is demonstrated by research that in some instances reveals a particular attitude may not influence learning whereas in other instances the reverse is true. This phenomenon supports the proposition that an individual's behavior tends to promote consistency of attitudes and beliefs. Thus the way a person interprets and perceives is associated with existing belief and value systems, variables not always obvious to the observer.

Given earlier comments on variability, we would expect to find a wide range of personalities within a normal group of adult learners. Purposive, selected, or membership groups may be more homogeneous than randomly composed groups, but even here some differences are likely to exist.

What does this mean for the adult educator? In most instances the purposes of educational activities do not include direct intervention to modify personality. Optimistically, many believe that wider educational experience may moderate extreme positions that prevent a learner from truly considering diverse information. Recognition that adult personality is difficult to modify is a primary response of the adult educator to the situation. A secondary response is to try to identify conspicuous attitudes, beliefs, and values that may interfere with learning and then to search for ways to mitigate their influence while expertly emphasizing the beliefs and attitudes that may encourage learning.

## Experiential Characteristics

The previous discussion of personality is directly related to adult experiential characteristics. Experience is potentially a significant consideration in adult learning. Kidd (1959) says

> . . . a principal factor—for some *the* principal factor—in adult learning is the comparatively richer experience of the adult and what use is made of this learning in the learning transaction (p. 45).

He continues to observe

> there are three related notions here: adults have *more* experiences, adults have different *kinds* of experiences, adult experiences are *organized differently* (p.45-46).

Assuming a constant rate of experiences across the life span, it is axiomatic that the oldest individual would have a greater number of experiences than the youngest. The effect of experience on cognitive strategies is implied in Gagne's suggestion that the skills of executive control are improved with practice; practice that may require years of refinement. Thus, Kidd's first premise is not difficult to accept.

Furthermore, if we accept the position that adults have *more* experiences that they can reflect upon in their learning activity, we have the prospects for a much richer learning environment. Joining this situation with Kidd's second premise, e.g., adults have different *kinds* of experiences, we have the potential for an extremely stimulating interaction. Furthermore, the idea suggests the possibility of great variability among experiences of adults, among all adults as a group, and between classes of adults that might be formed on the basis of age, education, sex or other variables.

Finally, Kidd's third principle, adults *organize* their experiences differently, can be applied to situations outside as well as within the classroom. At first reading we can assume that Kidd was distinguishing adult organization of experience from a child's organization. But, we can also extend his idea further and suggest because of the great variability among adults there will be organizational differences among adults.

Adult experience as it may relate to adult learning can be characterized in terms of *quantity* and *quality*. The mere possibility that ranges of quantitative differences exist among adult learners provides opportunities and challenges in adult learning. Perhaps even more profound in its consequences is the probability that the *quality* of adult experience is also differentially distributed among adult learners.

As a result of the interaction among experience (quantity and quality) and the various elements of personality, discussed earlier, a group of adult learners is extremely complex. In most fortuitously formed groups we should expect to find some individuals with personality and cognitive characteristics that are fine tuned to make the most of the learning opportunity. At the other end of the spectrum, we should also expect to find some adults for whom it will be very difficult to address the content, skill, or task to be learned. The situation may be somewhat muted, in terms of the more difficult learners, as in much of adult education the learner may choose to not continue. However, in mandatory situations the relationships established among learners, teacher, and content may be highly variable.

## Role Characteristics

Perhaps one of the most significant and least understood characteristics that may have implications for understanding adult learners concerns role. Briefly stated, a role is a socially ascribed set of rights and obligations. The development of roles helps large social groups function with limited dissonance. Pressures and rewards are frequently available to encourage us to properly discharge the rights and obligations of the various roles we occupy in society.

Understanding the concept of role is integral with understanding adult learners. First, the role of *learner* is often confused with the role of *student*. Second, the learner/student role is generally assigned to young people. Third, even when the learner/student role is assumed by adults, often it is a low priority role. Other adult roles such as parent, worker, and so forth are frequently more important. The relative emphasis is also a reflection of the continued identification of learner/student role with childhood where the learner/student role is often the highest priority role. Obligations associated with other roles such as sibling or child may be set aside in favor of the obligations of the learner/student role. Yet, this is not the case for most adult learners. Obligations of parent or worker take precedence over learner/student role obligations.

We are living in a period when some of these role relationships are changing. By 1999 the adult's worker role may be hyphenated to become the worker-learner/student role. This will be an improvement over the contemporary stressful situation. However, we may discover that the role transition tends to limit learning activities only to work-related content or skill.

In the meantime, if we are to have a better understanding of the adult learner, we are challenged to become more aware of the role conflict discussed above.


## SUMMARY

A major theme of this chapter on understanding adult learners is an emphasis on variability. The chapter does not contain a discussion of *the* adult learner because any composite profile inadequately represents a large proportion of adult learners.

The second major division of the chapter provides a brief overview of some selected physical characteristics of adult learners.

The third major chapter division describes psychosocial characteristics that have implications for understanding adult learners. Four subtopics are addressed under psychosocial characteristics: cognitive characteristics, personality characteristics, experiential characteristics, and role characteristics.

The point about wide ranges of differences among adult learners is made time and again in the discussion of the selected characteristics. The teacher of adults is especially challenged to be sensitive to the idiosyncrasies of each learner. Furthermore, educational and learning activities, to be most effective, must reasonably match the special characteristics of each learner.

## REFERENCES

Arlin, P. K. (1975). Cognitive development in adulthood: A fifth stage? *Developmental Psychology, 11* (5) 602-606.

Aslanian, C. B., & Brickell, H. M. (1980). *Americans in transition* New York: College Entrance Examination Board.

Boshier, R. (1971). Motivational orientations of adult education participants: A factor analytic exploration of Houle's typology. *Adult Education, 21* (2), 3-26.

Botsman, P. B. (1975). *The learning needs and interests of adult blue collar factory workers*. Ithaca: New York State College of Human Ecology.

Burgess, P. (1971). Reasons for adult participation in group educational activities. *Adult Education, 22*(1), 3-29.

Chiapetta, E. L. (1975, March). *A perspective on formal thought development*. Paper presented at the 48th annual meeting of the National Association for Research in Science Teaching, Los Angeles, California, (ERIC ED 108 862).

Cross, K., & McCartan, A. (1984). *Adult learning: State policies and institutional practices* (Higher Education Research Reports: Executive Summary, Report No. 1). Washington, D.C.: ASHE-ERIC Clearinghouse on Higher Education.

Dewey, J. (1933). *How we think: A restatement of the relation of reflective thinking to the educative process*. New York: D.C. Health and Co.

Gagne, R. M. (1985). *The conditions of learning and theory of instruction* (4th ed). New York: Holt, Rinchart and Winston.

Hilgard, E. R., & Atkinson, R.C. (1967). *Introduction to psychology* (4th Edition). New York: Harcourt, Brace and World, Inc.

Hollander, E. P., & Hunt, R.G. (Eds.). (1963). *Current perspectives in social psychology*. Buffalo: Oxford University Press.

Houle, C. O. (1961). *The inquiring mind.* Madison: The University of Wisconsin Press.

Johnstone, J. W. C., & Rivera, R. (1965). *Volunteers for learning.* Chicago: Aldine.

Kidd, J. R. (1959). *How adults learn.* New York: Association Press.

Knowles, M. S. (1984). Introduction: The art and science of helping adults learn. In M.S. Knowles & Associates, *Andragogy in action* (pp. 1-21). San Francisco: Jossey-Bass.

Long, H. B. (1971). *Are they ever too old to learn?* Englewood Cliffs: Prentice Hall.

Long, H. B. (1983a). *Adult learning: Research and practice.* New York: Cambridge.

Long, H. B. (1983b). Academic performance, attitudes and social relations in intergenerational college classes. *Educational gerontology, 9* (5-6), 471-482.

Long, H. B. (1985). Critical foundations for lifelong learning/lifelong education In H. B. Long, J. W. Apps & R. Hiemstra, *Philosophical and other views on lifelong learning* (pp. 63-92). Athens, Ga. Adult Education Dept., Univ. of Georgia.

Long, H. B. (1987). *New perspectives on the education of adults in the United States.* New York: Nichols.

Piaget, J. (1971). The theory of stages of cognitive development. In D.R. Green, M. P. Ford, & G. B. Flamer (Eds.), *Measurement and Piaget* (pp 1-11). New York: McGraw-Hill.

Piaget, J. (1972). Intellectual evolution from adolescence to adulthood. *Human Development, 15* (1), 1-12.

Sheffield, S. B. (1962). *The orientations of adult continuing learners.* Unpublished doctoral dissertation, University of Chicago.

Sherif, M. (1935). A study of some social factors in perception. *Archives of Psychology, 27,* 187.

Shibutani, T. (1963). Reference groups as perspectives. In E. P. Hollander & R. G. Hunt (Eds). *Current perspectives in social psychology* (pp. 97-106). Buffalo: Oxford University Press.

Spear, G. E., & Mocker, D.W. (1981). *The organizing circumstance: Environmental determinants in the non-formal learning.* Unpublished manuscript, Center for Research Development in Adult Education, School of Education, University of Missouri-Kansas City.

Travers, R. M. W. (1967). *Essentials of learning* (2nd Ed.) New York: Macmillan.

# CHAPTER 3

## Identifying Your Philosophical Orientation

LORRAINE M. ZINN

In the process of planning, conducting, and evaluating educational activities, adult educators have both the opportunity and the responsibility to make a number of decisions. Adult education is, to a great extent, minimally regulated in terms of what will be taught and what teaching methods will be used. Individual teachers often determine the content and scope of what they will teach, then choose methods or strategies and instructional materials they believe will best help the learner gain new knowledge, acquire a new skill, or change an attitude or behavior. Thus, adult educators often have the freedom, as well as the responsibility, to help set learner expectations, determine the purpose and outcomes of the learning activity, and conduct and evaluate the teaching/learning experience as they deem appropriate.

In the late 1960s, while working in an adult basic education program funded by the Office of Economic Opportunity, I began to be concerned about how educational and programmatic decisions were made. It seemed as if the primary influences were factors such as the availability, affordability, and attractiveness of instructional materials; the popularity of a particular teaching strategy (e.g., behavioral objectives) or a teaching device (e.g., a speed reading machine); or the stated objectives of a funding agency (e.g., citizenship education for immigrants). Since all of these elements were undergoing change, sometimes rapidly, I questioned whether there might not be something deeper than that, some set of values or beliefs which I might hold personally that might serve as a guide.

## THE IMPORTANCE OF A PERSONAL PHILOSOPHY

On what basis are decisions made and actions taken in the field of adult education? On what basis should they be done? Of what value might it be to the adult educator to go through a systematic process of exploring the basis for educational decisions and actions? If there are minimal guidelines or mandates, or if these keep changing, is there any primary factor that may be relied upon as a consistent basis for making choices in the practice of adult education?

There is evidence from a number of disciplines to suggest some positive relationship between an individual's beliefs, values, or attitudes and the decisions and actions that make up one's daily life. Psychological theories, though they differ, often draw a correlation between beliefs, values and/or attitudes, and human behavior. On the basis of such theories, certain forms of treatment or therapy are proposed to help individuals change undesirable, ineffective, and counterproductive behaviors through a process that involves examining, clarifying, and perhaps changing what one believes.

In an attempt to make sense out of the world, people formulate beliefs upon which they can rely as guides for the future. Individual beliefs generally fit into groups or categories with other similar beliefs, forming belief systems which, as a whole, comprise a life philosophy. Generally, adults have formulated some life philosophy which underlies their interpretation of the world and their actions within it. However, the life philosophy is often unrecognized and rarely expressed, though it may be understood implicitly. Goals may not be verbalized, direction is often unclear, and actions frequently are inconsistent with beliefs and values. A life philosophy is rarely static or inflexible; beliefs change to accommodate new needs and experiences. Yet, a person's philosophy of life does provide a framework by which to live and act.

## RELATIONSHIP OF PHILOSOPHY TO EDUCATION

When the adult educator engages in the practice of education, certain beliefs about life in general are applied to the practice. These beliefs constitute the basis for a philosophy of education. As with the life philosophy, the philosophy of education may be unrecognized, internally inconsistent, and only partially formulated. However, beliefs about education do provide some basis for selecting instructional content, establishing teaching/learning objectives, selecting and/or developing instructional materials, interacting with learners, and evaluating educational outcomes. In developing educational programs, deChambeau (1977) suggests that "the question of 'why' must precede questions of 'what' or 'how' " (p. 308).

Education has as a central focus an intent to effect change—whether that change be an increase in knowledge, the acquisition or improvement of a skill, or a change in attitude or behavior. The direction of change is based to a great extent on what individuals and the larger society believe should happen through education. Early citizenship classes, for example, were designed to "Americanize" immigrants, to acculturate them so they could better fit into American society. The black studies classes that emerged in the late 1960s were designed to instill and reinforce ethnic pride. Maria Montesorri's teaching system was intended to encourage individual growth, rather than to socialize children. "Back to the basics" movements in schools reflect a belief that the foundation of a good education includes a solid grounding in reading, writing, and arithmetic. The "behaviorist" approach to instruction was a direct result of Skinnerian theory regarding stimulus-response patterns; whereas Paulo Freire's "conscientizacion" clearly reflect its creator's belief that the primary purpose of adult education is to awaken critical consciousness that can be directed toward social change. To a greater or lesser extent, in more or less obvious ways, purposes and methods of education emerge from individual and/or shared perceptions of how things are and how they should be.

The role(s) of the adult educator may include transmitting information through a lecture, demonstrating new skills, assisting the learner in planning learning activities, facilitating a discovery learning process, directing the learner to other resources, leading the learner through a series of trial-and-error experiences, and a number of other possible ways of facilitating learning. In all of these cases, adult educators make decisions and act according to what they believe to be appropriate. Even if an educational institution dictates or regulates certain aspects of the teaching process, the individual educator may support, modify, reject, or conform to such mandates, based on personal beliefs and interpretations.

Since people enter the field of adult education with widely

varied backgrounds, there is also the likelihood that they will hold varied beliefs about how to teach, what to teach, and why adults are there to learn. With the proliferation of educational opportunities for adults and the increasing number of adults who will be engaging in educational activities, there will be a greater number of people who have some role in teaching them.

Adult educators are constantly faced with answering the questions, "What should I do?" and "How should I do it?"; "How can I accomplish X?" and "How can I change X to Y?" Answers to these questions can be sought in rational thought and educational theory; but other strategies are often used, such as acting on the basis of habit or following the latest trend. Unfortunately, these strategies (or lack of strategy) often lead to incongruence and inconsistency in actions. Elias and Merriam (1980) believe that "Theory without practice leads to an empty idealism, and action without philosophical reflection leads to mindless activism" (p. 4).

## PERSONAL VALUES AS RELATED TO EDUCATIONAL PHILOSOPHY

Rokeach (1968) and others clearly relate values to social psychology and the ways people act within society. People hold values regarding modes of conduct or "end-states of existence" which they consider personally and socially preferable to other modes of conduct and end-states of existence. "Once a value is internalized, it becomes, consciously or unconsciously, a standard or criterion for guiding action . . . " (p. 16). People are prompted to examine and perhaps change their values when they perceive inconsistencies within their total value system or between their values and their behavior. Changes in values would conceivably result in different modes of conduct or ways of acting in society.

A basic assumption underlying the teaching/learning process is that the purpose of education is to promote, guide, and/or facilitate some sort of change in individuals (Zinn, 1975). The adult educator is consistently and intentionally intervening in the lives of other adults. The changes which the adult educator is at least partially responsible for effecting in the learner "may hurt humans or evoke in them the truly beautiful and good" (White, 1970, p. 121).

The adult educator, acting in the role of change agent, often faces the dilemma of conflicting values.

The role of personal values in social change was noted by Warren (1971), who asserted that individuals orient themselves primarily toward one of two values—"truth" or "love"—when thinking of social change. However, "most of us carry both orientations around with us, applying them in different admixtures in this case or that . . . " (p. 273), resulting in an internal dilemma and external inconsistencies. People who attempt to promote social change are, thus, confused about what they are trying to do. "They seem to think it possible both to help people do what they themselves want to do (i.e., a 'love'/process orientation) and at the same time ensure that specific goals are met (i.e., a 'truth'/task orientation) . . . " (p. 290).

## WHAT WE SAY WE BELIEVE VERSUS WHAT WE DO

As adult educators begin to examine their own beliefs in relation to the practice of education, a word of caution is in order. There are frequently discrepancies between what people say they believe and what they actually do. Argyris and Schon (1974), working in the field of organizational development, looked for reasons why people have difficulty learning and adopting new theories of action. They suggested that this difficulty may represent conflicts with existing theories people have that already determine their practice. They called these operational theories of action "theories-in-use" to distinguish them from the "espoused theories" that are used to describe and justify behavior, and they questioned whether the difficulty in learning new theories of action is related to a disposition to protect the old theories-in-use.

When we are asked how we would behave under certain circumstances, the answer we usually give is an *espoused* theory of action for that situation. This is the theory of action to which we give allegiance and which, upon request, we communicate to others. However, the theory that actually governs our actions is the *theory-in-use*, which may or may not be compatible with our espoused theory; furthermore, we may not be aware of the incompatibility of the two (or more) theories.

Theories-in-use, however their assumptions may differ, in-

clude assumptions about self, others, the situation, and the connections among action, consequence, and situation. Lack of
congruence between espoused theory and theory-in-use may pre-
cipitate a search for a modification of either theory, since people
tend to value both espoused theory (image of self) and congruence
(integration of doing and believing). An awareness of discrepancies
between espoused theories (or values, beliefs, philosophy) and theories-in-use (or beliefs, values, philosophy as evidenced by behavior)
may prompt an examination of both what one says one values, and
what one actually does.


## BENEFITS OF CLARIFYING ONE'S PERSONAL PHILOSOPHY

In every phase of life, people believe certain things about the
activities they perform. The act of "philosophizing" is an attempt
to express such beliefs, whether for one's own clarification or to
communicate more clearly with others. We all "philosophize" when
we try to express the things we believe about our lives and about
our relations to the rest of life. "A myth seems to exist among
practitioners of many service-oriented fields that philosophy is the
exclusive domain of a few select academicians. However, the application (of philosophical thought) to real-life situations depends
on how willing practitioners are to reflect on why they do what
they do" (White & Brockett, 1987, p. 11).

The clarification of one's personal philosophy of education
may have the following benefits:

1.  Provide an integrated, consistent basis for making judgments
    and decisions (Stewart, 1973).

2.  Help separate what is worthwhile from what is trivial (Maxcy,
    1980).

3.  Develop methods of critical thinking (Phenix, 1958).

4.  Expand vision; enhance personal meaning in the individual
    adult educator's life (Apps, 1973).

5.  Assist in recognizing and resolving conflicts (a) within total life
    philosophy and (b) between beliefs and actions (Phenix, 1958).

6. Provide insight into relationships (a) between teacher and learner, (b) between learner and subject matter, and (c) between subject matter and the world at large (Maxcy, 1980).

7. Clarify how the adult educator's work relates to important problems of individuals and society (Apps, 1973).

8. Help the adult educator ask better questions and answer questions better, about educational programming (Apps, 1973).

9. Help the individual understand self in relation to vocation and employment, to resolve conflicts, to become self-directed, and to take leadership (Apps, 1973).

## Continuing and Extension Education

Apps has suggested that continuing education practitioners may benefit from philosophical analysis in five major ways:

> It can help us to become critically aware of what we do as practitioners; show us alternative approaches to program planning, teaching, budgeting, and so on; help us to become aware of how values, ethics, and esthetics can be applied to continuing education practice; illustrate to us the importance of our personal histories and how they influence what we do as educators; and free us from dependence on someone else's doctrine (Apps, 1985, p. 16).

Questions posed by Apps to guide in the development of a working adult education philosophy may be adapted to Extension education as follows: "What is human nature? What is the mission of Extension practice? What value does Extension have in our society? What is my role as an Extension professional?" (White & Brockett, 1987, p. 12). Philosophies which represent the field of adult education (Elias & Merriam, 1980) also have relevance to Extension programs and practice. White and Brockett suggested programmatic applications of these philosophical orientations (see Figure 3.1).

## Business and Industry Training

The essential function of a trainer in business and industry is one of adult education, i.e., "increasing the skills and knowledge of other workers so they can be more productive and efficient on the job" (Roth, 1987, p. 59). The trainer, as an adult educator, can

| Philosophy | Description | Application to Extension Practice |
|---|---|---|
| Liberal | Probably the most enduring of the major educational philosophies; stresses development of intellectual power of the mind. Emphasizes content mastery with the educator viewed as expert/authority. | Educational effort in pesticide education with agriculture specialist providing instruction via lecture with a test following presentation of material; content mastery is essential due to mandatory testing for licensing of pesticide applicators. |
| Progressive | Developed out of the ideas of John Dewey; stresses an experiential, problem-solving approach to learning. Emphasizes experience of learner in determining problem areas and solution to be considered. | Human resource specialist in interior design and household equipment designs an instructional approach directed toward household maintenance via a problem-solving process; participants identify, by experience, problems in home care and them determining appropriate procedure based on alternative suggested by the specialists. |
| Behaviorist | Emphasizes importance of the environment in shaping desired behavior. Behaviorism has contributed to the development of systematic instructional design models and emphasizes accountability. | Family economics specialist provides home study course in estate planning involving a systematic (step-by-step) approach to determining accountable end results; specialist serves as facilitator while participants take initiative to complete process and evaluate each step before proceeding to next step. |

| Humanist | Based on the assumption that human nature is essentially positive and that each person possesses virtually unlimited potential; places emphasis on personal growth and self-direction in the learning process. | Family development specialist designs instruction relevant to economic stress with emphasis on self-concept and self-esteem (worth of the individual). Small group workshops, seminars, and forums used to enhance "participatory" approach resulting in a positive feeling by individuals. Specialist serves as facilitator of the learning process. |
| --- | --- | --- |
| Radical | Stresses the role of education as a means of bringing about major social change; education is used to combat social, political, and economic oppression within society. | Public affairs specialist designs instruction relevant to public issues such as water policy. Forums, self-instructional packages, and other techniques are used to increase awareness of specific issues and, in turn, provide opportunity for possible community change. |

Figure 3.1 Adult education philosophy applied to extension practice.

Source: White, B., & Brockett, R. (1987). Putting philosophy into practice. *Journal of Extension, 25*, p.13. (Used by permission).

benefit from developing a personal philosophy of training, "a set of beliefs that guide the trainer and the training department . . . the heart of a training program . . . the foundation for decisions that can expand or improve training efforts" (p. 60).

Roth suggests two interrelated ways for the individual trainer to develop a personal philosophy of training. First, he presents a set of theorems proposed in the early 1900s by the National Society for the Promotion of Industrial Education, concerning standards for technical education. These ten concepts can be catalysts for developing a training philosophy. In addition, Roth poses a number of questions to guide the trainer in the development of a training philosophy. For example, "Should your training programs be accessible to all employees who want and can benefit from them? Should you develop training programs that can be adapted to the individual learning styles of the trainees? Should the goals and objectives of the training department reflect the broad purposes and mission of the company?" Answers to these and related questions may help the trainer to formulate the broad set of beliefs on which to develop a training philosophy. "Unless you can systematically identify what you value in a training program," suggests Roth, "you will never be able to justify the purpose for your training efforts" (p. 61).

## IDENTIFYING A PERSONAL PHILOSOPHY OF ADULT EDUCATION

Elias and Merriam (1980) provided a comprehensive overview of prevailing philosophies of adult education, which they categorized as follows: Liberal Adult Education, Progressive Adult Education, Behaviorist Adult Education, Humanistic Adult Education, Radical Adult Education, and Analytic Philosophy of Adult Education. They concluded their extensive discussion of these philosophies with a crucial question, "What stance should the adult educator adopt as his or her personal philosophy of adult education?" (p. 203).

Three alternate approaches are proposed. The first option is to choose one of the philosophies, or to determine that one has already espoused, perhaps implicitly, one of the theories discussed in their book. A second option is to formulate one's philosophy of adult education in an eclectic manner, choosing certain elements from different (though hopefully not conflicting) theories and operating according to those principles. A third option is to choose one particular theory as a framework upon which to build a personal educational philosophy. Within this structure, views from other theories can be incorporated that are not inconsistent with the basic position.

## Developing a Working Philosophy

Apps was one of the earliest proponents of the development of a personal philosophy by adult educators. In his 1973 monograph, he presented a rationale and proposed general guidelines for the adult educator to use to develop a personal "working philosophy of adult education." He stressed the importance of seeking answers to questions using a philosophic, as well as a scientific approach. Although educational decisions are often made on the basis of experience and common sense, Apps stressed that there is a need for a more systematic working philosophy, a method of looking at broad educational problems from a philosophic point of view.

Apps provided more specific guidelines for developing a framework for an educational philosophy. He proposed that the adult educator make a systematic analysis of his or her present "working philosophy" and then build on it where necessary. Using this approach, ideas from other general and educational philosophies would be incorporated into the working philosophy until they have been carefully analyzed.

In support of this approach, Apps quoted Eduard Lindeman (1926/1961, p. xxvii):

> Each of us must be allowed to possess two or three philosophies at the same time, for the purpose . . . of saving our thought from the deadly formality of consistency. No one can write about education, particularly adult education, without deserting at various points all schools of pedagogy, psychology and philosophy. Incongruities are obvious; one cannot, for example, be a determinist and at the same time advocate education; nor can idealism be made to fit the actualities of life without recognition of the material limitations which surround living organism. One cannot, that is, make use of these opposed points of view if they are conceived to be mutually exclusive.

Apps offered a framework that would enable adult educators to identify and state their beliefs related to adult education in a systematic way. First, he suggested that beliefs be identified in four categories:

1. *The Learner.* To develop one's working philosophy of adult education, it is essential that beliefs about the learner be carefully analyzed, and if necessary, developed. Ultimately, no matter what kind of adult education we are involved with, our concern is for the adult learner. What then do we believe about the adult learner?

2. *Overall Purpose of Adult Education.* What do we believe are the goals and the objectives of adult education? What is adult education trying to accomplish and why? Is it necessary that adult education have overall purposes?

3. *Content or Subject Matter.* What is to be learned? What are the sources of content? What do we believe about the role of content in adult education?

4. *Learning Process.* What do we believe about how adults learn? About providing opportunities for learning? About the role of instructional objectives in adult education? (pp. 11-12)

In a later work (1976), he added a fifth category: beliefs about the role of the adult educator. As a starting point for developing one's own adult education philosophy, he suggested a belief analysis process consisting of four phases:

1. Identifying beliefs held about adult education, by asking oneself the questions posed above, as well as other relevant questions in each of the five categories

2. Searching for contradictions among beliefs held

3. Discovering bases for beliefs, including sources of beliefs and evidence that supports beliefs

4. Making judgments about bases for the particular beliefs held

The process of analyzing one's philosophy, and subsequent synthesis which takes into account new and changing beliefs, is comprehensive and perhaps more complex and lengthy than most educators are willing to tolerate. However, it can certainly result in a comprehensive and consistent working philosophy.

## A Values Clarification Approach

Another alternative to formulating a personal philosophy of education incorporates the values clarification process, which became popular in the 1960s. Paterson (1964) suggested that "adult educational values are, in fact, nothing but our religious, moral, social, and other general values restated within the adult educational setting" (p. 48). If this is so, a process of systematically clarifying one's values may well lead to the clarification of one's personal beliefs about education, i.e., a personal philosophy of adult education. Proponents of values clarification believe that the process of clarifying values, especially as those values relate to certain activities or practices, is likely to reduce confusion, increase clarity and direction, and lead to more consistent behavior and decision making.

Major proponents of values clarification (Raths, Harmin, & Simon, 1966) have focused on the "process of valuing" rather than attempting to identify specific values. The method for clarifying values proposed by Raths et al. begins with the following list of criteria which indicate that something is indeed valued (p. 221):

PRIZING one's beliefs and behaviors

1. Prizing and cherishing

2. Publicly affirming, when appropriate

CHOOSING one's beliefs and behaviors

3. Choosing from alternatives

4. Choosing after consideration of consequences

5. Choosing freely

ACTING on one's beliefs

6. Acting

7. Acting with a pattern, consistency, and repetition.

Then, in a systematic manner, these criteria are applied to specific situations in which values are unclear and perhaps inconsistent. For example, a case study might be examined which presents educators with a dilemma and requires them to make a decision. In the process of making that decision, values stated and/or implied by the educators are examined against the valuing criteria. The educators might be asked to give examples of how they would give evidence of prizing, choosing, and acting on their beliefs. There are numerous values clarification techniques that might be used in this process (Simon, Howe, & Kirschenbaum, 1972). However, the values clarification process does not, in itself, result in a comprehensive statement of interrelated beliefs. Further steps would have to be taken to fit the clarified values into a broader framework or philosophical orientation.

## PHILOSOPHY OF ADULT EDUCATION INVENTORY

When I entered a graduate program in adult education and was asked to state my personal educational philosophy, I was stuck with a blank piece of paper. Even when I had succeeded in writing something about what I (thought I) believed and valued, it seemed rather esoteric and theoretical, somehow not connected to the reality of what I do as an adult educator.

A few years later, while enrolled in a doctoral program, I began to look for a practical and effective way to help adult educators identify their personal philosophical orientation related to adult education. As a result, a measurement instrument was developed and validated that could be used by an adult educator to identify a personal philosophy of adult education and compare it with prevailing philosophies of the field of adult education (Zinn, 1983).

The Philosophy of Adult Education Inventory (PAEI) © is designed to help you, as an adult educator, to begin a process of philosophical inquiry and reflection on your beliefs and actions.

The PAEI is reprinted in Appendix A at the end of this chapter. It is self-administered and self-scored, and guidelines are provided for interpretating your scores. You may want to take about 20 minutes to complete and score the PAEI before continuing with the rest of this chapter.

## Interpreting Your Results

What did you discover? Were you surprised? Or did the results confirm what you have generally believed to be your philosophical orientation? Do you recognize the various teaching methods, buzz words, and names associated with your primary philosophical orientation? Perhaps there are some new things to think about that will help your teaching and decision making in adult education to be more consistent with your beliefs and values.

Most respondents have either a clear primary philosophical orientation, or share two that are more prevalent than others. Typical combinations are Liberal and Behaviorist or Progressive and Humanistic. Some people interpret Radical Adult Education to be an extension and modification (or maybe an extreme form) of Humanistic Adult Education; thus, they might have high scores in both of these. It is highly unlikely that you would have high scores in both the Liberal and Radical categories. It is important to note that the terms "Liberal" and "Radical" should not necessarily be interpreted in a political sense. Instead of "Liberal," you may want to substitute "Classical" or "Tradition." "Radical" is used here to mean getting at the basis of something; an alternative term might be "Reconstructionist." If you find your scores fairly equal among all of the philosophies, or spread among three or more, you may need to work on clarifying your beliefs and looking for contradictions among them.

## Next Steps

Once you have determined how your personal philosophical orientation compares with others in the field of adult education, you may want to formulate a more comprehensive statement of your adult education philosophy. You might start by listing the actual statements which you rated as 1 in each of the fifteen items on the PAEI. Then, you could rearrange them into categories such as those proposed by Apps (i.e., beliefs about the learner, the purpose of adult education, content or subject matter, the learning process, and the role of the adult educator). Finally, you might elaborate on a few areas that do not seem to be covered by the items on the inventory. A note of caution: Be aware of contradictions in your statements of belief. Although it is not unusual that you might hold conflicting beliefs, examine your narrative belief statements to determine that they do not contradict the beliefs represented by your responses on the PAEI.

In order to get a more objective measure of the congruence between your beliefs and actions, you may want to arrange for a co-worker or supervisor to observe your teaching (and other activities you do as an adult educator) and help you make comparisons between their perceptions of how you behave or act and your stated beliefs.

It would be interesting to retake the PAEI from time to time, to notice whether there are changes in your philosophical orientation, and to reflect on the bases and consequences of such changes. You may find, for example, that when you move into a work setting, your philosophical orientation either conflicts with the new program or institution; or that it is supported in your new situation so that you feel more comfortable; or even that your philosophical orientation may change gradually as a result of exposure to different values and beliefs and different roles as an adult educator.

*Practical Application of the PAEI Results*

A recent study (McKenzie, 1985) which compared responses of twenty-two trainers in business and industry, forty-eight religious educators of adults, and thirty-two beginning graduate students in adult education sought to determine empirically whether a relationship existed between the philosophical orientations of adult educators and their experiences as educators in different adult education contexts. McKenzie did note some interesting differences that seemed to be related to the different contexts in which the respondents functioned as adult educators. He also observed that "many adult educators merely accept patterns of practice (and corresponding theoretical assumptions) without testing these patterns critically. It is not altogether uncommon for some adult educators to be enthusiastic about techniques, procedures, instructional aids, and fads while at the same time avoiding a critical examination of the philosophical grounds of practice" (p. 20).

You may want to use the PAEI with a group of co-workers.

Staff and team members of adult education programs have used the PAEI to identify and clarify their own beliefs regarding adult education, which has resulted in better understanding and communication, improved working relationships among co-workers, more effective planning and decision making, and a better fit between the adult educator's purposes and the needs of the adult learner.

## PHILOSOPHICAL ORIENTATION AND TEACHING/TRAINING STYLE

Increasing attention has been paid in recent years to teaching style, which may be defined as the operational behavior of the teacher's educational philosophy. A recent study revealed that teaching style makes a significant difference in student achievement (Conti & Welborn, 1986). They stressed the importance of teachers thoroughly analyzing their teaching behaviors and the consequences of their actions. In particular, it is important to practice a teaching style which consistently treats adults with dignity and respect.

The Philosophy of Adult Education Inventory is partially based on an earlier assessment instrument, the Training Style Inventory (Brostrom, 1979), designed as a tool to assist individuals who work in a training capacity to clarify their individual training style or orientation. The Training Style Inventory offers the trainer examples of choices that might be made in the process of planning, conducting, and evaluating training activities. The combined responses to the inventory result in a profile of the trainer, indicating the extent to which that person approaches training from a Humanist, Behaviorist, Functionalist, and/or Structuralist orientation.

## WHAT ARE THE CONSEQUENCES OF MY PERSONAL PHILOSOPHY?

How comfortable are you with "going against the grain" of American mainstream values? Podeschi (1986) identified a number of mainstream American values and categorized them under four of the philosophies identified by Elias and Merriam (1980): Liberal, Behaviorist, Humanistic, and Radical. He noted that the two philosophies which most strongly represent mainstream values are Behaviorist and Humanistic, which embody values such as progress,

change, optimism, individualism, self-reliance, practicality, productivity, technology, and measurability.

In contrast, Liberal adult education is historically associated
with the "elites," as well as with a population without much mainstream power: women. Values such as progress, change, newness,
optimism, activity, practicality, efficiency, measurability, and technology are *not* represented in the Liberal education tradition. Radical adult education also runs against the current of American value
patterns. "Pushing for political consciousness and social action,
radical philosophy emphasizes knowledge as power and a partner-
ship between teachers and students. This political thrust wants more
than the mainstream belief in 'equality of opportunity'; they want
an 'equality of societal conditions' " (Podeschi, 1986, p. 5). If you
find that your personal orientation tends more toward those philosophies which are less representative of mainstream values, you
may experience greater conflicts and dilemmas than those individuals whose philosophies are more in tune with current American
values.

There is nothing wrong with varying philosophies underlying
the field of adult education. Podeschi suggests that, "In its fervor
for identity and unity, adult education needs a reminder that plu-
ralism in a field is valuable and that philosophical differences
should not be neglected. This does not mean that it is wrong to
synthesize various ideas into a working philosophy. But uncritical
acceptance of methodologies is not the way out of genuine complexity" (p. 27).

Sometimes it is difficult to take time out from "doing" adult
education, in order to think about *why* you do what you do. However, a little effort in this direction from time to time can reap
valuable benefits. Philosophizing about adult education will probably not make a philosopher out of you, but it might help you to
be a better adult educator.

## REFERENCES

Apps, J. W. (1973). *Towards a working philosophy of adult education*. (Occasional Paper No. 36). Syracuse: Syracuse University

Publications in Continuing Education and ERIC Clearinghouse on Adult Education.

Apps, J. W. (1976). A foundation for action. In C. Klevins (Ed.), *Materials and methods in continuing education* (pp. 18-26). Los Angeles: Klevens.

Apps, J. W. (1985). *Improving practice in continuing education.* San Francisco: Jossey-Bass.

Argyris, C., & Schon, D. A. (1974). *Theory in practice: Increasing personal effectiveness.* San Francisco: Jossey-Bass.

Brostrom, R. (1979). Training style inventory. In J. E. Jones & J. W. Pfeiffer (Eds.), *The 1979 annual handbook for group facilitators* (pp. 92-98). La Jolla: University Associates.

Conti, G. J., & Welborn, R. B. (1986). Teaching-learning styles and the adult educator. *Lifelong Learning: An Omnibus of Practice and Research, 9*(10), 20-23, 24.

deChambeau, F. A. (1977). How? what? or why? Philosophy as a priority for educators of adults. *Adult Leadership, 25*(10), 308.

Elias, J. L., & Merriam, S. (1980). *Philosophical foundations of adult education.* Malabar: Robert E. Krieger.

Lindeman, E. C. (1961). *The meaning of adult education.* Montreal: Harvest House. (Original work published 1926).

Maxcy, S. J. (1980). How philosophy can work for the adult educator. *Lifelong Learning: The Adult Years, 4*(2), 8-9.

McKenzie, L. (1985). Philosophical orientations of adult educators. *Lifelong Learning: An Omnibus of Practice and Research, 9*(1), 18-20.

Paterson, R. W. K. (1964). Values in adult education. *Rewley House Papers* (pp. 48-51). Oxford, England: Oxford University.

Phenix, P. H. (1958). *Philosophy of education.* New York: Henry Holt.

Podeschi, R. L. (1986). Philosophies, practices and American values. *Lifelong Learning: An Omnibus of Practice and Research, 9*(4), 4-6, 27-28.

Raths, L. E., Harmin, M., & Simon, S. B. (1966). *Values and teaching: Working with values in the classroom.* Columbus: Charles E. Merrill.

Rokeach, M. (1968). A theory of organization and change within value-attitude systems. *Journal of Social Issues, 24*(1), 13-31.

Roth, G. L. (1987). Developing a personal philosophy for technical training. *Training and Development Journal, 41*(5), 59-61.

Simon, S. B., Howe, L. W., & Kirschenbaum, H. (1972). *Values clarification: A handbook of practical strategies for teachers and students.* New York: Hart.

Stewart, J. S. (1973). *Values development education. Part II: Final report.* An evaluation study of the high-school use films program of Youth Films, Inc., by T. W. Ward and J. S. Stewart. East Lansing, MI.

# APPENDIX A

## PHILOSOPHY OF ADULT EDUCATION INVENTORY

Lorraine M. Zinn, Ph.D.
The Philosophy of Adult Education Inventory©
is designed to assist the adult educator to
identify his/her personal philosophy of
education and to compare it with prevailing
philosophies in the field of adult education.
The PAEI © is self-administered, self-scored
and self-interpreted.

Validity and reliability test data are
summarized in *Dissertation Abstracts
International*, 44, 1667A-1668A (Zinn, 1983).
Copyright 1983 by Lorraine M. Zinn.
All rights reserved. Used with
permission of the author.

# PHILOSOPHY OF ADULT
# EDUCATION INVENTORY

## INSTRUCTIONS FOR COMPLETION

Each of the fifteen (15) items on the Inventory begins with an incomplete sentence, followed by five different options that might complete the sentence. To the right of each option is a scale from 1 to 7, followed by a small letter in parentheses. For the present, *ignore* the letters; use only the numbers on the scale.

To complete the Inventory, read each sentence stem and each optional phrase that completes it. On the 1-7 scale, CIRCLE the number that most closely indicates how you feel about each option. The scale goes from 1 (strongly disagree) to 7 (strongly agree), with a neutral point (4) if you don't have any opinion or aren't sure about a particular option.

Continue through all the items, reading the sentence stem and indicating how strongly you agree or disagree with each of the options. Please respond to *every option*, even if you feel neutral about it. THERE ARE NO RIGHT OR WRONG ANSWERS.

As you go through the Inventory, respond according to what you *generally believe*, rather than thinking about a specific class you may be teaching. HAVE FUN!

# PHILOSOPHY OF ADULT
# EDUCATION INVENTORY

|              | Strongly Disagree | Neutral | Strongly Agree |

1. In planning an educational activity, I am most likely to:

- identify, in conjunction with learners, significant social and political issues and plan learning activities around them.

  1  2  3  4  5  6  7  (e)

- clearly identify the results I want and construct a program that will almost run itself.

  1  2  3  4  5  6  7  (b)

- begin with a lesson plan that organizes what I plan to teach, when and how.

  1  2  3  4  5  6  7  (a)

- assess learners' needs and develop valid learning activities based on those needs.

  1  2  3  4  5  6  7  (c)

- consider the areas of greatest interest to the learners and plan to deal with them regardless of what they may be.

  1  2  3  4  5  6  7  (d)

2. People learn best:

- when the new knowledge is presented from a problem-solving approach.

  1  2  3  4  5  6  7  (h)

|                                      | Strongly Disagree | | | Neutral | | | Strongly Agree | |
| --- | --- | --- | --- | --- | --- | --- | --- | --- |
| • when the learning activity provides for practice and repetition. | 1 | 2 | 3 | 4 | 5 | 6 | 7 | (g) |
| • through dialog with other learners and a group co-ordinator. | 1 | 2 | 3 | 4 | 5 | 6 | 7 | (j) |
| • when they are free to ex-plore, without the con-straints of a "system". | 1 | 2 | 3 | 4 | 5 | 6 | 7 | (i) |
| • from an "expert" who knows what he or she is talking about. | 1 | 2 | 3 | 4 | 5 | 6 | 7 | (f) |

3.  The primary purpose of adult education is:

|                                      | | | | | | | | |
| --- | --- | --- | --- | --- | --- | --- | --- | --- |
| • to facilitate personal de-velopment on the part of the learner. | 1 | 2 | 3 | 4 | 5 | 6 | 7 | (d) |
| • to increase learners' awareness of the need for social change and to en-able them to effect such change. | 1 | 2 | 3 | 4 | 5 | 6 | 7 | (e) |
| • to develop conceptual and theoretical understand-ing. | 1 | 2 | 3 | 4 | 5 | 6 | 7 | (a) |
| • to establish the learners' capacity to solve indi-vidual and societal prob-lems. | 1 | 2 | 3 | 4 | 5 | 6 | 7 | (c) |

|  | Strongly Disagree |  | Neutral |  | Strongly Agree |  |
|---|---|---|---|---|---|---|

* to develop the learners'    1   2   3   4   5   6   7   (b) competency and mastery of specific skills.

4. Most of what people know:

* is a result of consciously    1   2   3   4   5   6   7   (h) pursuing their goals, solving problems as they go.

* they have learned through    1   2   3   4   5   6   7   (j) critical thinking focused on important social and political issues.

* they have learned through    1   2   3   4   5   6   7   (g) a trial-and-feedback process.

* they have gained through    1   2   3   4   5   6   7   (i) self-discovery rather than some "teaching" process.

* they have acquired    1   2   3   4   5   6   7   (f) through a systematic educational process.

5. Decisions about what to include in an educational activity:

* should be made mostly by    1   2   3   4   5   6   7   (d) the learner in consultation with a facilitator.

|  | Strongly Disagree | | | Neutral | | | Strongly Agree | |
|---|---|---|---|---|---|---|---|---|---|

- should be based on what learners know and what the teacher believes they should know at the end of the activity.

  1   2   3   4   5   6   7   (b)

- should be based on a consideration of key social and cultural situations.

  1   2   3   4   5   6   7   (e)

- should be based on a consideration of the learners' needs, interests and problems.

  1   2   3   4   5   6   7   (c)

- should be based on careful analysis by the teacher of the material to be covered and the concepts to be taught.

  1   2   3   4   5   6   7   (a)

6.   Good adult educators start planning instruction:

- by considering the end behaviors they are looking for and the most efficient ways of producing them in learners.

  1   2   3   4   5   6   7   (g)

- by identifying problems that can be solved as a result of the instruction.

  1   2   3   4   5   6   7   (h)

- by clarifying the concepts or theoretical principles to be taught.

  1   2   3   4   5   6   7   (f)

|  | Strongly Disagree | | Neutral | | | Strongly Agree | |
|---|---|---|---|---|---|---|---|

- by clarifying key social and political issues that affect the lives of the learners.

  1   2   3   4   5   6   7   (j)

- by asking learners to identify what they want to learn and how they want to learn it.

  1   2   3   4   5   6   7   (i)

7. As an adult educator, I am most successful in situations:

- that are unstructured and flexible enough to follow learners' interests.

  1   2   3   4   5   6   7   (d)

- that are fairly structured, with clear learning objectives and built-in feedback to the learners.

  1   2   3   4   5   6   7   (b)

- where I can focus on practical skills and knowledge that can be put to use in solving problems.

  1   2   3   4   5   6   7   (c)

- where the scope of the new material is fairly clear and the subject matter is logically organized.

  1   2   3   4   5   6   7   (a)

|  | Strongly Disagree |  |  | Neutral |  |  | Strongly Agree |  |
|---|---|---|---|---|---|---|---|---|---|

• where the learners have
some awareness of social
and political issues and
are willing to explore the
impact of such issues on
their daily lives.

    1   2   3    4   5   6   7    (e)

8.  In planning an educational activity, I try to create:

• the real world—problems
and all—and to develop
learners' capacities for
dealing with it.

    1   2   3   4   5   6   7    (h)

• a setting in which learners
are encouraged to exam-
ine their beliefs and values
and to raise critical questions.

    1   2   3   4   5   6   7    (j)

• a controlled environment
that attracts and holds the
learners, moving them
systematically towards
the objective(s).

    1   2   3   4   5   6   7    (g)

• a clear outline of the content and the concepts to be
taught.

    1   2   3   4   5   6   7    (f)

• a supportive climate that
facilitates self-discovery
and interaction.

    1   2   3   4   5   6   7    (i)

|  | Strongly Disagree | Neutral | Strongly Agree |
|---|---|---|---|

9. The learners' feelings during the learning process:

- must be brought to the surface in order for learners to become truly involved in their learning.  1  2  3  4  5  6  7  (e)

- provide energy that can be focused on problems or questions.  1  2  3  4  5  6  7  (c)

- will probably have a great deal to do with the way they approach their learning.  1  2  3  4  5  6  7  (d)

- are used by the skillful adult educator to accomplish the learning objective(s).  1  2  3  4  5  6  7  (b)

- may get in the way of teaching by diverting the learners' attention.  1  2  3  4  5  6  7  (a)

10. The teaching methods I use:

- focus on problem-solving and present real challenges to the learner.  1  2  3  4  5  6  7  (h)

- emphasize practice and feedback to the learner.  1  2  3  4  5  6  7  (g)

|  | Strongly Disagree |  |  | Neutral |  |  | Strongly Agree |  |
|---|---|---|---|---|---|---|---|---|
| • are mostly non-directive, encouraging the learner to take responsibility for his/ her own learning. | 1 | 2 | 3 | 4 | 5 | 6 | 7 | (i) |
| • involve learners in dialog and critical examination of controversial issues. | 1 | 2 | 3 | 4 | 5 | 6 | 7 | (j) |
| • are determined primarily by the subject or content to be covered. | 1 | 2 | 3 | 4 | 5 | 6 | 7 | (f) |

11.  When learners are uninterested in a subject, it is because:

|  |  |  |  |  |  |  |  |  |
|---|---|---|---|---|---|---|---|---|
| • they do not realize how serious the consequences of not understanding or learning the subject may be. | 1 | 2 | 3 | 4 | 5 | 6 | 7 | (e) |
| • they do not see any benefit for their daily lives. | 1 | 2 | 3 | 4 | 5 | 6 | 7 | (c) |
| • the teacher does not know enough about the subject or is unable to make it interesting to the learner. | 1 | 2 | 3 | 4 | 5 | 6 | 7 | (a) |
| • they are not getting adequate feedback during the learning process. | 1 | 2 | 3 | 4 | 5 | 6 | 7 | (b) |
| • they are not ready to learn it or it is not a high priority for them personally. | 1 | 2 | 3 | 4 | 5 | 6 | 7 | (d) |

|  | Strongly Disagree | Neutral | Strongly Agree |

12.  Differences among adult learners:

- are relatively unimportant as long as the learners gain common base of under-standing through the learning experience.     1  2  3  4  5  6  7   (f)

- enable them to learn best on their own time and in their own way.     1  2  3  4  5  6  7   (i)

- are primarily due to dif-ferences in their life ex-periences and will usually lead them to make differ-ent applications of new knowledge and skills to their own situations.     1  2  3  4  5  6  7   (h)

- arise from their particular cultural and social situa-tions and can be mini-mized as they recognize common needs and prob-lems.     1  2  3  4  5  6  7   (j)

- will not interfere with their learning if each learner is given adequate opportunity for practice and reinforcement.     1  2  3  4  5  6  7   (g)

|  | Strongly Disagree | Neutral | Strongly Agree |

13.   Evaluation of learning outcomes:

- is not of great importance  1   2   3   4   5   6   7    (e)
  and may not be possible,
  because the impact of
  learning may not be evident until much later.

- should be built into the   1   2   3   4   5   6   7    (b)
  system, so that learners
  will continually receive
  feedback and can adjust
  their performance accord-
  ingly.

- is best done by the learn-  1   2   3   4   5   6   7    (d)
  ers themselves, for their
  own purposes.

- lets me know how much   1   2   3   4   5   6   7    (a)
  learners have increased
  their conceptual under-
  standing of new material.

- is best accomplished when  1   2   3   4   5   6   7    (c)
  the learner encounters a
  problem, either in the
  learning setting or the real
  world, and successfully
  resolves it.

14.   My primary role as a teacher of adults is to:

- guide learners through   1   2   3   4   5   6   7    (g)
  learning activities with
  well-directed feedback.

|  | Strongly Disagree | | | Neutral | | | Strongly Agree | |
|---|---|---|---|---|---|---|---|---|
| • systematically lead learners step by step in acquiring new information and understanding underlying theories and concepts. | 1 | 2 | 3 | 4 | 5 | 6 | 7 | (f) |
| • help learners identify and learn to solve problems. | 1 | 2 | 3 | 4 | 5 | 6 | 7 | (h) |
| • increase learners' awareness of environmental and social issues and help them learn how to have an impact on these situations. | 1 | 2 | 3 | 4 | 5 | 6 | 7 | (j) |
| • facilitate, but not to direct, learning activities. | 1 | 2 | 3 | 4 | 5 | 6 | 7 | (i) |

15. In the end, if learners have not learned what was taught:

| | | | | | | | | |
|---|---|---|---|---|---|---|---|---|
| • the teacher has not actually taught. | 1 | 2 | 3 | 4 | 5 | 6 | 7 | (a) |
| • they need to repeat the experience, of a portion of it. | 1 | 2 | 3 | 4 | 5 | 6 | 7 | (b) |
| • they may have learned something else which they consider just as interesting or useful. | 1 | 2 | 3 | 4 | 5 | 6 | 7 | (d) |
| • they do not recognize how learning will enable them to significantly influence society. | 1 | 2 | 3 | 4 | 5 | 6 | 7 | (e) |

- it is probably because they
  are unable to make practical application of new
  knowledge to problems in
  their daily lives.

  1  2  3  4  5  6  7  (c)

## INSTRUCTIONS FOR SCORING THE INVENTORY

After completing the Inventory, go back to your responses and find the small letter in parentheses to the far right of each rating scale. This is a code letter for scoring the Inventory.

First, transfer each of your numbers on the rating scale to the matrix on the next page. For item # 1, if you circled a 5 for option (e), write the number 5 in the box for 1(e). Item # 1 has *five* different responses: e, b, a, c, d. Record *all five* of your responses for item #1, then go on to #2 and continue through #15. When you finish, there will be numbers in *every other square* in the matrix (like a checkerboard).

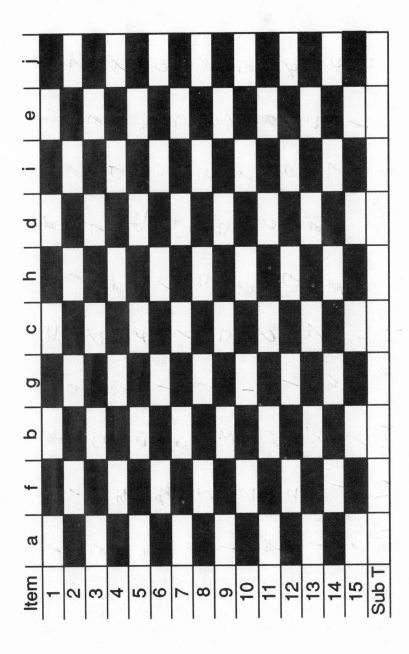

```
FINAL SCORE

a + f = L _____

b + g = B _____

c + h = P _____

d + i = H _____

e + j = R _____

Note: Final score
should be no higher
than 105; nor lower
than 15.
```

Now, add all the numbers by columns, from top to bottom, so you have *ten* separate subtotals. None of these subtotals should be higher than 56; nor should any be lower than 8. For your FINAL SCORE, add the subtotals from the columns as shown in the smaller box above.

## WHAT YOUR SCORE MEANS

Each of your scores reflects a particular philosophy of adult education:

L = Liberal Adult Education       H = Humanistic Adult Education
B = Behaviorist Adult Education   R = Radical Adult Education
P = Progressive Adult Education

On the next page, you will find a synopsis of each of these philosophies. You may want to write your score for each philosophy above the column that describes it. Your *highest* score reflects the philosophy that is *closest* to your own beliefs; your *lowest* score reflects a philosophy that is *least* like yours. For example, a score of 95-105 indicates a strong agreement with a given philosophy; a

score of 15-25 indicates a strong disagreement with a given philosophy. If your score is between 55 and 65, it probably means that
you neither agree nor disagree strongly with a particular philosophy.

Note that there is no "right" or "wrong" philosophy. The Inventory
is designed only to give you information about your own beliefs;
not to make judgments about those beliefs. You may want to give
some thought to how your beliefs influence your actions as an adult
educator.

PHILOSOPHIES OF ADULT EDUCATION*

|  | LIBERAL ADULT EDUCATION (CLASSICAL, TRADITIONAL) | BEHAVIORIST ADULT EDUCATION | PROGRESSIVE ADULT EDUCATION | HUMANISTIC ADULT EDUCATION | RADICAL ADULT EDUCATION (RECONSTRUC-TIONIST) |
|---|---|---|---|---|---|
| PURPOSE | To develop intellectual powers of the mind; to make a person literate in the broadest sense—intellectually, morally, spiritually, aesthetically. | To bring about behavior that will ensure survival of human species, societies, and individuals; to promote behavioral change. | To transmit culture and societal structure; to promote social change; to give learner practical knowledge and problem-solving skills. | To enhance personal growth and development; to facilitate self-actualization. | To bring about, through education, fundamental, social, political, and economic changes in society. |
| LEARNER | "Renaissance person"; cultured; always a learner; seeks knowledge rather than just information; conceptual, theoretical understanding. | Learner takes an active role in learning, practicing new behavior, and receiving feedback; strong environmental influence. | Learner needs, interests, and experiences are key elements in learning; people have unlimited potential to be developed through education. | Learner is highly motivated and self-directed; assumes responsibility for learning. | Equality with teacher in learning process; personal autonomy; people create history and culture by combining reflection with action. |
| TEACHER | The "expert"; transmitter of knowledge; authoritative; clearly directs learning process. | Manager; controller; predicts and directs learning outcomes. | Organizer; guides learning through experiences that are educative; stimulates, instigates, and evaluates learning process. | Facilitator; helper; partner; promotes but does not direct learning. | Coordinator; suggests but does not determine direction for learning; equality between teacher and learner. |

| | Liberal | Behaviorist | Progressive | Humanistic | Radical |
|---|---|---|---|---|---|
| CONCEPTS/ KEY WORDS | Liberal learning; learning for its own sake; rational, intellectual education; general education; traditional knowledge; classical humanism. | Stimulus-response; behavior modification; competency-based; mastery learning; behavioral objectives; trial and error; skill training; feedback; reinforcement. | Problem-solving; experience-based education; democracy; lifelong learning; pragmatic knowledge; needs assessment; social responsibility. | Experiential learning; freedom; individuality; self-directedness; interactive; openness; cooperation; authenticity; ambiguity; feelings. | Consciousness-raising; praxis; noncompulsory learning; autonomy; critical thinking; social action; deinstitutionalization; literacy training. |
| METHODS | Dialectic; lecture; study groups; contemplation; critical reading and discussion. | Programmed instruction; contract learning; teaching machines; computer-assisted instruction; practice & reinforcement. | Problem-solving; scientific method; activity method; experimental method; project method; inductive method. | Experiential; group tasks; group discussion; team teaching; self-directed learning; individualized learning; discovery method. | Dialog; problem-posing; maximum interaction; discussion groups. |
| PEOPLE/ PRACTICES | Socrates, Aristotle, Adler, Kallen, Van Doren, Houle; Great Books; Lyceum; Chautauqua; Elderhostel; Center for the Study of Liberal Education. | Skinner, Thorndike, Watson, Tyler; APL (Adult Performance Level); competency-based teacher education; behavior modification programs. | Spencer, Dewey, Bergevin, Sheats, Lindeman, Benne, Blakely; ABE; ESL; citizenship education; community schools; cooperative extension; schools without walls. | Rogers, Maslow, Knowles, May, Tough, McKenzie; encounter groups; group dynamics; self-directed learning projects; human relations training; Esalen Institute. | Brameld, Holt, Kozol, Freire, Goodman, Illich, Ohliger; Freedom Schools; Freire's literacy training; free schools. |

* Descriptions excerpted from J. Elias and S. Merriam (1980), *Philosophical Foundations of Adult Education.* Malabar, FL: Robert E Krieger Publishing Company.

# CHAPTER 4

## Identifying Your Teaching Style
GARY J. CONTI

Do some lessons seem to work much better than others? Are you puzzled about how to organize your next unit? Do you seem more comfortable using some techniques than others? Reasons for classroom situations such as these can be uncovered by exploring the concept of teaching styles.

Most of those who teach do so because they enjoy it. While some argue that the teacher is the most important variable in the classroom (Knowles, 1970), the question remains of whether it makes any difference what the teacher does in the classroom. Recent reports such as the *Nation at Risk* argue that educators have been remiss in their duties and that they are doing a terrible job of educating people. In many states, legislators who know nothing about learning theory or education are defining the curriculum and prescribing what teachers must do. To counteract this attack upon teaching and to regain control of their own profession, educators must ask, "Why are we as educators open to such a political attack, and why are we so inept in dealing with it?"

One major reason for such an attack is that teachers as a group are not able to clearly state their beliefs about teaching. What is our view of the nature of the learner? What is the purpose of the curriculum? What is our role as a teacher? What is our mission in education? Until we are able to clearly articulate our position on these types of questions, we will remain open to attack.

One way for teachers to begin to arrive personally at answers to these questions is to assess their own teaching style. Such an assessment will pinpoint their specific classroom practices and re-

late them to what is known about teaching and learning. As you
approach identifying your teaching style, you should be keenly
aware of how professional knowledge is created. Much of the formal knowledge for a profession is generated from basic and applied
research which is usually conducted within a university setting. Accepted knowledge is rather technical and is usually identified by
systematic, hypothesis-testing research. This type of knowledge has
been referred to as technical rationality. Unfortunately, real-world
problems do not present themselves in a clear, well-defined structure suitable for laboratory research. Unexpected situations force
practitioners to think in novel ways. They have to reframe the problems they face daily and construct a new reality for dealing with
them. By using their prior knowledge and experiences, they are able
to deal with new situations as they arise. As they reflect upon their
responses to these situations, they acquire new knowledge for future
action (Schon, 1987).

The reflection-in-action approach to professional practice is
a problem-solving process. It starts with people and their needs.
Importantly, it keeps people at the center of the entire process. In
doing so, it asks a different set of questions and a different type of
question from research. Significantly, it draws a different set of
conclusions from research. Rather than just suggesting conclusions
related to a narrow hypothesis or to additional types of research
that need to be done, it takes a chance at trying to explain what is
happening with the people being served. It views knowledge as
constantly developing and supports attempts to experiment with
that knowledge.

The teaching style research has been underdoing this developmental process. During the past decade, instruments have been
developed for identifying the teaching styles of adult educators, and
studies have been conducted to explore the impact of these styles
on the adult learners. A clear picture is beginning to emerge from
this research; it reinforces the need for teachers to assess their style
and to reflect upon the implications which that style has for their
learners in the classroom.

## WHAT IS TEACHING STYLE?

Teaching style refers to the distinct qualities displayed by a
teacher that are persistent from situation to situation regardless of

the content. Since it is broader than the immediate teaching strategies that are employed to accomplish a specific instructional objective, it cannot be determined by looking at one isolated action of the teacher. To identify one's style, the total atmosphere created by the teacher's views on learning and the teacher's approach to teaching must be examined. Because teaching style is comprehensive and is the overt implementation of the teacher's beliefs about teaching, it is directly linked to the teacher's educational philosophy. Lorraine Zinn's scale (see previous chapter) can be used to identify your exact educational philosophy. While several philosophy schools exist, the basic assumptions related to teaching can be divided into two major categories.

Much current educational practice can be categorized as either teacher-centered or learner-centered. The teacher-centered approach is currently the dominant approach throughout all levels of education in North America and is closely related to the ideas of B. F. Skinner. This approach to learning assumes that learners are passive and that they become active by reacting to stimuli in the environment. Elements that exist in this environment are viewed as reality. Motivation arises either from basic organic drives and emotions or from a tendency to respond in accordance with prior conditioning. Thus, humans are controlled by their environment, and the schools which are social institutions have the responsibility of determining and reinforcing the fundamental values necessary for the survival of the individual and the society. In this teacher-centered approach, the teacher's role is to design an environment which stimulates the desired behavior and discourages those that have been determined to be undesirable.

A teacher-centered approach is implemented in the classroom in several ways. Learning is defined as a change in behavior. Therefore, acceptable forms of the desired behavior are defined in overt and measurable terms in behavioral objectives. Outcomes are often described as competencies which the student must display after completing the educational activity. The attainment of the competencies is determined by evaluating the learner with either a criterion-referenced or a norm-referenced test. Through such a method, both the teacher and learner are accountable for the classroom activities.

Although a teacher-centered approach is widely practiced in adult education, the learner-centered approach is strongly supported in the field's literature. This approach is closely associated with the writings of Abraham Maslow and Carl Rogers. A learner-centered approach assumes that people are naturally good and that the potential for individual growth is unlimited. Reality is relative to the interpretations that individuals give to their surroundings as they interact with them. Consequently, behavior is the result of personal perceptions. Motivation results from people's attempts to achieve and maintain order in their lives. Their experiences play an important role in learning. In this process, learners can be expected to be proactive and to take responsibility for their actions.

In the classroom, learner-centered education focuses upon the individual learner rather than on a body of information. Subject matter is presented in a manner conducive to students' needs and to help students develop a critical awareness of their feelings and values. The central element in a learner-centered approach is trust; while the teacher is always available to help, the teacher trusts students to take responsibility for their own learning. Learning activities are often designed to stress the acquisition of problem-solving skills, to focus on the enhancement of the self-concept, or to foster the development of interpersonal skills. Since learning is a highly personal act, it is best measured by self-evaluation and constructive feedback from the teacher and other learners.

Teachers often practice elements from these two schools of thought. Some draw exclusively from one school while others prefer an eclectic approach. Whatever their approach, their "spontaneous, skillful execution of the [teaching] performance" can be referred to as "knowing-in-action" (Schon, 1987, p. 25). While this knowing-in-action may allow the teacher to get by on a daily basis, it does not address the important issue concerning the effectiveness of the style the teacher is using. To know if that style makes a difference in student learning, teachers must first identify their teaching style and then critically reflect upon their classroom actions related to that style.

## IDENTIFYING YOUR STYLE

As an adult education practitioner, you can assess your teaching style with the Principles of Adult Learning Scale (PALS) (see Appendix B at end of chapter). This forty-four-item instrument measures the frequency with which one practices teaching/learning principles that are described in the adult education literature. High scores on PALS indicate support for a learner-centered approach to teaching. Low scores reveal support for a teacher-centered approach. Scores in the middle range disclose an eclectic approach which draws on behaviors from each extreme.

Your teaching style can quickly be assessed with PALS. On a six-point Likert-type scale ranging from Always to Never, your responses indicate the frequency with which you practice the behavior in the items. The scale can be completed in approximately 10 to 15 minutes. Self-scoring involves converting the values for the positive items and then summing the values of the responses to all items. Scores may range from 0 to 220. The average for PALS is 146 with a standard deviation of 20. Although the instrument is classroom oriented and was originally designed for use in the adult basic education setting, the normative scores for PALS have remained consistent across various groups that practice adult education.

Your score can be interpreted by relating it to the average score for the instrument. Your overall teaching style and the strength of your commitment to that style can be judged by comparing your score to 146. Scores above 146 indicate a tendency toward the learner-centered mode while lower scores imply support of the teacher-centered approach.

Standard deviations refer to positions on the standard, bell-shaped curve. Most scores will be within one standard deviation of the mean; that is, they will be between 126 and 166. Movement toward these scores indicates an increased commitment to a specific teaching style. Scores that are in the second standard deviation of 20 to 40 points different from the mean indicate a very strong and consistent support of a definitive teaching style. Scores that are in the third standard deviation and are at least 40 points from the mean indicate an extreme commitment to a style.

The total score indicates the overall teaching style and the strength of the teacher's support for this style. While this score is useful for providing a general label for the instructor's teaching style, it does not identify the specific classroom behavior that make up this style. However, the overall PALS score can be divided into seven factors. Each factor contains a similar group of items that make up a major component of teaching style. The support of the collaborative mode in the adult education literature is reflected in the names for the factor titles. High scores in each factor represent support of the learner-centered concept implied in the factor name. Low factor scores indicate support of the opposite concept. Factor scores are calculated by adding up the points for each item in the factor.

The main factor in PALS is "Learner-Centered Activities." This factor is made up of twelve of the negative items in the instrument. These items relate to evaluation by formal tests and to a comparison of students to outside standards. If you scored low on this factor, it indicates a support of the teacher-centered mode with a preference for formal testing over informal evaluation techniques and a heavy reliance on standardized tests. It further indicates support for encouraging students to accept middle-class values. You favor exercising control of the classroom by assigning quiet desk-work, by using disciplinary action when needed, and by determining the educational objectives for each student. You see value in practicing one basic teaching method and support the conviction that most adults have a similar style of learning. However, if you scored high on this factor, you support the collaborative mode and reject these teacher-centered behaviors. Your opposition to these items implies that you practice behaviors which allow initiating action by the student and which encourage students to take responsibility for their own learning. Your classroom focus is then upon the learner.

Factor 2 is "Personalizing Instruction." This factor contains six positive items and three negative items. If you scored high on this factor, you do a variety of things that personalize learning to meet the unique needs of each student. Objectives are based on individual motives and abilities. Instruction is self-paced. Various methods, materials, and assignments are utilized. Lecturing is generally viewed as a poor method of presenting subject material to the adult learner. Cooperation rather than competition is encouraged.

Factor 3 is "Relating to Experience" and consists of six positive items. If you scored high on Factor 3, you plan learning activities that take into account your student's prior experiences and encourage students to relate their new learning to experiences. To make learning relevant, learning episodes are organized according to the problems that the students encounter in everyday living. However, this focus is not just on coping with current problems or accepting the values of others. Instead, students are encouraged to ask basic questions about the nature of their society. When this is screened through experience, such consciousness-raising questioning can foster a student's growth from dependence on others to greater independence.

Factor 4 is made up of four positive items related to "Assessing Student Needs." If you scored high in this areas, you view treating a student as an adult as finding out what each student wants and needs to know. This is accomplished through a heavy reliance on individual conferences and informal counseling. Existing gaps between a student's goals and the present levels of performance are diagnosed. Then students are assisted in developing short-range as well as long-range objectives.

Factor 5 is "Climate Building," and it also contains four positive items. If you scored high on "Climate Building," you favor setting a friendly and informal climate as an initial step in the learning process. Dialogue and interaction with other students are encouraged. Periodic breaks are taken. You attempt to eliminate learning barriers by utilizing the numerous competencies that your students already possess as building blocks for educational objectives. Risk taking is encouraged, and errors are accepted as a natural part of the learning process. In the classroom, your students can experiment and explore elements related to their self-concept, practice problem-solving skills, and develop interpersonal skills. Their failures serve as a feedback device for you to direct future positive learning.

The four positive items in Factor 6 relate to "Participation in the Learning Process." While Factor 2 focuses on the broad location of authority within the classroom, this factor specifically addresses the amount of involvement of the student in determining the nature and evaluation of the content material. If you scored high on this factor, you have a preference for having your students identify the problems that they wish to solve and for allowing them to participate in making decisions about the topics that will be covered in class. Encouraging an adult-to-adult relationship between teacher and students, you also involve the students in developing the criteria for evaluating classroom performance.

Factor 7 contains five negative items which do not foster "Flexibility for Personal Development." If you scored low on Factor 7, you see yourself as a provider of knowledge rather than as a facilitator. You determine the objectives for the students at the beginning of the program and stick to them regardless of changing student needs. A well-disciplined classroom is viewed as a stimulus for learning. Discussions of controversial subjects that involve value judgements or of issues that relate to a student's self-concept are avoided. If you scored high on this factor, you reject this rigidity and lack of sensitivity to the individual. You view personal fulfillment as a central aim of education. To accomplish this, flexibility is maintained by adjusting the classroom environment and curricular content to meet the changing needs of your students. Issues that relate to values are addressed in order to stimulate understanding and future personal growth.

## EVALUATING YOUR TEACHING STYLE

Instruments such as PALS are useful for describing one's style. However, more knowledge than scores on an instrument is needed in order to make judgments concerning the value of the identified style. The established theory base for adult education supports the collaborative mode as generally the most effective way of helping adults learn. However, it does not distinguish among the diverse audiences and settings in which adult education is practiced. When adult educators operate in this multitude of situations, their "knowing-in-action" tells them that this general rule needs more specificity. Four field-based research studies with PALS provide additional information for making judgments concerning teaching style and for translating the "technical rationality" of the knowledge base into theory-in-action.

While PALS has been used in numerous formal studies, four have directly linked teaching style to student performance. The relationship of teaching styles to student achievement was investigated in an adult basic education program (Conti, 1984). This program in South Texas had basic level literacy classes, high school equivalency classes, and English-as-a-second-language classes. The teaching style of twenty-nine part-time teachers in the program was measured and related to the achievement levels of their 837 students. The statistical results indicated that the teacher's style had a significant influence on the amount of the student's academic gain. However, the gains were not totally in agreement with the established adult education knowledge base. In the preparatory courses for the high school equivalency examination, the teacher-centered approach was the most effective. In these classes, students are very goal-oriented, and this goal has a short timeline. They want to pass the equivalency examination as soon as possible. The opposite situation exists in the basic level and English-as-a-second-language classes. Here, the students are concerned with the long-term process of acquiring reading, mathematics, and language skills. This process involves the student's self-concept, and acceptance by a caring teacher is important. Consequently, the learner-centered approach was most effective in these classes. Instead of suggesting that one style is superior to another as implied in the knowledge base, this study indicated that educators needed to switch their argument from a consideration of which style is best to one of when is each style most appropriate. It supported teacher's gut-level reaction from knowing-in-action that the situation and needs of the learner influence the effectiveness of different teachers.

A second study involved allied health professionals returning to college credit classes for continuing education purposes (Conti & Welborn, 1986). The 256 health professionals involved were nontraditional students attending classes outside the customary delivery schedule. Their academic success was related to the teaching styles of the eighteen instructors in the program. Once again, statistical evidence indicated that teaching style can affect student achievement. However, the findings once again modified the established knowledge base. As suggested in the existing literature, students of the learner-centered instructors achieved above average scores; however, the greatest gain was with the moderate learner-centered group rather than the intermediate learner-centered group which had higher PALS scores. For the other approach, students of teachers with a moderate or intermediate preference for the teacher-centered approach achieved less than all other students. Yet, students of teachers who had a strong preference for the teacher-centered approach and who scored the lowest on PALS achieved above the mean. Although this study was limited by a small range of teaching styles among the instructors, it provided further evidence that teaching style is an important variable influencing student performance. Furthermore, it revealed that either style could be effective when practiced to the proper degree in a given situation.

A third study examined a student performance other than academic achievement. In a study involving seventy-seven inmates and ten selected teachers, it was found that teaching style did in-

fluence a student's level of moral development (Wiley, 1986). Inmates who studied with learner-centered instructors progressed to
higher levels of Kohlberg's stages of moral development than those
who were with teacher-centered instructors. Most of the growth
was attributed to allowing the inmates to take responsibility for
determining how they would personally undertake their learning
once the broad parameters of the curriculum had been determined.

A fourth study was designed to overcome the limitation of
the small sample size of teachers of the three previous studies (Conti
& Fellenz, 1988). It involved eighty teachers from the tribally controlled community colleges of the Indian reservations in Montana.
This group contained a wide range of teaching styles; PALS scores
ranged from 2.5 standard deviations below to 2.5 standard deviations above the mean. When the sample of students for the study
was duplicated for each student completing a class, 1,447 cases
were available. The findings from this large group of students experiencing a full range of teaching styles provided clarity to the
findings of the previous studies. Unlike the other studies, the overall
teaching style score was not significant. However, the scores for
six of the seven factors in PALS were significant. When these scores
were placed on the same graph, the composite graph indicated a
general pattern of "M." The peaks of the "M" represented teachers
who scored very high in either approach to teaching; their students
tended to achieve higher grades than students with other type teachers. The middle of the "M" represents those who were less committed to one approach and who had a tendency to be eclectic;
their students tended to achieve about average grades. The bottom
of the outside legs of the "M" represent those who were extremely
high in their commitment to either teaching style approach; except
for the area of testing and classroom control, students of these
teachers tended to achieve below the average. Thus, while the
learner-centered approach was generally effective, above average
grades were obtained by students with teachers who were strongly
committed to a definitive teaching style regardless of whether it
was a teacher-centered or learner-centered style. These teachers believed strongly in a specific approach to teaching. In the classroom,
they consistently implemented complementary elements of a comprehensive educational philosophy. While they were consistent, they
were not extreme. They did not indoctrinate and were flexible

enough to consider human needs. As a result, students can anticipate and understand their actions.

## WHICH STYLE IS BEST FOR YOU?

As a teacher, you do not randomly select your teaching style, and you do not constantly change your style. Instead, your style is linked to your educational philosophy which in turn is a subset of your overall life philosophy. Therefore, your ethical, spiritual, and political beliefs will provide clues to possible elements of your educational philosophy.

Rather than picking a teaching style from the literature and seeking to emulate it, you should strive for consistency within your natural style which stems from your life philosophy. After identifying your general style, look for consistency within the various factors that compose that style. Your individual factor scores from PALS can highlight areas of inconsistency. Within each factor, look for items that have scores that are radically different from the other items in the factor; these will identify inconsistent areas in your classroom practices. Critical reflection is called for in areas that are inconsistent. Such reflection may lead to changes in either your educational philosophy or to a restructuring of your general life philosophy. The goal should be to have congruency among the basic assumptions upon which your philosophy is built.

## CONCLUSION

Educators have been a pawn in the political arena during this decade because they do not articulate a clear statement of what they do and why they do it. When attacked as being inept and accused of placing the nation at risk, they have not been in a position to retaliate with valid argument and to define the debate in their own terms. This professional void can be rectified by educators becoming reflective practitioners. You can begin this process by identifying your teaching style and relating your actual classroom behaviors to your educational philosophy. With an awareness and consistency of these, not only will you be able to speak and act as a professional, but also you can expect better results from your students.


## REFERENCES

Conti, G. J. (1984). Does teaching style make a difference in adult education? *Proceedings of the 25th Annual Adult Education Research Conference*, (pp. 44-49).

Conti, G. J. (1985). The relationship between teaching style and adult student learning. *Adult Education Quarterly, 35*(4), 220-228.

Conti, G. J., & Fellenz, R. A. (1988). Teaching and learning styles and the Native American learner. *Proceedings of the 29th Annual Adult Education Research Conference*, (pp. 67-72). Calgary, Alberta: University of Calgary.

Conti, G. J., & Welborn, R. B. (1986). Teaching-learning styles and the adult learner. *Lifelong Learning: An Omnibus of Practice and Research, 9*(8), 20-24.

Knowles, M. S. (1970). *The modern practice of adult education.* New York: Association Press.

Schon, D. A. (1987). *Educating the reflective practitioner.* San Francisco: Jossey-Bass.

Wiley, L. J. (1986). *The effect of teaching style on the development of moral judgement in prison inmates.* Unpublished doctoral dissertation, Texas A&M University, College Station.

# APPENDIX B

## PRINCIPLES OF ADULT
## LEARNING SCALE

*Directions*: The following survey contains several things that a teacher of adults might do in a classroom. You may personally find some of them desirable and find others undesirable. For each item please respond to the way you most frequently practice the action described in the item. Your choices are Always, Almost Always, Often, Seldom, Almost Never, and Never. On your answer sheet, circle 0 if you always do the event; circle number 1 if you almost always do the event; circle number 2 if you often do the event; circle number 3 if you seldom do the event; circle number 4 if you almost never do the event; and circle number 5 if you never do the event. If the item *does not apply* to you, circle number 5 for never.

| Always | Almost Always | Often | Seldom | Almost Never | Never |
|--------|---------------|-------|--------|--------------|-------|
| 0 | 1 | 2 | 3 | 4 | 5 |

1. I allow students to participate in developing the criteria for evaluating their performance in class.

2. I use disciplinary action when it is needed.

3. I allow older students more time to complete assignments when they need it.

4. I encourage students to adopt middle class values.

5. I help students diagnose the gaps between their goals and their present level of performance.

6. I provide knowledge rather than serve as a resource person.

7. I stick to the instructional objectives that I write at the beginning of a program.

8. I participate in the informal counseling of students.

9. I use lecturing as the best method for presenting my subject material to adult students.

10. I arrange the classroom so that it is easy for students to interact.

11. I determine the educational objectives for each of my students.

12. I plan units which differ as widely as possible from my students' socio-economic backgrounds.

13. I get a student to motivate himself/herself by confronting him/her in the presence of classmates during group discussions.

14. I plan learning episodes to take into account my students' prior experiences.

15. I allow students to participate in making decisions about the topics that will be covered in class.

16. I use one basic teaching method because I have found that most adults have a similar style of learning.

17. I use different techniques depending on the students being taught.

18. I encourage dialogue among my students.

19. I use written tests to assess the degree of academic growth rather than to indicate new directions for learning.

20. I utilize the many competencies that most adults already possess to achieve educational objectives.

21. I use what history has proven that adults need to learn as my chief criteria for planning learning episodes.

22. I accept errors as a natural part of the learning process.

23. I have individual conferences to help students identify their educational needs.

24. I let each student work at his/her own rate regardless of the amount of time it takes him/her to learn a new concept.

25. I help my students develop short-range as well as long-range objectives.

26. I maintain a well-disciplined classroom to reduce interferences to learning.

27. I avoid discussion of controversial subjects that involve value judgments.

28. I allow my students to take periodic breaks during class.

29. I use methods that foster quiet, productive desk-work.

30. I use tests as my chief method of evaluating students.

31. I plan activities that will encourage each student's growth from dependence on others to greater independence.

32. I gear my instructional objectives to match the individual abilities and needs of the students.

33. I avoid issues that relate to the student's concept of himself/herself.

34. I encourage my students to ask questions about the nature of their society.

35. I allow a student's motives for participating in continuing education to be a major determinant in the planning of learning objectives.

36. I have my students identify their own problems that need to be solved.

37. I give all students in my class the same assignment on a given topic.

38. I use materials that were originally designed for students in elementary and secondary schools.

39. I organize adult learning episodes according to the problems that my students encounter in everyday life.

40. I measure a student's long term educational growth by comparing his/her total achievement in class to his/her expected performance as measured by national norms from standardized tests.

41. I encourage competition among my students.

42. I use different materials with different students.

43. I help students relate new learning to their prior experiences.

44. I teach units about problems of everyday living.

## SCORING PALS

### Positive Items

Items number 1, 3, 5, 8, 10, 14, 15, 17, 18, 20, 22, 23, 24, 25, 28, 31, 32, 34, 35, 36, 39, 42, 43, and 44 are positive items. For positive items, assign the following values: Always = 5, Almost Always = 4, Often = 3, Seldom = 2, Almost Never = 1, and Never = 0.

## Negative Items

Items number 2, 4, 6, 7, 9, 11, 12, 13, 16, 19, 21, 26, 27, 29, 30, 33, 37, 38, 40, and 41 are negative items. For negative items, assign the following values: Always = 0, Almost Always = 1, Often = 2, Seldom = 3, Almost Never = 4, and Never = 5.

### Missing Items

Omitted items are assigned a neutral value of 2.5.

### Factor 1

Factor 1 contains items number 2, 4, 11, 12, 13, 16, 19, 21, 29, 30, 38, and 40.

### Factor 2

Factor 2 contains items 3, 9, 17, 24, 32, 35, 37, 41, and 42.

### Factor 3

Factor 3 contains items 14, 31, 34, 39, 43, and 44.

### Factor 4

Factor 4 contains items 5, 8, 23, and 25.

### Factor 5

Factor 5 contains items 18, 20, 22, and 28.

### Factor 6

Factor 6 contains items 1, 10, 15, and 36.

Factor 7 contains items 6, 7, 26, 27, and 33.

### Computing Scores

An individual's total score on the instrument is calculated by summing the value of the responses to all items. Factor scores are calculated by summing the value of the responses for each item in the factor.

Factor Score Values

| Factor | Mean | Standard Deviation |
|--------|------|--------------------|
| 1 | 38 | 8.3 |
| 2 | 31 | 6.8 |
| 3 | 21 | 4.9 |
| 4 | 14 | 3.6 |
| 5 | 16 | 3.0 |
| 6 | 13 | 3.5 |
| 7 | 13 | 3.9 |

# CHAPTER 5

## Strategies to Enhance Adult Motivation to Learn

RAYMOND J. WLODKOWSKI

One of the most helpful things to realize about motivation is that it is a *hypothetical construct,* an invented definition that provides a possible concrete causal explanation of behavior (Baldwin, 1967). Motivation cannot be directly measured or validated through the physical or natural sciences. Yet, it is an idea that helps us to understand human behavior and performance: Why did she study so hard for the exams? Why did he so do so much better than the other fellow even though they both had the same training and were at the same level of ability? Why was that team able to win against a superior opponent? To all of these questions motivation seems to be a likely part of the answer. Our daily lives seem to constantly tell us that we work harder, study more, and perform better when we are "motivated." Therefore, motivation as an idea makes sense to us. We want to know more about it and how to influence it. However, because the exact nature of motivation cannot be scientifically validated, differing opinions and definitions of motivation abound through the literature. Thus, as a field of knowledge, motivation can be quite confusing and is vulnerable to superficial explanation and gimmickery. What follows is a practitioner's distillation of current knowledge and research about how to strategically influence adult motivation to learn.

Most psychologists use the word *motivation* to describe those processes that can energize behavior and give direction or purpose to behavior. When we consider the human functions in learning,

such as attention, concentration, effort, perseverance, and intitia-
tive, we are dealing with motivational processes that are activated
and sustained through human energy. *What* we pay attention to or
expend our effort upon deals with the directional aspect of human
motivation. Since human energy is finite—there is a limited amount
we can give or apply—we constantly have to shift our attention
and effort to cope with the world about us. Thus, there is a dynamic
interaction between what is going on within us, such as needs,
feelings and memories, with what is going on outside of us, such
as the many environmental attractions and influences in our daily
lives.

This makes motivation very unstable. People not only frequently change their minds about what they want to do, but they
also usually vary in how they feel and how much effort they will
expend when they finally do what they have chosen to do. For
adults this is as true for learning as it is for work or play. Motivation
to learn can disappear in a microsecond. A room getting too warm,
a low score on a quiz, a sudden headache, a boring lecture, or the
anticipation of some important future appointment are all examples
of events that can instantaneously dismiss a person's interest in
learning.

One way to understand the instability of motivation is to see
the adult's world as filled with competitors for individual attention
and effort. Friends, family, job, sports, and the rest of the many
attractions and necessities of any normal adult's life all compete
with education for a part of the time and involvement that an individual may possess. Adult lives are filled with responsibilities.
The more compelling those responsibilities, the more any educational event has to display its merit or significant relationship to
those responsibilities if real interest and involvement are to be sustained during the lifespan of the course or training.

To gain the attention of adult learners is one thing; to hold
it is quite another. The teacher of adults faces a group whose attention may be easily lost, whose interest may wander, and whose
effort is parceled out with serious caution. This is normal. The
teacher's best initial preparation for working with adults is to be
personally convinced and readily able through the process of instruction to demonstrate that what is being learned could not possibly be considered a waste of time or unrelated to the lives and
values of the learners. Research consistently shows that adults are

highly pragmatic learners. They have a strong need to apply what they have learned and to be competent in that application (Knox, 1977). For a teacher of adults this translates into two questions:

1. How will my learners consistently know that what they are learning is vitally important to them?

2. How will my learners consistently know they can effectively use or apply what they are learning?

When these two questions are satisfactorily answered (within the process of instruction) by the teacher, the problems caused by the instability of motivation appear to be manageable.

## LEVELS OF ADULT MOTIVATION

In general, adults are mature responsible people who are capable of autonomous functioning in life and work. Adults engage in learning of their own volition. It may be that sometimes the circumstances prompting this learning are external, such as job loss or divorce, but the decision to learn is theirs (Brookfield, 1986). In fact, most adults are experienced self-directed learners (Tough, 1979). They have used their own resources to learn how to cook and repair, as well as how to rear their children, manage their money, and enjoy their hobbies.

Adults *need* to be successful learners. If there is a problem with expecting success, or experiencing success once the learning activity has started, their motivation to learn will usually be detrimentally affected. There are myriad theories and research studies to support this reality (Spence, 1983).

It is helpful to see adult motivation as operation on integrated levels, the first of which is *expectancy for success + a sense of volition*. It is critical for adults to feel willing to learn what they expect they can successfully master. This is the basic level of positive adult motivation for learning. To be realistic, a teacher may face reluctant adult learners. The course may be required or the training mandated. Sometimes there is hostility because of previous circumstances or conflicts. In any case, there are two strategic attitudes for the teacher to employ.

The first of these is: *Treat learners with a normal positive expectation that they will learn.* In most cases, it does little good to draw attention to student negativism or resistance. This simply amplifies the tension, reduces the teacher's spontaneity and sense of humor, and begins the momentum toward a self-fulfilling prophecy of doom and gloom. Negative adult learners are still curious and capable of being interested in learning something that they can successfully master and can see as important. By treating them in a manner that sensitively lets them know we see them as effective learners, we allow the power of our instructional prowess and relevant subject matter to overcome their initial reluctance and to connect with their still present motives for competence.

The second strategic attitude is: *Make the learning worthy of the adult learners' choice*—to teach in such a way that the learners will eventually think, "We may not have wanted this to begin with, but we do want it now." This cognitive shift can produce an emotional transformation from resistance to acceptance with benefit to both the learners and the teacher. People continuously have the experience where their initial negative expectations for something are not met. The same can be true for a negative expectation for learning when the quality of instruction provides for mastery of obviously important material. In such circumstances time is on the side of the teacher.

The second integrated level of adult motivation to learn is *expectancy for success + a sense of volition + value.* This means the adult learner does not necessarily find the learning activity pleasurable or exciting but does take it seriously, finds it meaningful and worthwhile, and tries to get the intended benefit from it (Brophy, 1983). Adults feel much better when they are successfully learning something they want to learn as well as something they value. This makes the learning something that can raise their self-esteem and incorporate their intrinsic motivation. At this level adults are aware that they are reaching beyond the trivial or superficial.

The last level is *expectancy for success + a sense of volition + value + enjoyment.* The adults are experiencing the learning as pleasurable (in the broadest sense of this word). Their pleasure may be coming from something as simple as an amusing game to something as profound as a life-changing insight. The beauty of learning is that its pleasures range from the delightfully absurd to the incredibly serious. To help adults successfully learn what they value and want to learn in a manner that allows for personal pleasure is the *sine qua non* of motivating instruction. Teachers who can help learners to reach this motivational level are truly masterful because they have made something difficult desirable. The myth in American education is that when students are motivated they will find learning to be *easy*. This is seldom the case and an even more remote possibility where excellent achievement is to be gained. Nobel laureates and Olympic athletes are seldom involved in easy tasks, but they often are committed to the pursuits of great pleasure within serious and demanding accomplishments.

The following concise overview of motivation planning and its related summarization of motivational strategies are methods that experienced practitioners and researchers have found to be an effective means to positively influence adult motivation to learn. Because research in this field is in its infancy and because most of the best teachers of adults do not write books, what is presented is, at best, a limited survey of the field. Yet, when one views or remembers a masterful motivating teacher, the presented strategies, in some number and in some design, are present.

## MOTIVATIONAL PLANNING

There appear to be at least six major factors that are supported by numerous theories of psychology and their related research as having a substantial impact on learner motivation—attitude, need, stimulation, affect, competence, and reinforcement. The following sections of this chapter will briefly consider how each of these motivational factors is a powerful influence on adult behavior and learning as well as how these major factors can be combined when using motivational strategies for instruction.

In general, an *attitude* is a combination of concepts, information, and emotions that results in a predisposition to respond favorably toward particular people, groups, ideas, events, or objects (Johnson, 1980). Attitudes are powerful influences on human behavior and learning because they help people to make sense of their world and give cues as to what behavior will be most helpful in dealing with that world. A teacher of adults can be quite assured that their attitudes will be an active influence on their motivation to learn from the moment the instruction begins.

A *need* is a condition experienced by the individual as an internal force that leads the person to move in the direction of a goal. The achievement of the goal is capable of releasing or ending the feeling of the need and its related tension. Thirst (a need) leads to a search for water (a goal). When enough water has been drunk, the need or tension of thirst is ended. All people live with an unending sense of need. Most often, needs act like strong internal feelings that push a person toward a general goal. The more strongly the person feels the need, the greater the chances the person will feel an accompanying pressure to attain the related goals. Accomplishing what one needs usually leads to satisfaction. When adults need what they are learning, they will tend to be highly motivated. Teachers can influence motivation based on need by being sensitive to apparent needs and by formulating how and what they present to adult learners in a manner that gratifies those needs.

*Stimulation* is any change in our perception of or experience with our environment that makes us active. We see something more colorful and are attracted to it. We hear something new and listen more carefully to the sound. A surprise jolts our emotions. All of these are stimulating experiences. They can be interesting, frustrating, invigorating, or irritating. Whatever their quality, they will get our attention and tend to keep us actively involved. Stimulation directly helps to sustain adult learning behavior. If a person does not pay attention to instruction, very little learning will take place. Also, when boredom sets in, fatigue and distraction are not far behind. Adults are more vulnerable to these two oppressors of learning because, unlike children for whom school may be their first priority, adults have other serious responsibilities and learning may be one more demand added on to an already stressful lifestyle. To be a stimulating instructor of adults is a great challenge and a real necessity.

The major motivational factor of *affect* pertains to the emotional experience—the feelings, concerns, and passions—of the individual learner or group while learning. No learning takes place in an emotional vacuum. Learners feel something while learning, and those emotions can motivate their behavior in a number of different directions. Teacher and learner emotions give meaning and relevance to learning. Affect can be an intrinsic motivator. When emotions are positive while learning, they sustain involvement and deepen interest in the subject matter or activity. If reading fine literature fills a learner with wonder and joy, that learner will very likely want to read more of the same literature. Harmony between emotions and thinking, so that they can influence motivation to learn as a supportive integrated force, is in the best interest of effective instruction.

According to White (1959), human beings inherently desire to gain *competence* over their environment. Competence theory assumes that people naturally strive for effective interactions with their world. By virtue of being a human being, a person is intrinsically motivated to master the environment and finds successful mastery of tasks to be gratifying. We are genetically programmed to explore, perceive, think about, manipulate, and change our surroundings to promote an effective interaction with our environment. Competence is both a symbol and a value of adulthood. We want to be effective parents, workers, and citizens. Thus, as stated earlier in this chapter, adults are especially prone to be motivated when they are aware they are mastering learning tasks which will make them more effective at what they value.

One of the most fundamental laws of psychology is the principle of *reinforcement*. Reinforcement is any event that maintains or increases the probability of the response it follows (Vargas, 1977). In countless studies with animals and humans, in laboratories, classrooms, and clinical settings, psychologists have found that behaviors can be made more or less likely to occur through the judicious application of positive reinforcement. People do seem to study with greater effort and learn more effectively when their specific learning behaviors are positively reinforced by their instructors. Praise, high test scores, academic awards, and instructor attention have been educational incentives for many years. Recent studies have indicated that *how* these reinforcers are applied must be carefully qualified. It is best that the reinforcers tell the adult learners something about their effectiveness and support their sense of self-determination for learning (Deci & Ryan, 1985). For example, grades administered would justly reflect clear criteria and *not* be used to coerce or manipulate learner behavior.

*Organizing the Major Factors of Motivation*
*for Maximum Usefulness*

Instruction is systemic in nature. It is a network of interactions between a teacher and learners that leads to learning. For example, learners listen to a lecture, which is followed by a discussion, which is followed by some problem solving based on the previous lecture and discussion. The learning objective is that the learner will correctly solve a certain kind of problem, and three learning activities were sequenced to reach this objective.

Every learning sequence, whether it lasts twenty minutes or twenty hours, can be divided according to a time continuum. There is always a beginning, a middle, and an end. There are effective things that can be done during each of these phases to enhance learner motivation. Each phase has a maximum potential for the enjoyment of motivational strategies that can optimally influence the learner's motivation. Each phase also relates to the others in forming a dynamic whole that, when proper motivational strategies are applied according to their particular phase, enhances the overall learning experience and catalyzes the learner's positive return to the learning situation. The various learning activities that make up the sequence can be analyzed in terms of when they occur and which motivational strategies they can incorporate in order to maximize their motivational influence throughout the sequence. The Time Continuum Model of Motivation (Wlodkowski, 1985) organizes motivational strategies according to this rationale (see Figure 5.1).

In the Time Continuum Model of Motivation the learning sequence or process is divided into three periods. For each of these periods, there are two major factors of motivation that serve as categories for strategies that can be applied with maximum impact during those periods of time.

1. *Beginning*: When the learners enters the learning process.
   *Attitudes*—The learner's attitudes toward the general learning environment, instructor, subject matter, and self.
   *Needs*—The basic needs within the learner at the time of learning.

2. *During*: When the learner is involved in the main content of the learning process.
   *Stimulation*—The stimulation processes affecting the learner via the learning experience.
   *Affect*—The affective or emotional experience of the learner while learning.

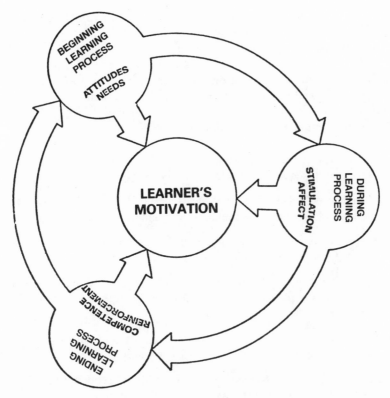

Figure 5.1 The Time Continuum Model of Motivation.
Copyright © 1978 by Raymond J. Wlodkowski, University of Wisconsin-Milwaukee.

3. *Ending*: When the learner is completing the learning process.
   *Competence*—The competence value for the learner that is a result of the learning behavior.
   *Reinforcement*—The reinforcement value attached to the learning experience for the learner.

   Although the Time Continuum Model of Motivation shows motivational influence in three separate phases, the overall influence of the major motivation factors is probably more dynamic and constant. Also, the six factors are probably not equal in their motivational influence upon the learner. Each is quite powerful. Therefore, the teacher can plan motivational strategies for at least one major factor in each time phase so that a continuous and interactive motivational dynamic is organized for maximum effective instruction. What is most critical is that each time phase (beginning, during, and ending) within the learning sequence includes significant positive motivational influence on the learner. If any of these periods is motivationally vacant, learners may have difficulty sustaining their motivation for learning. Six basic questions will help an instructor plan any learning sequence or experience:

1. What can I do to establish a positive learner attitude for this learning sequence? (emphasis on beginning activities)

2. How do I best meet the needs of my learners through this learning sequence? (emphasis on beginning activities)

3. What about this learning sequence and will it continuously stimulate my learners? (emphasis on main activities)

4. How is the affective experience and emotional climate for this learning sequence positive for learners? (emphasis on main activities)

5. How does this learning sequence increase or affirm learner feelings of competence? (emphasis on ending activities)

6. What is the reinforcement that this learning sequence provides for my learners? (emphasis on ending activities)

The primary value of the Time Continuum Model of Motivation is as an organizational aid. By continuously attending to its six related questions, the teacher can, in any learning situation, design motivational strategies for learners throughout the learning sequence. Each question pinpoints a major motivational factor and aids selection of motivational strategies from a wide array of motivational theories. At this time, for adult instruction, sixty-eight different strategies have been assigned to the Time Continuum Model of Motivation (Wlodkowski, 1985). Such strategies can be translated by the instructor into learning activities or instructor behaviors that are integrated into the learning sequence. Table 5.1 illustrates this process, applying it to an instructional objective in arithmetic in adult basic education.

A set of sequenced motivational strategies and related learning activities have been organized to create a positive motivational influence on the learners for each time phase (beginning, during, and ending) of the instructional process.

The model allows for as many strategies as the teacher believes are needed. The teacher's knowledge of learner's motivation, subject matter, instructional situation, and time constraints will determine the quality and quantity of the motivational strategies employed. The model also fits the actual process of instruction with sequenced activities and particular objectives. It provides a holistic, patterned framework that includes a time orientation, subjective viewpoint, and a logical method to combine strategies of motivational theories that are often set apart by their conflicting assumptions. With the use of this model, teachers can plan instruction which supports, strengthens, or increases the adult learners' motivation.

## MOTIVATIONAL STRATEGIES

Certain motivational strategies appear to be classic in their relationship to the instruction of adults. These strategies are well documented in the literature of psychology and their application appears to be widely supported by the wisdom of practice. They are realistic methods that have a logical probability of enhancing learner motivation. Here the strategies are categorized according to the major motivation factor to which they appear most directly related.

### Attitude

*Ensure Successful Learning.* It is difficult for anyone to dislike a subject in which they are successful. Conversely, it is rare to find anyone who really likes a subject in which they are unsuccessful. Competent learning in a subject is probably one of the surest ways to initiate a positive attitude toward that subject.

Some adults may need more time and effort to master what is being taught. We can positively influence their attitudes as well as those of our faster learners when we *guarantee* the following three conditions:

1. Quality instruction that will help them to learn if they try to learn

Table 5.1 Six Questions Based on the Time Continuum Model of Motivation as Applied by an Adult Basic Education Instructor.

Instructional Objective: After 2 weeks, learners will add and subtract mixed fractions at a 90% achievement level.

| Question | When Used | Motivational Strategy | Learning Activity or Instructor Behavior |
|---|---|---|---|
| 1. What can I do to guarantee a positive learner attitude for the learning sequence? | Beginning of the learning sequence. | Positively confront the possible erroneous beliefs, expectations and assumptions that may underly a negative. | Ask learners how many have heard that fractions are really difficult to do and discuss with them their feelings and expectations. |
| 2. How do I best meet the needs of my learners through this learning sequence? | Beginning of the learning sequence. | Reduce or remove components of the learning environment that lead to failure or fear. | Organize a tutorial assistance plan by which learners who are having difficulty can receive immediate help from the instructor or a fellow learner. |

| 3. What about this learning sequence will continuously stimulate my learners? | During main phase of the learning sequence. | Whenever possible, make learner reaction and involvement essential parts of the learning process, i.e., problem solving, games, role playing, simulation. | Use games and creative problems to challenge and invite daily learner participation. |
| 4. How is the affective or emotional climate for this learning sequence a positive one for learners? | During main phase of the learning sequence. | Use a cooperative goal structure to maximize learner involvement and sharing. | Have teams of learners solve fraction problems with one member of the team responsible for diagnosing the problem, another responsible for finding the common denominator, another for working it through, and another for checking the answer; alternate roles. |
| 5. How does this learning sequence increase or affirm learner feelings of competence? | Ending of the learning sequence. | Provide consistent feedback regarding mastery of learning. | Use answer sheets and diagnostic and formative tests to give feedback and assistance to learners. |

Table 5.1 Six Questions Based on the Time Continuum Model of Motivation as Applied by an Adult Basic Education Instructor.

Instructional Objective: After 2 weeks, learners will add and subtract mixed fractions at a 90% achievement level.

| Question | When Used | Motivational Strategy | Learning Activity or Instructor Behavior |
|---|---|---|---|
| 6. What is the reinforcement that this learning sequence provides for my learners? | Ending of the learning sequence. | When learning has natural consequences, allow them to be congruently evident. | Construct a "class test" where each learner creates a mixed fraction word problem for the other learners to solve. Each learner is responsible for checking and, if necessary, helping the other learners to solve the problem. |

Adapted from Wlodkowski, 1985, pp. 68-69.

2. Concrete evidence that their effort makes a difference

3. Continued feedback regarding the progress of their learning

For example, a weekly progress check in a word processing course where the learners can compare their recent work to that of previous weeks and calculate the hours of practice as a ratio to reduce errors and increases speed, e.g., 12 errors per 600 words in 15 minutes after 7 hours of practice, 10 errors per 620 words in 15 minutes after 10 hours of practice, and so forth.

*Make the First Experience With a New Subject or Topic Safe, Successful, and Interesting.* This strategy is based on the idea that "first impressions are important." According to Scott (1969, p. 67), "Organization inhibits reorganization." Therefore, the first time learners experience anything that is new or occurs in a different setting, they are forming an impression that can have a lasting impact. This could be the first day of a training session, or the beginning of a new unit of learning, or the introduction of a new piece of equipment. These are critical periods in determining the ways learners will respond. Making that initial contact as safe, successful, and interesting as possible will help the learners to form an attitude that will positively influence their future involvement with that subject. In this respect, a foreign language instructor might on the first day of class have each person learn some of the most essential expressions for traveling in the related foreign culture (hello, goodbye, where is the bathroom? etc.).

*When Accurate, Stress the Importance of the Amount and Quality of Effort Needed for Success in Learning Tasks Prior to Their Initiation.* Since effort is something over which learners have control, this emphasis establishes their responsibility, reduces their feeling of helplessness, increases their tendency to persevere, and helps them to feel genuine pride of accomplishment. Indicating the importance of effort for success in learning should be a matter of fact and not made in a threatening manner. For example, "Given the challenge of this assignment, it is going to take an hour of practice each day to reach the standard we set." In general, portray effort as an investment which will produce knowledge or skill development and thus empower learners, rather than as a means of avoiding failure or embarrassment (Brophy, 1987).

*Make the Learning Goal as Clear as Possible.* When learners understand exactly what they are to learn, confusion cannot detract from their expectancy to succeed. This may mean distributing instructional objectives, handing out a list of learning outcomes, or writing the purpose of a particular unit of study on the chalkboard—whatever it takes to clearly let the learners know what they are expected to learn.

*Make the Criteria of Evaluation as Clear as Possible.* For most adults, evaluation procedures will heavily influence their receptivity to feedback, their feelings of reinforcement, their sense of progress, and their self-confidence as learners. The criteria of evaluation have to be clear to them from the beginning of learning if they are to know which elements of their performance and effort are essential. When the criteria are clear, they have a "road map" to success and can self-direct and self-evaluate their learning as they proceed. The teacher's role is to explain as specifically as appropriate the standards of evaluation so that the learners can comprehend how these are applied and used as measures of learning. When possible, the distribution to learners of tests and projects from former courses which have had the same criteria of evaluation applied to them can dramatically help learners to understand what is expected of them.

*Promote the Adults' Self-determination Within the Learning Experience.* Because adults are inclined toward autonomy, giving them the opportunity to initiate and/or direct their own learning should enhance their positive attitude toward the learning endeavor. The boundaries for the application of this strategy will depend upon such factors as the learning objective, time limitations, and learner expertise in self-direction. So, to the degree possible, have learners plan and set goals for their own learning and make their own choices about what, how, and when to learn.

*Needs*

*Know and Emphasize the Felt Needs of the Learners Throughout the Instructional Process.* Felt needs are in the conscious awareness of the learner and they are needs that the learner wants or desires to gratify (Monette, 1977). A felt need of an adult in a woodworking class might be "to make something for my home," or a felt need for a parent in a family relations course might be "to learn how to discipline my children more effectively." Although felt needs may not represent all the real needs of adult learners, these needs are a fundamental part of the goals and interests that adults bring to a learning experience. The most direct method to survey these needs is to ask the learners through interviews, group discussion, or questionnaires what they most want to get out of this learning experience. The teacher then integrates these learner-felt needs into the learning activities.

*Plan Activities to Allow Adults to Share What They Have Learned and Produced.* When adults know form the beginning that their learning outcomes will be shared and available to their fellow learners, their motivation for the learning task is usually increased. Public attention means public evaluation. This activates their need for esteem with its accompanying motivational influence. However, the emphasis should be on sharing, gaining feedback, appreciating uniqueness, understanding personal differences, and learning from one another. Adults like to see how their peers solve similar problems, apply new skills, and evaluate their work. The spirit engendered by the teacher in these activities is, "These are the ways we respectfully learn from and with each other so that all of us can be more successful at what we value."

### Stimulation

*Provide Variety in the Processes and Materials Used for Learning.* Variety is stimulating and draws learner attention toward its source. People tend to pay more attention to things that are changing than to things that are unchanging. However, variety that disrupts necessary concentration is an unwise strategy. Timing an activity so it can serve as a cue or a needed change in function or form of learning is probably the best way to do it. Strategies to infuse variety include:

- Changing methods of instruction, e.g., lecturing, discussion, or games
- Changing materials used for instruction, e.g., books, videotapes, or slides
- Changing interpersonal learning patterns, e.g., individual, partners, or small groups

The general goal is to never allow the course or training to become a "daily grind."

*Use Disequilibrium to Stimulate Learner Involvement.* Cognitive disequilibrium is the tension people feel when they experience something that does not fit what they already know. This tension causes them to involve themselves with the new experience until they can understand or fit it into what they know or can do. This is a strong part of the attraction of new words, ideas, or skills. The novel engages people as long as it is not so strange as to confuse or scare them. For instruction, this works for both content and process. New topics, unusual class assignments, unfamiliar insights, surprising research, and unique skills will encourage learner involvement. The guideline for the teacher is: Continuously bring to learners information or processes that are different, novel, contrasting, or discrepant from what they already know or have experienced. This is what can make learning fascinating.

### Affect

*Make Abstract Content More Personal and Familiar.* To some extent this can be done by applying what is being learned to the daily lives of the learners, such as how new technology or new ideas are found in current events, local lifestyles, and regional media. Other ways include demonstrations using familiar objects, pictures, and movies as well as employing examples with famous people or events. When learners can see an ancient event as analogous to the Olympics or a historical leader as similar to a current president, they will more readily have some feelings about what they are learning. Also when they can see the human advantages of discoveries in the physical and natural sciences, they are more likely to want to know them and care about them. In general when people find any way to identify with what they are learning, they will more readily have their emotions involved in the learning process. This enhances their overall participation.

*Use Cooperative Goal Structures to Achieve Learning Outcomes.* A cooperative structure exists when learners work together to achieve joint goals (Johnson & Johnson, 1987). In cooperative groups, members seek outcomes that benefit both themselves and their colleagues. A common example is for a group of learners to produce a single product such as a research report, a problem solution, or a plan of action. In such groups, conditions are arranged so that every member has a substantive role to play and must participate actively. Research indicates that a cooperative goal structure, compared with competitive and individualistic ones, promotes more positive interpersonal relationships, higher emotional involvement in productivity, and a lower fear of failure (Johnson & Johnson, 1987).

## Competence

*Provide Consistent and Prompt Feedback to Learners Regarding Their Performance and Mastery in Learning Tasks.* Feedback is information that learners receive about the quality of their performance on a given task. Knowledge of results, comments about skill performance, notes on a written assignment, graphic records, and an approving nod are forms of feedback that teachers often use with adult learners. Feedback appears to enhance motivation because it allows learners to evaluate their progress, to understand the level of their competence, to maintain their effort toward realistic goals, to correct their errors with little delay, and to receive encouragement from their teachers.

*Whenever Possible, Use Performance Evaluation Procedures.* Performance evaluation procedures are the construction of situations in which the learner actually performs a sample of the behaviors with which a given learning experience is concerned. This is done in a manner resembling as closely as possible the ways in which what has been learned will ultimately be expressed (Knowles, 1980). This may be a real situation in which an actual learned behavior, such as operating a machine or carrying out a procedure, is performed and the performance is rated, timed, or otherwise measured. Also, it may be a simulated situation resembling real life as closely as possible. For example, if a teacher wanted to evaluate training in medical diagnostic procedures, there is the possibility of using actual patients or simulated cases. Performance evaluation procedures enhance adult motivation to learn because they realistically clarify competency, build self-confidence, and clearly lead to the transfer of learning to personal or professional life.

## Reinforcement

*Use Positive Reinforcers for Routine, Well-learned Activities, Complex Skill Building, and Drill-and-Practice Activities.* Routine, well-learned activities are situations where the learner has the basic skills but there is a need to improve the speed, rate, or persistence of the skill. Typing, monitoring instruments or machines, and various sport skills such as swimming laps are representative of this category. How to repair electrical equipment and how to operate high-tech machinery are illustrations of complex skill building. Drill-and-practice activities run the gamut from shooting free throws to solving a series of math problems. All of these learning activities have one thing in common—they usually follow some form of set sequence and process for effective learning and application. Positive reinforcement has been demonstrated as a very effective means to teaching such skills (Wlodkowski, 1985).

In such learning situations, extrinsic reinforcers usually are given immediately as positive feedback or rewards for successful completion of each step in the appropriate sequence. They take such various forms as money, comments, correct indicators, points, tokens, and tones and graphics on computers. The reason they are so effective is that they are very adaptable as a modality to precisely monitor, prescribe, and reinforce in a sequential manner. When such reinforcers are used to obviously confirm progress, they tend to be seen as informational about competence to adult learners.

*When Learning Has Natural Consequences, Help Learners to Be Aware of Them.* Natural consequences are the changes or results that the learners can perceive as produced by their learning behavior. Reading a book has the natural consequences of producing new insights. Solving a problem results in the natural consequence of a solution. The creation of any personal product through a learning activity such as a science experiment or creative essay is a natural consequence. Often learners are not aware of the natural consequences of their learning and teachers can help them by highlighting and emphasizing results. Also, by making learners active as soon as possible, natural consequences can occur to increase and maintain their motivation. Discussion, feedback, and comparison of learner progress with past work can positively draw the attention of adults to their learning accomplishments and enhance their sense of growing competence. "Look what you have done" can help a person to realize "look what you can do."

These classical motivational strategies are well documented and effective ways to influence adult motivation to learn. By applying them through a motivation plan, the teacher has a chance to systematically and consistently develop adult motivation to learn throughout the learning experience.

In conclusion, whether these strategies are offered as part of a motivation plan or as part of some other instructional approach, they have their best chance for success if they are within the repertoire of a person who teaches with *enthusiasm*. In educational research, enthusiasm enjoys a long history of being strongly and positively related to learner motivation (Wlodkowski, 1985). When we care about what we teach and this commitment is expressed in our instruction with appropriate degrees of emotion, animation, and energy, this tells learners we are teaching from our hearts as well as from our minds. This will not only attract the attention of adults but also will build the credibility that combined with effective expertise is the nurturing ground for inspired learning.

## REFERENCES

Brookfield, S. D. (1986). *Understanding and facilitating adult learning*. San Francisco: Jossey-Bass.

Brophy, J. (1983). Conceptualizing student motivation. *Educational psychologist, 18*(3), 200-215.

Brophy, J. (1987). Synthesis of research strategies for motivating students to learn. *Educational Leadership, 45*(2), 40-48.

Deci, E. L., & Ryan, R. M. (1985). *Intrinsic motivation and self-determination in human behavior*. New York: Plenum.

Johnson, D. W. (1980). Attitude modification methods. In F. H. Kanfer & A. P. Goldstein (Eds.), *Helping people change* (pp. 58-96). Elmford: Pergamon.

Johnson, D. W., & Johnson, R. T. (1987). Research shows the benefits of adult cooperation. *Educational Leadership, 45*(3), 27-30.

Knowles, M. S. (1980). *The modern practice of adult education: From pedagogy to andragogy* (Revised and Updated). Chicago: Follett.

Knox, A. B. (1977). *Adult development and learning: A handbook on individual growth and competence in the adult years*. San Francisco: Jossey-Bass.

Monette, M. L. (1977). The concept of educational need: An analysis of selected literature. *Adult Education, 27*(2), 116-127.

Scott, J. P. (1969). A time to learn. *Psychology Today, 2*(10), 46-48, 66-67.

Spence, J. T. (Ed.). (1983). *Achievement and achievement motivates*. San Francisco: Freeman.

Tough, A. (1979). *The adult's learning projects* (2nd ed.). Austin: Learning Concepts.

Vargas, J. S. (1977). *Behavior psychology for teachers.* New York: Harper & Row.

Wlodkowski, R. J. (1985). *Enhancing adult motivation to learn.* San Francisco: Jossey-Bass.

# CHAPTER 6

## The Art of Questioning

RAY E. SANDERS

Questioning is probably the most fundamental instructional methodology available. Questioning is used in conjunction with many other teaching methods; however, it is commonly the most overlooked method by inexperienced instructors. Questioning techniques afford two-way communication. Instruction without the proper use of questioning frequently results in exposing the learners to information without much learning occurring. The types of questions and the techniques used in questioning can help create reflective, active learners rather than parroting, passive learners.

### THE PURPOSE OF QUESTIONS

Questioning is a part of everyday communication. We ask questions of our spouses, children, colleagues, and even strangers. The focus of this chapter is on educative questions rather than everyday questions. The difference between educative questions and everyday questions lies in the amount of thought it takes to develop them. It requires no extra thought to ask an everyday question; that is, the question naturally occurs to us. Educative questions are designed to advance pedagogical purposes and therefore require much thought to be effective.

Taba (1988) described questioning as the single most influential teaching act because of the ability of questions to influence the learning process. Levin and Long (1981) reported that teachers ask as many as three hundred to four hundred questions a day. They also tend to ask them in rapid-fire fashion.

A question may serve several purposes simultaneously. Among the many purposes of questions are:

a. To gain the learner's participation in class.

b. To determine what the learner knows about a subject.

c. To focus attention of the learner.

d. To lead discussions.

e. To review subject matter.

f. To stimulate thinking.

g. To test the learner's knowledge of subjects covered in class.

## CHARACTERISTICS OF GOOD QUESTIONS

Questions should be clearly stated and easily understood. They should be worded in such a way that the learner knows exactly what is being asked. Ambiguous or unclear questions may lead to frustration and nonparticipation of the learners. In this vein, questions should also be as brief as possible.

Questions should be composed of common wording. Design questions so that the learners understand the terminology being used. Otherwise, learners will focus on terminology rather than on ideas. Instructors should never use questions to try to "trick" learners with rhetoric. Questions should focus on the major components of the lesson.

Good questions require much thought. Questions should be prepared in advance whenever possible. It may be necessary to try to anticipate discussions in order to prepare possible questions, depending of course, on the purpose of the questions. These carefully prepared questions should not take the place of questions which may be asked on the spur of the moment whenever the instructor believes that a question is appropriate, but they should provide a satisfactory skeleton around which good impromptu questions may be asked.

Questions should require the learner to take an active, reflective role in learning. Strategies and techniques which engage the learner should be used.

## A QUESTIONING PROCEDURE

Skillful use of questions which engage the learner comes with practice. However, there are a few strategies and techniques which may be used as general guidelines.

It is generally a poor method of questioning when the instructor asks questions and allows the entire group to answer in chorus. It may be a successful method of stimulating a dull class or encouraging shy students to participate; however, these good points are usually overshadowed by inherent disadvantages. This group method permits the learner's attention to wonder. It decreases individual thought. Further, the group method of asking questions does not allow the instructor to monitor feedback from individual learners.

One of the major deficiencies in instructor questioning is that there is generally no significant pause or wait time given for learners to think about the question and to organize their thoughts. Pausing or wait time is especially important to adult learners. A pause after an answer or several different answers to the same question may be valuable in order to permit the learner to think through the idea before a new thought is proposed by a new question (Miller & Rose, 1975).

Mental participation of the learners can be achieved through a simple five part questioning procedure. The procedure affords wait time which stimulates thinking.

1.  *Ask question.* The instructor should state the question clearly and concisely. When possible, the question should be well in mind before it is asked. If a question is complicated it may be necessary to state it more than once, varying the wording. It is imperative that the question is stated *before* naming the person to respond.

2.  *Pause.* After the question has been asked, pause so that everyone will have time to think about the question. It is important that enough wait time is given. Fifteen seconds may seem like an

eternity to the inexperienced instructor. It may be helpful to watch the learners for nonverbal feedback to determine how long to pause.

3. *Call on one learner by name.* When learners are faced with the possibility of being called on to answer the question, they are more likely to try to formulate an answer. Learners should be randomly selected to answer the questions. If the instructor develops a pattern of selecting learners to answer the question, the purpose of the technique has been defeated.

4. *Listen to the answer.* A good technique to ensure that all learners are focused on the idea presented is to ask someone else to respond to the answer given.

5. *Emphasize the correct answer.* This should be done without embarrassing the respondent. It may be necessary to ask probing questions to have the respondent clarify the response, to support a point of view, or to extend their thinking.

Because everyone is included, this questioning procedure can help ensure that all learners are thinking about the ideas being presented. When this procedure is not used, that is when the instructor calls on a student and then asks the question, everyone except the student called on may have the tendency to relax.


## LEVELS OF QUESTIONS

Sanders (1966) stated that good questions recognize the wide possibilities of thought and are built around varying forms of thinking. Good questions are directed toward learning and evaluative thinking, rather than what has been learned in a narrow sense. Some instructors intuitively ask questions of high quality, but far too many overemphasize those that require the learner only to remember, and practically no instructors make full use of all worthwhile questions (Sanders, 1966).

Questions can be classified in several ways. A universally accepted classification of questions in the cognitive domain was developed by Bloom et al. (1956): knowledge, comprehension, ap-

plication, analysis, synthesis, and evaluation. A brief explanation
of Bloom's taxonomy follows.

### Knowledge

Knowledge involves the recall of specifics and universals, the
recall of methods and processes, or the recall of a pattern, structure,
or setting. It is the lowest level in the hierarchy.

- *Knowledge of specifics.* The recall of specific and isolable bits
  of information, knowledge of terminology, and knowledge of
  specific facts.

- *Knowledge of ways and means of dealing with specifics.* This is
  knowledge of the ways of studying, organizing, judging, and criti-
  cizing.

- *Knowledge of the universals and abstractions in a field.* This is
  the knowledge of the major schemes and patterns by which phenomena and ideas are organized.

### Comprehension

This next level refers to a type of understanding or appre-
hension such that the individual knows what is being communicated
and can make use of the material or idea being communicated
without necessarily relating it to other material or seeing its fullest
implications.

- *Translation.* Comprehension as evidenced by the care and accuracy with which the communication is paraphrased or rendered
  from one language or communication to another.

- *Interpretation.* The explanation or summarization of a communication.

- *Extrapolation.* The extension of trends or tendencies beyond the
  given data to determine implications, consequences, corollaries,
  effects, etc., which are in accordance with the conditions described in the original communication.

*Application*

This level involves the use of abstractions in particular and concrete situations. The abstractions may be in the form of general ideas, rules of procedures, or generalized methods.

*Analysis*

This level includes questions concerned with the breakdown of a communication into its constituent elements or parts.

- *Analysis of elements.* Identification of the elements included in a communication.

- *Analysis of relationships.* The connections and interactions between elements and parts of a communication.

- *Analysis of organizational principles.* The organization, systematic arrangement, and structure which holds the communication together.

*Synthesis*

This level includes questions which focus on the putting together of parts to form a whole.

- *Production of a unique communication.* The development of a communication in which the writer or speaker attempts to convey ideas, feelings, and/or experiences to others.

- *Production of a plan, or proposed set of operations.* The development of a plan or the proposal of a plan of operations.

- *Derivation of a set of abstract relations.* The development of a set of abstract relations either to classify or explain particular data or phenomena, or the deduction of propositions and relations from a set of basic propositions or symbolic representations.

*Evaluation*

Questions at this level are used to develop judgments about the value of material and methods for given purposes.

- *Judgments in terms of internal evidence.* Evaluation of the accuracy of a communication from such evidence as logical accuracy, consistency, and other internal criteria.

- *Judgments in terms of external criteria.* Evaluation of material with reference to selected or remembered criteria.

Inherent in a taxonomy is that the higher levels subsume the lower ones. Thus comprehension subsumes knowledge; application subsumes comprehension, etc. This hierarchical nature of the taxonomy is important to remember when formulating questions at the various levels. Questions at the analysis level not only will guide learners in analysis but also will challenge them to function at the levels of application, comprehension, and knowledge. It is impossible for learners to analyze information without using some skills, without comprehending some ideals, and certainly not without having some base data.

## QUESTIONS AT THE VARIOUS COGNITIVE LEVELS

### Knowledge

Questions at this level can be considered to comprise the building blocks for other levels of intellectual functioning. Such questions tend to emphasize the parroting of information. They deal with the identification and recall of information such as who, what, where, when, and how. This does not mean that such questions are bad. If the purpose is to provide learners with a data base, then knowledge level questions are effective.

Questions at this level are easy to formulate. Instructors should know why they are asking questions at this level and be sure that they fit the learning objectives. An example of such a question would be: "What are two types of corrosive acid?"

### Comprehension

Comprehension questions ask the learner to show an understanding of the literal message contained in a communication (the learner is required to organize and select facts and ideas) or to discover or use a relationship between two or more ideas. The question at this level may give two ideas and ask for the relationship between them or it may give one idea and a relationship and ask for another idea that follows from the evidence. The ideas may be simple or complex.

Examples of questions and requests for information at the comprehension level include: "Restate the supervisor's responsibilities in your own words." or "What are the main ideas of sterilization procedures?"

## Application

Application questions require the learner to apply what has been learned to other situations and learning tasks. Exactly how the learner should function with the information is not explicitly related by the instructor. Part of the challenge lies in the learner's ability to determine the appropriate process to use. The central idea is that the learner deals with data or solves some type of problem (Hunkins, 1972). Application questions give practice in independent use of knowledge and skills.

Examples of application questions include: "Why is effective communication important?" "How are attitudes related to safety?" and "How is restating the speaker's ideas an example of active listening?"

## Analysis

Analysis questions require a lot of thought to formulate. They require the learner to separate a whole into component parts including elements, relationships, and orgnaizational principles. As stated earlier, before learners can deal with information at the analysis level they must have dealt with information at the lower levels.

Examples of analysis questions and requests for information are: "What are the parts or features of participatory management?" "Classify the enzymes according to their outcomes." "Outline/diagram/web the manufacturing process." and "How does the electron theory compare/contrast with the hole theory?"

## Synthesis

Synthesis questions encourage learners to engage in imaginative, original thinking (Sanders, 1966). These questions require the learners to organize the information they have obtained or considered at the lower levels of learning. In synthesis the learner must draw upon elements from many sources and put these together into a structure or pattern not clearly there before. Synthesis questions allow learners great freedom in seeking solutions to problems; however, a learning environment that seeks and rewards originality must be fostered for these questions to have their greatest impact. Instructors must make it clear that they have no definite answer in mind which the learner is to duplicate. Synthesis questions elicit divergent thinking which starts from a problem that offers a variety of possibilities radiating out to many satisfactory answers (Hunkins, 1976).

Some examples of synthesis questions are: "What would you predict/infer from the recent action of the board of directors?" "What ideas can you add to the retirement plan?" "How would you design a new information management system?" "What might happen if you combined the accounting department with the marketing department?" and "What solutions would you suggest for solving the high altitude engine stall?"

### Evaluation

These questions ask the learner to make judgments about the value, for some purpose, of ideas, works, solutions, methods, materials, etc. The answers involve the use of criteria as well as standards for appraising the extent to which particulars are accurate, effective, economical, or satisfying. Evaluation questions require the learner to set up appropriate values or standards and to determine how closely an idea or object meets these standards or values. The instructor must require both steps of the learner. Questions that specify the values for use in making a judgment are not evaluation questions but are rather interpretation questions.

Examples of evaluation questions and requests might be: "How would you decide about mandatory retirement?" "What is the most important long-range planning item?" "Do you agree with requiring safety shoes for all workers?" "Prioritize the department's goals." and "What criteria would you use to assess trainer efficiency and why?"

The level of questions should fit the curriculum objectives. Ask lower order questions if the curriculum objectives are at that level and ask higher order questions if the curriculum objectives are at that level. Higher order questions require active thinking on the part of learners. It is hard to imagine how people will learn to think without repeated opportunities to respond to higher order questions. Instructors should be cautious of expecting lower achieving learners to deal with higher order questions in the same manner as the higher achieving learners.


## SUMMARY

Questioning can be one of the most effective methods of teaching and is often used with other methodologies. Instructors should have a clear purpose in mind when asking questions. The questions should be well thought out and clearly and concisely stated.

Questioning strategies which engage the learner should be employed. Care should be given to ensure that learners take an active role in the learning process without feeling embarrassment.

Pausing is essential for thinking about ideas and the formulation of answers, especially for higher order questions. Higher order questions should be used to allow creativity and to foster critical thinking.

Questioning can be one of the most powerful teaching methods available when properly used. It is strongly suggested that persons in instructional roles practice strategies and techniques of questioning. Good questions and questioning techniques can make a fair instructor good and a good instructor great.


## REFERENCES

Bloom, B. S., Englehart, M. D., Furst, E. J., Hill, W. H., & Krathwohl, D. R. (Eds.). (1956). *Taxonomy of educational objectives, Handbook I: Cognitive domain*. New York: David McKay.

Hunkins, F. P. (1972). *Questioning strategies and techniques*. Boston: Allyn and Bacon.

Hunkins, F. P. (1976). *Involving students in questioning*. Boston: Allyn and Bacon.

Levin, T., & Long, R. (1981). *Effective instruction*. Washington D. C.: ASCD.

Miller, W. R., & Rose, H. C. (1975). *Instructors and their jobs* (3rd ed.). Chicago: American Technical Society.

Sanders, N. M. (1966). *Classroom questions: What kinds?* New York: Harper & Row.

Taba, H. (1966). *Teaching strategies and cognitive functioning in elementary school children.* San Francisco: San Francisco State College.

# PART TWO

# Methods
# and
# Techniques

# CHAPTER 7

## Learning Contracts

JUDITH M. O'DONNELL
ROSEMARY S. CAFFARELLA

*Sally Jones teaches in a continuing education program for nurses at a local community college. She has been asked to do a wellness update for the next semester. She realizes that the group of students in the course will be diverse in terms of age and experience. Her concern is that what she thinks is important to cover might be repetition for some and too advanced for others. She wants to make the class more responsive to the needs of the nurses and has thought about using learning contracts as one method for doing this. Sally wonders, though, if the participants in the course and her faculty colleagues will accept this form of instruction.*

In this chapter, the reader will be introduced to the instructional method known as the learning contract. As you will learn, the learning contract is an acceptable method for Sally Jones to consider. It is one which seeks to adapt educational needs to individual student needs and is a viable option when there is diversity in learner needs and interests. Sally's concern is also justified in terms of the participants' response. If the nurses are expecting primarily a lecture mode, the learning contract will take an adjustment on their part. Also her own colleagues, including the department head, may not like this type of method as they have the perception that it allows the learner too much freedom to learn what they want to learn rather than what they should learn.

The purpose of this chapter will be to focus on the use of contract learning in formal adult learning situations, such as

133

workshops, courses, conferences, and so on. However, the learning contract can be used by individual adult learners in their own self-directed or informal learning. This chapter addresses the underlying justifications of contract learning, suggests the advantages and disadvantages of the method, and through a discussion of the roles and duties of those involved, will assist both the educator and learner with the mechanics for utilizing the method. First, a working definition of the method will be discussed.

## WORKING DEFINITION

A learning contract is a formal agreement written by a learner which details what will be learned, how the learning will be accomplished, the period of time involved, and the specific evaluation criteria to be used in judging the completion of the learning. The learning contract is a method that is used to individualize the learning process.

The use of the word *contract* suggests that what is written in the agreement is important, legitimate, and fair to the party or parties concerned. The agreement, though not binding in a legal sense, can be a contract with an educator, a mentor, a small committee, a work supervisor, an educational institution, or with oneself for a self-directed learning project (Knowles, 1986; Lindquist, 1975).

As the definition suggests, the adult learner is responsible for establishing the parameters for the learning effort. However, as with other instructional methods, flexibility is important. There are many variations in how the learning contract format can be used (Knowles, 1986). Two of the most widely used variations are described below.

### Learner Constructs Entire Contract

Here, the entire learning activity is planned by the learner. There are no base line objectives which must be met that have been specified by an educator or supervisor. The learner is free to pursue a subject in any manner possible. An example would be Sally Jones deciding to let the nurses in the continuing education wellness program design their own learning situation including the content or subject matter. The input that Sally would make would be to serve as a resource to the participants in developing their learning plans.

## Learner Constructs Most or Part of Contract

The learner may plan the learning around course objectives, organizational orientation objectives, subject matter standards, and so on. In other words, the "what" to be learned may not be negotiable; however, how the learner achieves the "what" is open to individual discretion. In this case, Sally would develop a set of objectives which each nurse would need to accomplish by course end. How the nurses accomplish these set objectives would be their decision. In either case, or in any variations between, the adult learner is actively involved in the decision making relevant to both the product and process of learning.

Since learning is an active process, the contract allows the adult to participate as actively as possible. The decision to use a full or partial learning contract would be based on the instructor's knowledge of the subject matter, the student's knowledge, the instructor's beliefs about the role of the educator, the subject matter itself, and so on. These thoughts will be discussed in detail later in the learning contract discussion.

## Sample Learning Contract

What does a learning contract look like and what are its major components? One sample format for a learning contract is outlined in Figure 7.1. As can be seen in this contract outline, the learning contract provides a framework for describing what a participant will learn as a result of a learning activity. This sample contract consists of five sections which are generic to most learning contracts (Knowles, 1975; Lindquist, 1975):

1. Learning objectives

2. Learning resources and strategies

3. Target date for completion

4. Evidence of accomplishment

5. Evaluation of the learning

Learning Contract

——————————————————— Learning Experience ———————————————————

Learner

| Learning objectives (What are you going to learn?) | Learning resources and strategies (How are you going to learn it?) | Target date for completion | Evidence of accomplishment (How are you going to demonstrate that you have learned it?) | Evaluation of the learning (What are the criteria on which you will judge that your learning efforts have been successful and who will be involved in that judging process?) |
| --- | --- | --- | --- | --- |

Figure 7.1 A sample learning contract form.

Both parties in the contract agreement, learner and facilitator, agree to the five components of the learning contract.

*Assumptions Underlying the Use of Learning Contracts*

Effective instruction of adults calls for knowledge of the nature of the adult learner. The early writings of Lindeman (1926), made concrete by Knowles (1980), suggest four basic assumptions about the adult learner:

1. Their self-concept moves from being dependent toward being an independent self-directed human being.

2. They accumulate a growing reservoir of experience that can be used as a resource for learning.

3. Their readiness to learn is linked with the developmental tasks of their life roles.

4. Their time perspective toward learning shifts from postponed to immediate application and from subject-centeredness to performance-centeredness (Knowles, 1980, pp. 44–45).

A variety of instructional strategies have grown out of these assumptions. One such strategy is the use of learning contracts in adult education environments. Knowles (1986, p.41) suggests, "Contract learning is an approach to education that is most congruent with the assumptions about learners on which the andragogical model is based . . . " The learning contract is a means whereby adults can individualize their learning, and reconcile their own individual initiative and commitment with the expectations of school, employers, and/or supervisors (Smith, 1982). The learning contract is a good fit with the andragogical model.

## AUDIENCE FOR CONTRACT LEARNING

The learning contract can be used with diverse audiences. These audiences may include adult learners from a variety of settings such as higher education, business and industry, libraries, museums, hospitals, volunteer agencies, and public schools. Literature suggests that the primary audiences for contract learning has been higher education and professional groups. However, with modifications, the contract could be a viable approach with other types of learners. For example, one modification might include using verbal contract or having volunteers write contracts for learners with limited reading and writing skills. This modification might open the use of learning contracts to Adult Basic Education (ABE) or General Equivalency Diploma (GED) students.

The learning contract is particularly appropriate in situations when the goal is to help learners gain skills in learning as well as content. Contract learning makes the learning a personal experience since it involves the student in the decision making regarding the goals, methods of learning, and evaluation. It also tends to heighten motivation by placing the responsibility for the learning in the hands of the student (Buzzell & Roman, 1981). It helps to make visible the mutual responsibilities of the learner and the educator in meeting learning goals (Knowles, 1984). The learning contract is appropriate when one has the freedom to allow openness. It helps show people there are more resources than teacher procured resources (Knowles, 1980).

In addition, many of the dimensions of adult learning are very individual. A group of learners will quite often differ in the resources they prefer to use, the conditions under which they learn best, and their information processing style as well as personal abilities and characteristics. The learning contract is a mechanism for recognizing these individual differences and providing an optimal experience for each adult.

Sample learning contracts may be found in Figures 7.2 and 7.3. Figure 7.2 is designed for Adult Basic Education and Figure 7.3 is a partial contract for a graduate course in adult development and learning. These learning contract examples should be helpful in showing a range of audiences for the instructional strategy. However, as Combs (1964, p. 372) proposes, "Methods, like the clothes we wear, must fit the people we are". The educator must view the pros and cons of the method and evaluate the approach both in terms of educational appropriateness and personal fit.

## ADVANTAGES OF LEARNING CONTRACTS

There are four major advantages of the learning contract approach:

1. The flexibility of the approach makes it suitable for many learning experiences.

2. The learner is in control of the learning process.

3. Contract learning allows the development of instructional design skills by the learner.

4. Learners like the approach.

Each of these advantages will be explored in greater detail in the following sections.

## Flexibility of the Approach

The learning contract allows learners flexibility in meeting educator, institutional, or personal learning objectives. Learners are allowed to progress at their own pace, and there is no fear or anxiety caused by the feeling that one is falling behind other learners. Learners are proceeding at a pace which is comfortable for them.

Also in terms of flexibility, learning contracts are not immutable; they can be changed. The contract can be modified as goals change, as formative evaluation shows they should change, and/or as the learners' interests and needs change. Also, because of individual differences, learners may be able to study above and beyond what the minimum standards would indicate. Here, learners are not held back or bored with a minimum level of knowledge. Therefore, the learning contract allows the flexibility of differing levels of accomplishment.

## Control of the Learning Process

Smith (1982) suggests that the learning contract reinforces commitment, accountability, and the motivation to follow through on the learning effort. Basically, the approach emphasis is on the process of learning, which takes it out of the "teacher provides the content" structure. With this focus on process, the learners become actively involved, therefore, strengthening their interest in completing the work.

Knowles (1980) suggests that the learning contract induces learners to be more creative in identifying learning resources and developing strategies, and forces them to get better evidence of their

| Objectives | Learning Strategies and Resources | Evidence of Accomplishment | Evaluation of the Learning | Time Schedule |
|---|---|---|---|---|
| 1. List sources of employment information. | 1. View slide-tape presentation on job hunting.<br>2. Read a handout on "sources of employment."<br>3. Brainstorm with fellow class members on sources of jobs. | Class attendance; a list of places where I could go to find work. | The list will be realistic for my employment level and needs—validated by teacher and employment counselor. | November 1 |
| 2. Demonstrate that student can read and interpret employment ads. | 1. Work in class on reading want ads.<br>2. Collect want ads for one week and circle those jobs that might be appropriate. | Class attendance; submission of want ads. | The want ads circled will be realistic and appropriate—validated by teacher. | November 1 |
| 3. Demonstrate a basic technique of calling an employer on the phone. | 1. In-class participation.<br>2. Practice with class partner calling a potential employer. | Class attendance; actual participation in phone exercise. | The phone manner and conversation will be pleasant and correct-validated by teacher and fellow students. | November 8 |

| Objective | Learning Activities | Evaluation | Criteria | Date |
|---|---|---|---|---|
| 4. Write a letter of application for employment. | 1. In-class participation. <br> 2. Practice writing letters of employment. <br> 3. Write an actual letter to a potential employer. | Class attendance; submit set of practice letters and actual letters. | The actual letter to a potential employer will be clear and well written—validated by teacher and employment counselor. | November 15 |
| 5. Fill out a job application. | 1. In-class participation. <br> 2. Fill out at least five "mock" applications. <br> 3. Complete at least one real application for employment. | Class attendance; submit mock application and real application forms. | The real application form will be filled out correctly, neat, and legible—validated by teacher and employment counselor. | November 15 |
| 6. Describe what will happen in interview. | 1. In-class participation. <br> 2. Participation in at least two mock interviews. | Class attendance; completion of at least two mock interviews. | Manner and language used will be correct for a job interview; answers to questions will be complete and honest—validated by teacher and fellow students. | November 22 |

Figure 7.2 Sample learning plan: ABE student.

| Objectives | Learning Strategies and Resources | Evidence of Accomplishment | Evaluation of the Learning | Time Schedule |
|---|---|---|---|---|
| 1. Describe the major sociological, psychological, physiological and environmental factors which make adults distinct from earlier developmental levels. | 1. In-class work.<br>2. Complete required readings.<br>3. Complete a general review of the literature focused. | 1. Class attendance and participation<br>2. Submission of annotated bibliography cards<br>3. Submission of an annotated bibliography | 1. Active and relevant participation—validated by instructor and fellow students.<br>2. Annotated bibliography cards and list will be written in a clear and concise manner—validated by instructor.<br>3. A comprehensive review will be completed and written in a clear and precise manner—validated by Dr. Shoe and instructor. | 2. October 15<br>3. November 15 |

| | Learning Activities | Evidence | Validation | Date |
|---|---|---|---|---|
| 2. Gain a basic understanding of adult development theory from the life cycle perspective. | 1. In-class work. 2. Complete required readings. 3. Complete a paper comparing and contrasting the theories/writing of Levinson, Gould and Valient. | 1. Class attendance and participation 2. Submission of annotated bibliography cards 3. Submission of a 8- to 10-page paper | 1. Active and relevant participation—validated by instructor and fellow students. 2. Annotated bibliography cards will be written in a clear and concise manner. 3. The paper will be well written and reflect adequately the thinking of each author—validated by instructor. | 2. November 1 3. December 1 |
| 3. Identify and describe themselves as an adult person in terms of development phase and learning style. | 1. In-class work. 2. Complete a paper describing oneself as an adult learner. | 1. Class attendance and participation 2. Submission of paper | 1. Active and relevant participation—validated by instructor and fellow students. 2. The paper will be clear, well organized, and an honest reflection on self—validated by close friend and instructor. | October 1 |

Figure 7.3 Sample learning plan: partial contract for graduate course in adult development and learning.

| Objectives | Learning Strategies and Resources | Evidence of Accomplishment | Evaluation of the Learning | Time Schedule |
|---|---|---|---|---|
| 4. Interpret and distinguish between major learning theories; identify proponents of each and relate the theories to adult learners. | 1. In-class participation.<br>2. Required readings. | 1. Class attendance and participation<br>2. Submission of annotated bibliography cards | 1. Active and relevant participation—validated by fellow students and instructor.<br>2. Annotated bibliography cards will be written in a clear and concise manner—validated by instructor. | 2. November 1 |
| 5. Identify current concepts and resource materials regarding the needs, interests, motivation, and capability of adult learners. | 1. In-class participation.<br>2. Required readings.<br>3. Interview three practicing adult educators; collect resource people from these people, instructor, and others. | 1. Class attendance and participation<br>2. Submission of annotated bibliography cards<br>3. Develop a resource notebook on the needs, interests, and motivational techniques as these relate to adult learners. | 1. Active and relevant participation—validated by fellow students and instructor.<br>2. Cards will be written in a clear and concise manner—validated by instructor.<br>3. The resource notebook will be well organized and comprehensive in scope. | 2. November 1 |

accomplishments. The contract requires active involvement and dialogue between the student and facilitator which may not happen in other learning structures. This process can have the benefit of replacing the teacher-imposed learning discipline with self-discipline in learning. Caffarella and O'Donnell (1988) found that among professional trainers engaged in self-directed learning, the learner control of the learning project and its evaluation were important quality dimensions. Knowles (1986) suggests that the quality of learning is improved since the learner is actively involved in the decision making and so is more committed to the learning.

Hodgkinson (1975) also suggests that evaluation of the learning contract is usually more specific than general course work evaluation, since contracts usually involve focusing on specific problems and the evaluation is based around those problems. Also, the development of the evaluation criteria can prove to be both creative and motivating for the learner. The learner might involve other professionals or expert practitioners in the verification process, above and beyond the educator. For example, the learner could involve an immediate supervisor, not normally in an educational role, as part of the evaluation team. This would serve a number of purposes, one being an aid to the transfer of learning back on the job, another being that more interest is created with more people involved in the project.

## Development of Instructional Design Skills

Lindquist (1975) and Knowles (1980) suggest that contract learning develops the habit of lifelong learning. However, Caffarella and Caffarella (1986) found that the contract has little impact on developing readiness for self-directedness in learning, but does have some impact on developing competencies for self-directed learning. The competencies which increased were the abilities to: (a) translate learning needs into learning objectives, (b) identify human and material learning resources, and (c) select effective strategies for using learning resources. Caffarella and O'Donnell (1988) found that locating appropriate resources seemed to be a key as to whether one specific group, training professionals, termed their self-directed learning activities as quality experiences. Therefore, building competencies in the identification and use of resources would appear to be extremely useful in helping adults learn how to learn.

*Learners Like Contract Learning*

Learners appear to like the flexibility and independence, and the contract satisfies their desire to personalize learning (Lindquist, 1975). Caffarella (1983) in a study conducted with graduate students found that 83 percent strongly agreed that the learning contract placed the responsibility for learning more on them than other formats used in formal course work; 81 percent strongly agreed the learning contract assisted them in meshing their own learning needs/desires with the course requirements; and 76.2 percent strongly agreed that the learning contract gave them the opportunity to individualize their own learning. In another study, Polczynski and Shirland (1976) compared traditional grading and contract grading and found that student effort increased significantly using the contract method of grading. Basically, the students liked being treated as adults and being made responsible for their own learning.

## LIMITATIONS OF LEARNING CONTRACTS

There are four major limitations to the learning contract approach:

1. Discomfort with the unknown

2. Quality of the learning

3. Time pressures

4. Not suitable for all situations

Again, each of these will be explored in greater detail below.

*Discomfort with the Unknown*

Lindquist (1975) suggests that common to adopting new ways of doing things, there is some discomfort with the unknown. Using contract learning is often a new experience for both learners and teachers. The learner needs to go through a reorientation on what this type of learning is all about, while teachers need to redefine their roles as teachers. This often creates feelings of anxiety and uneasiness for both parties. Some students have reported (Buzzell & Roman, 1981) that they felt a lot of pressure when asked to write a learning contract for the first time. They felt they got caught up in the contract form, getting creative with evidence and verification of learning, and lost sight of what they needed to learn. The contract became an end in itself and not a means to an end.

When using learning contracts, it is important to set up a nonthreatening environment—a climate of mutual respect and a supportive attitude. Many adults have become so conditioned to having educators tell them what to do and when to do it, they become worried and anxious when confronted with taking an equal part of the responsibility for their own learning. In a nonthreatening atmosphere, the discomfort can be processed and adults can be helped to diagnose, plan, and conduct their own learning experience.

## Quality of the Learning

Educators are concerned about the academic quality of the learning that results from the contracting process. Is the learning of the same depth, breadth, or degree as that found with other instructional methods? There is a concern that because of the thrust of the approach, that of providing a forum for individual differences, learners may not learn what "they should" learn. Quality needs to be viewed as containing three aspects: learning product, learning process, and learning function (e.g., motivation, control, transfer of learning) (Smith, 1982). Therefore, if the learner is actively involved in designing a process of learning, has the learning under control, and is motivated to pursue a process and achieve a product, then the elements of quality are accounted for. Although the learning contract does not fit all situations, in the right learning environments it can well enhance the quality of learning. In general, the educator does not have to relinquish standards of quality when using a learning contract.

## Time Pressures

Lindquist (1975) also points out that use of the learning contract takes significant amounts of teacher/mentor time which can lead to a "does not pay" attitude on the part of educators, since the contracts distract them from other pursuits which may pay better returns. This is also related to the organizational support for the approach. Does the organization support the time needed to use learning contracts? Have new and different reward structures been introduced to recognize the use of innovative and/or different instructional methods?

### Not Suitable for All Situations

The learning contract may not be useful when the learning involves the development of psychomotor skills or interpersonal skills, or when the subject matter is new to the learner (Knowles, 1986). The learner needs enough familarity with the subject matter in order to be able to select resources and learning strategies.

The learning contract format also presents problems when the learners are highly dependent or when they are unmotivated. Here, however, the teacher/facilitator could work with the participant to develop the skills to use the contract learning format to their benefit.


## ROLES AND DUTIES OF CONTRACT PARTIES

Before the specific duties of the learner and facilitator(s) are discussed, we need to point out that the educator must gain the support of the sponsoring institution in order for the learning contract to be an effective instructional strategy. By its definition, contract learning is a process that is responsive to individual learner differences. If this kind of thinking represents a significant departure from normal operation procedure, then the process will need to be explained to the institutional hierarchy. For example, a student in higher education might decide that class attendance is not important to the completion of the learning contract. This would be perfectly acceptable behavior in contract learning but may not be seen as such by administrators unless it was explained in advance. Or, the orientation and professional development trainer in a hospital might find that learners want to interview the managers responsible for insurance claims rather than read the available brochures and other written materials on the subject. Again, this makes perfect sense unless the managers do not understand why three new employees are interviewing them.

The specific roles and duties of each party to the contract are discussed below. It would be helpful for the reader to use the two additional sample learning contracts as guides. Figure 7.4 is a workshop contract on conflict management and Figure 7.5 is a learning plan for visiting physician participants in clinical refresher courses. These sample contracts are the end result of the role and duty negotiations of each party to the contract.

*Roles and Duties of the Teacher*

In contract learning, the role of the teacher changes from being primarily a transmitter of content to learning facilitator and content resource person. Basically, the teacher/facilitator is responsible for the following.

1. Help the learner to develop the learning contract. The goal is to assist and supervise in order that the final package is complete and shows the promise of quality. If the learner has never been responsible for a learning contract, this orientation and coaching role is crucial. In general, the facilitator should make sure that the learning objectives are clear and realistic, that the learning strategies are reasonable, that the evidence of accomplishment is designed to be specific and appropriate, and that the evaluation procedures are clear and relevant.

2. Suggest learning resources which might be helpful to the learning project. These resources would include books, periodicals, people, and so on. The idea is to suggest what might be available and not to dictate specific resources.

3. Meet with the learner on an as-needed basis to review progress, supplement ideas and thinking, and perhaps negotiate a change in the contract. In some cases, it may be necessary to set up regular periodic reviews, especially in those situations where the learning contract is new to participants.

4. Evaluate the final work of the learner using the guidelines developed by the learner in the contract.

5. Give feedback on the person's learning to the appropriate parties; for example, by assigning a final grade or writing a memo to the employee's file.

*Role and Duties of the Learner*

The role of the learner shifts from being a passive receiver of content to being an active planner in the learning process. The

| Objectives | Learning Strategies and Resources | Evidence of Accomplishment | Evaluation of the Learning | Time Schedule |
|---|---|---|---|---|
| 1. Define the terms *conflict* and *conflict management*. | 1. Participation in sessions.<br>2. Reading of handout materials supplied by workshop coordinator.<br>3. Read at least five articles on conflict management. | 1. Session attendance and participation<br>2. Session participation<br>3. Development of annotated bibliography | 1. Active and relevant participation—validated by instructor and fellow participants.<br>2. Active and relevant participation—validated by workshop participant.<br>3. Annotations will be clear and precise—these will be shared with other participants—validated by fellow participants. | October 15 |

| 2. Identify and determine the basis of a conflict situation.<br>3. Identify and determine the scope of a conflict situation.<br>4. Outline the six major steps in the conflict cycle. | 1. Participation in sessions.<br>2. Reading of handout materials supplied by workshop coordinator. | 1. Session attendance and participation.<br>2. Session participation | 1&2. Active and relevant participation—validated by workshop leader and fellow participants. | October 15 |
| 5. Describe the four major strategies of dealing with conflict situations. | 1. Participation in session.<br>2. Interview at least three managers, asking them to describe how they deal with interoffice conflict. | 1. Session attendance and participation.<br>2. Share results of interview in session as part of a planned panel discussion. | 1. Active and relevant participation—validated by fellow participants.<br>2. The panel presentation will be well organized and complete—validated by workshop leaders and participants. | October 30 |

Figure 7.4 Sample learning plan: Combination in-service and independent study program on conflict management.

| Objectives | Learning Strategies and Resources | Evidence of Accomplishment | Evaluation of the Learning | Time Schedule |
|---|---|---|---|---|
| 6. Analyze two conflict situations, one involving interpersonal conflict, and one involving interorganizational conflict. Relate the concepts and ideas of conflict management to your specific area of practice, utilizing a real life situation. | 1. Participation in session.<br>2. Develop (with two other workshop participants) two case studies, one involving interpersonal conflict and the second, interorganizational conflict. | 1. Session attendance and participation.<br>2. Case studies will be written and presented to the workshop participants for analysis. | 1. Active and relevant participation—validated by fellow participants and workshop leaders.<br>2. Case studies will be clearly written and thought through with well-defined analysis questions—validated by fellow participants and workshop leaders. | November 15 |

Figure 7.4 Continued.

152

Name of Learner _____ Name of Facilitator _____ Department _____

AMA Category I Credit Hours Earned _____ Social Security Number _____ Date _____

| Learner's Objectives (What I propose to learn) | Learning Resources and Strategies (Resources, strategies and experiences I will use to learn this) | Evidence of Accomplishment (How I will know I have learned this) | Verification/Judge(s) (How I will verify I have learned this) |
|---|---|---|---|
| Pediatrics: to develop and review in-patient care of pediatric patients and to become acquainted with any new techniques and medications relating to this. | Spend a few days with pediatric housestaff and attending on teaching rounds, conferences, and direct patient care. The individuals will be observed for their approach to treating the patients that are currently being hospitalized in the Pediatric Ward and consulted for any questions concerning the diagnosis and treatment of these patients. | I would expect to spend these two days having seen clinical findings in much greater concentration than in the current practice that I have. In doing so I should feel as if I have reviewed a wide range of disease processes and physical findings that will be of great value to me in caring for patients in my present practice. | In being able to pick up potential problems in the pediatric population that I am seeing and feel more confident about treating these patients. |

_____
Signature of Facilitator

_____
Signature of Learner

(This contract is not binding, and may be negotiated at any time during the course by the Learners and Facilitator.)

Figure 7.5 Sample learning plan for visiting physician participants in MCV-CME clinical refresher courses (Office of Continuing Medication Education) Medical College of Virginia. Provided by Paul E. Mazmanian, Director, Continuing Education in Medical and Allied Health Professions, Virginia Commonwealth University, Richmond, Virginia. Reprinted with permission.

learner is responsible for diagnosing their own learning needs. Basically the duties are as follows.

1. State the learning objectives. Objectives are statements of what will be learned. If the learner has trouble wording objectives, the facilitator can recommend resources or work individually with the student on how to translate the learning need into the learning objective. Special attention needs to be paid to the action verb used in the learning objective. For example, will the learner "define" an area, be able to "describe" and area, be able to "apply" an area, or be able to "compare" an area? Each of these action words show a different level and type of learning.

2. Specify the learning resources and strategies. Resources are those materials or people which will be utilized, while strategies are the tools or techniques. For example, "I will interview (strategy) three agency volunteers (resources) on what they like about this agency." Frequently, a combination of resources and strategies are used to reach an objective or objectives. The more specific the learner is in describing the resources and strategies, the more helpful the educator/facilitator can be in making further suggestions. Some possible resources and strategies are given in Figure 7.6.

3. State the target date for completion. The learner needs to set realistic target dates for the accomplishment of each objective. The target dates help both the learner and the facilitator in the management of time.

4. Specify the evidence of accomplishment. In this section the learner describes what evidence will be collected to indicate that the objective has been accomplished. Some evidence must be collected for each objective. Evidence can take the form of written or oral reports, development of a videotape or poster presentation, and so on. The evidence of accomplishment for obtaining new knowledge can be demonstrated through a written report, an oral presentation, or by taking an exam. When learning a skill is the focus of the objective, the evidence of accomplishment might include performance exercises, videotaped performances, or some form of rating evidence by observers. Higher level objectives, those requiring evidence of

| Resources | Strategies |
|---|---|
| Teacher/Facilitator | Reading |
| Other Learners | Writing of research papers |
| Work Supervisors | Preparing an in-class presentation |
| Subject Matter Experts | Taking a field trip |
| Books | Developing a resource handbook |
| Journal and Magazine Articles | Preparing a case study analysis |
| Other Printed Materials | Writing a personal reflection paper |
| Audiotapes | Developing a performance exercise |
| Films | Completing a review of literature |
| Videotapes | Developing an audiovisual presentation |
| Computer Programs | Conducting interviews |
| Programmed Instruction | Preparing a case study |
| Videodiscs | Developing a role play |
| Case Study Materials | Conducting a game/simulation |
| Game/Simulation | |
| Skill Practice Exercises | |
| Photographs | |
| Records | |
| Television Programs | |

Figure 7.6 Examples of learning resources and strategies that can be used in carrying out a learning contract.

comprehension, application, synthesis, and so on, may be demonstrated by giving examples of using the new information, such as conducting research, developing a case study, writing a computer program, or any other actions project.

5. Specify how the learning will be evaluated. In this section the learner specifies how and by whom the evidence will be judged. Who will read the written report? What criteria will they use in judging it? The criteria will vary according to the type of objective. For example, appropriate criteria for knowledge objectives might include comprehensiveness, depth, precision, clarity, authentication, usefulness, scholarliness, and so on. For skill objectives more appropriate criteria may be poise, speed, flexibility, gracefulness, precision, imaginativeness, and so on.

The choice of judges will be dependent on the learning objectives and the context of the learning contract. The appropriate judge may be the teacher/facilitator, peers, a supervisor, or expert practitioners in the field of study.

6. Review the contract with the teacher/facilitator. This is the negotiation process for both the facilitator and the learner. The learner should enter into this discussion with an open mind. The facilitator may well have suggestions which could be added to the contract to help make it a better learning experience. Often, especially when the learner is new to learning contracts, the facilitator may need to cut down the number of objectives or the number of strategies employed. Another step in the review process may be to have fellow learners look at the learning contract. These fellow learners can help with clarifying objectives, suggest other resources and strategies, and in general, give feedback as to the clarity and relevancy of the contract.

7. Carry out the contract. Here the learner simply carries out what is specified in the contract. However, the learner is responsible for renegotiation any changes which can and do occur during the contract period.

8. Discuss the evaluation with the facilitator. Beyond the grade or memo to file which suggests that the learner has completed the contract, the learner would be well advised to discuss the entire contract package with the facilatator. This will help in designing future educational processes.

## Practical Hints for First Timers

Everyone is a first timer at some point. Based on our experience with learning contracts, we would like to share a list of helpful hints.

1. Expect that learners will react with anxiety, confusion, or even resistance. It is a frightening prospect to be made responsible for your own learning. Specific suggestions emanating from the Caffarella (1983) study were: (1) enlist the aid of more experienced fellow-learners in helping the beginner; (2) give those with no experience more time to develop their plans; and

(3) allow the less experienced learners to first develop a mini-learning plan and then complete a more in-depth one.

2. Give the learners very clear guidelines for developing learning contracts. However, do not distribute just one sample of a learning contract or it will be duplicated and given back to you. If you want to share examples, give the learners a number of very diverse samples.

3. When working with professionals, spend the time to acquaint them with the concepts and processes through doing practice exercises in contract writing.

4. Continue to read everything published about this approach. As a graduate student noted (Caffarella, 1983), "the instruction leader must be skilled at this approach to learning/teaching. The instructor must be a full-time learner, must understand this concept of learning, and must practice the concept correctly."

## EVALUATING THE LEARNING CONTRACT METHOD

Much more research is needed in order to evaluate the effectiveness of the learning contract approach with other approachers to teaching and learning. Chickering (1975) reports on a survey conducted at Empire State College where 46 percent of the students evaluated the learning contract as "superior" to traditional approaches; 26 percent rated it as "somewhat better," 13 percent as "comparable," and 2 percent as "somewhat inferior." Caffarella (1983) found that graduate students considered contract learning to be worthwhile and valuable. They were using the competencies gained from the process in both current teaching situations and in personal self-directed learning projects.

As with all instructional techniques, it is important for the educator to develop some criteria to see if the method was used properly, if the method was successful, and if changes need to be made to make the approach more usable in the future. Some points or criteria to cover in an honest appraisal would be:

1. Was the educator comfortable with the freedom of the learning contract? The adult educator needs to have confidence in any approach selected. This method is learner centered rather than teacher centered. Basically, this means the educator needs to

be secure enough in the subject matter to approach learning from the diverse needs and interests of the students. In making the learner centered/teacher centered decision there are three variables to assess: (1) the educator's levels of skill, (2) the maturity level of the learners, and (3) the complexity of the subject matter. Is it conducive to independent learning?

2.  Were the learners able to handle the learning contract? Some anxiety in writing a learning contract for the first time is inevitable. However, once over that hurdle, most learners enjoy the learning contract process. If they did not, then the educator needs to look at why this was so. Was it beyond their capability level? Were there external forces which limited the effectiveness of the approach? Could changes have been made to make it more effective?

3.  Did the learners achieve their objectives? This is the bottom line question. What were the results? Were there more cost effective ways (time and money) to achieve the same results? With learning contracts we are not evaluating the outcomes of teaching and the many problems associated with that approach to measurement. We are, however, evaluation something more concrete, whether the learner successfully achieved the learning objectives.

4.  Did the learning contract seem to fit the situation, time, place, and subject matter? The learning climate needs to be conductive to the development of learning contracts. There needs to be mutual trust, a realistic number of learners to work with, an opportunity to have independence between educator and learner, and so on. What might need to be revised in order to make the learning contract approach work better another time?

5.  What did the end of session evaluation show? Specific questions related to the use of learning contracts would prove beneficial in both using and modifying the approach to a specific situation.

## SUMMARY

This chapter has presented an analysis of learning contracts as an instructional method for adult learners. The concept of the learning contract was defined and a rationale was given in terms of its utilization. Advantages and disadvantages were discussed and the mechanics of using the learning contract approach were outlined. The educator was given some criteria on which to judge the merits of the method.

## REFERENCES

Buzzell, N., & Roman, O. (1981). Preparing for contract learning. In D. Boud (Ed.), *Developing student automony in learning* (pp. 135-144). New York: Nicholas.

Caffarella, R. S. (1983). Fostering self-directed learning in post-secondary education: The use of learning contracts. *Lifelong Learning: An Omnibus of Practice and Research, 1* (2), 7-10.

Caffarella, R. S. & Caffarella, E. P. (1986). Self-directedness and learning contracts in adult education. *Adult Education Quarterly, 36,* 226-234.

Caffarella, R. S., & O'Donnell, J. M. (1988). Self-directed learning: The quality dimension. *Proceedings of the 29th Adult Education Research Conference,* (pp. 31-36). Calgary, Alberta: University of Calgary.

Chickering, A. (1975). Developing intellectual competence at Empire State. In N. R. Berte (Ed.), *Individualizing education through contract learning* (pp. 62-76). Birmingham: The University of Alabama Press.

Combs, A. W. (1964). The personal approach to teaching. *Educational Leadership, 21,* 369-377, 399.

Hodgkinson, H. L. (1975). Evaluation to improve performance. In D. W. Vermilye (Ed.), *Learner-centered reform* (pp. 116-125). San Francisco: Jossey-Bass.

Knowles, M. S. (1980). *The modern practice of adult education* (rev. ed.). Chicago: Follett.

Knowles, M. S. (1984). *Andragogy in action: Applying modern principles of adult learning.* San Francisco: Jossey-Bass.

Knowles, M. S. (1986). *Using learning contracts.* San Francisco: Jossey-Bass.

Lindeman, E. C. (1926). *The meaning of adult education.* New York: Republic.

Lindquist, J. (1975). Strategies for contract learning. In D. W. Vermilye (Ed.), *Learner-centered reform* (pp. 75-89). San Francisco: Jossey-Bass.

Polczynski, J. J., & Shirland, L. E. (1976). Expectancy theory and contract grading combined as an effective motivational force for college students. *The Journal of Educational Research, 70,* 238-241.

Smith, R. M. (1982). *Learning how to learn.* Chicago: Follett.

# CHAPTER 8

## Lecture

SHIRLEY J. FARRAH

The thesis of this chapter is that the lecture is a legitimate instructional method for use by adult education practitioners. There is nothing inherently antithetical in the judicious use of oral discourse on the part of the teacher, and resultant learning on the part of the learner. Eble (1978) suggests that mediocre discussion classes, poor student reports, and ineffective panels or role playing are just as deadly as any lecture might be. Most of us have experienced good and poor lectures and lecturers, and we know when we hear and see them. A major point to keep in mind is that the purpose of the lecture is to *teach*—it is to be used as a teaching method, not just standing before a large group to speak (Hyman, 1974).

Learning can be facilitated through oral exposition and illustration without violating the basic principles of effective facilitation such as acknowledging the educational value of the learners' rich life experiences, fostering a sense of self worth, supportively challenging ways of thinking and believing, and encouraging critical reflection and application as well as active participant involvement. Much of the adult education literature would lead the practitioner to believe that somehow lecture negates any learning in the adult population. Yet most adult education practitioners know that lecture is one of the most frequently used methods. In fact, Darkenwald and Merriam (1982) reported that the lecture was the most preferred and most used instructional method in adult education.

As with each of the instructional methods, the choice of which method(s) to use is a function of the total teaching-learning situation—the objective of the transaction, learner preferences, preferences and skills of the teacher, and contextual variables such as time constraints, physical setting, and size of the learner group.

This chapter will begin with how to decide when lecture might be the method of choice and the advantages and limitations of this technique. Teacher qualifications and responsibilities of the teacher and learner will follow. The pattern of communication and seating arrangements will be addressed. Guides for the actual lecture preparation will be followed by tips on how to increase the effectiveness of the lecture. Finally, an evaluation strategy to determine the effectiveness of the lecture will be included.


## HOW TO DETERMINE WHEN TO USE LECTURE

A lecture is a carefully prepared oral presentation of a particular subject by a highly qualified individual (Bergevin, Morris, & Smith, 1963). Lecturing is informative speaking (Cooper, 1985). When the primary goal of the learning transaction is cognitive (information) transfer, the lecture method is well suited. Lecture is not the best approach to teach technical motor skills or modify attitudes (McKeachie, 1986; Verner & Dickinson, 1967). Lecture is appropriate when the information to be transmitted is not readily available or is scattered among diverse sources and when an expert has current information immediately desired or needed by a large group of learners in a short period of time (McKeachie, 1986). More specifically, lecture might be used when the purpose is to:

1.  Present information in an organized way in a relatively short time frame.

2.  Provide a framework for learning activities and further study which are to follow.

3.  Identify, explain, and clarify difficult concepts, problems, or ideas.

4.  Present an analysis of a controversial issue.

5.  Demonstrate relationships between previously learned and new information, and among apparently dissimilar ideas.

6. Model a creative mind at work, an expert's thought processes as the lecturer "thinks out loud."

7. Challenge the beliefs, attitudes, and behaviors of the learners.

8. Stimulate or inspire the audience to further inquiry (Bergevin, Morris, & Smith, 1963; Frederick, 1986; Sorcinelli & Sorcinelli, 1987).

If the purposes of the intended learning falls into any of these categories, lecture might be appropriate. But purpose is only one, albeit crucial, variable to consider. The qualifications of the speaker are paramount—not only in content expertise but in public speaking skills. Both are important. To be certain, we have all experienced deadly lectures (boring, monotone, erudite, and at times even read to us!) by imminent content scholars, well respected in their fields, who should probably stick to disseminating knowledge through publications or perhaps small group discussions. On the other hand, most of us have enjoyed the entertaining public speaker with charm, wit, and magnificent platform skills, but whose scholarship was superficial. It is doubtful that the learning objective was met in either situation. Again, both content knowledge and presentation skills are essential if lecture is to be an effective instructional method.

In addition to learning objectives and teacher qualifications, learner characteristics are a third consideration. Lecture tends to be more intelligible for learners with advanced educational levels; learners with above average education and intelligence demonstrate higher recall of the lecture content (Verner & Dickinson, 1967). Other factors to consider in deciding whether to use lecture are availability of appropriate physical facilities—adequate space with good illumination, functioning public address system, and audiovisual equipment—and the desired extent and nature of participant involvement. Although it is legitimate to anticipate active listening on the part of the learners, and in many cases critical analysis and thoughtful reflection upon what is being said, if verbal participation by the learner is essential, lecture is probably not the best method.

Many studies have compared the effectiveness of lecture to other instructional methods, with conflicting results. Verner and Dickinson's (1967) literature review of research on lecture over a fifty year period revealed that: (1) lecture is most suited to the transmittal of information for immediate recall; (2) a short (less than thirty minutes), carefully constructed lecture with meaningful examples, frequent summaries, simple language, and appropriate speed of delivery is most effective; (3) the specific learning task determines whether or not lecture is the method of choice; and (4) augmenting the lecture with other instructional methods and devices facilitates learning.

Oddi (1983) updated the literature review concerning the use of lecture in adult education in the fourteen years after Verner and Dickinson's work. She confirmed the appropriateness of lecture when the learning task is acquisition of knowledge.

To summarize, to the extent that the following contingencies are present, the use of lecture ought to be considered: the learning objective is to transmit information or to assist in the recall of facts; the learner cannot or will not use printed materials; the information is not immediately accessible in other formats; there is a time constraint; the group size is moderate to large; the presenter is a content expert, has information desired by the learners, and is comfortable in public speaking.


## ADVANTAGES AND LIMITATIONS OF LECTURE

### Advantages of Lecture

The actual delivery of the lecture is economical in time and energy—information can be shared with large groups of individuals in short periods of time, without having to repeat the information to several small groups. However, economy of scale does not equate with ease. The writer does not believe lecturing is as easy as some contend. Lecturing well is an art. To prepare and deliver an informative, useful, and stimulating lecture, particularized for a specific group of learners, at anything beyond an average level of competency is a feat accomplished by all too few educators. Considerable time, effort, and skill are required and some never master the art. But if it is appropriately used and done well, nothing can replace oral discourse as an "intellectual experience" exposing learners to "a window on the teacher's mind" (Frederick, 1986, p. 45). If you want the learners to be able to solve problems and reach conclusions, you can show them how to do it "out loud." Lecture provides an opportunity to let the learners "see" you think.

In addition to being an efficient instructional method, other advantages of lecture are:

1. The material may be presented in a clear, precise, and orderly format.

2. It is a well-known and acceptable method—most adults are familiar with and feel comfortable with the lecture.

3. It is useful for participants who will not or cannot use printed materials.

4. It may be used with large groups.

5. It provides for face-to-face contact with a talking, gesturing, feeling human being.

6. It is often easier for participants to listen than to read.

7. The speaker can use the lecture to stimulate and motivate the audience to further study and inquiry.

For too long, "active participation" on the part of the learner has become almost synonymous with verbal expression. An accomplished lecturer can intellectually stimulate, engage, arouse, and excite a learner's mind without the necessity for "talking" on the part of the learner. As Hyman (1974) suggested, there is no direct relationship between physical and intellectual passivity. It is entirely possible that learners may actively process information, reflect upon it, make judgments about it, and even act upon it without individual verbal dialogue with the instructor. Silent dialogue with the instructor is a possibility, especially for the motivated adult learner. Adult learners find it quite natural to dissect, decipher, and discuss the presented material with fellow learners (whether in formal or informal settings) and may have less need for direct one-to-one interaction with the instructor.

## Limitations of Lecture

The disadvantages of lecture are generally related to its misuse and overuse. Many of the limitations can be overcome by supplementing the lecture with other teaching methods and judiciously using audiovisuals. The following limitations of the lecture method frequently appear in the literature: (1) the audience is exposed to only one person's views; (2) there is the danger of inaccurate or biased information by careless or irresponsible speakers; (3) in its purest form, the lecture provides no verbal interaction between the audience and the speaker; (4) the lecture may discourage learner involvement in the teaching-learning transaction; (5) it is difficult to determine the effects of the lecture upon the audience in that feedback is often subtle, unless the teacher actively elicits it; (6) the speaker may not consider the audience's level of knowledge and education; (7) some speakers value "stage time" more than facilitating learning; and (8) too often speakers are judged on whether or not they entertain the learners rather than on the worthwhileness of the content (Bergevin, Morris, & Smith, 1963; Morgan, Holmes, & Bundy, 1976). Specific ways to compensate for these limitations are included later in the discussion of how to increase the effectiveness of lecture.

Some would argue that too much control is provided the instructor with the lecture approach and count it a liability; others would counter that the lecture is ego satisfying for the lecturer, who is viewed as expert and knowledgeable, and count it an asset. Perhaps there is an element of truth in both views. Clearly, the lecturer should not abuse the control and expert power provided by the lecture methodology. On the other hand, it is folly to presume that the teacher does not have a more intensive and extensive knowledge base with respect to the particular content area—if not, what are the meaning of credentials and why is the teacher teaching?

## TEACHER QUALIFICATIONS

The importance of teacher preferences and qualifications has generally been underestimated in choosing instructional methods. As discussed earlier, the two most important qualifications for an effective lecturer are content expertise and ease in public speaking. Both are necessary and, alone, neither is sufficient for an effective presentation.

Just as we develop specialized content knowledge and competence in a particular discipline through diligent study, application, and practice, so it is with developing and perfecting platform skills.

Although there are a few gifted individuals who seem to be genetically endowed as "naturals" for public speaking and a few others, at the opposite end of the "gifted continuum," who view public speaking akin to academic suicide, most of us fall somewhere in between. Although adult educators should strive for proficiency in several methods, it is the writer's contention that some individuals clearly prefer and excel in nonlecture settings. This is where they should focus most of their energies if at all possible, capitalizing on their strengths. Other educators experience an exhilaration, "a lecturer's high," in large group, didactic settings. Some of the most memorable learning experiences the writer has had involved outstanding lecturers who generated a passion and contagious enthusiasm for the subject matter. These lectures had the personality, heart, and soul of the lecturers, themselves.

Good public speakers are keenly aware of the importance of speaking loudly enough with clear diction, appropriate choice of words, and changing voice inflections for emphasis and variety. Their rate of speech reflects a sensitivity to the needs of the learner in that faster speech is better with simple, familiar material and a slower pace for more difficult concepts, with intentional pauses for the learner to process information. Silence is always preferred to meaningless uhs, ums, and okays. Age of the learner group also influences the teacher's delivery in that older individuals generally do better with slower rates and louder speech, all other factors being equal.

The proficient lecturer adapts the style of language (formal or informal, technical or commonplace) and level of content difficulty (basic or advanced) to the needs, interests, and background experiences of the learners. Relevant, meaningful examples are used to clarify and amplify the content. One of the major challenges confronted by the adult educator is a diverse learner group in terms of knowledge, skill, and experiential backgrounds. Using a variety of examples, including some basic and some advanced content, while gearing most remarks at the median audience level, and accommodating different learner preferences through the use of various visuals may help to bridge the gaps among learner backgrounds.

For those who are genuinely interested in improving their skills in oral exposition and illustration, colleague critique, invited learner feedback, and audio/video tapes of sample lectures should be helpful. Annoying mannerisms, distracting gestures, unnecessary jargon, and overused pet words will become apparent. All of these evaluative mechanisms require extra time and energy, some risk taking by all parties, and careful analysis and interpretation of data. But the potential benefits in improved instruction should be well worth the investment.

According to Weaver (1983), most delivery problems are due to two deficits: insufficient preparation and insufficient self-confidence. Techniques for lecture preparation appear later in this chapter. Building on the premise that a positive self-concept is an essential condition for effective presentations, the reader might find Weaver and Cotrell's (1985) article beneficial. The authors describe the use of imaging as a technique wherein lecture anxiety is systematically desensitized, then the image the lecturer wants to project is slowly built through a process of sensitization. The desired end result is a more confident public speaker.

Another requirement for the effective presenter is to stay within the given time frame. In all but the purest of lectures, where there is no allowance for questioning or discussion, it is difficult to prepare a lecture that has a perfect fit with the actual time allocation. Even in the pure lecture, skilled presenters gauge their speed of delivery, need for repetition, clarification, illustration, and summary on subtle cues from the learners and make on-the-spot adjustments. The best presenter cannot predict with any accuracy all these contingencies. Several suggestions are offered to assist the adult educator in conforming to the time constraint without losing needed flexibility and spontaneity. All of them require preplanning, preparation, and organization—essential ingredients of a good lecture.

One approach is to actually practice "talking" the presentation aloud. This is different than "reading" it aloud. By talking, the presenter is able to allow for normal pauses and changes in the speed of delivery. In general, going too fast is a much greater problem than speaking too slow. Pretend you are in the room with the learners. It may help to stand. Actually time yourself. Remember you are teaching, not talking to your spouse or best friend. *Go slowly!* You may need to time each section to determine which areas are being over- or under-emphasized. You can then rework the material as needed. Have another person, preferably at the same knowledge level as the intended learner, listen to you to see if your language, content, and rate of delivery are appropriate.

Another approach is to plan ahead for various "what if" scenarios. Ask yourself "what if" I have a lot of questions, a greater need for examples and explanations, a group of compulsive note-takers, or a speaker before me who exceeded the time frame? Conversely, what if I take less time than anticipated and run out of material? (Having too much time is not a common complaint among teachers who lecture). Both scenarios can be inconspicuously handled if your notes are in red, yellow, and green. This approach is analogous to the ABC approach to time management. The red means use only if needed; this is nonessential information. The yellow coded material should be used as time permits and includes "nice to know" information. The green material is the "need to know" core content which has priority over the yellow and red.

To summarize, knowing your content area well and being at ease with public speaking are the most important attributes of educators who effectively use lecture as a teaching method. The most important delivery problems are lack of preparation and lack of self-confidence. In response to the question, "What makes a good lecturer?" Eble (1978) suggests it is the ability of the presenter not only to embrace content, but to justify the endeavor by projecting both content and presence. He notes that voice command is as important as subject matter command. The lecturer's ability to relate to the learner's needs, values, and past experiences and to conform to given time constraints, without sacrificing flexibility and spontaneity, are also necessary.

## RESPONSIBILITIES OF THE TEACHER AND LEARNER

### Teacher Responsibilities

The need for content expertise and public speaking skills are teacher responsibilities. In addition, the adult educator has a professional and moral responsibility to use the lecture methodology only when it is an appropriate means of facilitating learning. This means it should not be indiscriminately used when other methods are more feasible and appropriate. Further, it should not be used as an intended means of undue control, intimidation, biased persuasion, or indoctrination by the teacher over the learner.

*Before the learning encounter.* Before the session begins, the instructor engages in careful content planning and preparation to meet the specified learning objectives. In many cases, it is the instructor who must ensure that a comfortable, accessible room of the right size, away from noisy distractions, with lighting that can be increased or decreased, and with convenient electrical outlets for audiovisual equipment is available. Adequate illumination is especially important for the aging learner; adults after fifty require 50 percent more light than do twenty year olds (Kidd, 1973). An appropriate seating arrangement for the particular group must be completed before the class begins. All materials to supplement the presentation—handouts, videotape, flip chart, chalkboard, overhead transparencies, slides, and demonstration materials—must be arranged for. All audiovisual equipment, including the public address system, should be checked out prior to the lecture, with extra bulbs and a glove that is readily available for changing hot, burned out bulbs.

*During the learning encounter.* During the learning transaction, the teacher's responsibilities are primarily related to the actual delivery. Sensitivity to environmental (temperature, illumination, excess noise) and learner (nodding of head in agreement or from dozing, facial expression, body position) feedback should help guide the presenter in meeting the particular needs of the collectivity. Most adult learning is voluntary and the learner comes with a preexisting "need to know." If not, the instructor must attempt to create that need. This might be accomplished by demonstrating relevance and application to the lives of the learners. For example, relate the content of the lecture to job requirements ("When you leave here today you ought to be better able to deal with difficult people in the workplace") or to changing adult role tasks ("The purpose of this class is to provide you with some current information on low cost, high protein foods" for a low income single parenting class). This may help gain the learners' interest by creating the perception that this class will help them personally.

For more structured learning environments, relating the content to follow-up evaluation activities where the learner has an opportunity to demonstrate learning is beneficial. For instance, if the lecture deals with certification preparation, you might say, "After the presentation, there will be a self-assessment quiz for each of you to practice and demonstrate what you have learned." Raising provocative questions and relevant controversial issues are other ways to stimulate interest (Sorcinelli & Sorcinelli, 1987).

*After the learning encounter.* After the encounter, the presenter should make every effort to be available for follow-up questions and interaction with the learners. This is of special importance if there was no questioning or other verbal dialogue during the lecture. As soon as possible after the learning transaction, the instructor should deliberately reflect on what occurred. To evaluate effectiveness, the following questions may be posed: "Did I stimulate interest and critical thinking? Did I allow controversy and freedom to disagree? Did the students question, discuss, or volunteer information? Did I cover the major points and use plenty of examples and visual aids? Did I help students focus on key issues and provide a framework for further study?" The wise instructor will immediately make notations on ways to improve the presentation the next time, while the ideas are still fresh. "Waiting until later" often results in vague recall of suggestions for improvement, or in doing no structured evaluation at all.

### Learner Responsibilities

Depending upon the nature of the situation, the learner's responsibility prior to the encounter might range from simply attending the lecture with a readiness to learn, to more extensive preparation involving reading assignments, questions to be considered, or written work. Although there is less opportunity for verbal participation by the learner during the lecture, nonetheless there is an obligation to engage in active listening. Ideally, the learners would move beyond listening and actively engage in critical thinking, identifying how the content relates to their own world views and what impact it might have on their lives. For some learners in some settings, note-taking is an important part of their learning. If questioning and discussion accompany the lecture, learners should participate by sharing their views and past experiences. After the transaction, the learners should reflect on what has been learned and how it might be incorporated into their own ways of thinking and behaving.


## PATTERNS OF COMMUNICATION

When lecture is used in its purest form, without accompanying questions or discussion, the flow of verbal communication is one-directional from the instructor to the learners. However, the flow of nonverbal communication is in both directions. Learners may laugh, smile, squirm, sit upright or slouch, nod, take notes, look at the speaker or the windows, appear interested or bored. There may also be nonverbal interaction among the learners.

Hyman (1974) notes that the unidirectional pattern of communication of the traditional lecture, depicted in Figure 8.1, may be altered to include a loop system, by the addition of questioning or discussion. Figure 8.2 displays the bidirectional flow of verbal communication with the loop resulting from the instructor posing

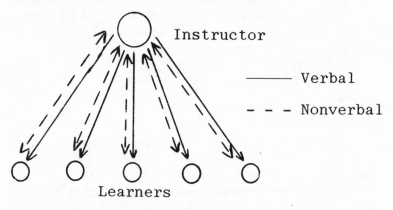

Figure 8.1  Unidirectional flow of communication in the traditional lecture.

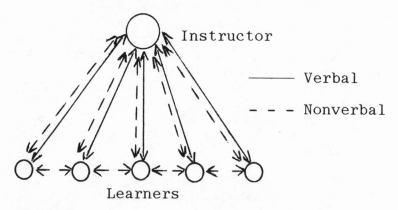

Figure 8.2  Bidirectional flow of communication with the addition of questioning.

questions, the learner responding, the instructor reacting to the learner's response, and the learner having an opportunity to provide feedback to the instructor's reaction.

With group discussion, communication assumes a multdirectional pattern with instructor to learner, learner to instructor, and learner to learner verbal interaction. As depicted in Figure 8.3, it is possible to create a loop system with multidirectional communication through the use of small or total group discussion.

Even with the traditional lecture, communication is enhanced by the intentional use of nonverbal cues such as direct eye contact and body movements. Some immobile presenters appear as if their feet are glued to the floor and the bottom part of their body is a lectern or their head is attached to a podium.

## ROOM SIZE AND SEATING ARRANGEMENTS

A room of the right size with the appropriate seating arrangement is an essential element for an effective oral presentation. The room must not only accommodate the learners, but also any audiovisual equipment to be used. Ideally, the room should be neither too large nor too small. A crowded small room has both physical and psychological drawbacks. Holding your note pad in your lap,

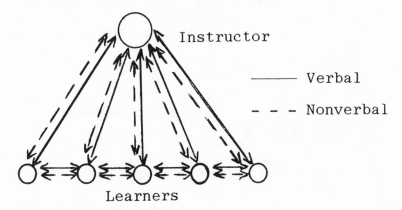

Figure 8.3 Multidirectional flow of communication with the addition of small group discussion.

laying your books and handouts on the floor, feeling claustrophobic and awkward because you can't cross your legs without kicking the person next to you, contribute neither to comfort nor to productive learning. Most classroom situations involving lecture require seating with tables and chairs or with movable desks that will accommodate adult-sized bodies!

A room that is too large presents problems in that learners tend to spread out and a sense of group cohesiveness is lost. It is difficult for the instructor to maintain audience eye contact and the distance itself is a physical barrier to communication. Learners may assume apparent anonymity.

There are many seating arrangements that might be used depending upon the size of the group, the length of the session, use of audiovisuals, and the extent of verbal interaction expected. Four of the most common setups include U-shaped, classroom, auditorium or theater, and amphitheater (see Figure 8.4).

*The U-Shaped Table.* This is best when you expect participation and verbal discussion. It is ideal for groups of twenty or under, but may be used for larger groups.

*Classroom.* This arrangement is suitable for audiences of almost any size. The herringbone pattern lets participants see one another and the tables provide plenty of workspace. Movable chairs encourage participant interaction, if desired.

*Auditorium or Theater.* This arrangement is used for large groups when you expect little or no participation. Your major concern is that your projection screen is large enough and clearly visible to all.

*Amphitheater.* This is the very best setting for presentations of short to moderate length. Here, the audience sits on elevated levels in half circles round the speaker. This configuration permits the seating of more people per square foot of floor space than other arrangements and everyone is relatively close to the presenter. In a well-designed amphitheater, acoustics are remarkably good, and the entire audience will have a clear view of the speaker and the projection screen. The amphitheater is ideal for presentations followed by a question and answer session.

Other groupings using the classroom style (with both tables and chairs) include fan-shape, diamond, and octagon. For very large groups, theater-in-the round or semicircular theater may be used.

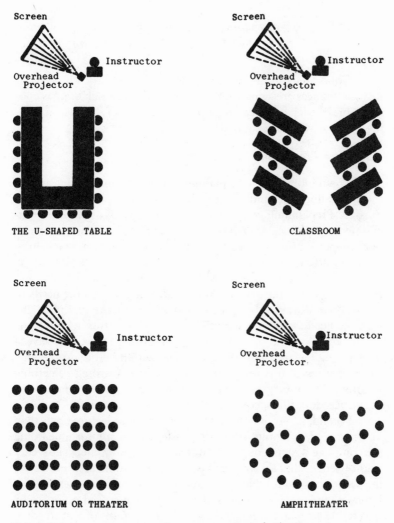

Figure 8.4 Four common seating arrangements for lecture.

Small semicircles and maple leaf arrangements are helpful if learners need to form small groups for discussion.

## HOW TO PREPARE AND DELIVER MORE
## EFFECTIVE LECTURES

Good preparation does not ensure good delivery, but without it, your chances are significantly diminished. Although there is considerable overlap between preparation and delivery, for ease in reading the two will be separated.

*Guides for Preparation*

The importance of preplanning, organization, staying within the time allotment, and concerted practice have already been addressed. Preplanning contributes to organization, organization facilitates compliance with time constraints, and practice enhances both preparation and delivery. In terms of organization, two helpful hints are offered.

First, don't be so rigid with your organization that you fail to change your game plan when needed. Sensitivity to the needs of the learners always takes precedence over your original plan. It's much easier to change a plan than to try to function without one at all. For example, if learners appear unsure, tense, or have a questioning facial expression, try to deal with it before proceeding. Your chances of teaching and of the students learning something worthwhile will be greatly enhanced. Success can't be guaranteed, but proceeding full speed ahead almost surely guarantees failure.

Second, it is probably better to outline your lecture notes than to write everything out in full. If you feel more comfortable doing the complete writeup, okay, but still develop the outline. (The writer acknowledges that the experts say to do the outline first. However, the writer has found that the sequence is not what makes the difference; the critical element is identifying the essential points to be covered.) Using an outline will decrease the chances of your reading the lecture, one of the deadliest things you can do. Again, it is okay to write out everything, just make sure you do not read it.

Remember, some things are meant to be individually read, such as this book; others are meant to be heard, such as a good lecture. To read aloud something that was meant to be individually read can succumb even the most inveterate insomniac. For those wanting more structure, it is often helpful to break the body of the lecture into distinctive components (e.g., identification, explanation, illustration, demonstration, questioning, and then application).

Preparation includes intentional plans for encouraging involvement of the learner. Specifically, you might consider the use of the following strategies.

1. Send the audience appropriate reading materials (case histories, annotated bibliographies, questions to be considered) prior to the presentation. This encourages thought on the content to be covered. If this isn't feasible, reading lists might be distributed at the class meeting for follow-up use.

2. Hand out a lecture outline with the key points, or place it on the board for students to copy. This not only encourages activity on the learner's behalf, but also provides an organizing framework, a prerequisite to learning. An outline facilitates note taking for those students so inclined. Learners tend to record in their notes what teachers write on the board or overhead transparency, believing it is important information (Sorcinelli & Sorcinelli, 1987). Consequently, be discriminating about what you note on the blackboard.

3. Intersperse intense, novel, or surprising information among the more mundane. A good beginning is crucial. You must capture the learner's attention. Make use of stimulating audiovisuals, autobiographical stories, real life illustrations, demonstrations, and provocative questioning. Pose leading questions or problems at the beginning of the lecture to provide direction for the learners as to what is most important and to stimulate interest and intrigue. One of the most effective demonstrations accompanying a lecture the writer has seen involved an inexpensive styrofoam ice chest, a zip lock baggie, and ice cubes partially melted, then refrozen. The point was to demonstrate an efficient way to tell when the temperature plunged below 32 °F., and the effect it had on commercial metal sheets. This memorable lecture was "seen" as well as "heard." All of these approaches can provide variety, substance, and insight, as well as

clarify and amplify the main points. But they do take time. Remember to plan ahead, allowing time for these strategies which can so effectively draw learners into the "lecture zone" with you.

Just a word about audiovisuals. Clearly, they enhance learning and assist in remembering. But, if audiovisuals cannot be seen and heard by everyone, don't use them. There is nothing more frustrating than an overhead transparency or slide with too much information to fully comprehend, or which cannot be seen. Consider the use of handouts in such situations. The importance of proper illumination, placing the screen so everyone can see, and giving the learners time to read the audiovisuals are other important factors to remember.

4. Draw listeners into the discovery process as you make your journey through the material. If you can provide for the learners a sense that you are discovering some basic truths and insights for the first time, they can enjoy the experience with you. A flair for dramatization, physical energy channeled in speaking, and body language can be used to engage the learner (Boman, 1986). You don't have to be ready for Broadway, but neither should you create a climate of boredom.

5. The appropriate use of humor is a wonderful means of stimulating attention and imagination. Appropriate humor illustrates as well as entertains. Developing a humor file consisting of collections of jokes, quotes, stories, and cartoons that have been used successfully is recommended. The ready availability of such materials eases the search process for the right touch of humor (Boman, 1986). Laughter not only activates the listener, but also provides much needed feedback for the teacher and enjoyment for the learner. Also, humor aids in recall of important information as it is often the funny story or anecdote that the learner first remembers. However, the link between humor and the point to be made must be strongly established such that the learner remembers the key point, not just the good joke or story!

A final item under preparation is familiarizing yourself with the target audience. This may be done vicariously, using individuals from a like group. For example, if you are to teach a stress management class to a group of reentry women for the first time, you might talk to other reentry women to determine some of their particular needs, interests, and concerns. This will help you anticipate the audience's attitudes and particularize your remarks to the specific learner group. Audience-centeredness on the lecturer's part is crucial to success.

### Tips for Delivery

There are several strategies to increase the impact of your delivery, ranging from those requiring little or no particular skill to those requiring persistent practice and reflection in order to do well.

1. *Set a learning climate.* Arrive early, be available at breaks, and stay after for those learners desiring more direct verbal interaction. Call the learners by name and maintain good eye contact. This communicates respect and value for the learners. Name tags with the first name written in bold large letters will help you and other learners remember correct names. Promote a sense of mutual trust, helpfulness, and acceptance. Provide the freedom to speak, to think, and disagree. Avoid authoritarian control, sarcasm or ridicule, and judgmental statements.

2. *Limit the amount of information.* Six or seven chunks of information (or major points) are as much as can be handled in a fifty minute class session (Eble, 1978). Any more than this leads to problems with listening, note taking, and retention (Sorcinelli & Sorcinelli, 1987). Don't try to teach the audience everything you know about the topic in one setting.

3. *Speak clearly, loudly enough, and at a pace appropriate for the learner group.* Going too fast is a common complaint about lecturers. Build in frequent pauses and summaries. Simple material is lost if the rate is too slow while complex material is lost if delivery is too fast (Verner & Dickinson, 1967). If the audience is over fifty-five, it is especially important to speak loudly and clearly. There is up to a 50 percent decrease in hearing intelligibility for older individuals and the situation is intensified with rapid speech (Kidd, 1973). Older adults need to set the pace of learning—they tend to go slower and the time required for learning new material increases with age

(Cross, 1981). Again, the importance of building in pauses and "think time" cannot be overemphasized. Rapid, monotone, and soft-spoken lecturers are one reason lectures have received a "bad rap."

4. *Use a conversational rather than pedantic, authoritative tone.* Raise and lower your voice using a range of intonations to provide emphasis for important points.

5. *Look at people.* Remember you are talking to, or better yet, with, *live learners*—not windows, ceilings, floors, projection screens, or lecture notes.

6. *Keep moving, but don't overdo it.* The use of the body to radiate enthusiasm, confidence, and interest is an art that can be learned. At times, exaggerated physical gestures are appropriate; in other instances, they fall flat. The point is that body language must be congruent for the point to be made and natural for the teacher. Gestures that appear rehearsed or "canned" are worse than no gestures at all. Good lecturers are good performers. Find skilled role models who have mastered the lecture method, solicit colleague critique, use videotapes, enroll in public speaking classes, and read books such as this. There are many inexpensive, accessible resources to help you.

7. *Complement the lecture with other instructional methods.* The pure lecture is most prevalent in formal presentations with large audiences where there is clearly an expert who is skilled in sharing information with a lesser prepared group of learners. In most situations, however, the instructor has some latitude to augment the lecture with other approaches. Using a multiplicity of instructional approaches appeals to a group of learners with different preferred styles of learning. Also, several studies indicate that learning increases when the lecture is modified to provide for more active involvment by the learner (Verner & Dickinson, 1967).

   *Lecture and Discussion.* The use of alternating mini-lectures (15-20 minutes) and discussions recognizes the conclusions of attention span studies by shifting the energy back and forth between the instructor and learner group (Frederick, 1986). Verduin, Miller, and Greer (1977) indicate that although some learner's attention span may be longer, for Adult Basic Education (ABE) or English as a Second Language classes, the instructor needs to adhere to the 15-20 minute presentation format followed by practice or discussion. Even in formal continuing professional education classes, where the academic level of the learner is advanced, the lecture should generally not exceed one hour.

McLeish (1976) points out that in a typical lecture, learner interest begins to decline in about 10 minutes, reaches a low point at 40 minutes, and increases during the last 10 minutes. The "middle sag" especially calls for changing strategies to hold the learner's attention. Any variation in stimulus is helpful. Since learners have better immediate recall of material presented at the beginning of the lecture than in the middle or at the end (Verner & Dickinson, 1967), the most important information might be placed early in the lecture.

Small discussion groups also account for the timid learner who might hesitate to question or discuss in front of the total group. Further, it makes use of learners who are familiar with the subject matter.

*Questioning.* For very large learner groups, you might pose a question or situation after making a series of points. For example, "Explain the most important points. What meaning do they have for you?" Ask the learners to mentally or physically write an individual response, followed by sharing with one or two people around them. You might even ask for responses from the group and offer your own analysis. Another approach using questions would be to ask participants to write out one or two questions for class discussion and bring to the next class meeting, or ask them to do so upon arrival (Sorcinelli & Sorcinelli, 1987). In addition to increasing in-class involvement, asking learners to bring questions with them to the class meeting serves two other purposes. To verbally formulate a question requires intellectually processing the content and, to do so ahead of time, provides confidence to the adult learner to raise the questions in class. Waiting until the end of the lecture to ask "Are there any questions?" seldom provides the type of learner participation desired.

The strategy of alternating short lectures with questioning, discussion, and other action-oriented formats is sometimes referred to as "feedback lectures" since it allows the instructor an opportunity to assess interest and understanding of basic concepts before moving on. If questioning and discussion are used, the instructor may need to repeat the comments from the learners in order for everyone to hear.

These variations on the theme of the traditional lecture can be used to increase learner participation in any large group setting, including the hallowed halls of academe with the bolted down seats.

8. *Provide an obvious end.* Summarization is essential to bring closure and highlight the most important points. It can be confusing and even annoying to have several "in conclusions" or "one more point." Timing is critical. Allow plenty of time for examples and audience responses. Ending on time is important because learner attentiveness decreases in direct proportion to the amount of time you continue beyond the intended closure. It is best for you to stop speaking *before* the audience stops listening.

## THE ANATOMY OF A LECTURE

To summarize, if the writer were to prepare a "lecture on lecturing," four major points would be emphasized. There are others, but these are crucial. They constitute the anatomy of a lecture.

Point 1:   Say a lot about a little.
Point 2:   Use a lot of examples.
Point 3:   Keep moving.
Point 4:   Capitalize on variety.

Although seemingly simple, these four points are difficult to master.

*Point 1: Say a Lot About a Little*

To say a lot about a little requires narrowing of the topic and identification of the three or four essential concepts. This is not easy, especially when there is "little time and lots to cover." One of the most difficult lessons to learn is that we cannot "cover" everything. Covering class material is not the same as learning material; this only deceives the teacher and frustrates the learner. As

Eble (1978) states, "Wisdom is in part learning what to leave out. . . . Sound preparation involves not only gathering material, but also throwing it away" (p. 47). Part of the presenter's responsibility is to assist the learner in focusing on what is of concern to the learner, what is most problematic or difficult to grasp, and what is critical. Generally the learner needs assistance in making these kinds of discriminatory judgments.

Once the most salient points have been identified, the lecturer can then do a lot with each one—make the point, illustrate it with real-life examples, elaborate it, reinforce it with audiovisuals, break the whole into parts, relate it to familiar material, draw implications for practice, put it back together again, summarize it, and move on to the next point. Explain one point at a time, then go on to the next, spacing your time so you don't have to rush through, or completely omit, the last point or two. Repeat the critical points, up to four to five times since repetition increases retention. Get as much mileage as you can from each major concept.

### Point 2: Use a Lot of Examples

Frequent use of examples, illustrations, and demonstrations requires that the lecturer not only know the content well enough to draw relevant, useful applications, but also have a sense of the learner's knowledge level, background, and life experiences. Examples related to financial management might include how to figure tax on a purchase or balance a checkbook for an ABE learner group, how to reconcile numeric financial management reports for a clerical reentry group, and how to invest for retirement for a group of middle-aged learners. Autobiographic examples and personal anecdotes are especially poignant in driving the point home.

### Point 3: Keep Moving

Moving about the room enhances both verbal and nonverbal communication. It requires that you know your material well enough to be able to leave the lectern, concentrate on the learner's responses, and make on-the-spot adjustments as needed. You may need to summarize, solicit feedback, go slower or faster, use more examples, or even depart completely from your planned remarks. Developing the ability to improvise requires some risk, and a lot of reflection and practice.

Moving about the room, increasing eye contact, and using a

conversational tone enhance a sense of connectedness with the participants. Calling the learners by name and using language and examples the group can relate to also facilitate bonding between the teacher and learners.

*Point 4: Capitalize on Variety*

Change alone is a major factor in holding a group's attention. Use audiovisuals, discussion, and questioning. Change your rate of delivery, tone of voice, and body gestures. You want variety in everything.


## EVALUATION

The importance of recognizing, interpreting, and responding to verbal and nonverbal cues during the actual delivery, as a method of evaluative feedback, has already been discussed. The two basic questions to be answered are: (1) What did the group learn? and (2) How well did I teach?

If structured feedback is deliberatively requested during the course (formative evaluation), needed adjustments can be made for that particular learner group instead of implementing their suggestions with the next group, whose needs and preferences might be significantly different. The nature and extent of the evaluation performed at the end of the class or course (summative) will depend on the time and financial resources available, the purpose of the evaluation, and the skill and inclination of the evaluator.

Sometimes, the evaluation will be very informal, relying primarily on verbal feedback from the learners. Honest, forthright feedback might be compromised if this is the only type of evaluation used. A simple paper and pencil questionnaire can be developed by the instructor, using a Likert scale, with a place for written comments. More honest and accurate perceptions will generally be elicited if signatures are optional.

The evaluation tool needs to include criteria with respect to whether or not (1) the speaker's content expertise was apparent, (2) the speaker was an effective lecturer, (3) the personal goals of the learner were met, (4) the audiovisuals aided learning, and (5) lecture was an appropriate teaching method for the particular situation. How participants plan to apply the material, factors which facilitated or hindered learning, likes and dislikes, suggestions for improvement, and general comments also provide helpful data.

The impact of the lecture may be difficult to assess since one of the primary purposes is to stimulate students to learn in their own way following the presentation. Consequently, attempting to measure learning immediately after the lecture may give a false impression of the overall impact of the lecture and reveal more about the "happiness index" of the learner group rather than any real learning.

## CONCLUSION

This chapter has dealt with learning situations in which lecture might be used as an appropriate instructional strategy, the advantages and limitations of lecture, responsibilities of the teacher and learners, communication patterns, and seating arrangements. A variety of useful tips concerning the preparation and delivery of effective presentations has been provided as well as approaches to evaluation. The most important point of this chapter is the realization that lecture is an appropriate instructional method in certain learning transactions. The staying power of the lecture has truly been remarkable in light of continual assaults by outspoken critics. It remains the most frequently used approach in higher and adult education settings. When there is an exceptionally well-qualified speaker, an audience with relatively little knowledge on the topic, and the learning situation requires a clear explanation and transfer of knowledge, lecture might be the ideal approach. At other times, more action-oriented methods would be ideal, but lecture is used due to its efficiency. In either case, there are particular ways to increase its effectiveness. There are many variations on the theme of lecture to make it a more stimulating, effective, and appealing instructional method.

## REFERENCES

Bergevin, P., Morris, D., & Smith, R. M. (1963). *Adult education procedures*. New York: Seabury Press.

Boman, J. (1986). Facilitating student involvement in large classroom settings. *Journal of Nursing Education, 25*(6), 226-229.

Cooper, P. J. (1985). *Teachers as public speakers: Training teachers
to lecture.* (Report No. CS 504 958). Indianapolis: Annual Meeting of the Central States Speech Association. (ERIC Document
Reproduction Service No. ED 258 302)

Cross, K. P. (1981). *Adults as learners.* San Francisco: Jossey-Bass.

Darkenwald, G. G., & Merriam, S. B. (1982). *Adult education:
Foundations of practice.* New York: Harper and Row.

Eble, K. E. (1978). *The craft of teaching.* San Francisco: Jossey-
Bass.

Frederick, P. J. (1986). The lively lecture—8 variations. *College
Teaching, 34*(2), 43-50.

Hyman, R. T. (1974). *Ways of teaching* (2nd ed.). Philadelphia:
J. B. Lippincott.

Kidd, J. R. (1973). *How adults learn.* New York: Association Press.

McKeachie, W. J. (1986). *Teaching tips: A guidebook for the beginning college teacher* (8th ed.). Lexington: D. C. Heath.

McLeish, J. (1976). The lecture method. In N. L. Gage (Ed.), *The
psychology of teaching methods* (pp. 252-301). Chicago: University of Chicago Press.

Morgan, B., Holmes, G. E., & Bundy, C. E. (1976). *Methods in
adult education* (3rd ed.). Danville: Interstate Printers and Pub-
lishers.

Oddi, L. (1983). The lecture: An update on research. *Adult Education Quarterly, 33*(4), 222-229.

Sorcinelli, G., & Sorcinelli, M. D. (1987). The lecture in an adult
education environment: Teaching strategies. *Lifelong Learning—
An Omnibus of Practice and Research, 10*(4), 8-10, 14.

Verduin, Jr., J. R., Miller, H. G., & Greer, C. E. (1977). *Adults
teaching adults.* Austin: Learning Concepts.

Verner, C., & Dickinson, G. (1967). The lecture, an analysis and
review of research. *Adult Education, 17*(2), 85-100.

Weaver, II, R. L. (1983). *Understanding public communication.*
Englewood Cliffs: Prentice-Hall.

Weaver, II, R. L., & Cotrell, H. W. (1985). Imaging can increase
self concept and lecturing effectiveness. *Education, 105*(3), 264-
270.

# CHAPTER 9

## Discussion
### STEPHEN D. BROOKFIELD

Of all the methods most favored by adult educators, it is discussion which has perhaps become enshrined as the adult educational method "par excellence." The exalted methodological status granted to the method has arisen mostly because of its democratic associations. Discussion as a teaching method seems both inclusionary and participatory. Those who proclaim its benefits do so because it appears to place teachers and learners on an equal footing, because it imples that everyone has some useful contribution to make to the educational effort, and because it claims to be successful in actively involving learners. To educators of widely varying ideological hues, discussion is revered as the educational method which is the most participatory and the most respectful of learners—crucial components in both the liberal humanistic and radical traditions. Almost all activities which are cited as exemplary of the best traditions of adult education—Freirean culture circles, the Highlander Folk School, the Junto, the Canadian Farm Forum, Swedish study circles, the American Great Books program, the British Workers Education Association, Danish folk high schools, the Antigonish movement—rely for their methodological centerpiece on some variant of discussion. Additionally, American adult educators have claimed for the use of the discussion method a significance which extends far beyond the classroom. Lindeman (1945) claimed the neighborhood discussion group to be essential to the maintenance of democracy and, hence ultimately, to world peace. If citizens participated in discussion groups they would learn democractic habits, they would be able to see through the inflated claims of demagogues, they would detect when propoganda was being foisted on them, and they would develop the kind of critical judgment necessary to informed political activity. Essert (1948) advised Americans to regard participation in discussion groups as a substitute for the experience of community which had been denied to so many as industrialism advanced, as extended families declined, and as occupational and geographical mobility increased.

To neophyte adult educators, therefore, the use of the discussion method has become an unchallenged pedagogical given. Paterson (1970) comments that generalizations about the value of discussion form "chief articles of the catechism in which novices to liberal adult education are expected to verse themselves" (p. 28). In noticing the prevalance of the method, Brunner and others (1959) remarked that the generally favorable attitude towards discussion among American adult educators meant that it was used for its own sake, irrespective of its merits or suitability for particular pedagogic or curricular purposes. To accept such an indiscriminate use of any educational method is dangerously misconceived. No matter how much our democratic impulses might suggest the natural preeminence of discussion as a teaching method to be used with adult learners, we should not uncritically accept this as obvious. Uncritically accepting handed-down orthodoxies in teaching is lazy and dangerous, as it is in any other aspect of life. Before rushing to embrace the discussion method as the obvious and natural one to be used with adults, we need to look long and hard at its chief purposes and central features.


## PURPOSES OF DISCUSSION

### Cognitive and Affective Benefits

Many different reasons for using the discussion method emerge in the literature (Paterson, 1970; Legge, 1971; Osinski, Ohliger & McCarthy, 1972; Fawcett Hill, 1977; Bridges, 1979; Hyman, 1980; Brookfield 1985; Bligh, 1986). One of the most frequently cited argues that discussion is suited toward achieving particular cognitive and affective ends, particularly those of problem solving, concept exploration, and attitude change. In problem-solving discussions the purpose is to understand the nature of a particular problem, and then to investigate alternative solutions. In concept exploration discussions the purpose is usually to revise concepts introduced through lectures or assigned readings. In attitude change discussions the purpose is to engender in learners what teachers define as desirable attitudes. These three kinds of discussions are sometimes described as "guided," "controlled," "directed," or "teaching" discussions and are treated as forms of discussion to be used when discussion leaders have specific pedagogical objectives in mind.

But this approach to discussion illustrates a fundamental contradiction. If discussion methods are adopted because of their democratic nature, then the ideas of guided or teaching discussions become contradictions in terms, self-negating concepts. As I have argued elsewhere "a necessary condition of discussion is that there be no preconceived agenda, no cognitive path to be charted, no previously specified objectives either for substantive knowledge to be transmitted or for process features to be exhibited. Hence, guided discussion is conceptual nonsense in that discussion is free and open by definition" (Brookfield, 1985, p. 57). In problem solving, concept exploration, and attitude change forms of discussion, leaders have in mind various cognitive and affective purposes which the discussions are intended to achieve. But for facilitators to enter discussions with preconceived agendas of aims, objectives, or outcomes is to be guilty of an insidious manipulation. It is also to run the very real risk of being perceived by learners as dishonest and inauthentic.

Rogers (1977) maintains that "it is not possible to chart too closely in advance the form the discussion should take, for the essence of a valuable discussion is the unexpectedness and originality of the new territory which should constantly be explored" (p. 179). Yet in problem-solving discussions, the problems to be solved are usually selected by leaders beforehand, as is the range of alternative solutions to be considered. Rarely do groups engage in problem posing (Freire, 1970) or problem setting (Schon, 1983); that is, in collaboratively identifying problematic aspects of reality such as major discrepancies between ideals and actuality, or between rhetoric and action. In concept exploration discussions the cognitive outcomes of the activity have usually been specified in advance by the leader. Watkins (1975) describes the situation in

which "the tutor's sense of responsibility for the group—his determination that the ground should be covered—can deter individual students from clarifying their own experience of the material
under discussion. In other words, the learning which takes place is
that sanctioned by the tutor and not necessarily what the student
most needs" (p. 7). Finally, in attitude change discussions the attitudes which are to be assimilated are defined in advance by discussion leaders. These kinds of guided, controlled, or directed
discussions are frequently insidious exercises in learner manipulation. This manipulation will soon enough be perceived by learners
who, depending on the context and the power relationships in play,
will challenge the leader, try to feed back to the leader what they
perceive to be the correct attitudes, or simply opt out of the activity.
If leaders do have a set of purposes in mind, it is more honest and
more authentic for them to declare these to group members at the
outset. Not to do this risks destroying the trust between leaders and
learners so necessary to the halting and often painful scrutiny of
values, beliefs, and behaviors which comprises genuine discussion.

*Participatory Learning*

A second reason which is frequently cited for using discussion
is that it encourages active, participatory learning. Legge (1971)
declares that "as an educational method, in fact, its importance lies
in the way in which it impels class members to participate" (p. 58).
Gulley (1965) writes that "to call an activity discussion, all or most
members of the group must participate" (p. 4). The assumption
underlying such assertions is that "the more members who are active
in the discussions, the better the retention of active and inactive
members" (Davis, 1961, p. 135). Facilitators who use discussion
generally do so with the belief that most members must be actively
involved for the discussion session to be at all successful. A twelve
member group in which most of the verbal interchange occurred
between two or three especially articulate members would not be
regarded as a full fledged discussion group, whereas a session in
which ten of the twelve members contributed (irrespective of the
worth of the contributions) would qualify for such a description.

The problem with this participatory rationale for using discussion is that it comes dangerously close to a cocktail party concept
of discussion. Valuing verbal contributions and active participation
for their own sakes means that it becomes tempting to judge the

success of a discussion session by the number of contributions made. Yet, as Rogers (1977) points out, "Not all discussions need to be noisy or obviously vigorous to be educationally valuable. A good discussion may be quiet, apparently low key, with a lot of thoughtful silences" (p. 188). Additionally, discussion groups have a powerful psychodynamic dimension to them. Participation patterns tend to be created early in the group's life. By the third meeting of discussion courses, discrepancies in communication between garrulous and silent members are usually well established. This pecking order of communication is self-fulfilling; the longer a discussion member remains silent, the more intimidating is the prospect of eventual participation.

Discussion groups can easily become competitive emotional battlegrounds with participation a highly threatening experience. Group members compete for recognition and affirmation from peers and teachers. American culture places great emphasis on the confident extrovert so that the glibly articulate group member is often regarded as an educational success compared to a more quiet but reflective colleague. Learners invest discussions with considerable emotional significance and performing well (talking frequently and confidently) becomes inextricably bound up with their self-esteem. In such an atmosphere divergent viewpoints and critical comments from other participants can be interpreted as personal attacks. When disagreement is treated by group members as an act of aggression in the competition for status within the discussion group, then reflective thinking becomes virtually impossible. Such a situation is often created when continuous assessment of learner participation becomes one criterion by which leaders judge learners' achievements. In this context the pressure on participants to contribute for contribution's sake becomes irresistible as they strive to establish themselves as effective, competent performers in their teachers' eyes. Allocating 20 or 30 percent of an overall course grade for "participation" may seem like an effective way to prompt learner participation and to avoid what are interpreted as unfortunate silences. But silence is not equivalent to intellectual inactivity. It is an essential contemplative element in the praxis of reflective learning.

For what educational purposes is discussion most effective? The following are suggested as the most impelling cognitive purposes for which discussion should be used:

1. To expose learners to a diversity of perspectives on an issue, topic, or theme

2. To help learners to externalize the assumptions underlying their values, beliefs, and actions

3. To assist learners in perspective taking; that is, in coming to see the world as others see it

4. To introduce learners to elements of complexity and ambiguity in an issue, topic, or theme

The overarching purpose of discussion is to help learners to explore their experience so that they become more critical thinkers (Brookfield, 1987); that is, to help them to become contextually aware, to develop reflective skepticism, to be able to unearth and analyze the assumptions informing their values, beliefs, and actions, and to explore alternative ways of thinking and acting. Although, as we shall see, flexibility and risk taking are crucial components of discussion, there are various preparatory steps which can be taken to increase the chances that discussion sessions will be perceived by learners as open ended and charged with meaning and excitement.

## PREPARING FOR DISCUSSION

### Setting Discussion Themes

Themes, issues, questions, and topics for discussion should not be too factual or uncontroversial, nor should any questions be raised which learners are able to answer in the course of their preparatory reading. Legge (1971) proposes that "discussion is most appropriate to those subjects concerned with controversial issues about which there are different but equally tenable opinions" (p. 78). It is also useful to present groups with questions to be considered, rather than abstract themes. A program director of a course for new adult education instructors would be better advised to ask participants to consider "Do lectures promote retention of knowledge?" than to ask them to attend a discussion on "The Lecture as a Teaching Method."

## Providing Resource Materials

Merely because adults are gathered together for the purposes of discussion does not guarantee that any worthwhile activity will take place. Discussions can quickly degenerate into noncommunicative intolerance—"numbers of people slamming shut their minds in one another's faces" (Brew, 1956, p. 325)—if participants merely exchange entrenched prejudices on the basis of mutual ignorance. If learners have access to materials for scrutiny well before any meeting, then a common pool of concepts, ideas, factual information, and explanations exists to inform their discussion. This reduces the risks that discussions will meander aimlessly, that learners will become intolerant of minority opinions or that sessions will become emotional battlegrounds for the furtherance of individual self-esteem.

## Evolving Consensual Rules

Miller (1964) believed that participant training was so crucial to success in discussion groups that the first sessions in any series of meetings should be devoted to evolving procedural rules and codes of conduct to guide discussion in subsequent meetings. Bridges (1979) specifies epistemological underpinnings of discussion and proposes a moral culture to guide this activity. He emphasizes the values of reasonableness (openness to others' arguments and perspectives), peaceableness and orderliness, truthfulness, freedom, equality, and respect for persons. It is important to evolve clear rules of conduct for the group's interaction. These rules of conduct should try to ensure that minority opinions are respected, that no one is allowed to dominate the group, that silent members are not bullied into participation, that divergent viewpoints are allowed expression, and that there is no pressure to reach premature and artificial solutions to problems posed. There can be time limits set on the length of any individual contribution. There can be rules set for the order in which participants can initiate new themes and respond to others already raised. And there can be agreement on the importance of ensuring the confidentiality of opinions expressed within the group.

## Personalizing Discussion Topics

Attemps to foster discussion on broad themes may well flounder as a result of participants' perceiving such themes as being

unrelated to their own individual lives. This is particularly the case
where the discussion of social and political issues is concerned.
People frequently perceive themselves to be helpless in the face of
overwhelming social forces. They regard their individual lives as
relatively insignificant brush strokes when viewed against the background of the broad canvas of social, political, technological, and
economic changes. The connections between individuals' personal
lives and wider changes—between the personal and the political—
is either wholly unfathomable or completely ignored. If points of
connection can be uncovered between learners' experiences and
broader themes, or if learners can be encouraged to imagine themselves in hypothetical situations and dilemmas and describe the actions they would take and the reasons for these actions, then the
exploration of broad themes becomes more immediate and charged
with significance. Asking participants to think in these personalized
ways about a general theme, and perhaps to make a few brief notes
on these musings for consultation in the discussion session, is an
important preparatory step leaders can take.

### Attending to the Group's Composition

Group dynamics are an important factor to be considered in
the use of the discussion method. Aside from the need to evolve
consensual rules to govern group members' interactions, two important preparatory steps can be taken. Firstly, the group's size
should be kept to a reasonable maximum. Opinions differ as to the
optimal size for interaction, but the consensus seems to be that
somewhere between ten and twenty members offers the best chance
for provocative discussion. A group smaller than this can easily
become unnecessarily introverted, with selected members periodically repeating their particular obsessions. A group larger than this
can be intimidating to those members who find public speaking
difficult. Secondly, it is important to attend to the participants'
backgrounds and experiences. Because of the largely white, middle
class composition of adult education discussion groups, there may
easily be a homogeneity of opinion on many discussion issues. It is
important to try and assemble groups containing members with
diverging backgrounds, experiences, and world views. Where a
homogeneity exists in regard to these, one approach is to ask people
to undertake imaginative projection so that they try to address an
issue from a perspective quite different from the one they generally

inhabit. Although not quite a role play it is surprising just how effectively adults can, with careful encouragement, immerse themselves in another's perspectives and bring these to bear on discussion themes.

## FACILITATING DISCUSSION

Any guidelines for facilitating discussion must, of necessity, be speculative. Discussion is by its very nature unpredictable. If we knew exactly what was going to happen in a session it would cease to be a discussion in any meaningful sense. Every discussion group is a universe unto itself, a unique constellation of personalities. How these individuals will perceive, and react to, preparatory reading, a leader's comments, and other group members' contributions, cannot possibly be anticipated in advance. Discussion leaders have to make innumerable decisions during meetings which are wholly contextual. For example, when should an overly garrulous participant be restrained so that others can have their say? How strongly should silent members or isolates be prompted to contribute? At what point should one try to move a discussion into another area? After how long do group silences for periods of contemplation and reflection become embarrassing rather than welcomed? When does vigorous, passionate, and honest disagreement cross the line to become personalized insult? When is it useful to follow up an apparently irrelevant line of discussion because of the benefits that might result? How do you react when a participant makes a statement which seems obviously racist? Does quelling racist contributions contradict a leader's assurances that all viewpoints should be respected?

In the course of dealing with the kinds of situations outlined above, each facilitator evolves a personal theory in use of discussion leadership. A theory-in-use (Schon, 1983) is a collection of hunches, insights, and intuitions concerning what works when and why. It is context specific, being borne out of distinctive experiences and crafted within particular situations. But elements of a theory-in-use can be generalized to connect to a range of contrasting situations. What follows is my own theory-in-use of discussion leadership. This comprises the guidelines I would give to anyone new to facilitating discussions who asked me for advice on this activity. It comprises five components.

1.  Be wary of standardized approaches.

2.  Use a diversity of approaches.

3.  Welcome the unanticipated.

4.  Attend to the emotional dimension.

5.  Be authentic in the group.

## Be Wary of Standardized Approaches

There is no one model of discussion leadership suitable for all groups or all curricula. Although particular variants of discussion such as the circular response technique are useful for particular purposes, no prepackaged approach can be presumed to be appropriate for all situations. Ambiguity, diversity, and conflict are givens of discussion, just as they are of all attempts to assist learning. Every learning group comprises individuals with idiosyncratic personalities, diverse learning styles, different cultural backgrounds, varying expectations, and a multiplicity of motives for learning. To expect one approach to be perceived by all group members as being relevant, congenial, and connected to their own experiences is wholly unrealistic. There will always be participants for whom the theme under discussion, the method used, or the apparent purpose of the activity appears pointless or confusing. If discussion leaders equate success with meeting all the learning needs of learners as they have defined them, then they are assigning themselves to a permanent professional purgatory of self-induced guilt at their apparent failure to be constantly perfect teachers.

## Use a Diversity of Approaches

As a general rule it is a good idea to use a diversity of approaches in discussion sessions. Have a reservoir of possible questions, discussion leads, and different materials ready. The principle already described of personalizing the discussion of broad themes is a good one. Variants of the life history method can be used or one can try critical incidents. In the critical incidents approach learners write down very brief (usually no more than half a page) descriptions of situations in which something significant has occurred and read these out to the group. For example, in a professional development course for teachers of adults, one might want to discuss how teaching and learning might be evaluated. Instead of opening a discussion by posing a general question—"How should you evaluate teaching and learning?"—one might ask learners to write down a brief description of the last time they left a classroom feeling a real "high" of fulfillment and satisfaction. In reading out their descriptions of what events and situations caused teachers to feel so excited about what they were achieving with learners, participants can probe each other's descriptions for general evaluative criteria which seem to undergird their incidents. Such a personalized, descriptive approach to discussion is far less intimidating, and arguably more compelling, than posing generalized questions about the philosophical aspects of evaluation.

## Welcome the Unanticipated

The cardinal principle underlying discussion is that of flexibility. Leaders and learners should be ready to depart from the general aim of the session, or the prevailing line of discussion, to follow up themes which arise unexpectedly. A great deal of significant learning cannot be anticipated in advance, so discussion leaders should be courageous in encouraging learners to explore the unexpected and to take risks themselves. When people recall the most significant aspects and events of educational experiences in which they have participated, they frequently cite skills, knowledge, and insights which were not part of the official purpose of the course. The most vivid events recalled are often those focusing on a teachable moment charged with risk, uncertainty, and excitement. Someone raises an issue which is not part of the group's agenda, but which has great significance for group members, and the resulting interchange has a dramatic quality missing from some of the more planned discussions. Without a willingness to embrace risk and to venture into unanticipated intellectual territory, discussions can easily become bloodless exercises with no real meaning or significance to participants.

## Attend to the Emotional Dimension

Attending to the emotional dimension in discussion is crucial. Learning is a highly emotional phenomenon involving joy, pain, excitement, anger, anxiety, fear, pride, frustration, boredom, and relief. Education, similarly, is a passionate undertaking. It never ceases to amaze me how comprehensively textbooks on educational

method can bleed dry of passion what are emotionally charged
activities. One reads of methods, techniques, and devices to be used
with learners which make no reference to emotions, either of teachers or learners. It is as if there are no feeling beings in education,
merely role functionaries called teachers and learners. These are
presumed either to be emotional ciphers bereft of feeling, or to
exhibit such a homogeneity of emotional response that one can
safely predict the reactions to materials, methods, and content.

As those who have burnt themselves in the fiery crucible of
pedagogic experience know, discussions can be highly charged,
competitive emotional battlegrounds. They can also be the forum
in which people let down their defenses and reveal aspects of their
personalities which they generally regard as highly personal and
private. Groups can become bitterly factional in a very short time
with members spending their energy replaying aggressive patterns
fixed in the first few meetings. Or, groups can become cohesive
units, characterized by a deeply felt bonds of commitment, love,
and obligation among members. Learners weep tears of joy, of
frustration, of hostility, and of relief. It is not uncommon for me
to leave a discussion session feeling completely drained, emotionally
wrung out. I am tired, exhilirated, depressed, puzzled, and excited
all at the same time. I find it difficult to talk to anyone and like
to shut myself away in privacy for an hour or two. If the session
has been held in the evening I take at least two to three hours to
wind down. It is at these times that the videotapes of the "David
Letterman Show" that have been piling up get watched.

These emotions are not uncommon and facilitators need to
be prepared enough so they are not thrown into total disarray when
they experience such reactions. They also need to remember that
although their learners are probably feeling many of these same
emotions, this may not immediately be evident. It is true that boredom is usually readily detected (the snoring generally gives it away),
but many learners have learned the lesson that overt displays of
emotion within formal classrooms are to be avoided. Indeed,
"you're getting too emotional about this" is one of the most effective
put-downs a teacher can use with a student. So it is not surprising
that learners consciously try to adopt a mien which appears, calm,
considered, and serious. The presentation by learners of this apparent emotional calmness or vacuity means that charting the emotional temper of a group is one of the most difficult of all pedagogic

tasks. Yet if accomplished it can be invaluable. Teachers can come to see how the meaning and significance of ideas and concepts can be connected directly and dramatically to learners' own lives. Apart from relying on the direct evidence of one's own eyes (principally the body language of learners) it is possible to use learning journals to record the emotional life of the group. Learning journals are confidential personal diary entries made by learners regarding their perceptions of educational activities. It is a very simple task after a meeting to ask learners to write down the most fulfilling and the most distressing aspects of that meeting, and to describe the activity which had most personal meaning for them. By reading these brief journal entries (after assuring learners of their confidentiality) facilitators can gain a much more informed idea of the emotive dimensions of the group's discussions.

## Be Authentic in the Group

One of the most damaging mistakes facilitators can make in leading discussions is to pretend to a personality they don't possess. It is very easy to erect a role model of the ideal discussion leader— warm, incisive, animated—a combination of Phil Donahue, Ted Koppel, and Johnny Carson or Barbara Walters, Judy Woodruff, and Lily Tomlin. Facilitators then feel they have to become these hybrid creations and learn a set of communication skills (make eye contact with all members on a regular basis, use your body language vigorously, smile frequently, constantly alter the tone and temper of your voice to enhance the dramatic dynamic of classroom communication) in a highly routinized way. In my opinion these attempts to model the perfect facilitator are perceived by learners as blatantly inauthentic, hollow, and misconceived. It is far better to acknowledge one's own personality as a facilitator and build on whatever strengths one possesses. In my own case I have a "low key" style, so to attempt to turn myself into the Rodney Dangerfield of discussion would be disastrous. I would come across as failing to be someone I wasn't. This is not to say that one should not pay attention to how one might better communicate in a discussion. One of the best teaching improvement exercises is to watch oneself leading a discussion group on video tape. The scope for improvement rapidly becomes evident. But to try to role play a personality type which feels unfamiliar to the facilitator will only impart an air of unreal artificiality to the group's activities.

## EVALUATION

Don't evaluate by learner satisfaction. Given that so much adult education practice is informed by the felt needs rationale—that the duty of educators is to meet as fully as possible those learning needs expressed by learners themselves—there is a real tendency to evaluate the success of discussions by the extent to which learners enjoyed them. This is misconceived for two reasons. Firstly, a great deal that is educationally valuable occurs long after the educational event itself. Learners may leave a session feeling puzzled or disturbed because questions have been raised, or perspectives illuminated, which they had not considered before, and which throws their dearly held givens, common sense beliefs, and values into doubt. It may take weeks, months, or years before learners find some meaningful connection between the events within a discussion session and their own lives. And during that time they may feel frustration and perplexity regarding the discussion's format and content. Yet, in the long run, the sense of having one's unquestioned givens challenged, of being shaken out of habitual ways of thinking, are some of the most significant and valuable of all educational activities. Secondly, with learning, as with other things in life, we tend to enjoy the familiar, the comfortable. A discussion which learners leave feeling comfortable may well be one in which their prejudices are confirmed and their habitual patterns of reasoning are reinforced. Such sessions may be pleasant social occasions, but they are hardly educational.

How then might we evaluate whether or not a discussion session is educationally worthwhile? As with so many educational activities, multiple criteria come into play. For me, the overarching criterion by which I judge the educational worth of any activity has nothing to do with social dimensions. It is, quite simply, whether or not people have been helped to learn by the activity. More specifically, an educational activity is successful to the extent to which it encourages people to think critically. This is why I consider discussions which are characterized by periods of confusion, painful self-scrutiny, and anxious recognition of the fragile, tenuous, and culturally formed nature of our "common sense" knowledge, to be educationally successful, even though participants may resist and dislike many of these activities. So the fundamental criterion for evaluating a discussion—whether or not people are being prompted to think critically—is the fundamental criterion for judging all educational activities, and it has nothing to do with social arrangements. There may be many times when learners are silent, or when discussion is halting, tentative, and intermittent. Yet these silences and interruptions may be caused by learners contemplating critically their previously unquestioned values and beliefs. Such reflective interludes, or provisional formulations, are crucial to critical thinking, yet they certainly do not conform to the ideal of discussion as a continuous, informed, and smoothly flowing conversation.

With regard to evaluating the social dimension to discussion, the criterion of fairness must prevail. All members of a group should feel that their right to contribute is safeguarded. They should also keep in mind that they do not have the right to dominate the discussion, no matter how much they are convinced of the rightness of their viewpoint. With regard to the order in which participants speak, I would urge leaders to discriminate positively in favor of the less frequent contributors. In other words, if several group members are vying for the floor, the leader should intervene to allow the quieter member to speak. Again, while the most preferable option is for leaders not to have to orchestrate the discussion, there will be times when it is necessary to intervene to establish an order in which participants will speak.

## CONCLUSION

Discussion facilitation is essentially a question of balance. Balance between examining the declared themes of the discussion and exploring uncharted intellectual terrains. Balance between accepting the contributions of confident and articulate group members, and arranging exercises which provide silent members with the chance to speak. Balance between supporting and appreciating the inchoate, stumbling efforts at critical analysis of group members, and challenging the intellectually lazy to stretch their minds to consider alternatives. Balance between making sure every member's contributions are respected and making clear that racism and bigotry are unacceptable. Balance between facilitators expressing their own opinions honestly and openly, and keeping these private so as not to give messages to participants regarding "approved" or "acceptable" views. Balance between emphasizing the connections of discussion themes to the immediate circumstances and concerns of adults' lives, and prompting learners to consider ideas and explore perspectives which they had previously rejected as being of no immediate relevance to them. Balance between meeting the declared felt needs of learners, and asking them to engage in activities which they initially resist. And balance between learners feeling enlivened by the joy of learning and being ready to face the anxiety and painful self-scrutiny sometimes involved in critical thinking.

To participate in discussion—in the collaborative effort to find meaning in, and make sense of, our experience—calls for courage and hard work on the part of learners and leaders. It asks adults to examine critically the cultural contexts within which their beliefs and values have been framed and to query the universal validity of these. It also requires that the distinction between learners and leaders be forgotten as much as is humanly possible, though in formal educational settings it can never be completely erased. As a student I remember well my own scepticism at teachers who declared that their discussion groups were democratic and leaderless, while all the time subtly controlling the interactions and judging the worth of each person's contributions through the award of end-of-semester grades. But it is possible for discussion leaders to demonstrate through their actions—in particular their willingness to admit their faults and to undertake the same critical scrutiny of their own ideas and contributions as they do of others—that an atmosphere of openness, trust, and confidentiality prevails. For example, I regularly require learners to identify points of ambiguity in my arguments, internal contradictions, omissions, and poorly expressed ideas. To aid them in this I make copies of critical reviews of my work and I try to take on the perspective of my critics. This is not an extended masochistic exercise in intellectual self-flagellation. At least I don't think it is. It is an effort to demonstrate through my actions that I mean it when I say that the discussion method provides one of the best forums in which to develop critical thinking.

When conducted authentically, discussion is not an easy or soft option. It entails learners identifying and externalizing the assumptions underlying their taken-for-granted, common sense ideas and their habitual actions. It also involves people in a critical examination of the extent to which these uncritically accepted assumptions are found to be valid in adult life. It is intellectually taxing and emotionally unsettling. It requires participants to attend carefully to what others are saying. It places the responsibility for the success of the activity in learners' hands, for even the most animatedly enthusiastic and experienced leader can do little if participants refuse to respond. Participants have to present their own ideas as clearly as possible, they have to respond thoughtfully to people's reactions to these, and they then have to interpret other learners' ideas which might be expressed in highly personal and ambiguous ways. And all this in an atmosphere which may be highly competitive and in which there is no chance to rehearse one's contribution so that it comes out smoothly and confidently. Small wonder, then, that participating in the sprawling, wayward, emotionally charged activity we know as discussion represents for many adult learners the quintessential adult educational experience.

## REFERENCES

Bligh, D. A. (Ed.). (1986). *Teaching thinking by discussion*. Guildford, England: Society for Research into Higher Education.

Brew, J. M. (1956). *Informal education: Adventures and reflections*. London: Faber and Faber.

Bridges, D. (1979). *Education, democracy and discussion*. Windsor, Berkshire: National Foundation for Educational Research.

Brookfield, S. D. (1985). Discussion as an effective educational method. In S. H. Rosenblum (Ed.), *Involving adults in the educational process* (pp. 55-67). New Directions for Continuing Education, no. 26. San Francisco: Jossey-Bass.

Brookfield, S. D. (1987). *Developing critical thinkers*. San Francisco: Jossey-Bass.

Brunner, E., Wilder, D. S., Kirchner, C., & Newberry, J. S. (1959). *An overview of adult education research*. Chicago: Adult Education Association of the United States.

Davis, J. A. (1961). *Great books and small groups*. Englewood Cliffs: Free Press.

Essert, P. L. (1948). The discussion group in adult education in America. In M. L. Ely (Ed.), *Handbook of adult education in the United States* (pp. 269-275). New York: Teachers College Press.

Fawcett Hill, W. M. (1977). *Learning thru discussion*. Beverly Hills: Sage.

Freire, P. (1970). *Pedagogy of the oppressed.* New York: Continuum.

Gulley, H. E. (1965). *Discussion, conference and group process.* New York: Holt, Rinehart and Winston.

Hyman, R. T. (1980). *Improving discussion leadership.* New York: Teachers College Press.

Legge, D. (1971). Discussion methods. In G. W. Roderick & M. D. Stephens (Eds.), *Teaching techniques in adult education* (pp. 75-89). Newton Abbott, Devon: David and Charles.

Lindeman, E. C. (1945). World peace through adult education. *The Nation's Schools, 35,* 23.

Miller, H. L. (1964). *Teaching and learning in adult education.* New York: Macmillan.

Osinski, F. W. W., Ohliger, J., & McCarthy, C. (1972). *Toward Gog and Magog: A critical review of the literature of group discussion.* Syracuse: Syracuse University Publications in Continuing Education/ERIC Clearinghouse on Adult Education.

Paterson, R. W. K. (1970). The concept of discussion: A philosophical approach. *Studies in Adult Education, 2,* 28-50.

Rogers, J. (1977). *Adults learning.* Milton Keynes: Open University Press.

Schon, D. A. (1983). *The reflective practitioner.* New York: Basic Books.

Watkins, R. (1975). Co-operative learning in discussion groups. *Teaching at a distance, 2,* 7-9.

# CHAPTER 10

## Mentorship

LAURENT A. PARKS DALOZ

Ever since the first appearance of Mentor as the embodiment of wisdom and guardian of young Telemachus in that great journey tale, *The Odyssey,* mentors have been recognized as guides on a lifelong journey. In recent years, since they caught the public imagination in Gail Sheehy's *Passages* (1979), mentors have become as familiar—and nearly as popular—as microwave ovens and Granny Smith apples. Dozens of articles and several books have appeared extolling their virtues or sniffing at their defects. There is even an international association of them and a journal (Fagan, 1987). The business world in particular has noted their importance, suggesting that mentors play an import part in helping young aspirants to scramble up the corporate webwork. Not far behind, researches in academia have pointed to the numerous ways in which the professoriate helps former students advance into the upper reaches. And in sports, music, and the arts, mentors have long played germinal roles even though more often known simply as "coach" or "teacher."

Most of the emphasis has been on the ways in which mentors turn up in a "natural" setting and on how they help their protégés to advance in the external world—to gain more power, earn more money. As used in that research, the term, "mentor" generally designates an informal role in which the teaching function is recognized primarily as a means to personal and institutional advancement and only secondarily as a contribution to the overall well-being of the protégé.

Yet the relationship between mentorship and learning is a

crucial one for educators, especially those who would like to see a closer conceptual tie between education and development. Because it acknowledges some legitimate role for authority without the parental connotations that can color the education of children and adolescents, mentorship is of particular concern to adult educators, and in the growing numbers of programs designed especially for adults, "mentor" often refers to a faculty member who has a more formal and explicitly didactic role than does a mentor in a "natural" setting. The mentor may be an academic advisor, an independent study tutor, or a counselor who teaches the student as well.

The role was pioneered in the 1950s by Goddard College and was later modified by such institutions ad Empire State College and the Fielding Institute. While responsible for conveying a certain amount of academic content, mentors of this ilk tend to value their subject matter as much for its part in enhancing the overall intellectual and ethical development of their students as for its intrinsic worth. They are committed to promoting such generic abilities as critical thinking, the capacity for empathy, the power to take diverse perspectives, and the will to take positive action in a tentative world. Seeing the job as one of cultivating their students' growth, they don't "push" or "pull" so much as *align themselves in relation* to their students. Their work is to empower their students by helping to draw out and give form to what their students already know. They call out the best parts of their students. They serve as midwives or guides rather than solely as sources of knowledge.

The aim of effective mentorship, then, is to promote the development of the learner. For our purposes here, "development" may be taken to mean an increase in the ability to perceive and hold complexity, to tolerate ambiguity, to experience one's own and others' feelings more richly, to see oneself and others in a broader context, and to make wholehearted commitments in a complex, tentative, and interdependent world. In the following discussion, I have assumed that most students are undergiong a developmental shift from relatively tacit, unexamined ways of knowing and a sense of the self as a passive receiver toward a more critically reflective stance on their culture and a more active notion of themselves as learners. Malcolm Knowles (1970) has described this form of growth in detail, and it is frequently referred to in the developmental literature as the "three-four shift." While not the only developmental transition of adulthood, it is almost certainly the most common one experienced by the returning adult student.

Although mentors may appear in a variety of garbs, in this chapter we will look only at how mentors operate in an academic setting when in a one-to-one relationship—perhaps as academic advisor, perhaps as particularly valued teacher, or perhaps as "mentor" in a special program tailored to adult students. Thus, one might imagine a mentor sitting in an office with a student discussing a paper, meeting in a classroom to go over independent study plans, or perhaps having a cup of coffee and talking about how a business accounting course relates to the student's struggle with an alcoholic spouse.

When students come to higher education, they are in a real sense *changing environments*. If the college is doing its job, it expects more rigorous thinking as well as more considered moral actions from its students. If education is what it should be, it represents an intensification of and expanded reflection upon the best aspects of everyday life. As such it requires of its students a different way of being if they are to adapt successfully to the new environment.

In such a situation, mentors serve the important function of introducing students to the new world, interpreting it for them, and helping them to learn what they need to know to flourish in it. Mentors are, thus, *interpreters of the environment*. They help students to understand how higher education words and what it expects of them.

But mentors are also an important part of the environment itself. They may be doing some of the teaching, they model expected behavior, and most certainly they speak the language of the new world and understand its peculiarities. They thus provide a kind of special "test environment" for their students. According to Robert Kegan (1982), environments affect human development in three ways: they *confirm* (it's OK to be where you are), they *contradict* (it's not OK to be where you are), and they *provide continuity* (when you move, I'll still be here). If we translate these three functions to what a mentor does, we see that mentors can do three things for their students as they work. Mentors can *support* their students in their present ways of being, they can *challenge* their students toward more appropriate adaptations to the higher education environment, and they can *provide vision* for students to help them see where they have been and also where they are going.

It is no surprise that the work of mentorship has been described as a "balancing act" (Schneider et al., 1981), for mentors spend much of their energy helping their students to negotiate the delicate balances in their lives between an old world and a new one, between the expectations of the work world and those of school, between demands of family and of study, and between too much and not enough pressure to ask provocative and profound questions about how they make meaning in their lives. To help students mediate these tensions in the mentor's art. Effective mentors do this by delicately calibrating the mix of support and challenge they offer their students while holding open the larger questions of ultimate purpose (Parks, 1986).

In Figure 10.1, notice that when both support and challenge are low, rather little happens. The student remains where he is. This may be fine in situations where the only goal for the student in the acquisition of knowledge or skills. But if we want more for the student, we need to consider what happens if we alter the balance (Daloz, 1986).

If we offer lots of support but provide little challenge, the

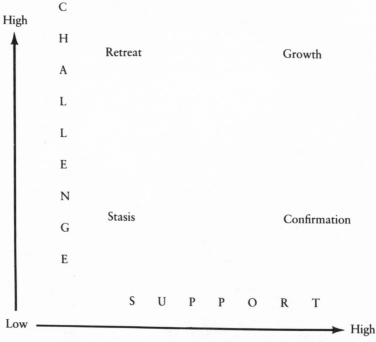

Figure 10.1 Dimensions of Response to Environmental Variation.

student will experience a sense of confirmation. For students who come to the program with deep injuries to self-esteem (a distressingly common phenomenon among adult students), this may be just what is necessary to allow healing to begin. There are times when people simply need to be "held," when even a little challenge can be too much.

Yet too much challenge with too little support can simply drive people back into earlier, less adequate ways of interpreting the world. Much current "fundamentalist" thinking seems to be this form of "retreat" (Perry, 1968) in which people have chose to see a fluid and complex world in black and white terms because the complexity and ambiguity of the modern world are simply too demanding.

Viewed this way, it becomes clear that what we seek as mentors is to provide a balance of support and challenge such that our student feel *safe to move*. To risk leaving home they must know that it is safe to return. But they must also know, or at least have a general sense of, their destination. They must have a vision which places their journey in a larger context and invokes purpose from their lives.

How, then, do mentors support, challenge, and provide vision to their students? We will look at these function separately, but the reader should bear in mind that mentors usually do these things simultaneously.

## MENTORS SUPPORT THEIR STUDENTS

Most good teachers instinctively know that even though they may disagree with what a student is saying or may see weakness in a student's work, it is necessary to pick the time to make the point. It is a lot harder for one to hear criticism if one is already feel vulnerable. Effective mentors begin be encouraging their students. Students have to know they have done something right before they can hear that they have done something wrong. To support a student is to affirm that person's essential integrity, to say that no matter what is to come, that person is fundamentally OK. Beyond this, of course, support assures students that what they have done right they can do again. The mentor must be able in a fundamental way to say, "I am on your side; we are in this together."

*Call Out the Inner Voice*

The most basic tool of the effective mentor is the ability to listen well to the students. Listening does two important things. It allows the mentor to gather information on the basis of which to move ahead, and it assures the students that they have something to say, that they have a degree of control in the relationship, and that their voices will be heard. Effective mentors often spend a lot of their early listening time helping students to think through more deeply their reasons for returning to higher education. They may evoke the students' individual stories, encouraging them to talk about how school fits into their lives and what they see ahead for themselves. In order to understand the context of a student's study, the mentor might inquire about family and friends, noting especially who helps and who hinders the schoolwork. And moving more deeply, some mentors urge their students to use this precious time to explore their "burning questions" about life. This is not simply small talk, or a device for "establishing rapport." It is a powerful way of learning about what moves the student and of enhancing that individual's inner voice, of helping the student to tell and retell his or her story, a profoundly important aspect of the process of evolution. Listening is an active intervention. Not only is it the first step a mentor and student take together, it lies at the heart of all of their work.

*Provide Appropriate Structure*

All students need structure. The question is how much comes from outside authority and how much from within. In this, people vary widely, usually in accord with their developmental level. Knowing just how much and what kind of structure to provide is delicate work, best informed by a good knowledge of the student's developmental journey.

In general, students who view knowledge as concrete and fixed will tend to seek authority from outside sources rather than from within themselves. Thus, such students will tend to feel supported by specific assignments with clearly defined tasks and expectations. For them, "truth" is found rather than constructed, and the source of truth lies with authority. Mentors are usually more successful with such students when they conform to see extent to the students' authoritarian needs and act like "real teachers." On the other hand, students who are a bit farther along developmentally are more likely to view knowledge as fluid and relative. Since for them their own experience provides relevant "knowledge," they may tend to discount or modify the role of outside authority in favor of subjective "truth." For such students support means having their own personal insights validated. The effective mentor here will take a less authoritarian stance, using carefully chosen empirical information to raise questions, and pressing students to construct a way of knowing that can coordinate multiple truths.

Thus, mentors need to be able to read their students accurately and then to place themselves at the appropriate position, providing enough confirmation of the student's existing worldview to give a feeling of safety, but enlisting a kind of benign doubt as a spur to further growth. It is in this sense that the mentor serves as transitional figure, confirming the world as it is, but pointing ahead to a more complex, inclusive, and ultimately adequate perspective.

## Express Positive Expectations

When students look back to describe the most significant contribution of their mentors, they often recall some variant of the message: "You can do it. I know you can." Notice how different this is from "You must do it; I expect it." In the former case, the mentor is making a personal affirmation of the student's ability while retaining the expectation. In the latter, affirmation of the student's worth is made contingent on fulfillment of the expectation. The implied threat is seldom lost on students.

To express positive expectations requires not so much a sunny (and possibly hypocritical) imagination for the student as a determined connection with and responsibility for the student's ability to make some sort of movement. Moreover, while effective mentors surely can see their students' shortcomings, they tend to place those limitations in the broader context of their students' promise. Thus, rather than dwell upon what their students did wrong, they will tend to talk about how the students can improve. Said on mentor, "I find that students improve much faster when I tell them what they did well instead of pointing to all their flaws."

## Advocate and Explain

The world of higher education, with its control over credentials, its credit and distribution requirements, its specialized jargon, and its overwhelming aura of authority, can be intimidating to many students. An important task of mentorship, particularly in the early stages, is to explain the arcane mysteries of academia to the student. Too often, overburdened advisors forget how bewildering their world can appear to a newcomer, especially to an adult who may have been away from school for years. Effective mentors take the time to be sure that their students at least know where to go for help—the registrar's office, financial aid, or students services—if they themselves cannot provide the answers.

In addition, many adult degree programs expect the mentors to advocate for the student during the program approval process. It is important to be aware of how vulnerable students feel when their degree plans or final evaluations are in the hands of a strange committee. At such times the mentor's calm assurance is a much needed gift.

## MENTORS CHALLENGE THEIR STUDENTS

If support affirms students where they are, challenge often sows the seeds of discontent. It seems to work because as meaning-making creatures, human beings need to make sense of things. When new information calls old structures into question, we strive to close the gap, either by denying the discrepant information or by construing the world in a more adequate way to hold the new data. Thus, when mentors challenge students, they do so by providing new, disruptive information or by assigning tasks which will lead to the discovery of such information. One might say that if support involves using the strength of relationship to empower learning, then in a sense, challenge strengthens learning by placing the present form of the relationship at risk.

### Set Tasks

The most common "challenge" function is the setting of tasks, from homework assignments to papers to field research. Mentors set tasks in the hope that their students will learn from them. But the purpose of these tasks may not always be obvious. The young Rilke was told by his mentor, August Rodin, to go to the zoo and simply watch the animals. It was only as Rilke began to reflect on the meaning of this act, and to write about it, that the power of the exercise became manifest. Thus, effective mentors are mindful about how they design the tasks for their students. Of course they are concerned with tasks which will result in knowledge acquisition, but they also want their students to reflect upon the meaning of the tasks themselves, to use them as exercises in reflection, in analysis, in the reconstruction of a former way of thinking. Thus, they usually have some notion in mind about how the task can help the student move ahead. To do that, of course, they need to have a clear idea of what "ahead" means. For some, the student needs to learn to "think more broadly," for others, the student may need to "find her own voice," or for still others, the need may be to "think in less absolute terms."

### Provide an Alternative Voice

Another important form of challenge is to provide an alternative voice to the one the student conventionally hears. To the relatively unsophisticated student, this can come as a surprise, for the assumption is that there is only one truth, and authorities know what it is. When the mentor, an authority, questions another assumed authority, the student has to make sense of the new ambiguity. Some will simply reject the mentor and stick with their earlier truth; others will reject it and cleave to the mentor. The mentor's long-term goal, however, is not to gain a convert but to help the student understand that what seemed once to be "truth" is better understood as a particular point of view, a particular way of making sense of the data.

At another point in student development, the mentor may suggest alternative interpretations to the student's own voice. This must be done delicately, and the mentor must read carefully whether the voice being disconfirmed is an old one that needs disturbing, or a more recent one that wants comfort.

An effective way to encourage students to explore different perspectives is to ask them to express a point of view which differs from their own in such a way that someone who "really" held that position would agree that it was an accurate replay. Again, the task must be give with care, for some students are simply not yet ready to do it. The ideas of convincingly arguing for something they do not believe seems senseless. They have yet to separate themselves from their ideas, an important piece of work.

Thus, for students in early developmental positions, alternative voices serve to raise necessary doubts about the monolithic nature of truth. For those in later positions, actually trying these voices on can help them to see that each truth rests on its own assumptions and contains a unique logic. To recognize this inner structure of ideas is an important insight and of profound importance in the developmental journey.

### Help Students to Identify Their Assumptions

Many students come to higher education carrying as unexamined "truth" the beliefs of their parents, their communities, their culture. Often, before they entered the rarified air of higher education, their beliefs went unchallenged. But if an important purpose of higher education is to help students to form their own considered views based on reasoned argument, then they must go about the sometimes painful business of critically examining long-held beliefs. A primary way for them to do this is to identify the assumptions which underlie their tacit belief systems. Such assumptions are "the seemingly self-evident rules about reality that we use to help us seek explanations, make judgments, or decide on various actions" (Brookfield, 1987, p.44). By becoming aware of a formerly unseen assumption, the student has a choice that did not exist before.

Mentors may do this in a number of ways, but central to all is the need to listen carefully as the student talks, or to read written work closely. For it is out of the specifics that the assumptions can be drawn. Once the assertions are made, a number of questions can arise:

- How does the student value it?

- What would happen if it were continued indefinitely?

- What is satisfying (or right, or good) about the situation?

- Should this apply to everyone?

And often, taking an assumption and expanding on it, the mentor can then ask "Then do you think that . . . ?"

An important result of identifying assumptions is that it relates a given position to others and helps students to recognize that each position is constructed from a certain foundation. This represents an important developmental step beyond simply taking the world as given to be "the only" or "the best" way.

### Encourage Hypothetical Thinking

An important conceptual leap occurs when we come to think in hpothetical terms, when we become able to take a particular assumption which we know is not true and spin off a set of implications from it. As we learn to do this, our thinking gets "off the ground" in a sense and can be exercised without any necessary constraint of "reality." Although there are clearly limitations to such thinking, the ability to function in such an abstract manner is nonetheless a valuable tool. For it lies at the heart of the ability to imagine a world that is more than merely practical. Hpothetical thinking makes utopian thought possible. It allows us to "play with ideas" and is thus central to the creative imagination. As Fowler (1981) explains it, reality becomes a subset of possibility rather than the other way around. "Thought," he tells us, "takes wings" when we develop the ability to reflect upon our own thought, when we can think about thought.

The kind of "as if" thinking often used in computer simulations, statistics exercises, or in certain simulation games is a good way of exercising this capacity. Many students find i pointless at first to play simulations in class. "What can you learn from a game?" they ask. But it is just such exercises which, if well-designed and appropriately processed, can help students to develop their ability to see that even though a situation may not be "real," they can still learn from it.

### Provide Specific Positive Feedback

One of the most frequently commended yet seldom used techniques is simply to be very specific about feedback. And although there are clearly times when it is appropriate to be clear about a student's errors, many mentors maintain that most of the time the student will learn far better if they ignore the weaknesses and emphasize his strengths. Yet important as it is to tell students when they have done a job well, it is still more important to let them know what it was that they have done well. Thus, when speaking with a student about a particular paper, it helps to tell the student where a particular idea was handled deftly or how two ideas were lined together insightfully. "This is a great job of identifying Bly's three main points!" might go in the margin of a paper, or when discussing a student's plan for a special project, the mentor might say, "I like the way you are going from a specific incident, to an analysis, to your summary." The point is to be specific so that students knows when they have done well so they can do it again.


## MENTORS PROVIDE VISION

In addition to challenge and support, mentors also can help their students to see the way ahead, to gain the insight they will need to further their own educational journey rather than remaining dependent on teachers. In a sense, vision is the larger field on which the challenge and support are played out. Effective mentors are not satisfied with superficial or instrumental answers to their question, "Why are you doing this?" The press; they ask, "So what? Why is that important? What difference will that make in the long run?" Such questions force students to construct a reasoned, thought-out, and named context for the ways they have chosen to invest their lives. And it is by helping student to be clear about their long-term purposes that the mentor frees students from his or her own influence and creates the possibility for them to become their own mentors.

### Offering a Map

Most mentors have some idea of what constitutes "growth" for their students. Depending on the context, it may mean increasing their skills (say in accounting or music), it may mean deepening their personal insight (in the study of literature or psychology perhaps), or it might mean sharpening their ability to understand complex ideas (as in science or business). But beneath the specific dimensions of "growth," there is usually the sense that "growth" means a kind of movement, a journey of some sort. Perhaps it was with this in mind that Carl Jung (1958) remarked that mentors are people who ask us who we are and where we are going. Thus, if mentors are to be guides on a journey, it would seem a good idea for them to carry maps.

The social sciences have given us several valuable maps of development, some descriptive of patterns of lifelong growth, and some more normative. One of the most useful such maps in William

Perry's (1968) description of the journey from a simple black and white world to a stance of commitment in a reconstructed, contextual, and relativistic world. Another is Robert Kegan's (1982) vision of the movement from an interpersonal world of tacit belief to an institutional one of explicit choice. And a third, particularly helpful for work with women is that of Belenky, Clinchy, Goldberger, and Tarule (1986) who describe the growth in a sense of "voice" for female learners from a condition of passive silence and receptivity through to a recognition that truth emerges from a dialectical conversation. But different mentors in different circumstances may find other models of value. In any case, such maps help mentors not only to be more purposeful in helping their own students move through transitions, but they also can prove helpful to the students themselves. I have found that students benefit greatly when they are helped to understand the model of growth that I value, or when they find one that makes particular sense to them.

Thus, with one student it may make sense to discuss in abbreviated form what the "journey" is like as we move from black and white thinking toward a more richly textured way of knowing; for another the image of "leaving the tribe" (Daloz, 1988) might be appropriate; and for still another, that of "gaining a voice." The point is that when students are provided with some sense of what it means to "grow intellectually," they gain more control over the process itself and are better able to conduct their own journeys.

## Keeping Tradition

It is for good reason that mentors are often depicted as aged people. Age connotes both continuity and wisdom. In certain ways, age is an analogue for a mentor's stability. Although they may be the medium through which profound transformation can take place, mentors are in a curious way quite conservative. Because it is they who must have a foot on either bank as they swing the traveller across the chasm, mentors must have a perspective that the student may lack. Thus, the mentor will often steer the student back toward the more profound and firmly grounded work in the field; the mentor may consciously remind the student of the lessons of history or may press the student to consider more broadly the implications of that student's ideas for the whole human family. In this way it is the mentor's role to provide continuity for the student.

## Suggesting New Language

Language is a powerful indicator of our forms of thought. As those forms change, so does the way we use language. Effective mentors learn much about how their students make meaning from the way they talk and write. At early developmental positions, for example, people tend to use frequent absolutes. Later, their language may turn sharply personal and subjective. A rambling narrative style may replace a slavish parroting of authority. Later still, phrases like "it depends" and "assuming" appear, indicating a new sensitivity to hypothetical thought.

By suggesting more appropriate use of language, we can help our students name their emerging world views more effectively. Thus, we can flag such unqualified language as "always," or "true," suggesting language like "in many cases," "in this context," or "appropriate." And we can help them see the relative nature of such terms as "progress," "objective," or "success" by insisting that they frame them in quotation marks, thus acknowledging their contingent definitions. For students emerging from a tacit, personal way of knowing, the language of systems can have special power: "the system," "ideology," "model," "paradigm." These and other abstract terms help students to hold their nascent awareness that ideas in themselves have the power to shape reality. In a similar vein, exercises in the creative and original use of language, such as those suggest by the poet, Cora Brooks (1987), can help students to recognize the power we have as human beings to name the world afresh and thus to recreate our reality over and over.

## Providing a Mirror

It is no secret that we come to define ourselves in large part through they eyes of others. As particularly important "others," teachers often contribute an important part of our self-image, especially our intellectual image of ourselves. Thus, mentors have a lot of power to influence how students think of themselves. How we use that power is of central importance, for we inevitably distort the mirror. The question is whether we distort it in ways that ultimately serve our students or not.

Socrates used the mirror to draw out his students in long sequences of "if/then" reasoning, inexorably leading them toward logical conclusions from their initial assumptions, helping them to comb their ideas, to realize their implications, reducing them to the absurd as a way of baring the bones of the arguments. Effective mentors may find themselves doing this, asking questions about the ramifications of their positions, pushing their assertions at the edges, asking them, "Then would you also say that . . . ?" This may lead to qualifications and enhanced richness. More, it can lead toward students' coming to see their own thought, recognizing it as a phenomenon in itself.

By providing "feedback" to our students in the form of a slightly titled reflection of their own ideas, we can help our students to see their own positions from several different perspectives and thus to expand the scope of their thinking. One valuable device is the "learning style inventory" (Kolb, 1981), a simple, self-administered test that students can use to determine whether their own style tends more toward concrete or abstract thought, toward reflective or active engagement with their learning. By helping students discover yet another way to understand their own approach to learning, it effectively tilts the mirror so they can know themselves from a fresh angle and thus develop a more complex picture of who they are in the world.

## THE LIMITATIONS AND PROBLEMS OF MENTORSHIP

Thus far, the bulk of the literature on mentorship ranges from favorable to euphoric. But most people can cite numerous examples of the dark side of mentorship. Some of the problems include a need for control and misuse of power by the mentor, charges of favoritism and rivalry among proteges, desertion by the mentor, excessive emotional dependence by either party, differing ethics, and a vulnerability to hero worship which can restrict the further growth of student and mentor alike.

Most of these problems come into focus when we consider that a healthy mentor-protégé relationship will tend to move from a more or less hierarchical form in which mentor and protégé have complementary roles toward a more symmetrical one in which each contributed equally. Levinson (1978) notes that many mentorships end unhappily. Other research qualifies this. But since a certain tension is implicit in the evolution of the two roles, it is no surprise that the evolution of the relationship can become stuck.

Sometimes, for example, the mentor becomes enamoured of his own power and finds it too much to handle when the protégé begins to question some of his corner on the truth. The protégé's very understandable need to have an idea of his own, to find his own voice, may be the catalyst for the challenge to earlier forms of the relationship.

At other times, a problem may arise because the protégé wants more from the mentor than the mentor is willing to provide. Demands for time or attention become excessive—or at least too much for the mentor's own level of tolerance. The result again is to challenge the form of the relationship.

At still other times, one of the other partner simply "drifts away." Perhaps the most common resolution, this becomes understandable when we recognize that mentors are not so much "found" as invented. We create mentors when our developmental needs call for someone to help us to make a transition. Unless there was more to the relationship, it will understandably fade away once that transition is made. This seems to hold most often in the case of formal, institutional mentorships, founded as they are on an essentially instrumental basis. The formal role structure itself tends to insulate the partners from the kind of personal hurt that can result from a harsh ending, and while many teachers continue to maintain close, caring relationships with former students, the expectation, at least, is otherwise. When the course or the independent study is over, so also is the relationship.

## GIFTS TO THE MENTOR

The advantages of mentorship to the student have been fairly clearly spelled out above. Mentors provide a personal connection in an often impersonal and threatening world. They replicate certain and appropriate aspects of an earlier parenting relationship and as such help the student to resolve earlier separation/attachment issues and to continue "growing up" emotionally as well as intellectually. They offer a powerful form of role modeling, a direct form of teaching, and an effective means of making the transition in a new and wider world.

There are advantages for the mentor as well. Much of what is best and most rewarding about teaching can be found in a good mentoring relationship. Mentors can work in a truly responsive and interactive way with the student, shaping their responses directly to the student's, blending support and challenge in an optimally appropriate way.

Moreover, the rewards of seeing a student share one's own excitement about a subject, of revisiting familiar intellectual pathways with a new companion, of being an important part of another's growth, can be rich. Noting the importance for human development of the capacity to nurture, Erik Erikson calls teaching one of the most profound affirmations we can make of our own hope for and trust in the next generation. "Man needs to teach," he writes, "not only for the sake of those who need to be taught, not only for the fulfillment of his own identity, but because facts are kept alive by being told, logic by being demonstrated, truth by being professed" (Erikson, 1964, p. 131).

## EVALUATING THE MENTORING METHOD

There exist "objective" assessment instruments for evaluating the effectiveness of mentorship at an institutional level (Fagan, 1987). But as a practical matter there appear to be three primary voices which can help us learn how well we have done: those of our students, our own, and those of our colleagues.

### Student Assessment

Students may assess both their own progress and the helpfulness of the mentor. Programs which value student-centered learning and intellectual growth highly tend to place considerable importance on student self-assessment, arguing that such reflection encourages the ability to think about, name, and thus enhance one's own development. The problem is that in the glow that can often follow a good learning experience, students may tend to generalize about their own growth and heap indiscriminate praise upon the mentor, leaving everyone feeling good but no one knowing why. While a vast array of student assessment instruments is available, those which encourage specificity—about the student's new skills and the mentor's interventions—are likely to do a better job both of educating the student and of informing the mentor.

*Self-assessment*

Since effective assessment measures accomplishment against intent, how good we feel about our work with a particular student depends in part on what we set out to accomplish—and that will appropriately vary with each person. But in most cases, if our map is clear we can at least determine the extent to which the student has moved along it. The tendency of many mentors at first is to overestimate how much students will change; with experience we learn that the changes may appear in small ways if at all, and that student self-reports must be well salted. Sometimes, indeed, a student may appear to have actually regressed as a new loyalty to truth replaces slick platitudes with halting affirmations. It is important for us as mentors to be able to see the difference.

One of the best ways to combine the virtues of both student and mentor self-assessment is to conduct a "debriefing session" in which the two partners talk over the previous work together. As the power in such situations almost always appears to rest with the mentor, it is incumbent on the latter to help set an environment of openness and inquiry. This will be enhanced to the degree that the mentor can indicate that the conference will be a place for *both* partners to learn from the experience. Well conducted, such conferences can be of major educational value in themselves.

*Collegial Assessment*

How might our colleagues participate in the evaluation of our work? At first glance, the essentially private nature of a mentor-student relationship might seem to preclude the participation of others as evaluators, and indeed, much of the power of good mentorship hangs on the privileged character of the conversation. Yet if the evaluation process is understood as a learning opportunity and if an effort is made to hold regular meetings for discussion of student case studies, much can be learned by the faculty as a whole. Moreover, in situation where competitiveness is low and a sense of collegial learning is high, it might even be possible for small groups of mentors to hold debriefing sessions with students to discuss "how the study went" and what interventions did and did not work well.

## CONCLUSION

Effective mentorship is akin to guiding the student on a journey at the end of which the student is a different and more accomplished person. In a formal learning situation, mentoring functions can be understood as variously providing *support, challenge,* and *vision.* Supportive activities include listening, providing structure, expressing positive expectations, and advocating. Challenged include setting tasks, proving alternative perspectives, unmasking assumptions, encouraging hypothetical thinking, and giving specific feedback. Vision is provided by offering a developmental map, by honoring tradition, by suggesting new language, and by providing a mirror. Although there are potential problems in any mentor-student relationship, when practiced in the context of care for the student and commitment to the learning, mentorship can be a powerful human experience for student and mentor alike.

## REFERENCES

Belenky, M., Clinchy, B., Goldbergerm, N., & Tarule, J. (1986). *Women's ways of knowing: The development of self, voice, and mind.* New York: Basic Books.

Brookfield, S. (1987). *Developing critical thinkers: Challenging adults to explore alternative ways of thinking and acting.* San Francisco: Jossey-Bass.

Brooks, C. (1987). *The sky blew blue.* Norwich, VT: New Victoria.

Daloz, L. (1986). *Effective teaching and mentoring: Realizing the transformational power of adult learning experinces.* San Francisco: Jossey-Bass.

Daloz, L. (1988). Beyond tribalism: Renaming the good, the true, and the beautiful. *Adult Education Quarterly, 38*(4), 234-241.

Erikson, E. (1964). *Insight and responsibility.* New York: Norton.

Fagan, M. Ed. (1987). *International Journal of Mentoring.* Dept. of Behavioral Sciences, Kentucky Wesleyan College, Owensboro, Ky 42301.

Fowler, J. (1981). *Stages of faith: The psychology of human development and the quest for meaning.* New York: Harper & Row.

Jung, C. (1958). *Psyche and symbol.* New York: Doubleday.

Kegan, R. (1982). *The evolving self: Problem and process in human development.* Cambirdge: Harvard University Press.

Knowles, M. (1970). *The modern practice of adult education: Andragogy vs. pedagogy.* New York: Association Press.

Kolb, D. (1981). Learning styles and disciplinary differences. In Chickering, A. (Ed.), *The modern American college* (pp. 232-255). San Francisco: Jossey-Bass.

Levinson, D. (1978). *The seasons of a man's life.* New York: Knopf.

Parks, S. (1986). *The critical years: The young adult search for a faith to live by.* San Francisco: Harper & Row.

Perry, W. G. (1968). *Forms of intellectual and ethical development in the college years: A scheme.* New York: Holt, Rinehart, and Winston.

Schneider, C., Klemp, G., & Kastendiek. S. (1981). *The balancing act: Competencies of effective teachers and mentors in degree programs for adults.* Chicago: Center for Countinuing Education, Univ. of Chicago.

Sheehy, G. (1976). *Passages: Predictable crises of adult life.* New York: E. P. Dutton.

# CHAPTER 11

## Case Study
### VICTORIA J. MARSICK

An almost universal dictum of good adult education is that it be experiential in several ways. First, it should draw on the past experience of participants. Second, it should be participatory in nature, thus adding to past experience by involving adults in current activities that either provide new experience or that help learners reinterpret their prior experience. And finally, it should have an action component, which is a link to future experience. The case study is used by educators in a variety of ways to meet one or more of the above criteria. At its core is the concept of learning from and through experience—from the *past,* on which the case study is built; through the *present* interaction of participants who bring their own life experience to bear upon the case; and for the *future,* by building skills that are presumed useful to the learners.

This chapter first describes what the "classic" case study is, for whom it is appropriate and why, and how an educator should design, use, and assess the success of this method. The author then discusses advantages and disadvantages of the method and describes variations that compensate for some of its limits.

## THE "WHAT" OF CASE STUDIES

The terms "case study" and "case method" are sometimes used interchangeably. However, "case study" is also used in research to mean the in-depth study of a problem or situation, whether or not it has direct implications for practice. "Case method," on the other hand, almost always refers to a method of instruction based on real-life examples. The case method was developed by Christopher Langdell of Harvard's Law School in the 1880s and later introduced into Harvard's Business School. For many, Harvard is still most closely identified with the case method even though it has been adopted and adapted by many other fields, for example, medicine, social work, engineering, theology, communications, and management development.

The case method can be used throughout a course or only for selected activities. In law schools, cases are frequently the backbone of a course, with separate cases used throughout the course period. An overarching case is often used throughout a long course in other fields to tie all components of the subject matter together. Each time learners meet, new material is introduced that expands on the nature of the problem. The case is not fully resolved until the end of the course. At other times, shorter cases might be used for specific activities to illustrate concepts and provide opportunities to apply new material. Cases might also be used by individuals in self-paced courses, using written materials or computer-based simulations.

Cases typically include three interrelated components: a case study or report, case analysis, and case discussion. The case discussion is sometimes supplemented by a report written by the learners.

## Case Report

The classic case report is based on an actual situation and typically consists of a set of researched, predesigned written materials supplemented at times with slides, videos, or other audiovisuals. As discussed below, the case report has been altered in variations, as for example in "live" case studies, the use of hypothetical rather than real situations, and cases as springboards for behavioral change activities. The strength of the classic case is its true, rich description of a complex problem and the decisions taken to resolve it—against which learners can test their understanding of the situation and their own decision-making process.

This report is centered around a complex problem or dilemma about which various participants in the case hold different views. One of the original purposes of the case method was to help learners analyze the strands of the problem in order to name it, identify and analyze alternative solutions, and think through the steps and possible consequences of implementation. Thus, the case method usually differs from simple problem-solving exercises where the problem is identified in the opening paragraph.

The key to the case's success is the selection of the right problem situation. It must be relevant both to the interests and experience level of learners and to the concepts being taught in the activity. Included in the case report are facts about the problem itself, the environmental context (e.g., the organization, its clients and community, or special conditions bearing on the problem), and the characters of the people in the case. Insofar as possible, the case report is factual, although opinions and views held by people in the case should be included. Cases include realistic details, much as does a good novel, to help put the reader into the situation itself: conversations, maps, correspondence, policy statements, organizational charts, and pictures. The information included in the case is limited only by the time available for its analysis, since its purpose is to simulate a real-life situation in which problems and conflicting perceptions are not clear. The case report includes a description of the actual solution to the problem, but this is not handed out to participants until they have reached their own conclusions and wish to compare their results with the decision taken in real life.

### Case Analysis

The analysis of the case is discussed more fully below in guidelines for its implementation. Evans (1980) compares this phase to a good detective novel in that it is a search for clues to underlying principles and problems, and their assembly into a reasonable explanation of the situation. Because the case is by definition complex, the analysis must help the learners tie their insights to other facets of the case that should also be taken into consideration. The key to a good analysis is thus its grounding in the facts, which limits idle speculation.

Case analysis can be carried out in many ways, depending on the purposes and length of the activity. The analysis may be done by learners before a class meets, either by working on their own or informally with members of a study group. Frequently, questions are provided in the case materials that help the learner begin the analysis. Even if individuals have prepared the case before coming to class, time is often provided for groups to work on their own to brainstorm their perceptions of the case before the case discussion begins.

## Case Discussion

The third component of the case method, discussion, is examined later in this article as well as by Brookfield in Chapter 9. The Socratic method is at the heart of this phase, that is, a probing, critical discussion that raises new perspectives and digs for underlying assumptions that may not be apparent. In the field of law, this phase is typically a dialogue between two people, the student and professor. Even in law, however, there are advocates for more effective *group* process such as Reed (1984) because of the way in which the perspectives of others can broaden the learner's viewpoint. In most other fields, the case discussion is ideally a highly participatory activity.

Usually, discussion involves both process and task issues. Groups must decide how they will work together and who will assume the various roles needed to facilitate and record discussion. The educator managing the activity cannot assume that group members will have the skills needed to keep the discussion on track, to involve all learners in the task, and to probe skillfully into the case. Unless one purpose of the course is to train learners in these process skills, the educator in charge has certain responsibilities: (1) to help learners as a whole decide on criteria for problem solving and decision making, (2) to provide clear instructions for group discussion when learners work independently, and (3) to manage the discussion of the entire group so that the case gets properly analyzed.

Case discussion is, to some extent, an art. Since its purpose is simulation of reality, the discussion leader must make sure that all perceptions and proposed actions are anchored in the data. The leader helps learners arrive at broad consensus about the nature of the problem. Together, they probe the case data to understand the perspectives of different stakeholders, decide what the problem is, and evaluate various solutions to the problem. The discussion does not usually end with a decision. Learners get practice in laying out plans for implementing the solution, including a discussion of timing, strategies, obstacles, responsibilities of key people, and possible intended and unintended consequences. After they have developed their own solutions, the learners examine the real case: how the problem was formulated, analyzed, and solved, and when possible to determine, what the consequences were of that decision.

Case discussion can be combined with other methods. Learners may be asked to present their findings to the rest of their class in a panel discussion, for example. Role play is commonly used. Learners may role play solutions to the case and ask for feedback from other members of the class. The educator managing the case may have learners role play dialogue between people in the case with different perspectives to determine whether or not proposed actions are consistent with the characters. If a purpose of the case is to improve learners' writing presentation skills, groups can also be asked to write up their analyses—individually, as separate groups, or in one composite report.

## THE "WHO" AND "WHY" OF CASE STUDIES

Case studies simulate the real world. They can thus be used to orient learners to a new profession, organization, or social world. Since cases can be written at varying levels of complexity, they can be used with both the relatively inexperienced and the highly sophisticated learner. Variants of case studies are used to prepare professional at the university level, to teach literacy and vocational skills, to integrate immigrants or the emotionally handicapped into mainstream societies, and to develop technical skills. Cases are frequently used in business and other organizations to orient new employees and to teach a range of managerial, sales, marketing, and personnel skills.

Thus, in a sense, case studies can be used to teach anyone. However, since they take much time to prepare, case studies should not be used if a simpler activity can be designed to provide learners with skills practice or to solve simple, nonambiguous problems for which there are clear "right" answers. Case studies sharpen analytical skills and help socialize learners so that they can "think like" people in a profession or role to which they aspire where the rules are not clear.

For example, cases help future lawyers organize complex bodies of facts and information on their own and to inductively arrive at principles and apply them to new situations. Cases also socialize new lawyers into both a problem-solving process and an environment in which new twists and turns must always be considered as a lawsuit unfolds. Other professions use case studies for different kinds of analytical, problem-solving, and socialization purposes. Engineers, for example, use cases to introduce students with a mastery of technique to the organizational worlds in which they will work. They will have to communicate their proposed solutions to a mix of clients with multiple backgrounds and organizational roles and will frequently address ill-defined problems with provisional solutions. Business schools and other socially oriented professions also use cases to help students master the ambiguity of the worlds in which they will work and at times, to build teamwork and group process skills. Thus, while cases are used universally to simulate the real world, the needs of different professions suggest different uses of the case method.

## THE "HOW" OF CASE STUDIES:
## DESIGN, USE AND EVALUATION

### Designing Case studies

The principles of good learning design apply to case studies as much as to any other method. In other words, you should identify in advance the learners and their needs, what you want the learners to gain by using this case, clear objectives for the activity, the mode of delivery, and the methods by which you will assess the learning. However, there are some considerations unique to the case method.

*Focusing on the Problem.* The problem has to be real, typical, complex, and researchable. The case's "punch" is its trueness to life, with all the accompanying shades of gray that people with different perspectives and values bring to a problem. Its critical ingredients are a problem statement and factual content.

Your problem is not likely to be stated in your opening paragraph, unless your purpose is to focus on solving problems more than understanding them. It is more likely that you will use it as a guide for selecting and limiting what you will include in your case. While you should include rich detail, too much information can be distracting unless there is a tie-in with your focus. A clearly written problem statement will lead to scenarios that accurately project this problem.

As Pigors and Pigors (1987) note, the Harvard case studies are well known for the extensiveness and quality of their research, which can take years of staff preparation time, almost to the point where they are too detailed and time-consuming. The reports must balance the need for information with the amount of learning time available for the activity and the level of ability of learners. However, cases must be researched sufficiently to be believable, even when—as discussed below—they are hypothetical composites based on different situations. Interviews and participant observation are ideal methods for researching cases, but much information can also be gathered by reviewing such documents and relevant reports as minutes of meetings, policy documents, personnel files that are not confidential, and other training materials.

*Dramatizing Real Life.* The case must be developed dramatically to represent a slice of life with which the learners want to identify. Start with what you want to achieve and work backward, so that from your opening paragraph onward you develop a tightly woven story. To avoid confusion, limit the number of characters in your story to four or five and also limit the relative number of complications they face.

Develop character sketches for each person in the case, so that your portrayal of their thoughts, words, and actions is believeable. A character sketch is a paragraph that describes the person's education and background, his or her values and beliefs relevant to the problem, language he or she might use, and positive and negative traits. Characterization might not be used verbatim, but it can be used to describe thinking or provide dialogue that makes the story come alive.

The case is intended to stimulate the thinking of the learners. Thus, it should end at a dramatic juncture, leaving the learners with a challenge to which they must respond. The tone of the cutoff suggest a need for action even though the decision to be made is not immediately apparent.

*Designing to the Learner.* The case should be written with the learners in mind, and what it is they should most gain from this activity. Some cases are designed primarily to acquaint learners with the professional knowledge and problem-solving methods they must use in a job. Much of this knowledge is ambiguous and must be gained experientially, frequently through the feedback gained in the case analysis and discussion. Guidelines for case analysis would be open-ended to stimulate the learners' discovery of the problem. Even in situations where the objectives are more specific, learners should be allowed to take the lead in exploring the problem and its alternative solutions to simulate real-life conditions.

Because so much reliance is put on the learner, the designer should make sure that the experience level required for the case analysis matches that of the learners or they will quickly become frustrated. When the case is written for those relatively new to a field or organization, the designer should be careful to explain unfamiliar terms, concepts, and procedures needed to interpret the case. Such information can be put into appendices or placed on reserve in a central location. Conversely, when the case is written for the very experienced, the designer should build in details that will challenge their thinking.

*Designing to the Mode of Delivery.* The case should be written with the mode of delivery in mind. Cases require that you allow enough time for people to fully understand the nature of the problem and the situation. Using video or other relevant audiovisuals will cut down on the time needed for understanding, but will increase your design time. If you have only one class period, you case study should be no more than two pages in length. Cases of more than three pages in length can be used for longer periods of time, especially if you plan to build your case over several sessions, with new information presented each time.

Keep in mind the case's location within the course. If it is introduced at the beginning, you can link insights to concepts introduced in subsequent activities. If you want learners to build gradually on their knowledge and skills, place it at the end of the course and use a final, culminating problem to pull it all together. At times, a case may be used for a learner's self-assessment or evaluation by the education. Law students, for example, are given hypothetical cases that pose new situations. When a case is used for evaluation, specify the criteria on which the learners will be evaluated. In law cases, for example, the critical factor is the student's ability to reason logically, define issues, distinguish among facts, and apply legal principles. Cases can also be used to evaluate the learner's ability to identify or solve problems, to demonstrate familiarity with concepts relevant to the course, to understand different points of view, or to work well with team members.

Most cases rely on group work. Determine how large each group will be and whether each group will work on the same case or on different segments. Also determine whether you will make all or only part of the information needed available. In a straight case, everyone works on the same problem and has access to all necessary information. The difficulty with this design is that learners quickly become very familiar with the case, thus losing the ability to ask questions from fresh perspectives, as would perhaps happen in real life. This drawback is somewhat offset in a simultaneous case, in which subgroups work on different segments of the problem. This makes the presentation more interesting but may also make it more difficult to manage. An incident case is one in which only partial information is available, thus forcing the learners to determine what else they need to resolve the issue and to seek out this information, as they would have to do in a real situation. The disadvantage here is that it takes more time.

*Developing Administrative/Support Materials.* If someone other than yourself is going to lead the case, provide materials to assist them in managing each step of the process. Objectives and a course outline will be needed, along with timing for different phases of the process, steps the case leader should take, briefing guides for groups, reference or support materials, evaluative materials if needed, and a checklist of administrative materials needed, such as teaching aids or suggested room arrangement.

Materials should include teaching notes to ensure that the problem and issues are clarified, to help groups decide on criteria by which they should make decisions, to supplement the rationale for the actual solution, and to identify relevant concepts that can be used to interpret the groups' findings. Sample questions should be developed to guide the discussion at various phases of the case analysis, along with relevant points of the case that should not be missed. Several alternative decisions can be identified, along with factors that could be incorporated into strategies for implementing those decisions.

*Revising and Field Testing.* A good case must be complete, but not overly detailed; clear, but not simplistic; storylike, but believable. Even more than other materials, the case must therefore be revised and field tested to ensure that it accomplishes its aims within the desired time period. Before field testing, check the case several times for completeness, clarity, brevity without losing essentials, and a style that prospective readers can understand. Check for ambiguous terms and sections where dialogue or characterization is misleading. Try out the materials on an audience as close to your real target population as possible, but include specialists if needed to verify the accuracy of information and learning specialists to help you monitor and evaluate feedback. When field testing, allow ample time to stop and debrief the participants. You should review the case for content validity, reliability, objectivity, and comprehensiveness. In addition, if someone other than you is going to administer the case, you should check the clarity and completeness of any instructional guides. Pay particular attention to the questions provided to the case leader to guide discussion, making sure that they stimulate desired responses and provoke a stimulating, deep discussion. Learners should fully understand as well as solve the problem, if that is the aim of the case. Ensure also that instructions provided to the groups about what to do in each phase of the discussion are understood and achieve results.

### Using Case Studies

*Arranging the Room(s).* Room arrangement depends to some extent on the number of people participating in the activity and the availability of separate breakout rooms. The ideal is separate breakout rooms, preferably small areas in which people can sit around a table. If classrooms must be used, desks or chairs can be arranged in a circle so learners can talk directly to one another.

You can manage the activity within the same room, although the noise level will be high, by seating people in groups around tables as indicated in Figure 11.1. By arranging tables in a herringbone fashion, participants will be able to see one another and not have to sit with their backs to others. Even if groups use breakout rooms, you may wish to arrange the main room in this manner because it facilitates group interaction.

Each group will need either a flipchart or transparencies on which to record their findings for presentation to others. Figure 11.1 illustrates the placement of optional flipchart easels and overhead projectors. Arrange for more than one flipchart easel or overhead projector in the main room so several sets of ideas can be

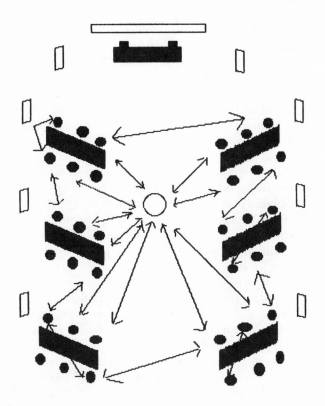

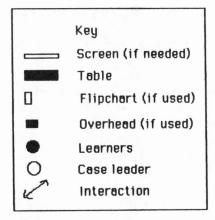

Figure 11.1 Room arrangement for case study.

considered simultaneously when the entire group reconvenes for discussion. Even if group discussion takes place in the main room, you will want at least one additional flipchart easel at the front of the room for your own use.

*Assigning People to Groups.* Divide the learners into subgroups. You may wish to arrange the groups before the activity begins and list their names on the blackboard, flipcharts, or handouts. Groups should ideally range from three to six members; if you put more in a group, everyone will not participate equally. Diversity—of age, function, gender, ethnic background, and work experience—is the guiding principle for group composition in order to obtain as many different perspectives as possible on the problem. The only exception to this rule might be status differences. If learners do not perceive themselves on somewhat the same level of power and authority, these differences might interfere with full participation by all members.

*Clarifying Roles.* Clarify your own role as leader vis-à-vis both the process the group will follow and the help you are willing to provide on the task itself. If the purpose is to stimulate reality, the learners should do as much work as possible on their own to identify and understand what the problem is. However, limitations in time and learner experience might prompt you to be more directive. Furthermore, some cases place more emphasis on finding solutions to problems than defining them. Others focus on applying concepts to develop skills. In these situations, the leader's role may involve providing feedback to the learners regularly as discussion progresses.

Clarify the roles to be taken by group members and brief the class on what these roles entail. Do not assume that participants are adept at group process even if some have worked in groups before. Establish procedures for selecting leaders and recorders, for ensuring that everyone participates equally, and for identifying action each group must take to address the task. These steps are especially important when the learning of group interaction skills is as important an outcome as understanding concepts or receiving practice in a particular kind of problem solving process.

*Managing the Case.* Introduce the case and relate it to the experience of the learners as well as its purpose and placement in the course. Explain the mode to be used in the case (discussed above): straight, simultaneous, or an incident process. Distribute the problem and materials, and show any audiovisuals if you are using them. Explain procedures to be used in analyzing the case and check that learners understand instructions: what the groups are to accomplish, logistics and timing, reporting procedures, and your availability as a resource person. You will probably use the same pattern of group work followed by plenary discussion whether the case is a short one to be conducted in one phase, or a longer one to be conducted in several successive phases.

As the groups work, rotate among them to answer questions and check on their understanding of the issues. As the time draws near for the end of each phase of the activity, alert the groups to time limitations and determine whether to adjust the time to allow for sufficient discussion. Do not, however, allow all available time to be taken up in groups since the plenary analysis is equally as important.

In debriefing the case, start by asking groups to report on their understanding of the case details and the problems or issues involved in the decision. You may wish to ask each group successively for one or two salient points rather than exhaustively discussing the report of one group before going on to the next. In this way, all groups will remain interested and no one will feel that they have nothing to add to the discussion. Minority and conflicting viewpoints should always be elicited. Always bring the discussion back to the facts of the case. At times, groups will feel it necessary to talk about the process by which they arrived at a conclusion. Do not discourage this since it sheds light on the reasoning process people in the case might also have used.

Once the facts of the case have been thoroughly discussed, you can either move to the consideration of alternative decisions and plans of action as a whole group or through another round of small group discussions. This depends somewhat on the degree to which the case emphasizes problem formulation or problem solving. There is no need for groups, or for the class as a whole, to arrive at a consensus decision on action to be taken unless one of your purposes is to foster this kind of collaboration. Otherwise, after the alternatives have been outlined, you can move to the presentation of the actual steps taken by the persons in the case and a discussion (either in plenary or in subgroups) of the differences between the solutions agreed to by the groups and the action taken. As noted above, you may also wish to ask the learners to write up their analysis of the case—individually, in subgroups, or as an entire class—if your purpose is also the development of writing skills because these would be needed in the actual situation.

In concluding the case, you will want the learners to sum up the learning points from the case. As you wind down the discussion, make sure that these "learnings" are related to concepts covered in the course (unless this is a standalone activity), to other similar problems and challenges in the area covered by the case, and to the learners' back-home worlds of work or personal development.

*Evaluating Case Studies*

Your evaluation will depend on your purpose and objectives. To name a few, these might include: identifying a problem when faced with a welter of conflicting facts and opinions, seeing a situation from multiple viewpoints, assessing the unwritten norms of a complex organizational system, analyzing the problem, laying out action steps to implement a solution, understanding and relating concepts or principles to new situations, reasoning clearly, gaining confidence in one's ability to work in groups, or presenting information to potential clients of different disciplines or perspectives. In addition, you may wish learners to gain practice in highly specific skills and possibly change their attitudes toward certain kinds of problems.

Pigors and Pigors (1987) identify long-term milestones by which to measure the case method. One milestone is effective teamwork, which they define as team spirit, smooth group interaction, and effective verbal and nonverbal communication. Another milestone is "case-mindedness," which they see as an ability to step back and view a situation objectively, differentiate between feelings and facts, make short-term decisions within the context of long-term goals, and identify apparently trivial incidents that can be explosive if left unattended. Perhaps the most complex of these milestones is "a triple blend of understanding" that includes "intellectual capacity . . . sensitivity, empathy, and interpersonal skills . . . (and) common sense" (pp. 426-428). In short, they believe the case study method can enable learners to reach a deep level of personal and professional development grounded in reality.

Unfortunately, many of these longer-term developmental effects cannot be measured within the period of the course or activity. Short-term assessment can be undertaken in several ways. If you are familiar with the learners, you will undoubtedly observe progress as the case is being analyzed and discussed. However, since many activities will at times take place simultaneously, you may wish to supplement observation with learner ratings. You can develop a short feedback form asking learners to rate the extent to which they achieved desired objectives, the success of their group's interaction, and factors in the design and implementation of the case that will help you improve its delivery. This type of assessment can also be carried out less formally in the subgroups in which learners worked, followed by a general discussion of the case's value.

Evaluation can also be oriented to in-depth self-development if enough trust has been developed in the subgroups. Ask each person to list the information and skills he or she has gained, and the areas in which he or she still feels a need for improvement. If you wish, assist the learner in this by developing checklists covering expected gains in knowledge, skills, and attitudes with respect to the substance of the case, problem identification and solving methods, and group process. Working in their subgroups, learners should then take turns discussing their self-assessments with their peers. Ask each learner to identify first personal strengths and then perceived weaknesses. Peers should then give additional feedback on both strengths and weaknesses. If this method is used, make sure that assessment begins with achievements before going on to weaknesses to counteract the notion that criticism is only valuable if it is negative. Also, make sure that everyone participates equally or else those speaking may feel exceptionally vulnerable.


## ADVANTAGES AND DISADVANTAGES

The strengths of the case study are many. It emphasizes practical thinking. Through the case method, learners both identify principles after examining a welter of facts and apply those principles in new situations. They thus learn to formulate problems as well as solve them. As in real life, learners must make decisions under time pressure with an inadequate stock of information. However, because they are in a laboratory situation, they have time to reflect and think more critically than they might under pressure. They must take risks in front of their peers, present their reasoning on-line, and argue their point of view. Case discussion can question the notion that there is "one right answer," and broaden the learner by encouraging a wide range of viewpoints from others. However, an assumption is made in this process that participants will be similar enough to the range of people one would encounter in a real-life incident, which is not always true, especially if learners come from the same discipline.

Many of the advantages of the case method can be looked at as disadvantages from another point of view. For example, one key strength is clearly the method's simulation of reality: both the ambiguity of the professional or personal world into which learners are entering, and the more socially oriented work world of organizations in which group work is key to decision making. On the other hand, the complexity of these cases also mean that they take a long time to prepare and a long time for learners to fully comprehend. The benefits to be gained by simulating the real world clearly must outweigh the time needed to do a case, even if it is an abbreviated case, as discussed below.

Another advantage is that the case method is participatory in nature. A related disadvantage, however, is that the facilitator must be skilled in leading case analyses and discussions and must be able to develop group skills in the learners so that all participate equally in the discussion. Even with advance preparation, the facilitator must think on-the-spot with the learners and cannot anticipate many of the responses a case will elicit. Moreover, in order to encourage participation, it is easy to fall into the trap of accepting ideas offered by the learner without adequate probing and critique. The case leader must challenge and probe to go beyond a superficial level of analysis, especially if the learners do not already have the kind of experience that would enable them to see deeper nuances.

In a similar vein, the case method can be used to simulate real-life conditions, particularly when learners begin to challenge one another as if they were in the actual situation. Sometimes role play can be used to enhance the reality of these interactions. On the other hand, the case leader must feel comfortable in dealing with unanticipated confrontations and possible conflicts. The case leader can and should draw up a lesson plan for discussions, but should also be prepared to depart somewhat from the agenda if learners raise other issues relevant to the case in which the majority have a great interest.

## VARIATIONS IN THE CASE METHOD

The case method has been adapted in many different ways to needs not shared by its original designers. Common variations include changing the method of presentation, using fictitious or abbreviated cases, and guiding more fully the group process. Some examples are discussed below.

### Method of Presentation

*The "Live" Case.* An early variation of this type, the "live" case, was developed by Walter B. Murphy in the early 1950s at the Wharton School of Finance and Commerce (Pigors & Pigors, 1987, p. 416). Instead of using written materials, executives were invited to discuss the case in person, thus heightening a sense of realism and providing an expert resource who could give additional information as needed. The original format, discussed below, has since been modified but the spirit of this adaptation is retained.

Students received a brief written statement in advance of the class session to set the context. The executive spent about an hour presenting the case and answering questions. Students then met in small groups to discuss the situation. Each student individually wrote an analysis of the problem, a suggested solution, and a one-page executive summary before the next class meeting. The second class meeting was a student-led discussion. Based on this, the instructor selected and forwarded the ten "best" reports to the executive. The executive commented on the reports and returned them before meeting with the class a final time to present the historical solution to the problem, comment on students' solutions, and participate in a final general discussion.

*Technological Presentations.* A common variation, made more feasible by technological advances, is an audiovisual packaged presentation using video, film, or computer simulation. Delving into the details of this approach is beyond the scope of this chapter. Readers are referred to Chapter 15 by Linda Lewis and Chapter 18 by Barbara Fiorini for some discussion of these tools. Packaged materials, including cases or variations of them, can be purchased off-the-shelf from vendors. Often, such cases are fictitious, as discussed in the next section, and are used primarily as a projective stimulus for learner discussion or other activities.

One example of video-based case material is Adkins Life Skills

Program (Adkins et al., 1985), which addresses personal and social needs rather than professional development. It also combines case analysis with behavioral change skill development. Video cases are used in the first "stimulus" stage of the process. They are realistic life vignettes that dramatize problems or dilemmas that the socially disadvantaged might encounter. The second "evocation" stage is a facilitated group discussion in which learners identify the problems depicted in the video and relate them to their own life experience. In the third "objective inquiry" stage, learners typically investigate the problem and make some decision relevant to their experience of it. In the final "application" stage, action is taken to carry out their decisions. Sample learning activities include a personal experience inventory, role playing, surveys, structured exploration of jobs, interviews, and action plans.

*Fictitious and Abbreviated Cases*

Pigors and Pigors (1987) warn against the use of fictitious and abbreviated cases, in part because they believe case leaders may become tangled in their own web of inventions and cause learners to lose faith in the reality of the problem or its consequences. However, fictitious and abbreviated cases are frequently used in business and industry. They are often based on "stories" collected from trainers or the target group to be trained, the experience of course designers, and documents already available in the corporation. These cases often begin by identifying the problem since time may be too short for lengthy explorations and needs to be spent on skills practice. Trainers often use these cases for performance evaluation of principles taught in the course. Cases are shortened because training usually takes place within three to five days rather than three to five months. Sample cases of this nature used for human relations training, for example, can be found in Pfeiffer and Jones (1973-79).

Cases can follow the more classic format with respect to length and style, but still be fictitious. For example, a colleague (Srinivasan, 1988) develops composite "case stories" under the direction of the Sterling Institute. His cases are approximately twelve to twenty pages in length, are written in prose style but backed by technical information, and are typically divided into three parts. Based on a composite of research drawn from several different problem situations, these cases are written as fiction to disguise the sources and serve learning needs. Each case ends with several questions for group (and individual) consideration, which can be supplemented by questions or activities designed by the case leader.

In the first part of the case story, the writer describes the dilemma, introduces the characters, and creates tension due to conflict between the goal and various forces behind the dilemma. In groups, learners then describe the dilemma, identify options, and propose next steps. In the second part, the main character's analysis of the situation is presented along with his or her decision and actions. Learners then compare their analysis with that of the case, discuss risks and benefits, evaluate the character's action, and propose their own next steps. The third part describes the main character's subsequent actions, consequences, and implications for the future. This last discussion focuses on an overall evaluation of the case, things learners would have done differently, the relationship of the case to the experience of the learners and principles covered in the training, and action plans.

### Guided Group Process

The group process methods needed in case analysis and discussion may be as important as the content of the case itself in situations where these skills are critical to success in real life. Muñoz (1981), for example, highlights the importance of social skills in business and critiques the case method when used to educate Hispanic business students because it often favors students already adept at interaction and ignores the development of these crucial skills in others. The case writer might want to build group skills by writing guidelines for group interaction into the case study. Wales and Stager (1978), for example, developed a Guided Design Approach which structures the steps within each phase of the group's work to reward cooperation, develop collaborative skills, and help the group plan for each step of the process.

Pigors and Pigors (1987) have developed a guided case method process that incorporates several unique features: written materials are kept to a minimum, as in the "live" case; techniques are built into the process to aid group process; leadership responsibilities are shared; and successive subgroup meetings are progressive.

The Pigors Incident Process (PIP) begins with a one page description of an incident and the suggestion that learners adopt the role of the manager who must deal with this problem. Learners must read between the lines to understand the total situation. In step two, learners question the case leader for details, sort through and summarize the facts, and identify the problem. Learners then use diagrams to explore relationships among facets of the case. They then subdivide into small groups of like-minded members to make decisions and plan action. Groups then make, present, and test their opinions and the reasons that have led them to these conclusions. Finally, the entire case is reviewed for further, deeper learning. Subgroups reexamine the favorable features of the case, shortcomings or situational flaws, and needs and opportunities with respect to long-term organizational goals.

In the PIP, the case leader acts as a role model for leadership skills. A teammate acts as observer to provide feedback on the group process that otherwise would be missed. This approach is later imitated by subgroups. Gradually, students are introduced to their group process roles and assume increasing responsibility for leading the case discussion.


## CONCLUSION

This chapter shows that, while the core of the case method is a "slice of life," there are as many different interpretations of the method as there are areas of practice that use it. Even more diversity can be achieved if cases are explored that, in fact, summarize an incident in the life of the participants instead of drawing on materials predesigned by outside experts.

One example of this approach is that used in action science, where participants write dialogues about complex, difficult, recurring situations in which problems are not resolved to the satisfaction of the participant (Argyris & Schön, 1974). A case leader and colleagues in the group help the learner identify paradoxes and dilemmas that impede effectiveness. Role playing helps develop new responses to break old habits that prevent success. Some experiential learning programs go even further by asking learners to undertake real-life projects, individually or in pairs or small teams, which then become the subject of case analysis. The theory is that the closer the learners are to real-life conditions, the more likely it is that they will develop abilities actually needed outside the classroom.

The adult education literature does not emphasize the case

method although it is included in inventories of methods, perhaps because the field is highly interested in the learning process whereas those using the case method are more interested in the development of professional knowledge and skills. Since group process is instrumental to these goals, the field of adult education might contribute to strengthening this method by its process orientation.

## REFERENCES

Adkins, W. R., Cullinane, M. C., Davis, D. D., Lovett, A. B., & Manuele, C. A. (1985). *Adkins life skills program* (2nd ed.). New York: Institute for Life Coping Skills, Inc.

Argyris, C., & Schön, D. (1974). *Theory in practice: Increasing professional effectiveness.* San Francisco: Jossey-Bass.

AT&T. (1987). Case studies. In AT&T, *The trainer's library: Techniques of instructional development* (pp. 227-336). Reading: Addison-Wesley.

Barton, B. F., & Barton, M. S. (1981). The case method: Bridging the gap between engineering student and professional. In D. W. Stevenson (Ed.), *Courses, components, and exercises in technical communication* (pp. 22-33). (Report No. ISBN-0-8141-0877-6). Urbana, IL: National Council of Teachers of English. (ERIC Document Reproduction Service No. ED 200 996).

Caulley, D. N., & Dowdy, I. (1981). *Legal education as a model for the education of evaluators* (Report No. NWREL-Rep-51). Portland, OR: Northwest Regional Educational Lab. (ERIC Document Reproduction Series No. ED 206 680).

Evans, R. A. and Others. (1980). *Case studies in higher education ministries.* Lafayette: National Institute for Campus Ministries. (ERIC Document No. ED 207 387).

Muñoz, R. J. (1981, November). *Special needs of Hispanic business students: Teaching methodologies to develop social skills.* Paper presented at the 3rd Annual Symposium on Hispanic Business and Economy, Chicago, IL. (ERIC Document No. ED 211 634).

Pfeiffer, J. W., & Jones, J. E. (Eds.). (1973-79). *A handbook of structured experiences for human relations training.* La Jolla: University Associates.

Pigors, P., & Pigors, F. (1987). Case method. In R. L. Craig (Ed.),

*Training and development handbook* (pp. 414-429). New York: McGraw-Hill.

Reed, R. M., (1984). Group learning in law school. *Journal of Legal Education, 30* (4-5), 674-696.

Srinivasan, C. (1988). *The case story: A tool for interactive training.* Memo and personal correspondence.

Wales, C. E., & Stager, R. A. (1978). *The guided design approach.* Englewood Cliffs: Educational Technology Publications.

Williams, G. (1985, August). *The case method: An approach to teaching and learning in educational administration.* Paper presented at a symposium on The Professional Preparation and Development of Educational Administrators in Commonwealth Developing Areas, Barbados. (ERIC Document Reproduction Services No. EA 018 979 and ED 276 135).

# CHAPTER 12

## Nominal Group Technique
### LLOYD J. KORHONEN

### GROUP TECHNIQUE/GROUP PROCESS

The use of group technique has been one of the most widely utilized instructional techniques in adult education. Effectiveness, leadership, instruction, democratic principle, adaptation, productivity, and many other concepts have been tied to the principles of effective group action. These multiple uses of group technique make definition a problem. Beal, Bohlen, and Raudabaugh (1962) defined a group technique as " . . . a predesignated pattern for human instruction that offers a better potential for progress toward goals than does instructured random behavior" (p. 44). This definition presupposes that there are defined goals. These goals might be either individual or group derived, but in either case, they must satisfy both the needs of the individual in the group and the needs of the group as a whole. It is a logical instructional assumption that adult educators would utilize techniques that support the goals of all adult students in the most effective and successful manner.

A subset of group technique—group process—can be defined as the factors which are concerned with how persons learn together (the way) as contrasted to what they learn (the content). The choice of a group process method should be based upon a set of principles that guide that selection (Bergiven, Morris & Smith, 1963). The choice of group process method can be based upon a set of agreed principles.

247

1.  The appropriateness of the method in relationship to the knowledge, ability, and skill of the participants

2.  An understanding of the internal dynamics of groups in relation to the needs of the individual participants

3.  The realization of the setting and organizational factors that are important to the process

4.  The purpose to which the outcome is to be used

5.  The understanding that group process should be used as an instructional or problem-solving method, not as recreational activity

## THE DEVELOPMENT OF NOMINAL GROUP TECHNIQUE

The nominal group technique was developed by Andre Delbecq and Andrew Van de Ven in the 1960s as a problem-solving technique. Its strength is derived from the power of individuals each generating, exploring, and communicating ideas. Although, as will be described later in this chapter, there are a variety of adaptations, the technique as explained by Delbecq and Van de Ven uses a six stage process (Van de Ven & Delbecq, 1974) as depicted in Figure 12.1.

1.  *Formulating the nominal group technique question.* The question to be utilized by the nominal group must be carefully designed. The design process should take place prior to the introduction of the nominal group technique.

2.  *Generation of ideas.* In this step the question is presented to the group members. Enough time is provided for participants to write down ideas about the problem. This step is done individually by each group member; group interaction is not used during this step.

3.  *Round-robin listing.* Group members are asked serially to disclose their individual ideas. A careful recording of the ideas on a flip chart or overhead transparency is important. The ideas must be visible to all group participants.

4. *Discussion of ideas.* This step provides the opportunity for clarification. Agreeing or disagreeing with ideas generated must be accompanied by a logical arguement. This discussion is meant to clarify similarity or differences between the individual ideas.

5. *Voting on individual ideas.* A numerical system for voting is designed that is suited to individual group setting. This can be accomplished by giving the highest rated items the largest numerical value.

6. *Tabulating the voting.* The final result of the nominal group process is a numerical ranking of individual ideas based upon the totalled individual rankings of the members.

## ADAPTATIONS OF THE NOMINAL GROUP TECHNIQUE

Adaptations of this methodology have used as few as three steps. In the variety of applications explored in preparation for this chapter, three, four, five, six, and seven step models were reported to be utilized and identified as nominal group technique methodology. All the adaptations have three common elements.

1. Individuals in the group work independently of others during the initial formation of responses although in the presence of others.

2. All responses are written and the ideas generated are sequentially shared by the individual group members.

3. Some form of ranking, ordering, or valuing is designed to fit the particular situation.

### Three, Four and Five Step Nominal Group Technique Models

*Three Step Model.* The fewest numbers of steps decribed as a nominal group technique appeared in a report by Sharbrough (1982) on increasing student involvement using nominal grouping to generate formal report topics.

## Preparation for the Process

Leader Role
Carefully prepare the
question for discussion
by the group.

Learner/Participant Role
No role

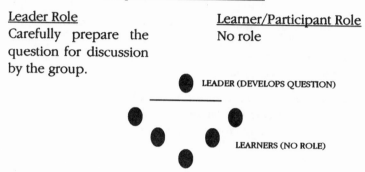

## Generation of Ideas

Leader Role
Present the question to
the participants. Clarify
question if necessary.

Learner/Participants Role
Individual members write
down ideas about the problem. No group interaction
is used.

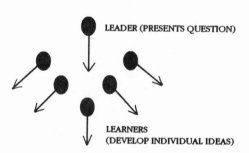

Figure 12.1 Six stage process.

### Round-Robin Listing

**Leader Role**
Carefully record all individual responses in a visible manner. A flip chart, chalkboard, or overhead projection can be used.

**Learner/Participant Role**
Individual members each disclose their ideas for listing. There is no discussion among participants at the time.

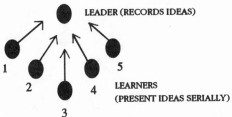

### Discussion of Ideas

**Leader Role**
No role

**Learner/Participant Role**
Members participate in an open discussion of ideas, agreeing or disagreeing for clarification of meaning. No resolution is made at this time.

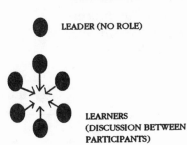

Figure 12.1 Six stage process. (continued)

## Voting on Individual Ideas

### Leader Role
Design and present the numerical voting procedure. Provide for a private way for individuals to vote. This could be by ballot. Remember the process must allow for rank ordering.

### Learner/Participant Role
Individually rank order the ideas generated by the individual group.

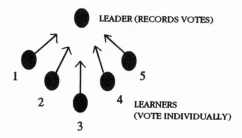

## Tabulating the Voting

### Leader Role
Total all responses with equal weight given to each participant's response. Present the final ranking based upon the process designed for the particular question explored.

### Learner/Participant Role
No role

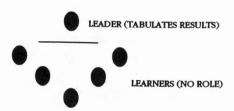

Figure 12.1 Six stage process. (continued)

1. Listing (of individual ideas)

2. Recording

3. Voting on ideas generated

His report suggests that student involvement in developing formal report topics can be stimulated by using a nominal group technique. Reducing the number of steps in the process does not shorten the time needed to efficiently utilize the technique.

*Four Step Model.* Ludden and Wood (1986) in their research report on "The Adult Literacy Needs of Indiana: Utilization of the Nominal Group Technique" use a four step model.

1. Participants are asked to respond to a question or statement by generating a written list of responses.

2. The group facilitator asks each member to contribute an idea from their list in a round-robin approach.

3. Group members are given the opportunity to discuss and clarify any of the ideas that have been selected.

4. Group members are asked to rank or rate each item.

*Five Step Model.* A five step nominal group technique was described by William Price (1985) as a needs assessment methodology in marketing education.

1. Introduction to meeting

2. Select generation of ideas in writing

3. Round-robin listing

4. Discussion for classification

5. Ranking of items

It should be clear to group leaders that the more experience people have with a method the more likely they are to abbreviate the steps. All the models presented in this section whether they use three, four, or five steps utilize all the components of the original six step technique. If the technique is new to the instructor, all six steps should be utilized for consistency.

## ADVANTAGES AND LIMITATIONS OF
## THE NOMINAL GROUP TECHNIQUE

The choice of a group technique demands a knowledge of the application and purpose for its use. As discussed earlier in this chapter, there are clearly defined uses for a nominal group process.

*Advantages*

1. It restricts the influence of the group leader.

2. It reduces, to a great degree, the influence of dominant group numbers.

3. It provides a format for closure. By voting and ordering there is a calculated decision-making mechanism.

4. It is efficient in its use of time. Where other group processes demand a great deal of time, there is efficiency in this technique.

*Disadvantages*

1. It demands that the question posed to the group be well-formed. If the question is ill-formed there is little chance to recover. This technique does not allow for the process of initial generation of the discussion topic.

2. It is not a concensus model. There exists the possibility that the decisions reached will not provide the basis for entire group commitment.

3. The group leader is limited to the role of facilitator.

4. It limits the emergence of group leadership by restricting the decision-making process.

It must be remembered that the nominal group technique is best utilized (1) where there is a well-formed question that is of interest to the participant, (2) where it is important that a decision be made, and (3) where time is a restraining factor.

## GROUP LEADER AND LEARNER/PARTICIPANT RESPONSIBILITIES

The roles and responsibilities of the group leader and the learner in this technique are well-defined. They are also, for the most part, serial. When the leader has a role the learners are not involved and when the learners are active the leader should remain uninvolved.

The roles utilized in the nominal group process are firm. Remember the role of the leader is to form the question and then facilitate the synthesis and tabulating. The role of the learner is to generate ideas, interact, and vote on the results of those processes.

## NOMINAL GROUP TECHNIQUE SATISFACTION MEASURES

The use of group learning process demands that there be an assessment of potential satisfaction with the method prior to its utilization. Group process methods, including the nominal group technique, are subject to a variety of criticism. This criticism is generally based upon the central concern that group methods lack efficiency. The nominal group technique minimizes the problem of efficiency by utilizing a ranking format that both forces and focuses on closure.

There has been very little research in regard to generalizable measures of satisfaction with the nominal group technique. Ian Gresham, in a 1986 study utilizing 206 adult conference participants, reported four research findings in regard to satisfaction with the nominal group techniques (Gresham, 1986).

1.  The level of satisfaction with the nominal group technique was high across all the groups studied.

2.  The professional background of the group members did not appear to influence the degree of satisfaction with the nominal group technique.

3.  The degree of understanding of the purposes and procedures
    of the nominative group technique *did* have a significant effect
    on attitude toward the effectiveness of the nominal group tech-
    nique.

4.  There was a consistent thread of dissatisfaction with the use of
    the nominative group technique among individuals within the
    groups studied.

Measures of group satisfaction are inclined to point out the
deficiencies that may exist within one method, without an analysis
of the relative merits in comparison to other choices. Most studies
of group process have indicated that adult learners have a high
degree of satisfaction with interactive learning models. Situational
characteristics, however, are a better indicator of which method
would be most valuable, resulting in a high degree of satisfaction
among the learners.


## NOMINAL GROUP TECHNIQUE FOR EVALUATION

The process of evaluation is important to a variety of activities
involving adult learners. Evaluation models can be utilized to measure process, product, individual, or group behavior outcomes. The
nominal group technique provides a format for accomplishing a
variety of evaluation tasks. As an evaluation process the nominal
group technique has the following advantages:

1.  *It restricts the influence of the group process leader.* Due to the
    nature of the group interaction, the nominal group technique
    diminishes the importance of expert intervention. The method
    demands that the leader's input into the process be limited.
    This does not prevent the leader from framing the initial ques-
    tion or introducing the process.

2.  *It encourages respondents to frame their own responses.* The
    individual input feature of a nominal group technique allows
    for either written or oral generation of ideas. Ideas formed in
    this way utilize the language, logic, and understanding of the
    individual without initial modification by others.

3. *It sustains individual autonomy during group pressure.* Once committed to a point of view, the participants are much less likely to be influenced by the individual beliefs of others in the group. It must be remembered that the consensus portion of the model is not derived from the changing of individual input, but rather by a ranking method that provides for the autonomy of the individual input of group members.

4. *It provides the respondents with knowledge of the full range of possible responses.* The power derived from this model is based upon the number of individual items presented (the breath of input) and the strength of response of the items (the number of times an item may be presented by different individual group members) (Lomax, 1984).

## GROUP TECHNIQUES THAT CAN BE USED IN COMBINATION WITH THE NOMINAL GROUP TECHNIQUE

A variety of group process techniques can be used in combination with the nominal group technique. Various input processes can provide different outcomes or can aid in validation. This is not meant to be an exhaustive list, but only illustrative of what combinations can be used to broaden or focus the participation process.

### Brainstorming

Developed by Alex F. Osborn, brainstorming is a technique for generating new ideas. It is especially useful in formulating the initial question. Because brainstorming does not provide a ranking or voting process, by itself it may not be a satisfying or synthesizing method. It does however contribute to the classification of the question by providing for structured input in a short amount of time (Srinivasan, 1977).

### Synetics

Synetics is a group process that is intended to join together different and apparent irrelevant elements. As defined by W. J. Gordon of the Cambridge synectics group it is intended to direct imagination to the solution of technical or theoretical problems.

Since it is an analogous system based upon feeling, it makes the unique contribution of providing an escape for emotional, basically nonrational processes. This can be especially important in question formation and discussion. As explained by the authors it has the potential to "make the strange familiar" and to "make the familiar strange." This allows for unique insight into seemingly distant or difficult problems (Srinivasan, 1977).

*Delphi Technique*

The Delphi technique as explained by Linstone and Turoff (1975) is an especially useful technique in combination with the nominal group technique. It has a variety of uses. For example, it has the potential to develop the question for this group process prior to the group getting together. The use as a validation tool can also be helpful. In addition, it can be utilized to continue a process after group members have left the group setting. When people leave a group setting there is occasionally an emotional letdown. The continuing nature of a Delphi technique allows for continuing contact. It does not, however, provide the same sense of closure as a nominal group technique. It also does not provide strong group identification.

Other methods can be successfully utilized in combination with a nominal group technique. The setting and the imagination of the adult learning leader are the only restrictions to potential uses.

## APPLICATION OF NOMINAL GROUP TECHNIQUE

As with many other methods of interaction used in the instruction of adults, the nominal group process has some strong advantages. It fills a particular need of adult learners who request group interaction, but it also demands closure. It is best used for clarification of group goals and actions. When used in this way it provides a predictable pattern of instruction. Since defined closure is an integral element of the model, it provides better individual satisfaction and group action. It is very important that the questions framed for the nominal group technique be clear and applicable to the problem being addressed. The model can be used for curriculum building, job task analysis, group cohesion activities, and for introduction of new change process. As with any other group technique it should be used with a defined purpose in mind, not as an activity. The nominal group technique is also a useful tool in combination with other processes. The leader should not be afraid to experiment once familiarity with the process has been achieved.

## REFERENCES

Beal, G. M., Bohlen, J. M., & Raudabaugh J. N. (1962). *Leadership and dynamic group action,* Ames: The Iowa State University Press.

Bergevin, P., Morris, D., & Smith, R. M. (1963). *Adult education procedure.* New York: Seabury.

Gresham, J. N. (1986). *Expressed satisfaction with the nominal group technique among change agents.* A Summary Report of Research. Departmental Information Bulletin, Texas A & M University, College Station, Texas.

Linstone, H. A., & Turoff, M. (1975). *The delphi method: Techniques and applications,* Reading: Addison-Wesley.

Lomax, P., & McLeman, P. (1984). The uses and abuses of nominal group technique in polytecnic course evaluation. *Studies in Higher Education,* 9 (2), 183-190.

Ludden, L., & Wood, G. S. Jr. (1986). Identifying the adult literacy, research needs of indiana: utilization of the nominal group technique. *Proceedings of the Midwest Research-to-Practice Conference in Adult, Community and Continuing Education.* Muncie: Ball State University.

Price, W. T. Jr. (1985). The nominal group techniques: A needs assessment methodology for vocational education. *Journal of Vocational and Technical Education,* 2 (1), 11-25.

Sharbrough, W. C. (1985). Increasing student involvement: using nominal grouping to generate formal report topics. *ABCA Bulletin,* 45 (2), 44-45.

Srinivasan, L. (1977). *Perspectives on nonformal adult learning.* New York: World Education.

Van de Van, A., & Delbecq, A. (1974). *Group decision-making effectiveness.* Kent: Kent State University Center for Business and Economic Research Press.

# CHAPTER 13

## Demonstration and Simulation
JERRY W. GILLEY

Marienau and Chickering (1982) noted that the principles of adult learning stress "the role of experience, freedom to make judgments, and responsibility for the consequences of choice and action" (p. 8). Long (1983) furthered stressed the value of experience as a part of an adult education process. In perspective, "adult learners have experienced some learning" and "all adults have some experiences that may be related to their learning" (p. 223). Thus, there is the implication that experience plays a strong role in the process of learning in adults.

Another implication for the use of experience as a method of instruction is described by Knowles (1978). An experiential exercise in a "learning-how-to-learn" activity is a primary facilitating tool in promoting the self-directed learning process. Further, one of Knowles's four assumptions of andragogy is that adult learning differs from pedagogical learning because experience plays a primary role.

Little (1981) suggested that the objectives in experiential learning are especially adaptable to adult learners. Experiential learning can develop in adults the ability to learn in a self-directed fashion. This is encouraged by the opportunity to see real consequences of one's actions, to feel the exhilaration of success as well as the frustration of failure. Second, adults can develop functional skills and attitudes necessary for effective adult life. These include skills of interpersonal interaction, group processing, intracultural communication, coping with ambiguity, and working on real-life problems with other adults. Experiential learning may be used to develop an ethical stance, to develop moral reasoning or judgment in complex situations.

According to Jernstedt (1980), demonstration and simulation are methods based upon experiential learning. They provide adult learners the opportunity to observe the exact way of performing a skill. Learners can observe actual practice and utilize their experiences in real life situations. This fosters and enhances learning by providing the time to develop mastery of a skill or the conditions by which personal adaptation and awareness can be developed. This is most easily accomplished through the utilization of past experiences. As a result, adult educators should seriously consider demonstrations and simulations when using experiential learning exercises.

## DEMONSTRATION

Much of learning is concerned with acquiring some combination of knowledge and skill. Lectures and discussions are incomplete as techniques for providing a combination of knowledge and skill. Demonstrations, however, show adults how something works and the procedures followed in using it. Demonstrations can supplement content and translate descriptive material into actual practice. Demonstration of the skills is also often required in order for the learner to fully comprehend as well as apply the new knowledge, competencies, skills, concepts, and/or truths.

As an example, a traditional apprenticeship consisted of telling the learners how, showing them how, letting the learners attempt the task, and then evaluating the performance. The demonstration portion of a formal learning program uses this same procedure, applied to a larger number of learners.

Demonstration can be defined as an accurate portrayal of a procedure, technique, or operation (Laird, 1986). It is a method which requires special skills and abilities in order to perform effectively. For example, a demonstration is a method of instruction in which the adult educator actually performs an operation. As a result, it requires adult educators who are highly skilled in the material or process to be demonstrated. Therefore, the utilization of this method should be limited to those who maintain a mastery of the material and/or process being studied.

Demonstrations serve two purposes in instruction. First, they may be used to provide a model of a skill. Second, they may be used to support an explanation of an idea, theory, belief, concept, or skill.

Laird (1986) reported that a demonstration is merely an illustrated lecture or presentation. By contrast, demonstrations may be used to show the use of rules or problem-solving skills. Quite simply, then, a demonstration may be any well-chosen example of something the learner should be able to do. An implicit criterion in the demonstration is the standard of performance that will be required of the learner. Thus, the preparation and skill-level of the adult educator performing the demonstration cannot be overemphasized.

There are five basic types of demonstrations, ranging from relatively simple to increasingly complex and sophisticated (Sredl & Rothwell, 1988).

1. Instructor. The instructor bears the full burden of showing and telling.

2. Participant Volunteer. A volunteer demonstrates a task, a process, or a behavior and then discusses it.

3. Full Participation. All learners are required to demonstrate and one or all to discuss the experience.

4. Job Instruction Training (JIT). This type calls for a demonstration sequence in which:

    a. The instructor introduces a task and demonstrates it.

    b. Participants explain the same task and demonstrate it.

    c. The instructor provides feedback on how well participants performed the task, then introduces another task and demonstrates it.

    d. These three steps are repeated through an entire chain of related behaviors or tasks.

5. Behavior Modeling. This type requires a sequence of demonstrations.

a. The adult educator introduces a topic and "models" effective and ineffective behavior.

b. The adult educator shows a videotape or film that simulates job conditions and "models" effective and ineffective behavior.

c. Learners discuss the behavior and then demonstrate it themselves.

d. The adult educator and/or learners critique the demonstrations.

These steps are repeated until mastery occurs.

## Appropriateness of Demonstrations

In terms of the learning process, a demonstration serves the purpose of arousing interest or motivation and directing attention to the skill, behavior, and/or knowledge to be learned. Demonstrations may also be used to support a verbal explanation of a principle or physical process. When used in this way, the demonstration may provide a visual image that contributes to encoding of information.

Demonstrations are also appropriate when the topic or skill lends itself to observation. Adult educators can develop learning situations which foster participation and involvement and allow the learners to observe their individual performance as well as development.

Demonstrations provide for an economical use of time, materials, and equipment. Although a one-on-one teaching situation would be desirable, it is often impossible to have a group consisting of a small number of participants. Also, the expense of some materials, equipment, and supplies calls for wise and economical use. Demonstrations provide a means to illustrate and clarify an approach, skill, and method to many adults at one time, without having all the adults attempt the procedure. In addition, demonstrations can be effectively used to show a procedure as it would happen over a long period of time. The process can be speeded up to show the entire procedure, as in the case of a motor skill.

This method is also appropriate when there is a need to show a process in action. For example, interviewing skills and techniques would be difficult if not impossible to develop without the opportunity to observe correct approaches and the opportunity to demonstrate and practice them. The learner can experience what it is really like to conduct an interview and see "how" and "why" certain skills and techniques are used.

In addition, demonstrations are appropriate when there is a need or value in providing step-by-step guidance in performing a task or using a skill. An example of this might include a complex process such as designing a learning program or a simple process such as teaching someone how to use an overhead projector. In both situations, exact step-by-step procedures must be followed in order to accomplish the desired goal.

Finally, demonstrations prepare adult learners for practice sessions and drill exercises. Both require adult learners to practice for skill improvement. Learners watch the adult educator perform the specific skill and then practice the skill themselves.

## Advantages of Demonstrations

Demonstrations are an excellent way to illustrate points which enable the learner to comprehend complex and difficult material in a short period of time. In formal training environments, time is important; this is especially true in corporate settings. When properly prepared, several minutes of demonstration may accomplish more than hours of lecture.

Another advantage is that demonstrations help reduce the gap between theory and practice. Adult educator can provide practical examples which reflect actual practice. By providing a demonstration, complex models and processes become real.

The first three types of demonstrations discussed earlier are relatively easy to develop and usually inexpensive to design and produce. They do, however, require the adult educator to maintain a mastery level of knowledge and skill in order to develop demonstrations which reflect practical and real life situations. They also require an understanding of verbal communications and a high degree of psychomoter skill.

Demonstrations enable more than one of the senses to be activated which enhances learning. In many cases, a demonstration will involve visual, aural, haptic, and kinenistic learning styles. By providing adult learners the opportunity to focus upon a preferred learning style, the learning situation becomes more personalized and individual. In addition, a combination of various learning styles fosters comprehension and improves recall and transferability (Galbraith, 1987).

Another advantage of demonstrations is that they provide variety to learning situations. They allow both learners and educators to focus attention upon something different which enables both to relax and enjoy the learning exchange.

Demonstrations allow the learners to see the exact manner in which a skill or behavior is to be performed. Adult educators should, therefore, provide ample practice time in order for the learners to develop a mastery level of performance. This is an advantage because adult educators must provide the necessary time required to develop such a skill level, an emphasis which should improve recall as well as application.

Finally, demonstrations are similar to the "for example" parts of a book. They can enable learners to understand that people have different perspectives of ideas, concepts, and truths which are based upon individual experiences. Demonstrations also provide a needed break from complex material which is difficult to comprehend.

### Disadvantages of Demonstrations

Other than providing the learners an overview of a task, skill, or process, some critics believe demonstrations offer few positive benefits. For example, many learners are negatively motivated after a demonstration because they are unable to perform the skill as well as the facilitator. They are thinking, "Wow, there is no way I can ever do it that well." This of course establishes barriers for the adult educator to overcome and present psychological resistance to practicing the skill or behavior.

Adult educators who do not possess a mastery level of skill or cannot demonstrate the correct procedure and/or behavior should not attempt this method. First, it can confuse the learners but more importantly it can discourage them. They may feel overwhelmed if the "teacher" cannot demonstrate the correct procedure, skill, or behavior. Not only might they resist attempts at mastering the skill, but they may also lose respect for an inept instructor.

Another disadvantage is that it is often difficult to isolate tasks, skills, procedures, and behaviors in a step-by-step manner. Some skills are difficult to break down into components and thus are not good candidates for this methodology. Also, some skills and behaviors are best understood from a holistic perspective.

While demonstrations may accomplish outstanding results which otherwise might take several hours of lecture time, they can be time consuming because they require time for practice and review. In many learning environments, little time is available for such activities if the entire course outline is to be covered. This is a realistic concern in corporate and organizational learning environments. In many situations, however, the learners can practice the tasks, skills, and behaviors on their own, which allows for more content to be covered during formal class sessions. Under these circumstances, the responsibility for mastery is solely upon the learners while the adult educators are viewed as content experts responsible for providing the maximum amount of material in the time available.

Because the demonstration method is best with small groups, there is a cost-benefit factor to consider. In some learning situations, it may well be prohibitive on a cost/time basis. However, before discarding it, adult educators will want to be certain that its substitute will fulfill the identified learning objective satisfactorily in terms of costs and results.

Finally, it is difficult for even the most skilled and talented adult educator to provide timely, detailed feedback on performance to each individual in a group situation. This is further compounded when there is only one instructor for several learners. This method also requires that adult educators possess the communication skills necessary for adequate feedback.

## Responsibilities of the Demonstrator

Careful planning and preparation are essential to the performance of an effective demonstration. This includes a clear understanding of the learning objectives which the demonstration will address, since presentation may vary according to the learning objective.

Certain qualities and skills are essential for the demonstrator. Demonstrators should first determine which of these qualities they possess and at what level of expertise. It is their responsibility then to design an individual development plan for those qualities that they either do not possess or have at a low level of expertise. Adult educators are essentially responsible for their own self-development prior to using the demonstration method.

The demonstration should be designed so that it can be broken down into small, manageable steps. To reproduce the performance, learners need to be able to recognize the distinct phases or steps of the activity being demonstrated and identify the skills associated with each. It is the demonstrator's responsibility to rehearse the demonstration until each step is correct in every detail. According to Laird (1976), the following are responsibilities of the demonstrator:

- Analyze the process, breaking it into small sequential steps.

- Make sure everyone can see each step of the presentation.

- Have all material in place.

- Check the operation of all equipment before the demonstration.

- Position or scale the models so all learners can see all parts all the time.

As a demonstration proceeds, the demonstrator explains the next steps. It may be helpful to provide information sheets outlining the steps for the learners to follow or provide detailed illustrations to focus their attention on important aspects of the demonstration. This helps ensure that all the steps are understood and followed. It also helps learners to check their progress as they practice the task, skill, or behavior.

The instructor may intersperse the demonstration with questions to help learners focus their attention as well as deepen their understanding of the importance of various steps. Questions will help the learners relax and can also provide opportunities for critical self-reflection. To summarize, good demonstrators:

- Rehearse the presentation prior to delivery to make certain that information is correct and clear.

- Explain the goals of the demonstration at the beginning, in a two-way discussion with the learner.

- Present the operation one step at a time and explain each step as the demonstration proceeds.

- Allow the earliest possible tryout of the demonstrated skill, procedure, or behavior.

- Reinforce everything learners do correctly in their practice session. (Laird, 1986, p. 186)

## *Responsibilities of the Adult Learner*

It is important that each of the steps of the demonstration be performed correctly in order to ensure that the learners are duplicating the performances correctly. The learners must practice the special techniques associated with demonstrating skills, even if they are already expert performers. Failure to practice may result in a marginal performance with an ensuing loss of confidence and credibility as well as respect on the part of the learner.

Learners must concentrate on each skill, task, or technique. It is important that the learners perform the skill, task, or technique exactly as demonstrated prior to adjusting for personal preferences and talents. It is also the learners' responsibility to communicate to the demonstrator any difficulty or problem related to the demonstration. Failure to communicate may result in the improper development of the desired skill. This can cause a loss of time and money as well as of self-confidence.

## *Communication Patterns*

Just as lectures require learners to listen, demonstrations require learners to watch. Therefore, the learners' role is essentially a passive one. The lines of communications are one way from the demonstrator to the learners during the early stages of a demonstration. It is often suggested that lectures be followed by questioning to give the learners an opportunity to respond actively to the content of instruction. In the same way, demonstrations should be followed by practice sessions. Practice sessions give learners an opportunity for performance and feedback. This fosters two-way communications and incorporates the interactive learning style.

Demonstrations can integrate verbal, visual, and interactive stimulus into one process. The verbal stimulus comes first, then the visual, and finally the interactive.

Each of the components of a demonstration requires either one-way or two-way communication between the demonstrator and the learners. A two-way interactive communication pattern is best because it enables the learners to ask specific questions regarding their area of concern. This fosters a collaborative learning environment.

## Room and Facilities Layout

Room and facilities arrangements for a demonstration are best determined on a case by case basis. One thing is essential: the learner must always be able to see all steps of the demonstration and be close enough to observe even the smallest details and components. Figure 13.1 shows several examples of room layouts for a demonstration and the directional lines of communication between the demonstrator and learners.

In each example, two-way communications are employed. The demonstrator gives the necessary information to the learners and the learners ask questions or make comments freely. This enhances the demonstration and helps the learners remain active.

## Evaluation of Demonstrations

It is important to conduct an evaluation to determine if the demonstration method was used effectively. This can be accomplished by including as criteria the qualities of a good demonstrator discussed earlier. In addition, adult educators should determine if they have provided adequate time for learners to practice the task, skill, or behavior as well as provided encouraging and timely feedback to each individual.

A good demonstration should be:

1. Clearly presented

2. Visible to all participants

3. Presented in small manageable parts

4. Capable of being duplicated

5. Relevant to the situation, topic, and/or subject being discussed

These are good criteria upon which to evaluate the effectiveness of a demonstration.

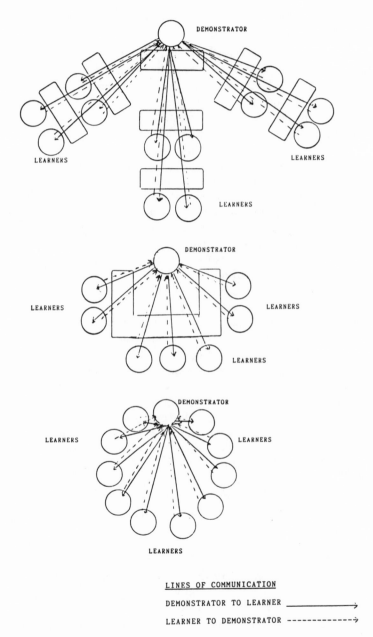

Figure 13.1 Demonstration room layout and lines of communication.

## SIMULATION

Many adult learners participate in learning activities in order to address problems or to obtain the needed skills, competencies, and/or knowledge required to solve problems. As a result, they demand relevant and accurate learning situations. They are less tolerant of theoretical and nonpractical exercises which cannot be applied. Kolb (1984) noted that there is a renewed interest in and attention to instructional methods which translate abstract ideas of academia into the concrete realities of peoples' lives. In addition, adult learners approach learning situations with a great deal to lose. In other words, their self-esteem is placed at risk during each learning activity. This may prevent an open and honest exchange as well as a sharing of experiences and awareness. Therefore, a search must be undertaken for an alternative method which is practical and reflects realism as well as one which preserves the dignity of the learner. One such method is simulation.

Simulation is a technique which enables adult learners to obtain skills, competencies, knowledge, or behaviors by becoming involved in situations that are similar to those in real life. The most common simulation techniques used in adult education are role playing, case study, critical incident, and in-basket activities. It is a dramatic representation of reality. In addition, simulation is a method which attempts to address problems under real life conditions and to discuss them completely afterward. This requires adult educators to possess real life practical experience prior to the use of this method. If adult educators fail to maintain such experience, they will be unable to actually construct the real life situation needed to maximize learning. Adult educators must also possess the facilitation skills required to process the learning results after learners have participated. The lack of practical experience and adequate facilitation skills often limits the effectiveness of this method.

### Appropriateness of Simulations

One of the values of simulation is its potency and its ability to get learners involved cognitively as well as emotionally. This enables adults to share valuable insights which can deepen and enhance learning. A simulation might also include policies and procedures already understood. Since learners are more comfortable with situations which resemble their everyday lives than with unfamiliar situations, this method provides a "safe" but relevant environment to test ideas, beliefs, and assumptions against personal experience.

A successful simulation is based on identifying an appropriate learning objective and then designing a learning activity which accomplishes that objective. Thiagarajan (1980) suggested that simulations were appropriate for five learning objectives:

1. To develop highly complex cognitive skills such as decision making, evaluating, and synthesizing

2. To impact positively on the learner's values, beliefs, or attitudes

3. To induce empathy

4. To sharpen human relations skills such as interpersonal communication skills

5. To unlearn negative attitudes or behaviors (p. 38)

In order to accomplish a learning objective, the facilitator should plan activities that include:

1. Appropriate background information

2. Establishment of the correct physical and/or psychological environment

3. Correct characterization of the participant which includes appropriate casting of roles and dialog

4. Identification of a relevant and realistic problem or situation

5. Incorporation of the decision-making process

6. Utilization of the feedback process as a learning tool

7. Adequate time for participants to evaluate the experience (Thiagarajan, 1980)

Chiarelott (1979)suggested that four principles should be considered in the development of simulation activities. First, the selection should be based upon the continuity and interaction of the learners' past, present, and future experiences. Second, the sequencing of activities should be based upon an "experience continuum" in which the learners use knowledge gained from one experience to understand the meaning of the new experience. Third, action and reflection should be used in reviewing learning experiences. Fourth, the subject matter should be discovered by the learner through a process of inquiry, exploring the significance of each experience.

*Advantages of Simulations*

According to Waddel (1982), several advantages of a simulation can be identified. First, it provides an opportunity to apply learning to new and rewarding situations which allows for new discoveries. Second, the learners are active participants in the learning process rather than passive recipients of information. In addition, the learners can gain from simulations without paying the consequences for a wrong decision which would occur in a daily routine.

Another advantage is that discussions are realistic and focused upon observed behaviors. Feedback is immediate, which provides for a built-in reward system that encourages involvement. Learners are also more receptive to new ideas and attitude changes when they are exposed to them in real life situations as provided through simulations. Simulation is a cost effective method because it enables a number of learners to participate in a learning experience rather that only a few.

Learners may adopt a more worldly view through sharing and making generalizations and applications of the new information. Finally, simulations are more relevant that other methods because they represent real life situations and circumstances.

*Disadvantages of Simulations*

Several disadvantages result from the use of simulations. First, a simulation demonstrates how people may behave rather than how they will behave. This should be addressed by the facilitator before a simulation begins. In addition, an effort to depict appropriate behavior that is directly related to real life situations, whether it be personal or professional, should be made.

In some situations, the results of a single simulation are used as the sole basis for generalization of behaviors or actions. This misapplication of the method leads to mistrust and often inappropriate behaviors or actions. Confusion may also be created by introducing overly complex situations and circumstances to the learners. This can cause a lose in confidence and self-esteem because of the failure to perform successfully. As a result, negative learning can occur and transferability to the real situation may become more difficult.

The facilitator must thoroughly prepare the learners for the simulated experience in order for them to adequately develop the knowledge, skills, and attitudes desired. The facilitator must be able to shift from role to role—from a disseminator of information to a facilitator of learning. Many adult educators have not developed the skills necessary to make this transition.

Finally, simulations can be very expensive to design and develop as well as very time-consuming to conduct. For example, "high tech" simulations used in continuing education or training and development settings may cost thousands of dollars to design and develop. As a result, the cost of such simulations becomes a major disadvantage to its use.

Each of these disadvantages should be carefully considered prior to the design, development, and utilization of simulations.

## Responsibilities of the Facilitator

It is the responsibility of the adult educator to make certain that the simulation meets the learning objectives desired. The following checklist will be useful:

1. Are the participants completely prepared and ready to engage in a simulation?

2. Are the instructions short, clear, and understandable?

3. Is the purpose of the exercise understood by each of the participants?

4. Are the rewards for participating in the exercise apparent?

5. Is the simulation relevant to all participants?

6. Is the exercise a close representation of real or potential situations?

7. Does the simulation meet an immediate need or solve a specific problem?

8. Does the simulation involve problem-solving and decision-making processes appropriate to the level of the learners?

9. Does the exercise provide for adequate interaction and feedback?

10. Is the simulation sufficiently disguised to avoid possible embarrassment for participants as well as observers?

The adult educator should also make certain that the learning environment represents an actual real-life situation. In addition, the facilitator sees that all participants meet their personal responsibilities and assignments before, during, and after the simulation.

Before the exercise begins, the adult educator must provide clear and understandable instructions and delegate the principal components of the exercise to the learners. This includes the roles, the dialogue, and the problems which must be addressed or behaviors which must be analyzed. In addition, the adult educator should determine the context of the situation, identify the objectives of the simulation, provide the resources needed to conduct the exercise, and structure the sequence of interaction that must occur. Each of these must either be communicated to or provided for the learner prior to the beginning of the exercise.

During the exercise the adult educator must provide essential feedback at critical points as well as encouragement and any needed clarification or explanations. The adult educator may provide feedback on an individual basis or may request the entire group of participants to share and discuss their perceptions of the activity.

It may be appropriate to follow a five step process designed by Goldstein and Pfeiffer (1983) when using a simulation. These five steps also apply to an experiential exercise. They include: 1) the experience (simulation), 2) sharing, 3) processing, 4) generalizations, and 5) application.

*The Experience.* The first step is doing the exercise. During this phase, small groups of four or five participants are often appropriate. This encourages increased involvement and sharing. Normally, exercises are undertaken without long introductions which could bias the participants. It is important that participants each identify their own purpose of the exercise rather that be told in advance its meaning or goal. This will help in increasing the variety of conclusions reached.

*Sharing.* The second stage involves participants sharing their experiences after the exercise is concluded. Members are encouraged to share both their observations of what when on as well as how they felt about the activities or events. Often, the feelings are more important to reveal than comments about objective events. The adult educator should not comment on either the process or the meaning of the exercise during the sharing phase, but rather take a facilitation role and encourage increased sharing.

*Processing.* The third stage in this experiential learning process involves processing the information gathered during the sharing stage. Unlike sharing, which is done in small groups, this is generally accomplished with all the participants. The goal at this point is to identify commonly shared experiences or perceptions and to identify common themes among the group members.

*Generalizations.* Next the adult educator guides the group into drawing broad implications from the experience and resulting discussion. This is the most important phase of the entire process, and if left out, the learning will appear to be superficial to the participants. The idea during this phase is essentially to answer the question, "What is the point?" Participants are led to understand what has happened in the exercise and how it applies to their specific work situations or personal lives.

*Application.* The final stage of the process addresses the question, "Now what?" The adult educator's role at this point is to help the participants think of ways to apply the new generalizations to future situations. Many adult educators like to have participants return to their initial exercise groups to develop these ideas for application. A participant from each group may be appointed to report on the results.

A variety of questions will help facilitate applications. For example, the adult educator may ask the participants how they will use the new information in specific situations or ask them to set job related goals. In addition, learners may role play new behaviors based upon the new information, or they may discuss new ways of handling a situation in the context of a case study. Overall, the application phase is designed to give participants a chance to apply the new concepts, feelings, and ideas.

## Responsibilities of the Learners in Simulations

As a result of a simulation, the learners should have an increased awareness of themselves and be able to apply new knowledge, skills, or attitudes to real life situations. It is, therefore, the learners' responsibility to participate in all activities as well as to provide personal insights. They should also encourage their fellow learners to participate openly and enthusiastically. They should develop an atmosphere of sharing and support for each other and provide essential feedback to one another. When a fellow learner fails to accomplish the objectives of the simulation or reaches the "incorrect" answer, it is important to be noncritical. Finally, the learners should give the facilitator open and honest feedback regarding the realism, rigor, and complexity of the simulation. From this critique future simulations can be made more realistic, challenging, and stimulating.

### Room and Facilities Layout

The learning environment is an important component of simulations. It is impossible to establish exact criteria and conditions that must be followed since each simulation is different and requires very different resources and materials. The learning environment must be realistic and ideally will model the type of situation in which the learner is expected to perform during real life interactions. It should also be free of distractions and be relatively private because many learners find it difficult to perform in unprotected and embarrassing environments.

### Communication Patterns

Before the simulation, the adult educator communicates the purpose and objectives of the simulation to learners. This normally is done through a one-way line of communication from the facilitator to the learners. During the simulation, several communication patterns may develop. Most will be two-way communications between the facilitator and learners, and between the learners and/or groups of learners. After the simulation, a two-way communication pattern continues with the facilitator providing feedback to learners and learners asking questions or describing their understanding of the concepts, ideas, procedures, experiences, skills, or abilities developed as a result of the simulation.

### Evaluation of Simulations

The evaluation of a simulation should meet the following criteria: 1) active involvement, 2) realism, 3) clarity, 4) feasibility, 5) repeatability, and 6) reliability (Dean & Gilley, 1986).

Active involvement helps all the participants become motivated. They identify with the situation and this fosters learning. Each participant should be able to describe the dynamics of the exercise as well as comment on its effectiveness.

A simulation must possess sufficient realism to convey the essential truths, ideas, skills, competencies, behaviors, and/or knowledge desired. This can be assessed by how closely it resembles real life situations.

Clarity refers to the decision-making process in terms of the choices made. In other words, are the decisions made because of the clear consequences and causes or are they selected by chance through the "best guess" approach.

Feasibility measures the cost in terms of materials, space, and time against the achieved outcomes. This cost/benefit approach is essential in formal learning environments such as corporate training programs where learning programs are required to improve overall organizational efficiency. In less formal learning environments where time is a very real constraint, it is important to select instructional methods which can produce the best results within the time available.

Repeatability and reliability are important because it is essential that a simulation be repeated with the same degree of reliability relative to its outcomes. This will improve the accuracy of the learning as well as the credibility of the simulation. This also enhances the consistency of learning for one group to another.

After the simulation is completed, the adult educator provides a debriefing in order to allow maximum learning to occur. Questions to foster enhanced learning include:

1. What kinds of decisions were made?

2. What influenced the group during the simulation and did it affect the outcomes of the experience?

3. What constraints were felt by the participants?

4. What did the participants learn from the exercise?

5. What types of interaction occurred between the participants?

6. Did the simulation accomplish the stated purposes?

7. What changes should be incorporated into future simulations?

8. How closely did the simulation approximate a real situation?

9. What kinds of uncertainty were experienced by the participants?

10. What personal reactions did the participants have to each other during the context of the simulation? situation?

## CONCLUSION

Demonstrations and simulations both foster experiential exercises and learning. Participants can develop new insights and awareness as well as utilize those past and present experiences which will impact future learning. Both methods require active learner involvement. They also require adult educators to develop and maintain facilitation skills as well as advanced interpersonal skills. Demonstrations and simulations are very effective alternatives for the learning situation. They should only be used when deemed appropriate, however, since both require adequate time and resources to develop and produce. These two methods provide a unique type of "learner ownership."

## REFERENCES

Chiarelott, L. (1979). *Basic principles for designing experiential-based curricula.* Paper presented to the annual meeting of the American Educational Research Association. San Francisco.

Dean, R. L., & Gilley, J. W. (1986). A production model for experiential learning. *Performance and Instruction Journal, 25*(3), 26-29.

Galbraith, M. W. (1987). Assessing perceptual learning styles. In C. Klevins (Ed.), *Materials and methods in adult and continuing education* (pp. 263-269). Los Angeles: Klevens.

Goodstein, L. D., & Pfeiffer, J. W. (1983). *The 1983 annual for facilitators, trainers, and consultants.* San Diego: University Associates.

Jernstedt, G. C. (1980). Experiential components in academic courses. *Journal of Experiential Education, 3*(2), 54-59.

Laird, D. (1986). *Approaches to training and development* (2nd ed.). Reading: Addison-Wesley.

Kolb, D. A. (1984). *Experiential learning*. Englewood Cliffs: Prentice-Hall.

Knowles, M. (1978). *The adult learner: A negelected species* (2nd ed.) Houston: Gulf Press.

Little, T. C. (1981). *History and rationale for experiential learning*. Unpublished manuscript.

Long, H. B. (1983). *Adult learning: Research and practice*. New York: Cambridge.

Marienau, C., & Chickering, A. W. (1982). Adult development and learning. In B. Menson (Ed.), *Building on experiences in adult development* (pp. 62-84). New Directions for Experiential Learning, no. 16. San Francisco: Jossey-Bass.

Sredl, H. J., & Rothwell, W. J. (1988) *The ASTD reference guide to professional training roles and competencies*. New York: Random House Professional Business Publications.

Thigarajan, S (1980). *Experiential learning package*. Englewood Cliffs: Educational Technology Publications.

Waddell, G. (1982). Simulations: Balancing the pros and cons, *Training and Development Journal, 36*(1), 80-83.

# CHAPTER 14

## Forum, Panel, and Symposium
### BURTON R. SISCO

Perhaps no method is more central to the adult education tradition in the United States than the forum and its derivations the panel and the symposium. So integral is the forum in U.S. history that it could be added to mom, apple pie, and hot dogs as uniquely American. Such initiatives as the lyceum, the New England town meeting, and the Des Moines public forums are all examples of where the forum has been championed as a tool for citizens to practice and participate in democracy. Though we live in more hurried times today, the forum, panel, and symposium are still utilized in much the same way they were in times past. In fact, they are popular adult education methods at many civic, professional, and educational events throughout the United States and abroad. The purpose of this chapter is to consider why the forum, panel, and symposium are revered by educators of adults, to define and illuminate the distinguishing characteristics of each method, to consider some of the uses to which the forum, panel, and symposium are often put, and to assess the relative merits of each approach.

## SIGNIFICANCE OF THE FORUM, PANEL, AND SYMPOSIUM

Advocates of the forum and its closely related brethren, the panel and the symposium, typically cite the social and educational advantages of these methods, particularly in the context of an enlightened citizenry. For example, John Studebaker saw the public forum as essential to the preservation of democracy. In *The American Way*, Studebaker (1935) argued that the forum was a means "whereby we can redevelop the ability ably to discharge our responsibilities as citizens of a democracy, retaining our birthright of unhampered freedom to learn while molding the new economic order" (p.17). Similarly, Bryson (1935) saw the forum as "one of the best methods for dealing with controversial questions in politics, economics, or public affairs" (p. 90). Hewitt and Mather (1937) were so taken by the forum that they declared it to be " . . . the principal medium in the United States for obtaining active audience participation" (p. 150). Writing more recently, Poznar (1982) argued that open and continuing forums are needed on university and college campuses to promote serious inquiry and widespread debate on vital issues.

If we stood still for a moment and looked about us, we would see many illustrative examples of the forum, panel, and symposium at work today. The local newspaper carries an account of a public forum sponsored by the League of Women Voters on "Toxic Waste Management." On the radio, a news story is read about a university panel discussion on group activism and lobbying. In the mailbox rests an advertisement for an upcoming professional conference that includes among many activities, a symposium dealing with "Ethical Issues in Professional Practice." And the list goes on.

Clearly, the forum, panel, and symposium are evident in our daily lives; they are all about us. There is a historic as well as a contemporary tradition upon which each method rests. While there are many similarities in how the forum, panel, and symposium are organized, there are distinct differences in purpose, tone, and level of audience participation. In the next two sections, we will look at how each method is defined and then discuss how each is different.


DEFINITIONS OF FORUM, PANEL, AND SYMPOSIUM

There are nearly as many definitions of the forum, panel, and symposium as there are writers who have examined each method. Some writers tend to note few differences among the methods and thus group them together, whereas other writers suggest distinct differences. For purposes of this chapter, each method is seen as distinct and some precision will be offered when using each term.

A *forum* is best defined as an open discussion carried on by one or more resource persons and an entire group. It is used when large groups of twenty-five persons or more meet for the purpose of diffusion of knowledge, information, or opinion. The forum tends to be semiformal in nature and is directed by a moderator. The moderator is responsible for guiding discussion during which the audience is encouraged to raise and discuss issues, make comments, offer information, or ask questions of the resource person(s) and each other. There are many variations on the forum, such as the panel forum or symposium forum, which is why the methods are sometimes seen as identical.

A *panel* is defined as a small group of three to six persons, who sit around a table in the presence of an audience and have a purposeful conversation on a topic in which they have specialized knowledge. The panel is typically informal in nature, usually lasts under an hour, is guided by a moderator who starts the session and sustains discussion, and has no audience participation other than watching and listening. Because of the latter characteristic, the panel is usually followed by a forum which does allow verbal participation by the audience.

A *symposium* is defined as a series of presentations given by two to five persons of notable authority and competence on different aspects of the same theme or closely related themes. The symposium tends to be formal in nature because of the authoritative presentations. However, once the presentations are given, questions from the audience are encouraged and accepted. Rarely, do the invited speakers converse with one another and almost never does one of them interrupt another during the formal presentation of ideas. A program chair typically organizes the symposium and is in charge of the actual proceedings. Usually, speakers are limited to a maximum of twenty minutes each so that time for audience questions and comments can be included. Thus, most symposiums run between sixty to ninety minutes in length.

## DIFFERENCES BETWEEN FORUM, PANEL, AND SYMPOSIUM

As noted earlier, the forum, panel, and symposium are often used interchangeably. This is understandable since all three methods share the commonality of organized sessions for medium to large groups and are guided by a moderator or chairperson. However, there are notable differences in the purpose, tone, and level of audience participation in each method. This has caused confusion as to whether there are any differences between the methods.

One way of clearing up such confusion is to place each method on a continuum of formality and level of audience participation. At one end would be the panel and at the other end would be the symposium. Somewhere near the middle would be the forum.

The panel is the most informal in nature and is designed for purposeful conversation among three to six persons on an assigned topic or theme. The panel works best when a number of views or opinions on the assigned topic are presented and where there is no final solution in sight. The thinking of the panel members may evolve as discussion on the topic occurs. Although the tone of the panel is informal, little audience participation is permitted since the focus is on the conversation of panel members and not the audience.

At the other end of the continuum lies the symposium. It is clearly the most formal in design and nature. A symposium is like a speech in that the audience listens to prepared presentations from two to five persons from a platform. A chairperson normally opens the meeting and then introduces each speaker. The chief difference between the symposium and the panel is that the speakers do not converse with one another; they make presentations to the audience. Another difference is that when the presentations are completed, audience participation is encouraged in the form of questions and comments.

Near the middle of the continuum lies the forum. It is semiformal in nature because one or more resource persons are involved and a moderator leads the meeting. The forum is intended to promote audience participation. The function of the resource person(s) is to supply technical information, answer questions, or offer comments to further discussion. The chief difference between the forum and the panel and symposium, aside from the tone of the meeting, is the level and extent of audience participation; the panel has little or no audience participation, the symposium moderate, and the forum great. In fact, the ultimate success of a forum is the extent to which the audience shares ideas, raises and discusses issues, and asks critical questions of each other and the resource person(s).

As we can see from the foregoing discussion and Figure 14.1, the forum, panel, and symposium are indeed distinct methods for adult education practice. It is important to understand the differences and similarities when deciding what method is most appropriate to use and under what circumstances. The next section will look at each method in some detail.

| Method | Purpose | Tone | Level of Audience Participation |
|---|---|---|---|
| Forum | Meeting of 25 or more persons gathered for open discussion among members of the entire group and one or more resource persons. | Semi-formal | Great |
| Panel | Meeting of 3 to 6 persons seated around a table in the presence of an audience with aim of having a purposeful conversation on a given topic or theme. | Informal | Limited |
| Symposium | Series of formal presentations given by 2 to 5 persons of notable authority on different aspects of the same theme or closely related themes. | Formal | Moderate |

Figure 14.1 Chief characteristics of forum, panel, and symposium.

## THE FORUM

### When Should a Forum Be Used?

There are any number of occasions when a forum should be used. It may be used as a follow-up to clarify or explore information given in another technique such as a lecture or panel presentation. It may be used to promote free and open audience participation by contributing ideas and opinions. It can stimulate broad based discussion among and between audience members and resource person(s). The forum may also be used to identify community needs and interests to be addressed by further programming.

### Who Is Involved in a Forum?

Three distinct parties are involved in a forum, each having certain roles and responsibilities.

1. **The moderator** is responsible for introducing the program and guiding discussion. This person should be an adept facilitator capable of clearly articulating the goals of the program, leading discussion, and encouraging audience participation;
2. **The resource person** or persons supply information, answer questions, stimulate audience thinking, and offer insights and ideas for continued discussion. They do not make a formal presentation but provide some brief remarks as a way of focusing discussion. Resource people should be competent and interested in the topic under consideration;
3. **The audience** should be both interested and knowledgeable about the topic so that intelligent conversation can occur.

### What Are the Advantages of the Forum?

The forum method has numerous advantages. Perhaps the most significant is the interactive nature of the method; audience members have an opportunity to participate verbally with the resource people as well as with each other, and thus are more likely to be active participants. Another advantage is that resource people are typically well-prepared because of their role and are more likely to consider the needs and interests of the audience. An additional advantage lies in the opportunity for audience members to clarify points made by the speakers.

## What are the Limitations of the Forum?

The chief limitation of the forum rests with its size. With a large audience, the time needed for each audience member to make a contribution may be hampered. Some audience members may be intimidated from speaking because of the sheer size of the group. Also, it is sometimes difficult to provide adequate facilities such as auditoriums or meeting rooms that are conducive to large group discussion. In additional, it is essential to have a moderator who is skilled in handling large group discussion; otherwise the program may be dominated by one or two outspoken members of the audience.

## What Are the Usual Lines of Communication?

Figure 14.2, adapted from the work of Bergevin, Morris, and Smith (1963), depicts the typical lines of communication in a forum. Note how the forum promotes discussion by a large audience among and between the moderator, the resource personnel, and each other.

## What Are the Duties of the Personnel Involved in a Forum?

The moderator, the resource person(s), and the audience each have specific duties and responsibilities both prior to and during the forum which will be explicated below.

*What Does the Moderator Do?* The secret to a successful forum usually lies with the moderator. The responsibilities are many but typically involve such preparatory duties as organizing the topic(s) to be covered, generating guiding questions for the discussion, understanding how the forum works, identifying appropriate resource persons and getting to know them so a proper introduction can be made, arranging for a suitable physical space that is conducive for audience comfort and discussion, and understanding the makeup and composition of the audience. The moderator also prepares a brief presentation that introduces the topic and the resource people to the audience, describes how a forum works, notes the

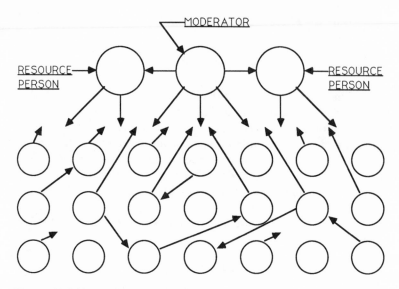

Figure 14.2 Lines of communication.

amount of time available for the forum, and outlines the responsibilities of the audience.

Once the forum begins, the moderator gives the introduction and sets the tone of the meeting by offering a guiding question for discussion. The moderator monitors the discussion by encouraging audience participation, keeps in mind the goals of the program, makes certain that everyone has a chance to participate verbally, avoids a monopoly of talk, uses humor to speed discussion along, and suggests the next course of action at the conclusion of the event.

*What Do the Resource People Do?* Like the moderator, the resource persons have a number of duties prior to the forum and during it as well. They should study the mechanics of the forum, understand the nature of the topic(s) to be discussed, become acquainted with the audience, and be prepared to participate informally and flexibly.

Once the forum begins, the resource persons should make brief opening remarks. They should use lay terminology to avoid being perceived as dominating or authoritarian. Their main role is to encourage audience participation through questions and comments. Resource people should avoid heated confrontations and deal with comments in a constructive manner. Above all, they should acknowledge when a question is beyond their competence, and be prepared to refer the participant to another source for appropriate information.

*What Does the Audience Do?* Prior to the forum, the members of the audience should become informed about the topic(s) to be discussed and understand their role in a forum. During the forum, they should listen intently and participate by asking questions, raising issues, offering comments, requesting further information, and helping to clarify for others. Above all, audience members should be judicious in their remarks, be courteous to others, and avoid monopolizing the discussion. In short, they should treat others as they would expect to be treated.

### What Does the Layout of the Room and Facilities Look Like?

Figure 14.3, adapted from Bergevin, Morris, and Smith (1963) gives a typical physical layout for a forum. The moderator and resource persons are usually seated on a stage or platform in front of the audience. They are seated before a table and microphones are provided so that the audience may hear any comments from the platform. The audience is seated in concentric semicircles so as to promote optimum discussion in front of the platform. An alternative to this arrangement would be audience members seated around round tables that accommodate approximately twelve individuals each.

### How to Evaluate the Forum

Any number of techniques can be employed to evaluate the effectiveness of the forum. These include questionnaires, checklists, interviews, and observations. Each technique has certain strengths and certain weaknesses. For example, the questionnaire asks for opinions and feelings of the participants which are completely subjective. Experienced programmers know that almost any group contains chronic complainers. A checklist can be helpful but it may be too exclusive and miss important information. Thus, it is important to use multiple evaluation techniques such as a questionnaire coupled with a small number of randomly assigned participant interviews when determining program effectiveness.

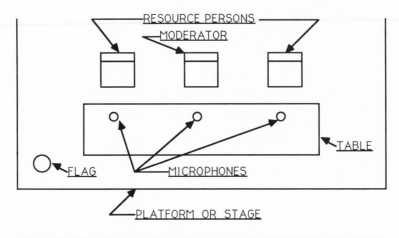

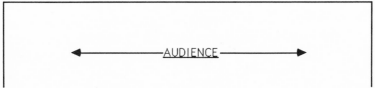

Figure 14.3 Room layout.

## THE PANEL

### When Should a Panel Be Used?

The panel method is most effective when the goal is to bring several points of view before an audience. It may be used to stimulate interest in a topic, identify and clarify problems and issues, or chart a course of action. It may also be used to promote a wide variety of informed opinion. The nature of the panel is conversational and informal.

### Who Is Involved in a Panel?

A successful panel involves three distinct parties: the moderator, panel members, and the audience. Each party has certain roles and responsibilities which are described below.

1. **The moderator** is responsible for arranging the panel, selecting the panel members, and guiding discussion. This person should

be thoroughly familiar with the topic so that discussion can be facilitated among the panel members.

2. **The panel members** are persons who possess specialized knowledge of the topic at hand, can articulate verbally in a clear manner, and have an interest in the program. They should be willing to carry a conversation among themselves, be flexible, and avoid preaching. Panel members are selected to represent various points of view, levels of experience, and backgrounds. Thus, they may not be experts in an academic sense, but rather authorities on the basis of their knowledge and experience.

3. **The audience** is composed of a variety of backgrounds and interests. Their involvement in the program is an indication of some interest. For this reason, the panel should be organized in a manner that reflects the needs and interests of the audience.

### What are the Advantages of the Panel?

The main advantage of a panel is the opportunity to hear a variety of opinions or points of view from several knowledgeable speakers. Another advantage is that the informal, unrehearsed nature of a panel often results in spontaneity between speakers. This can produce a dramatic quality that stimulates further interest and learning among audience participants.

### What Are the Limitations of the Panel?

The panel method has numerous limitations. One of the most incriminating is a poor moderator who fails to keep panel members on the topic. Another limitation is finding available panel members who are not only knowledgeable, but are effective speakers. An additional limitation is the proclivity of some speakers to do most of the talking at the expense of other panel members. This can result in audience members getting agitated and losing interest. Since the panel method is informal and conversational by nature, it can sometimes be perceived as chaotic and unsystematic. A skilled moderator is needed to avoid this situation.

### What are the Usual Lines of Communication?

Figure 14.4, adapted from Bergevin, Morris, and Smith (1963), shows the typical lines of communication during a panel. Note that the conversation flows among the moderator and panel members and not the audience. Conversation may also be among panel members directly without the assistance of the moderator. Audience members only listen and observe.

### What Are the Duties of the Personnel Involved in the Panel?

The three parties involved in a panel—the moderator, the panel members, and the audience—each have certain duties and responsibilities prior to and during the panel which will be described below.

*What Does the Moderator Do?* Without a doubt, the success of any panel lies with the moderator. Prior to the meeting, it is vital to understand the topic at hand, the goals of the program, the amount of time available, and how the panel will be used. In addition, the moderator should study the characteristics of the audience that will likely attend the meeting, keeping in mind what they will be expecting. The moderator prepares questions for the panel that will guide discussion, gets to know panel members so that a proper introduction can be made, and explains to them the

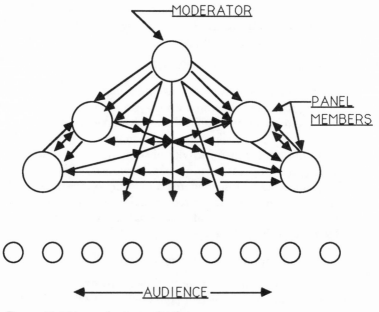

Figure 14.4 Lines of communication.

nature of a panel and their responsibilities as panelists. The moderator also selects the facility for the panel, noting that it is sufficiently large enough for the anticipated audience and ensures that the proper physical setup will be made. Finally, this person plans an introduction noting the topic at hand, who the panelists are, the purpose of the panel and how it will be operated, and the time limits.

During the panel discussion, the moderator is responsible for giving the introduction and setting a relaxed, informal tone so that all in attendance can feel comfortable. The moderator guides discussion among panelists, acts as a timekeeper, and guards against domination by one or two panel members. At the conclusion of the panel, the moderator summarizes what has transpired and encourages appropriate follow-up study.

*What Do the Panel Members Do?* Prior to the meeting, panel members should apprise themselves of the panel method, taking note as to what their respective responsibilities are as discussants. They should familiarize themselves with the goals of the program and try to understand what the audience is looking for. Finally, panel members should prepare themselves to be relaxed and flexible.

Once the meeting begins, panel members should try to make their comments as meaningful as possible to the audience. They should be brief and articulate and above all, avoid dominating the discussion. They should also remind themselves that spontaneous conversation is desirable and often welcomed by the audience.

*What Does the Audience Do?* Prior to the panel discussion, the audience should study the topic and goals of the meeting. They should understand the purpose of the panel and be willing to hear disparate points of view.

During the panel, the audience should try to become as involved as possible by taking mental notes for further study and listening actively. The audience should also try to relate the discussion to their own experience and in the process, be critical consumers. Finally, audience members should be mindful of additional topics for further study.

### What Does the Layout of the Room and Facilities Look Like?

Figure 14.5, adapted from Bergevin, Morris, and Smith (1963), depicts the typical physical arrangements of a panel. Note that the panel members face each other so as to promote conversation and dialogue with each other. Also note that the moderator is nearby to foster and guide discussion among panel members. The audience, while present, is in a position of observation only; audience members do not participate verbally.

### How to Evaluate the Panel

Multiple evaluation techniques can be employed to determine the success of the program. These include questionnaires, interviews, checklists, or observations. As was discussed earlier, the use of one evaluation technique should be avoided since it may provide erroneous information. It is important to utilize multiple measures such as a checklist, observations, and a participant questionnaire to determine if the program was ultimately successful.

## THE SYMPOSIUM

### When Should a Symposium Be Used?

The symposium method is appropriate for any number of occasions. It tends to work best when the purpose of a meeting is

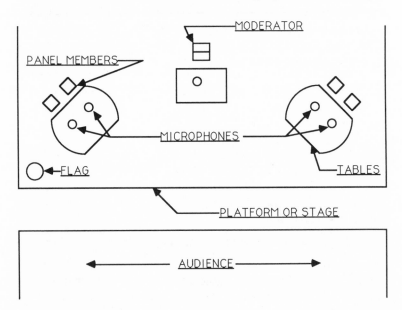

Figure 14.5 Room layout.

to present several sides of one question or to approach a central theme from several different perspectives at a single session. It works well when disparate points of view are brought together on a controversial topic. The symposium also can be used to help people understand how related parts of a topic contribute to the topic as a whole. An additional use of the symposium is to stimulate fresh thinking on a topic.

### Who Is Involved in a Symposium?

Like the forum and panel, there are three parties involved in a symposium: the chairperson, the speakers, and the audience. Each party has distinct roles and responsibilities which are described below.

1. **The chairperson** is responsible for organizing and presiding over the symposium. Important qualifications include some knowledge of the topic, a good speaking voice, and the ability to facilitate large group meetings. In addition, the chairperson should be able to tolerate ambiguity and deal with spontaneous situations that may arise during the symposium.

2. **The speakers** are responsible for preparing their remarks and presenting them in a clear and concise way. They should have a firm grasp of the topic at hand and try to learn as much as they can about the audience to which they will be speaking.

3. **The audience** is usually comprised of interested individuals who want to attend the meeting. Because of this, every effort should be made to organize the symposium in a manner that stimulates thought among audience participants and contributes to their further understanding of the topic at hand.

### What Are the Advantages of the Symposium?

The symposium offers many advantages. It brings together knowledgeable speakers who present a variety of opinions on a given topic. Even though each speaker's time is short, it is often possible both to identify and to explore problems quite thoroughly. The audience has the benefit of hearing disparate points of view that can be challenging and stimulating. Audience attention is usually greater since the number of speakers tends to mitigate boredom.

*What Are the Limitations of the Symposium?*

There are a number of limitations with the symposium method. The formal structure tends to promote passivity among audience members since there is little room for active participation. Sometimes the symposium members fail to check with each other prior to the meeting which results in repetition of information, confusion, and deviations from the assigned topic. Also, it is sometimes difficult to find enough competent speakers to cover the topic adequately.

*What Are the Usual Lines of Communication?*

Figure 14.6, adapted from Bergevin, Morris, and Smith (1963), clearly shows the lines of communication between the chairperson and the speakers. Note that communication during a symposium is characterized as one-way; the chairperson and the speakers are talking to the audience.

*What Are the Duties of the Personnel Involved in the Symposium?*

Each party has certain roles and responsibilities both prior to and during the symposium that will be described below.

*What Does the Chairperson Do?* To ensure a successful meeting, the chairperson fulfills many responsibilities before the sym-

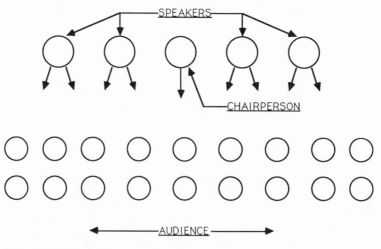

Figure 14.6 Lines of communication.

posium takes place. This person serves as supreme organizer of the event, identifies the theme or topic to be covered, selects the appropriate speakers, and works out an acceptable timetable with each speaker. The chairperson reviews what the purposes of a symposium are, becomes familiar with the goals of the program, gets acquainted with the speakers, and secures their biography so a proper introduction can be made. Other responsibilities include selecting the appropriate physical space for the meeting and trying to understand the characteristics of the audience likely to attend the event. The chairperson also prepares an introduction that makes clear what the symposium is about, who the speakers are, how much time is allotted, and the responsibilities of the audience. For example, the chairperson might ask the audience to write down questions for the speakers to answer in a forum to follow the symposium.

Once the symposium begins, the chairperson presents the introduction, makes sure that each speaker starts and stops each presentation as scheduled, and summarizes the various speeches at the conclusion of the meeting. The chairperson also suggests next steps and closes the meeting.

*What Do the Speakers Do?* Before the symposium begins, the speakers should organize their speeches in a manner that considers audience needs and interests. Speakers should plan their remarks so that nonspecialists can understand what they are presenting, should avoid the use of highly technical jargon, and should keep the length of their speech within agreed upon time limits.

Once the symposium begins, the speakers should make logical and organized presentations. They should keep their remarks brief or at least within accepted time allotments, and pay attention to audience reactions.

*What Does the Audience Do?* Prior to the meeting, the audience should become as informed as possible about the program and understand what the purposes of a symposium are.

Once the meeting starts, the audience should listen carefully to each speech, take mental notes for follow-up questioning, and try to relate the material to their own experiences.

### *What Does the Layout of the Room and Facilities Look Like?*

Figure 14.7, adapted from Bergevin, Morris, and Smith (1963), shows the physical setup for a typical symposium. The stand or podium is placed on the stage for use by the chairperson and

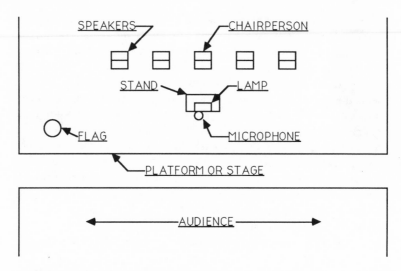

Figure 14.7 Room layout.

the speakers. This layout clearly shows the formal nature of the symposium where speeches are directed to the audience from the platform or stage. There may be a period for questions from the audience following the speeches, but this is up to the chairperson and the design of the program.

*How to Evaluate the Symposium*

We have previously discussed the need to use multiple evaluation measures such as a participant questionnaire, interview, and observation, and this truism holds with a symposium as well. The program planner will then have a much better idea of the ultimate success of the symposium because a variety of data can be analyzed.

## CONCLUSION

The purpose of this chapter was to examine three specific adult education methodologies—the forum, panel, and symposium—in some detail. We began by noting that these methods have been championed by educators of adults for many years, particularly as a means of promoting enlightened citizenship. We too noted that some confusion exists in the literature as to whether the methods are the same or different. We took the position that there are distinct differences in each method in terms of purpose, tone, and level of audience participation. We then examined each method in some detail noting their respective characteristics and described how they could be used. We described the advantages and limitations of each method, typical lines of communication, personnel involved, possible physical arrangements, and finally how to evaluate the effectiveness of the method.

The ultimate success of any adult education enterprise lies with a firm understanding of when and how to use specific educational methodologies. It is hoped that this chapter contributes to this understanding particularly as it relates to the use of the forum, panel, and symposium.

## REFERENCES

Bergevin, P., Morris, D., & Smith, R.M. (1963). *Adult education procedures: A handbook of tested patterns for effective participation*. Greenwich: The Seabury Press.

Bryson, L. (1936). *Adult education*. New York: American.

Hewitt, D., & Mather, K. F. (1937). *Adult education: A dynamic for democracy*. New York: D. Appleton-Century.

Poznar, W. (1982). The college as forum. *Educational Record, 63*, 26-28.

Studebaker, J. W. (1935). *The American way*. New York: McGraw-Hill.

# CHAPTER 15

## Computer-Enriched Instruction
LINDA H. LEWIS

Just as books have served as traditional adjuncts to instruction, computers are fast becoming enhancements to the teaching-learning transaction that are shaping our vision of the future. While computers have many potential educational uses, the most challenging, and sometimes the most threatening, is their use as a medium for delivering instruction. The question is, to what extent can computers become the primary teaching source, and to what degree does the medium support the cognitive processes necessary and sufficient for learning?

While the critical differences between computer-based instruction and traditional modes of knowledge presentation remain unspecified, computer-enriched instruction has matured during the past decade to the point where its instructional benefits can be tested and compared with components of traditional instruction. A meta-analysis of 199 comparative studies of computer-based instruction (Kulik & Kulik, 1987) found that, while computers did not have positive effects in every area studied, individuals:

1. generally learned more in classes when they received help from computers;

2. learned with less instructional time;

3. liked class more when they received computer help; and,

303

4. developed more positive attitudes toward computers when they received computer assistance in an educational setting.

A recent analysis of published reports on computer-based instruction suggests that the disparate findings relative to the merits of computer-assisted instruction (CAI) are due, in part, to the failure of researchers to adequately report data (Gillingham & Guthrie, 1987). Of the 220 studies published since 1980, identified in the ERIC database by the descriptor CAI, only 13 reported positive or negative evidence of the effects of computer-based instruction on learning (Gillingham & Gurthrie, 1987). In fact, research studies on the impact of computer-based instruction do not link their findings to the contributions of specific instructional components. Additionally, evaluations of the effectiveness of computer-based instruction tend to vary as a function of the evaluation design used to measure effectiveness. While anecdotal accounts touting the efficacy of computer-based learning exist in sufficient volume, successes tend to receive more publicity than failures. Thus, the reality is that little support exists for the suggestion that computer-based instruction produces greater gains in achievement relative to other forms of instruction.

The purpose of this chapter is not to grapple with the issue of superiority, but rather to suggest that there are more relevant and meaningful questions to be asked about computer-based instruction. For example, how well-suited is the medium to the needs of learners? How much of what is learned through computers transfers to the real world setting? How does computer-assisted instruction facilitate the acquisition of knowledge for special-needs populations such as adults with learning disabilities or speech and auditory impairments? What factors should dictate whether computer-based instruction or more traditional instructional methods are preferable? All these questions suggest that judging the effectiveness of computer-based instruction may simply mean assessing the relative merits of a particular approach, for a particular population, with particular subject matter, against a particular measure of benefit. "The computer-driven screen should be viewed simply as another medium available to the teacher and capable of doing certain things well and others poorly or not at all" (Hagler & Knowlton, 1987, p.87).

## ACRONYM ALIENATION

One problem that plagues those wishing to converse about computers and adult learning is terminology. Not only are different terms constantly bandied about to refer to the use of computers for facilitating learning, but rarely is there agreement as to their meaning. In part, this confusion is due to similarities in functional characteristics; however, it is important that meaningful and consistent definitions be developed in order to avoid misunderstandings and improve communication.

The oldest and most commonly utilized term, familiar to most educators, is computer-assisted instruction (CAI). While still used extensively, the acronym is somewhat dated. CAI is a term that was prominent at a time when more naive and often unsuccessful approaches were employed in computer-based lessons. With the advent of the microcomputer revolution in the mid-1970s, renewed interest in CAI led to advances in the technology accompanied by lower cost and greater sophistication. However, despite the introduction of new approaches such as LOGO, the term CAI still carries a negative connotation for many educators.

In an attempt to find an appellation that could help to define the strengths of the medium, computer-based education (CBE) was coined to help expoit its success. CBE includes computer-managed instruction (CMI), computer-based testing (CBT), instructional applications of computers (IAC), and administrative applications of computers (AAC). The variation in terminology suggests the continual differentiation of computer-based technology, as well as the wide range of potential uses. Yet the advantage gained by developing specific terminology is lost as the number of acronyms increases. For example, it is common to define computer usage in terms of its applications function. The descriptor CAI refers to situations in which computers are used in direct support of an instructional function involving subject matter, learners, and teachers. On the other hand, computer-supported instruction (CSI) is employed to describe computer applications in support of instruction, i.e., using computers as classroom aids to assist instructors in the accomplishment of educational objectives. Last, noninstructional support (NIS), the application of computers to assist outside the classroom, is gaining favor. NIS includes the use of computers for scheduling, evaluation, guidance, grading, report preparation, or as ancillary utilities for problem solving or library retrieval.

Before proceeding, one additional definition must be added to the locution of high technology. When viewing computers as a means for freeing educators from tasks requiring human skill, computer-managed learning (CML) is a commonly used designation. CML refers to the use of computers to guide the entire learning process by assuming an administrative role. While the content may be delivered by computer, the use of books, video recording, programmed text, or other material might also be employed. In fact, CML systems may be so well integrated that learners may be unaware of switching from one mode to another.

CML decisions are made for individual learners. Not only can each learner follow an individually designed course, but testing an individual's knowledge leads to a prescribed plan that specifies what unit or module a learner should do next. In addition to testing, routing, and remediating, the computer keeps records and produces reports. Some CML systems are written specifically for one course. Others are flexible and can teach a variety of subjects.

Regardless of how one arranges the alphabet soup, the multiplicity of terms underscores the level of sophistication that is being developed. While the list of acronyms describing computer-based instruction goes on and on, the term used throughout the remainder of this chapter is computer-enriched instruction (CEI) because of its generic connotation and inclusiveness of a plethora of computer-enhanced learning opportunties. This singular designation suggests that computers are to be used in an educational setting to make instruction deeper, exemplified, or more meaningful. CEI also conveys the idea that computers are adjuncts to instruction—an additional medium to be used in concert with a variety of additional media, stategies, and techniques. An ancillary benefit to using the term CEI is that it inhibits individuals from limiting their concept of the computer's role to the idea that computers are simply vehicles for programmed instruction. As this chapter will illustrate, there are numerous ways to incorporate microcomputers with adult learning so that they become extensions of the present with unlimited potential for enriching the learning process for both teachers and learners.

## ADVANTAGES OF COMPUTERS
## FOR FACILITATING LEARNING

In any engagement between teacher and learner, the teacher is ultimately the one who is responsible for the guidance of the learning for the acquisition, enhancement, or refinement of knowledge. Good teachers guide practice, motivate and involve learners, manage attention, assess proficiency, and evaluate progress. These same attributes should apply equally to computer-enriched instruction. However, there are differences that help to distinguish teachers and computers with respect to how they teach as opposed to what they teach.

Today's approach to CEI is learner-centered. The focus is on individuality. Individually tailored programs make it possible to compose a lesson and customize it to the needs of the student. The flexibility afforded by CEI permits learners to choose both the time (day, night, or weekends) and the place (home, office, or classroom) for their learning. Self-directedness is encouraged as individuals control the instructional time, adjust the speed at which information is transmitted, and choose among learning options. Opportunities for self-diagnosis and self-study offer learners a degree of freedom rarely afforded in traditional learning environment.

Adaptive computer-based instruction is interactive and includes initial diagnosis or prescription, rediagnosis, and apportionment of the amount and sequencing of instruction. Computers can anticipate student errors, classify them by type, and provide appropriate remediation. "Properly programmed, computers can match the pace and timing of a presentation to a learner's requirments at a given moment. The result is a saving of time; an average time-saving of one-third is typically found in comparing CBI programs with conventional ones" (Walker, 1983, p.104).

Today's computer programs possess many noteworthy technical qualities that contribute significantly to the positive characteristics of the medium. Computers possess the ability to deliver information with a program contingent upon a learner's response. Unlike teachers, computers have total recall whereby information stored in a fluid, electronic matrix can be held in reserve and presented to learners in any order, not just from beginning to end.

One feature commonly found in drill and practice programs,

called "increased ratio review," allows for the distribution of practice in any given computer program. When a learner answers incorrectly, the example doesn't go to the end of the stack as it might if one were using flash cards; instead, a new ordering is reformed on the spot, and the missed item (or its variant) is inserted at several review positions with increasing numbers of intervening items between the review and the iteration (Siegel & Davis, 1986). A similar procedure is followed for each item that is missed. Thus, there is not only random sequencing, but a tireless effort on the part of the computer to continue to provide learning opportunities and practice until mastery is attained.

While some balk at the use of microcomputers for drill and practice, this rudimentary use is oftentimes more involving than a printed page that neither acknowledges responses nor provides feedback. Adult learners, pragmatic in their approaches to learning, like to see the results of what they have done. Computers not only provide corrective and constructive feedback based on individual input, but ensure that learners do not receive more instruction than needed. Additionally, computers offer the ability to learn from experience as in the case of computer simulations whereby individuals discover relationships, act on them, and see the consequences of their actions. Another advantage of computers is that they can aid in the development of abstract and conceptual skills by affording learners an opportunity (through graphics and simulations) to experience abstracts, gain the power to internalize the information, work with random processes, and think conceptually. Computers also make it possible for learners to receive information in varied sensory and conceptual modes through the use of color, shapes, sound, graphics, and a variety of peripheral input devices such as drawing pads, light pens, joysticks, and the like. In addition, computers can be linked with a variety of electronic media to further enhance their merit as educational tools.

One of the adjunct benefits of CEI is that adult educators are looking at what they have been doing and determining what works and what doesn't. Computer-enriched instruction not only gives teachers and learners an opportunity to experiment, but it prompts researchers to conduct further inquiry into the science of learning, intelligence, and human thought. Cognitive and educational psychologists, along with classroom teachers, administrators, and counselors, now have the potential of working together to bridge the gap across disciplines by seeking answers to such questions as: What is the best way to sequence information? How often should review occur? What is the optimal use of the computer for accommodating to different cognitive styles? How is self-directedness best encouraged? Although new questions emerge daily, CEI is providing the impetus for exploration into ways of teaching higher-order reasoning skills and for the improvement of instructional practice.

## LIMITATIONS OF COMPUTER-ENRICHED INSTRUCTION

The quality of software is a concern to many educators. Although some programs are of a high caliber, there are still tutor-style materials developed twenty-five years ago that do not always combine principles of good instructional design and subject matter expertise. While features such as increased ratio review are incorporated into computer programs, nonadaptive lessons are still on the market. Such programs take students through the material in the same order, are unimaginative, and offer no assurance that individuals have learned what is being taught. Some computer-based programs control learners by drilling rather than by putting them through their paces while other programs can not anticipate perfectly reasonable student responses. The scarcity of excellent courseware means that teachers oftentimes utilize parts from a variety of different programs. Teachers' keen evaluative skills are important in order to assess the features and qualities of the various programs currently available. Later in the chapter, specific guidelines are provided for software evaluation and selection.

In addition to concerns about the quality and appropriateness of software for adult learners, cost is often a factor that precludes the use of CEI in a variety of educational settings. The potential for obsolescence is an additional barrier that has inhibited the purchase of hardware to support instruction. Rapid changes mean that teacher time needs to be continually dedicated to updating expertise beyond the initial energy that was expended to learn the technology. The lack of standardization, the question of return on investment, and the resistance of some humanists and educational idealists to CEI are supplemental factors that contribute to slowing the widespread use of computers to facilitate learning.

Much remains to be worked out in developing appropriate strategies for integrating computers into an educational setting. CEI not only heralds the need for curricular revision, but in some instances, presents a threat to traditional and established routines. In fields such as the arts, humanities, literature, or even complex mathematics that require a deep understanding not easily taught with computers, CEI is less common. While newer and more complex models are being developed daily to incorporate sophisticated branching options, most programs currently found in adult, continuing, and vocational education settings handle rule-based procedures. The use of computers in this fashion helps to illustrate a critical difference between working with a qualified teacher versus using a computer. While computers draw on information that has been specifically programmed into them for handling a task at hand, they cannot call upon the life experiences of the learner or make use of new information. Another problem is that CEI is often seen as a substitute for, rather than an enhancement to, conventional education. The difficulty with relying on any singular mode of learning, whether it be independent study, distance learning, or computer-based education, is sustaining motivation and participation in the absence of a teacher or a social structure. The use of computers to promote learning is diminished if they are employed to the exclusion of other media or personal interaction.

The multiple ways in which computers can be utilized is addressed in the section that follows. An enumeration of the uses of CEI underscores the versatility of the technology and suggests how computers can truly provide enrichment and promote learning when appropriately and meaningfully integrated into an educational setting.

## FACILITATING LEARNING THROUGH COMPUTER USE

In order to simplify what could be a complicated explanation of the various applications of computer-enriched instruction, a tripart classification has been developed. By categorizing computers as instructional vehicles, tools, and resources, many possible educational applications emerge that help to promote further understanding of the computer's educational utility.

## Computers as Vehicles for Instruction

Computers used as "teaching machines" assist with the acquisition of basic factual or theoretical knowledge. Through the logical presentation of material or theory, the computer instructs, permits practice, provides feedback, assigns instruction based on user response, and tests comprehension. Today sound, high resolution color graphics, and increased interactivity are combined to permit the computer to direct learning just as an adult educator might do in the classroom.

Computer-enhanced instructional programs can be instruction-centered, practice and evaluation-centered, or assessment-centered (Herrmann, 1988). In addition, numerous computer-based instructional modalities (optional lessons) can be employed. For illustrative purposes, placing each option at a point along a continuum helps to differentiate one instructional mode from another. At one extreme is drill and practice, the most mechanical type of lesson, which relies primarily on prescriptive response modes. At the other extreme is programming, a learning option that utilizes the teaching of programming skills to develop additional competencies. In the middle lie tutorials, simulations, games, and dialogue. While each is a convenient way of describing the different types of computer-based lessons, such categorizations are oversimplifications because the different modes overlap. Each instructional option includes differing amounts of structured lessons as well as student-designed, self-directed content. The idea of the continuum is not meant to suggest that any one mode is preferable to another, but rather that a variety of computer-based lessons are available. It is this variety that helps to maintain interest and to sustain motivation.

In order to assist educators in selecting the option most appropriate for a given individual, the various instructional modes are explained in the sections that follow. Each may be more or less valuable depending on the ability of the particular lesson or program to meet the needs of individual learners.

*Drill and Practice.* Using computers for drill and practice can help to reinforce concepts introduced in class or to help with skill building. In drill and practice the computer guides, controls, and monitors the repetition of a specific set of tasks in order to develop a predetermined level of proficiency in a skill. Different levels of difficulty are built into the programs themselves, allowing for the tailoring of instruction to the needs and abilities of the individual user based on performance. Programs can offer multiple choice options and provide successive clues and hints; however, the inherent limitation in even the most sophisticated programs is that there is only one right answer.

Drill and practice can be used for self-diagnosis, memorization, or for learning facts, routines, and rules. This option is particularly useful for adults who may fear being embarassed in front of a group. Working individually with the computer allows them to make mistakes without risk or public acknowledgment. Drill and practice programs are also a tremendous aid to teachers who cannot always keep careful track of the areas needing remediation. Additionally, their use frees educators to focus on the development of higher order, less redundant learning.

While drill and practice lessons are good for teaching structured, drill-oriented subjects such as math, spelling, and grammar, such programs are most beneficial for those who prefer structure and who need information delivered in small, incremental pieces. However, not everyone learns best in such a fashion. "As much as half the population has the sort of cognitive structure that resists the acquistion of knowledge from the highly linear and orderly process of the computer" (Gueluette, 1982, p.181). Given this consideration, along with the suggestion that no singular instructional mode be relied upon as the sole basis for learning, drill and practice should be seen as supplemental instruction that is reinforcing in nature (Suppes, 1966).

*Tutorials.* A more complex form of drill and practice, tutorials introduce, as well as reinforce, concepts. They are generally used for presenting new material rather than for supplementing previous knowledge. Because tutorials can be used to teach a subject, they incorporate a number of broader objectives. While some refer to this mode as the automation of programmed text by the computer, the format can also incorporate short answers and interpret responses. Tutorials employ multiple choice, vary the amount of information presented at any one time, and provide branching and nonbranching options (i.e., reactive versus nonreactive responses). In this mode the computer presents information in text and pictures and then queries learners to assess comprehension and to ascertain their ability to apply the information. Tutoring consists of a dialogue in which each successive element depends upon an interpretation of what preceded it, thus escalating the number of response combinations. Yet, despite the increased complexity of such lessons, the number of possible responses to any pertinent question is limited.

Tutorial programs are closely related to "expert systems" that combine simulation with the tutorial mode. Some early examples of such programs developed for medical diagnosis have gained prominence as being particularly beneficial for bridging the gap between theory and practice by developing an understanding of cause and effect. As work in the area of artificial intelligence continues, computer tutoring may someday hold additional promise by making it possible for students to have their own mentors. "In a few more years, millions will have access to what Philip of Macedon's son Alexander enjoyed as a royal prerogative: the personal services of a tutor as well informed and responsive as Aristotle" (Suppes, 1966, p.206).

*Simulations and Games.* Simulation promotes an understanding of interrelationships among parts and helps to develop a relationship between theory and its application. By permitting the manipulation of reality, learners are afforded the opportunity to observe effects, reflect upon practice, develop problem-solving and decision-making skills, and enhance integrative abilities. Simulation lessons are most widely used in science and math, particularly in teaching physics, biology, and chemistry. However, their use is by no means restricted, as excellent simulations have been developed for the arts and humanities. One program used in theater arts allows for the staging of an entire production by using a computer that permits individuals to move actors and manipulate props and scenery (Turner, 1986).

The advantage of simulations is that they expose individuals to reality in a way that would not otherwise be possible given factors such as time, cost, safety, resources, and the like. They are fun, promote the transference of skill to the real world, and actively involve the learner. Simulations are particularly advantageous for individuals who are worried about making mistakes because they allow for experimentation in a penalty-free environment. This learning option is opportune for adults who are oftentimes reluctant to take risks. In addition, simulations provide opportunities for individuals to work together and cooperate through role playing or bargaining as they work through processes and discover what it "feels like" to be in a particular situation.

While simulations promote group cohesiveness and offer collegial learning opportunities, they are, of necessity, an oversimplification of reality. Therefore, teachers must take care in pointing out the differences between simulations and the real world situations that they simulate. Time-consuming and sometimes expensive, simulations are not always consistent or compatible with instructional goals, and their use rarely fits into a typical class period. However, simulations are excellent learning vehicles for those who prefer a fair amount of guidance but who still like to experiment. They afford the adult educator an opportunity to maintain control over the learning while simultaneously permitting students to explore and discover on their own.

Simulations can be used to promote group or individual competition, and some include written materials to which a single person or group must respond. There are also board simulations that make use of cards or game boards to trigger problems. This form of simulation moves closer to category of "games" which is often included under the simulation rhubric. Computer games provide an opportunity to apply concepts by creating situations requiring individuals to manipulate an environment. Although there are those who take exceptions to their use in an educational setting, computer gaming can be effectively employed to promote teamwork, develop social skills, and stimulate an individual's or group's competitive spirit.

*Dialogue and Programming.* Dialogue is a highly refined use of the computer as a teaching machine. In this mode the computer not only presents lessons, provides practice exercises, and asks questions, but it also allows students to exchange true conversation with the computer. In this Socratic option the ability to initiate questions is afforded both the learner and the computer. Using appropriate, well-designed software that has been developed by experts with both programming and subject matter expertise, the computer can tailor its presentation to accommodate a wide range of student differences.

In those instances where the programming option is appropriate, the computer acts like a tutee, i.e., the learner does the tutoring. Individuals first learn to program and then communicate with the computer in a way that it understands. In this fashion individuals learn what they are trying to teach the computer. Thus, the programmers (who are also the learners) not only discover more about how computers work, but learn more about their own thinking processes. Because no predesigned software is necessary, programming is an inexpensive, but highly sophisticated option that can only be used with a select group of learners.

While the aforementioned instructional options of drill and practice, tutorials, simulations, games, dialogue, and programming can supplement instruction, or even change the relationship between the learner and the teacher, their use does not eliminate the need for basic interaction between the two. "Involvement of the teacher with a student remains essential. In fact, proper use of the computer can intensify this relationship in a most effective way" (Lynton & Elman, 1987, p.124).

## Computers as Resources

Computers can be invaluable resources for promoting learning. While a certain degree of skill development is necessary to implement the commands and routines necessary to run programs, to network with people, or to access data bases, computers can aid in promoting self-direction and efficiency. By accessing information from among the 3,000 data bases currently in existence, individuals can use the computer to network with others and seek answers to their questions as they converse through a communications link.

Cost often precludes the use of computers as resources in many instructional settings. Since charges for accessing data bases accrue based on subscription surcharges and telephone time, many educational programs can simply not afford such open-ended learning opportunities. An additional prohibitive factor is that adults using the computer in this fashion need to have fairly cogent writing skills and usually have to teach themselves the nuances of accessing the different data bases.

For those who want to choose the way in which they master competence, utilizing the computer as a resource works very well. It allows learners to identify and select their own resources, time their own learning, and work independently. For those who enjoy a consultative approach, using the computer as a resource can be rewarding for both the teacher and the learner.

*Computers as Tools*

The difference between the use of computers as resources rather than tools is that as tools, computers don't deliver instruction, they facilitate it. Used as developmental tools, the tireless computer can be employed in an educational setting to assist with writing (word processing), computation (statistical programs), data management (spreadsheets), graphics (visual production), and the like. A variety of programs widely available in the marketplace can be easily incorporated into existing structures. They not only save time, but help learners to organize, gather, classify, and analyze data once they learn the necessary commands. Such programs are best for those who desire to apply their own learning to real world situations, who like to initiate, and who are oriented more toward the practical rather than the theoretical. Providing opportunities for learners to use their own skills effectively for whatever projects they wish allows for the maximum use of computers for encouraging self-direction.

## COMPUTERS AND INSTRUCTIONAL DESIGN

The true value of computers in adult education is dependent upon how the hardware and software are ultimately utilized by both teachers and students. To the extent that computers support the cognitive processes necessary or sufficient for learning, the medium makes a significant contribution to learning.

When considering the integration of computers into a learning environment, the concern about instructional design takes on new meaning and respectability. The employment of CEI calls for a linking science between psychology and instructional practice in order to determine the following:

- What instructional design best fosters the acquistion of knowledge that promotes better performance?

- How do facilitators of learning effectively combine work in class with work at home using computer-based technologies?

- What is the best way to ensure that group processes are incorporated in computer-enriched education?

- What content should be teacher-faciliated as opposed to computer-assisted?

Research suggests that learners scoring high in general ability and prior knowledge do especially well with instruction that is incomplete, as it affords them an opportunity to elaborate and organize the learning themselves (Snow & Lohman, 1984). Conversely, less able students tend to benefit from explicit, structured instruction that is aimed at developing their learning strategies and skills. Thus, it becomes clear how computers and programs are more or less beneficial based on the educational level of a particular population, the preferred learning style of the student, and learning objectives. While as yet there are no definitive answers on how to implement CEI, adult educators are encouraged to experiment and continually evaluate to determine the proper integration of the technology with more traditional teaching-learning methods. One alternative is to follow a progression similar to the one suggested in Figure 15.1. The steps that are outlined help to ensure that attention

---

1. Develop learning objectives.
2. Determine the skills, knowledge, and abilities the student needs to develop.
3. Ascertain as much as possible about the student's educational cognitive style.
4. Strategize possible learning opportunities, i.e., home-based, in-class, group, or individual.
5. Decide how the computer will be used for instructional enhancement: tool, resource, or instructional vehicle.
6. Determine the mode of computer inquiry most appropriate for individual learners, i.e., drill and practice, simulation, tutorial, or dialogue.
7. Preview and evaluate a variety of software using specific evaluative criteria.
8. Select and utilize only those programs that are appropriate for adult learners and which are in concert with objectives, needs, and learning strategies that have been defined.

---

Figure 15.1 Protocols for effective instructional design.

is directed toward developing specific protocols when integrating computers into an educational setting.

When considering which of the modes of CEI corresponds most closely with specific instructional or educational objectives, it is useful to analyze the degree to which each modality contributes to the development of different skills, knowledge, or abilities. Utilizing Blooms's taxonomy of the cognitive domain for classifying educational objectives, Figure 15.2 suggests the extent to which the most frequently employed modes of CEI (drill and practice, tutorials, and simulations) contribute to encouraging or emphasizing various intellectual outcomes. Similar charts can also be developed for the affective and psychomotor domains. While such a classification is useful, it should be noted that the extent to which soft-

| Objective | Drill and Practice | Tutorial | Simulation |
|---|---|---|---|
| KNOWLEDGE | Strong | Strong | Strong |
| COMPREHENSION | Good | Strong | Strong |
| APPLICATION | Weak | Good | Strong |
| ANALYSIS | Poor | Weak | Strong |
| SYNTHESIS | Poor | Weak | Strong |
| EVALUATION | Poor | Weak | Good |

Knowledge—ability to recall previously learned information

Comprehension—ability to understand the meaning of oral or written material

Application—ability to select and use information and theory in concrete situations

Analysis—ability to divide material into parts in order to understand the meaning

Synthesis—ability to combine parts so as to form a new whole or original idea

Evaluation—ability to judge the worth of material for a specific purpose

*Note:* From *Taxonomy of Educational Objectives: Cognitive Domain* by B. S. Bloom, Editor, 1956, Vol. 1, New York: McKay.

Figure 15.2 Strength of the most frequently employed modes of CEI for accomplishing cognitive objectives.

ware emphasizes different cognitive objectives varies from program to program. Thus, despite the generalizations that can be made based on an "ideal" program, it is possible that an outstanding tutorial may emphasize higher order skills to a greater degree than a lesser quality simulation program.

## Organization of Computer Resources

The physical placement of computers within an educational setting in large measure dictates usage patterns. Computers can be integrated with instruction through their placement in a classroom, computer laboratory, learning/resource center, or any combination thereof.

Whatever arrangement is used to provide access to computers, their placement should allow for use at varying times. Whenever possible, computers should also be placed in locations other than those traditionally associated with computer use. For example, locating a computer in arts and humanities classrooms, in counseling offices, and libraries is one way of debunking the myth that math is a requisite skill for computer use or that only the hard sciences are best served by the technology. In addition, care must be taken in arranging rooms so that computers are not positioned in a manner that reinforces the assumption that they are isolating devices. Strategies that encourage students to pair with one another, share ideas, and establish support networks are facilitated by configuring computers in a fashion that promotes interactivity. To summarize, the placement of computers should facilitate both dyadic or group work, as well as individualized usage of the medium.

*Computers in the Classroom.* To some extent classroom use of computers limits options as it usually means that only a few computers (often just one or two) are available to learners. Consequently, not much hands-on time is afforded individual students, and care must be taken to construct paired or shared use to allow for increased utilization, expanded access, and equitable usage. The advantage of having computers in the classroom, however, is that CEI can be more closely linked with the curriculum. Not only does this distribution of hardware cause relatively little disruption to the classroom routine, but it allows teachers to control work groups, interact with students, and respond to any questions that arise. It also allows students to become leaders and trainers who can assist their peers in using the technology and assimilating content.

Placing computers in the classroom also allows for flexible usage. For example, someone who finishes an assignment quickly, or who already possesses the competencies being addressed in the class, can use the computer. In this way, the computer becomes another resource available to students, just as books or filmstrips are, to use as time permits or as individual needs dictate. It should be noted that the maximum use of computers in the classroom occurs when they are linked to other technologies, such as video or large screen monitors.

While classroom teachers are the key to the potential success of the classroom model for accessing computers, adult educators differ widely in their ability to use computers, their familiarity with available courseware, and their attitudes toward the technology. When teachers display their own enthusiasm or dislike of computers, students tend to follow the model that is put forth and become more or less willing to use the medium despite their own true feelings. Thus, the greatest challenge that exists for integrating computers into the classroom is countering negative attitudes and tradition. The traditional environment is not always compatible with the potential of high technology nor is it always hospitable to its entry. Fear of change, uncertainty, inertia of the educational system, and concerns about the technology itself often contribute to the incompatibility between facilitating learning and integrating computers into an educational setting.

*Computer Laboratories.* Sharing computer resources is becoming more and more common. Often times public adult educational programs that utilize space in elementary and secondary schools can avail themselves of hardware already located in computer laboratories. In other instances, community colleges or vocational schools may have their own computer laboratories in which large numbers of computers, peripherals, and software are housed. Such an arrangement allows for the utilization of resources by individuals on a flexible basis.

Most often a computer lab coordinator and lab assistants are available to assist learners. Although these individuals can help with the mechanics of running programs, they are not necessarily content experts. Teachers themselves, however, may opt to reserve the computer lab for large group instruction so they can participate directly with their own students in facilitating the teaching-learning transaction. Some labs include large monitors or projection systems that allow teachers to display computer-generated output on a large screen. In addition, there may be conference room space that permits adjunct activities, such as discussions, debriefings, or small group work, to take place.

The disadvantage of the computer lab is that the mere placement of computers in laboratory environment isolates learners from activities that are part of the regular classroom curriculum. Rather than encouraging students to view the computer as another way of learning, their placement in the lab may suggest that the medium is something to be used only at a particular time of the day. It also preempts the productive interaction that can occur between teacher and student when the computer is actually tied to the curriculum with computer-enhanced activities taking place in the classroom. In some labs, assistants inexperienced in working with adults serve as monitors. This can be frustrating for those who need additional support in gaining comfort with the technology or who have a learning style preference for personal interaction and tutorial assistance. In addition, computer labs are often overfilled. Rather than providing opportunities for individualized work, they can become environments in which students compete for scarce resources.

*Resource Centers.* Learning resource centers, central storage areas for instructional resources, allow for the easy access of materials by both teachers and students. While many resource centers house a great variety of print media (and therefore bear more resemblance to a library), they also contain additional resources such as films, maps, and games, as well as computers. The advantage of resource centers is that they are central collection points that ensure materials are housed in one reasonably accessible place. Resource centers can be used by individual teachers or entire classes needing a variety of materials, equipment, or technology. Often times resource centers have computerized data bases listing materials within the center and at other locations. Students and teachers can also use the electronic data base to research special topics.

Teachers who are working toward becoming facile with computers, who are interested in previewing available software, or who wish to plan integrated lessons can work independently in this generally under utilized setting. Students can also come to the center and request teacher recommended software to reinforce concepts previously covered in class. Learning resource centers are not meant for large groups but rather for individual or small group work.

Unfortunately, many centers were not designed originally for computer use and cramped quarters make interaction with more than a few people difficult. On the other hand, a resource center is often a positive environment in which a few students can come together to work on a project without disturbing others, as might be the case in a computer lab or classroom.

A resource center can also serve as a location for training staff. In fact, many teachers, concerned about undertaking their own learning in front of their students, may find the resource center a positive environment for experimention and self-instruction. Security systems, already in place, help to secure the hardware and software. Resource librarians and other assistants who maintain and update software listings serve as valuable resources. Thus, resource centers not only serve as dissemination and information centers, but they can help teachers to inform their practice while simultaneously encouraging student utlization.

## STRATEGIES AND METHODS FOR
## IMPROVING LEARNING WITH COMPUTERS

Attention is certainly a prerequisite to learning; when an individual is motivated, attention is voluntary. Therefore, the question is, beyond the intrinsic capabilities of computers to capture the learner's attention, what else can be done to increase motivation and promote the efficacy of computer-based learning?

Cognitive psychologists have identified a variety of factors that contribute to heightened learning and can be applied to computer-enriched instruction. The following are suggestions for enhancing learning with, and through, computers so as to maximize the potential of the technology.

### Identify Benefits

Prior to computer usage, explain the benefits that can be expected to accrue for learners if they devote attention to the material. For some adults, this may necessitate addressing short-term goals. For example, a student might be told, "If you work on these programs that are designed to develop your skill at doing word problems, you should be able to enter the carpentry class as soon as you've gained mastery." A discussion of long-term benefits might suggest the professional advantages students could gain by mastering the computer-delivered material.

## Develop a Set of Questions

Researchers report that twice as much learning can take place when individuals are asked questions or are shown curiosity-provoking, ambiguous information (Berlyne, 1971). Pre-even questioning techniques set up conditions that can influence the effectiveness of subsequent reinforcing events. In the case of computer-enriched learning, this means that asking questions of students prior to their engaging in computer-based instruction could help to heighten drive or curiosity. Such arousal is satisfied when answers to questions are received. Thus, the careful development of an initial inquiry process can help to establish an atmosphere of intellectual curiosity and entice learners to seek answers through the programs at their disposal.

## Utilize Advanced Organizers

As an instructional device, advanced organizers have been proposed to assist learners in formulating the relationship between their existing knowledge and the new material encountered in a lesson. Better post-test results are achieved. In other words, using advanced organizers to provide a conceptual framework can help a learner to link existing knowledge with the new learning being encountered. For example, when applying such a technique to the use of simulation programs, an advanced organizer can assist learners in fitting increasingly difficult material into their own cognitive structures. This not only facilitates the recall of previously learned material, but also increases the breadth of application in working with new material.

While advanced organizers are not particularly effective for the acquistion of simpler, factual information, they have been found to aid learners working in unfamiliar situations with the assimilation and integration of material. This is, in part, accomplished by activating the appropriate domain of existing knowledge, and by providing certain key ideas (anchors) which promote an association of the new material with existing knowledge. Thus, learners engage in CEI only after the provision of organizers.

## Develop Group and Individual Learning Opportunities

Computers can not satisfy the needs of all students all of the time; however, by varying the ways in which the medium is used, many learners will make computers compatable with their preferred learning style. For example, those who prefer to engage in self-directed, independent learning activities can be directed to programs specifically selected to meet their needs. Others who prefer a collegial learning atmosphere can work in dyads or small groups on computer-based assignments, projects, simulations, and the like. The key is to vary the approach and allow for a variety of instructional strategies. In some instances learners can be "stretched" if the objective is to promote self-directedness, while at other times, the goal may be to allow learners to capitalize on their strengths and work in their preferred mode. Whatever strategies are employed to integrate computers into the learning environment, adult educators must ensure that time is allocated for learners to come together for face-to-face interaction with other students. Just as learning labs in which individuals came and went independently failed to build a sense of belonging, using computers as the sole learning vehicle can endanger continuing participation. Whether it is someone who has been absent from a learning environment for many years, a low literate adult who is upgrading basic skills, or an individual pursuing continuing professional development, interaction among learners, teachers, and peers is critical for establishing a positive learning environment.

## Critically Evaluate and Selectively Utilize Software

The availability of software influences both the direction and the breadth of computer usage. Therefore, it is imperative that educators develop keen evaluative skills for selecting appropriate software for adult learners. While numerous sets of guidelines and criteria have been developed to assist with software selection, the learning facilitator can best determine the suitability of a particular program for an intended population. The truest test of programs, however, comes when teachers observe learners using the software. Such observations can be invaluable when deciding whether or not to integrate a particular program into the curriculum.

Exemplary educational software should fill a specific need, fit existing curricula, contain specific design features, and actively engage the learner (Malone & Levin, 1984). Critical for promoting achievement are features that provide opportunties for problem solving, corrective feedback, elaboration, visual and graphic cues, control of the routine by the learner, immediate feedback, and appropriate wait time between input and response. From the educator's point of view, software can be evaluated from the perspective of program quality (what the features are of a good program) or in terms of teaching requirements (how the program will improve the quality of education). While space does not permit an elaboration of the latter, Figure 15.3 enumerates the types of questions that should be posed when critically evaluating the suitability of software for use by adult learners.

## DEVELOPING AN AGENDA

Current experiences show that the most successful implementation of computers in a learning environment puts teacher training first, consideration of the software second, and the selection of hardware that best accommodates the software, third (Williams & Williams, 1984). In a progression that places people before programs and programs before machines, it is clear that time, energy, and money must be dedicated for professional continuing education to enable adult and continuing educators to become expert in the application of CEI. In addition, the tendency for planning and acquisitions to be equipment-oriented must be abandoned, and instead curricular and student needs must dictate what hardware and courseware should be utilized.

As the use of computers in adult and continuing education expands, it is imperative that a fuller understanding of the effects of computing on educational outcomes be gained. Studies need to be undertaken to explore the relationship between learning and the alternate form of representation the computer offers. Research on student achievement needs to be initiated that considers the mode of computer use, learners' characteristics, and the design of the instructional materials before statements can be made as to the efficacy of CEI. And finally, widely acknowledged strategies for integrating microcomputers into the learning environment must be developed.

The reality is that continuing education's conception of the

CONTENT

Is the content accurate?

Is the content meaningful for adult learners?

Is the content useful?

Is there congruence between the content presented and course objectives?

Are the objectives of the program clear?

Is the content free of gender and racial bias?

INSTRUCTIONAL QUALITY

Does the program motivate and stimulate the interest of adults?

Does the program integrate adults' life experiences?

Is there provision for recording students' progress?

Do both students and teachers have access to record keeping?

Is student testing in the program appropriate and useful?

TECHNICAL QUALITY

Is help available to the user?

Are pacing and sequencing controlled by the user?

Are illogical or incorrect entries rejected?

Can the user exit from the program when desired?

Can the program be modified by the teacher?

Are the instructions clear and easy to follow?

DOCUMENTATION

Is written information provided with the program complete?

Are supplementary instructional materials available?

Does documentation include suggestions for integrating courseware into the curriculum?

Is the documentation clear and easy to use?

PROGRAM ELEMENTS

Are the following features/elements appropriate, motivating, and relevant for adults: graphics, color, feedback, sound, voice, humor, surprise, examples, and highlighted text?

Figure 15.3 Questions to be asked in evaluating the suitability of software for adult learners. *Questions are derived from items contained in a courseware evaluation form developed by L. Lewis and C. Murphy, 1987, University of Connecticut, School of Education, Storrs, CT 06268. Copies of the courseware evaluation form can be obtained by writing to the authors.*

computer is just beginning to take shape. As CEI continues to evolve, it behooves adult and continuing educators to develop expertise as facilitators of computer-enriched learning, as well as critical evaluators of the technology. "To point out the dangers of excessive reliance on the new technologies is not to reject their use but to call for discrimination and perhaps some caution in their application" (Lynton & Elman, 1987, p.131).

## REFERENCES

Berlyne, D. E. (1960) *Conflict, arousal and curiosity.* New York: McGraw-Hill.

Gillingham, M. G., & Guthrie, J. T. (1987). Relationships between CBI and research on teaching. *Contemporary Educational Psychology, 12,* 189-199.

Hagler, P., & Knowlton, J. (1987). Invalid assumption in CBI comparison research. *Journal of Computer-Based Instruction, 14*(3), 84-88.

Heermann, B. (1988). *Teaching and learning with computers.* San Francisco: Jossey-Bass.

Kulik, J. A., & Kullik, C. L. (1987). Review of recent research literature on computer-based instruction. *Contemporary Educational Psychology, 12,* 220-230.

Lynton, E. A., & Elman, S. E. (1987) *New priorities for the university: Meeting society's needs for applied knowledge and competent individuals.* San Francisco: Jossey-Bass.

Malone, T. W., & Levin, J. (1984). Microcomputers in education: Cognitive and social design principles. In F. D. Walk & R. D. Hess (Eds.) *Instructional software: Principles and perspectives for design and use.* Belmont: Wadsworth.

Siegel, M. A., & Davis, D. M. (1986). *Understanding computer-based education.* New York: Random House.

Snow, R. E., & Lohnman D. F. (1984). Toward a theory of cognitive aptitude for learning. *Journal of Educational Psychology, 76*(3), 347-76.

Suppes, P. (September, 1966) The uses of computers in education. *Scientific American,* 207-220.

Walker, D. F. (October, 1983). Reflections on the educational potential and limitations of microcomputers. *Phi Delta Kappan*, 103-107.

Williams, P., & Williams, V. (1984). *Microcomputers in elementary education: Perspectives on implementation*. Belmont: Wadsworth.

# CHAPTER 16

## Internship
SUSAN B. PREMONT

In recent years, internships have become an important instructional methodology for adult learners in training and development, continuing education administration, public service, and counseling, to name but a few career fields. Internship as a method for teaching adult learners, however, can be traced to the medical profession in the late 1800s. By the turn of the century, a few medical schools required student doctors to practice their future profession under the guidance and supervision of a qualified physician (Davies, 1962). As the medical schools recognized the value in such experiential learning, more medical degree programs adopted the concept of putting theory into practice. Later other professions, such as public administration, social work, teaching, surveying, the ministry, nursing, law, and engineering adopted a form of internship to prepare adults students for practice in their fields (Alperin, 1981; Hoppack, 1976; Davies, 1962). Today internship is widely used in many disciplines.

This chapter discusses internship as an instructional method in an academic setting. The major potential audiences for this method are described. Additionally, the advantages and limitations are analyzed from the point of view of the intern, the academic supervisor, and the sponsoring agency. The required lines of communication are detailed; also, the various duties and responsibilities of the internship participants are presented and discussed. Finally, the issues and problems concerning intern and program evaluation are reviewed. Effective and efficient evaluation methods are suggested as a means of assessing the intern's performance and estimating his potential for success in the particular career field.

## DEFINITION

The definitions and concepts of internships are as varied as the number of fields offering them. Medicine, education, ministry, law, engineering, social work, and public affairs are but a few examples of fields utilizing internships as a method of instruction. Internships are designed to "bridge the gap" between the theoretical world of academe and the "real world" of professional practice (Macala, 1986). They can be found in government agencies, nonprofit organizations, public and private corporations, and civic groups. Krush (1965) notes that they may have other names:

1. *Field study or practicum*—generally academically credited experiences required by degree programs for a particular professional training program such as teacher certification.

2. *Cooperative education (co-op)*—experiential programs, often in technical fields, which alternate academic semesters with work periods.

3. *Work-study*—a funded program in which students work on or off campus, part time during the academic year or full time during the summer.

Internships may be paid or voluntary; they may or may not involve academic credit. They can be part time or full time. The length of internships many range from a few months to a year or more. They are open to high school students, undergraduates, graduate students, and continuing education students (Stanton & Ali, 1987).

In spite of this diversity, internships have three basic characteristics in common (Simmons & Haggarty, 1980). First, they are short term; most internships range in length from a few months to a few years. They may extend for an academic year, a semester, or a summer. Second, internships offer students an opportunity to observe and work in professional work situations, not simulations. Finally, internships represent an "on the job training" or "learning by doing" experience for the student. Such professional experience may be required before professional practice, as in a medical internship, or may serve to enhance the student's employment potential.

Internships require three components: the academic institution, the sponsoring agency, and the intern (Profughi & Warren, 1984). Internships are effective only when this triad systematically plans, reassesses, and communicates work goals and expectations. In bridging the gap between the academic institution and a professional career, these three groups must continually assess the internship experience in relation to the generalization of academic subject matter.

## What an Internship Is Not

In examining internship as a method of instruction, one often hears the terms "apprenticeship" or "externship." These terms are not interchangeable. Apprenticeships, while perhaps as long in length, do not offer students intensive and extensive work experiences. Apprenticeships are intended to provide career guidance. Apprentices are given largely elementary and exploratory activities; the goal is for the students to decide whether or not they wish to pursue further education and training in a particular field. Externships, in contrast, only allow students to observe a professional in the work situation; the students do not actually work. Examples of externships include pre-student teaching observations and "shadowing" assignments where students follow and observe a competent practitioner on the job. While both apprenticeships and externships offer invaluable experience for learners, this chapter will only deal with actual work experiences designed to refine, enhance, and complete the formal academic training for professional practice—the internship.

## AUDIENCE

In utilizing internships as an instructional tool, the academic institution and the sponsoring agency must recognize the divergent audiences that will participate. Generally, interns fall into two broad categories (Griswold, 1977). The most traditional group consists of students who are nearing the end of their academic programs or who have just graduated. In "bridging the gap" to professional practice, the internship serves to synthesize for the students the academic subject matter and the practical work experience. In so doing, the internship helps the students and the advisor identify any weak areas requiring further study prior to professional practice. Secondly, the academic advisor and the sponsor can evaluate and assess each intern's potential for success within the field. This work experience provides a proving ground for the students; indications of strength or weakness often surface during this trial period. Also, the advisor and the sponsor can share ideas, analyze findings, and prepare feedback for the interns. The academic program can be supplemented or the work assignment modified to accommodate the professional development needs of the interns.

The second possible audience for internships are those students making a career change or beginning a professional career sometime after completing a formal degree program. These students are often older than the traditional intern. They may already have work experience and understand the fundamentals of other career fields. These individuals participate in an internship to be retrained for new careers in new fields or to prepare themselves for what has become a delayed entry into a first career. Rapidly changing technology, and its effect on the workplace, will result in growing numbers of people making one or more career changes during their lifetime. It is estimated that the average worker in the United States will make six career changes during a lifetime (Healy, 1982). These occupational changes may often require a practical field experience to supplement the academic preparation. These workers will recognize internships as a relevant and goal oriented part of the retraining process. Other interns will be volunteers who want a new professional career. Still others may be required by their employers to seek retraining as part of their organization's retraining program or training development process.

## ADVANTAGES

Whether the internship represents a first career experience or a career field change, it has numerous advantages for the interns, the academic institution, and the sponsoring agency. As a transition from academe to professional practice, the internship affords student interns many practical benefits. First, and foremost, the field experience is *experience* with real responsibility. In an era of limited employment, internships offer students a means of obtaining job experience. This often assists in avoiding the "no experience-no job" dilemma. Secondly, interns, by virtue of the field experience, develop a more comprehensive view of the profession. Interns who have served as continuing education administrators or social workers have a more realistic and holistic view of the career field. They have a clearer understanding of what a professional in their chosen field actually does. The typical routine of the professional is no longer abstract or theoretical; having experienced the real work situation, the interns appreciate the nature of the work they have chosen. Finally, the experience allows the interns to prove to themselves and their potential employers their ability to perform. The internship provides students with a valuable proving ground for their skills.

In the field experience, the interns also benefit from the experience of the agency sponsor. By working closely with the sponsor, interns each have a unique opportunity for extensive one-to-one guidance from an experienced professional. Working with this mentor encourages the intern to begin building professional relationships and developing a personal network of colleagues. These contacts often prove as beneficial to the intern as the actual work experience. Additionally, these daily contacts with colleagues help the sponsoring agency transmit the "culture" of the agency and the profession as a whole. The intern learns the shared values and ethics of the organization and profession. The unwritten rules of what is expected of a worker are passed on to the student. Through these contacts, the intern learns how workers are expected to behave, work, and play. The traditions, rituals, and ceremonies of the organization are passed on. Exposure to the organization's culture is a distinct benefit to the intern. Without understanding and accepting this culture, the intern has little or no chance of success with the organization or profession. Most employee failures are not due to an inability to do the job, but rather to a misinterpretation of the organization's culture (Ouchi, 1981).

Finally, the internship has certain practical advantages for the students. First, internships often provide financial aid. While the amount of money is generally not substantial, it does serve to help meet the tuition and living expenses of the students. Secondly, in many instances, students with practical field experiences receive higher starting salaries than do their contemporaries without any internship experience (Little, 1983). As positions become scarce and budgets remain limited, this added benefit of the internship will become increasingly important to students entering professional practice. Lastly, from a practical standpoint, internships give students a certain amount of control over their work experience, goals, and scheduling time. Interns are actively involved in the design of their learning experiences. The ability to control such practical factors as scheduling is extremely important for adult students (Cross, 1981).

Advantages of internships are not limited to the interns. The academic institution and the academic sponsors also receive many potential benefits. The nature of internships require the academic advisors to keep in almost daily contact with the sponsoring agency. This communication gives the professors daily contact with reality and forces them to keep up to date with the latest advances in their professional fields. The interaction with the agency also provides the advisors with feedback on the academic program. This feedback from the field provides the department with accurate and professional guidance in revising the pre-service academic training of students.

The academic institution receives additional benefits from participating in various internships. To begin with, the variety of field experiences enhances student placement (Freidson, 1973). Since job opportunities are increasingly limited, any institution welcomes the chance to improve its record of student employment. Second, internships provide the institution with much needed public relations. Successful internships offer the institution the opportunity to market its professional development programs as relevant and important to career placement or enhancement. Such good public relations also serves to improve the interface with the local community and minimize "town-gown" disputes. Active internship relationships with local agencies show the community the best side of the institution's professional development program, while highlighting the interdependence of the institution and the community. Last, and most important, internships allow the institution to reassess and revise its programs continually (Davies, 1962). The institution ultimately benefits from internships by developing exceptional programs of professional development.

The sponsoring agency also benefits from the intern program. First, the intern program provides an inexpensive vehicle for professional recruitment. The agency gets a free or inexpensive look at potential employees before making a commitment to hire them. If the agency chooses to hire an intern, it has the chance to train the individual prior to employment, once again at no or little cost to the organization (Profughi & Warren, 1984). Regardless of whether the agency is able or willing to hire the interns, the organization benefits from the "new blood" they represent. Also, the agency receives the added services and labor from the interns at little or no cost for the duration of the internship. Many organizations find this added labor pool well worth the time needed to supervise the student interns. Finally, the internship permits the sponsor the chance to fulfill the professional obligation to help train others in the field. Many educators, engineers, doctors, social workers, and government employees take great pride in assisting in the professional development and training of future practitioners in their field. The agency sponsor also has the advantage of constant access to the academic institution's ideas, theories, and often, resources in supporting the internship. These valuable professional contacts allow the agency to modify its operation and stay current in much the same way as the academic institution revises its academic program.

The internship experience offers a variety of advantages and benefits to the intern, the academic institution, and the sponsoring agency. These benefits are valuable, but not without cost.

## LIMITATIONS

In spite of the numerous advantages of internships to all parties, several limitations must be considered. The impact of these limitations and the possible strategies for their resolution or reduction depend on the role of the individuals involved. To the intern, the most commonly cited limitation is "go fer" work, that is "go for the coffee" or "go for the file" (Stanton & Ali, 1987). Often interns are given rather trivial clerical tasks. Adults who have completed academic preparation for a profession find this use of their abilities inappropriate. Some routine filing, copying, and telephone duty may actually be part of the job. If everyone in the office has to do a share of clerical work, interns should certainly be expected to do their share. Interns should not, however, become the permanent typists or phone monitors. A clear understanding of the intern's duties before the beginning of the internship will minimize this misuse of talent. Continuous communication and feedback among the intern, sponsor, and advisor will also assist in redirecting an intern's assignments should a problem occur.

Students may find that the internship seriously limits the time available for completing other university requirements. The interns should address any problems arising from the time constraints of the work situation with the academic advisor immediately. Usually, the advisor can work with the other faculty members or with the sponsor to modify or rearrange a student's work load.

Additionally, interns are often pressured into meeting production schedules. Not only does such pressure to perform get in the way of learning, the use of interns for production is totally inappropriate. Interns are working in the sponsoring agency to learn; they are not there to help the sponsoring agency meet production deadlines. Interns require much training, assistance, and guidance. Academic advisors must realistically advise potential sponsoring agencies of the amount of work that can reasonably be expected from an intern (Macala, 1986; Griswold, 1977).

Another limitation for the intern may be in the scope of the work experience. Occasionally, an intern will spend the entire program working on one project or a limited number of activities. Although there are advantages to in-depth training, the breadth of the intern's experience must not be sacrificed. Once again, an early understanding of the proposed internship assignment and close communication among the three principal parties will ensure a quality field experience.

Finally, some interns find problems with coworkers to be a serious limitation. If the sponsoring agency has a policy of "promoting from within," coworkers may view interns as a threat to their career progression. In organizations with labor problems, reductions-in-force, or other adverse personnel actions, interns may accurately be viewed as unwanted competition. In such cases, the sponsor should take the initiative in explaining the role of the intern in the organization to minimize the misunderstandings.

The academic institution also experiences several limitations in establishing, maintaining, and managing internships. First, the entire process of selecting interns, locating sponsors, and supervising the field experience, is time consuming. Faculty members are already overburdened with classes, advising, service responsibilities, and research. Additionally, internships generally do not count against the faculty member's class load. For the faculty member with several interns, this may be an unacceptable burden. Secondly, faculty members and administrators may consider the granting of academic credit for internships inappropriate. Many faculty members regard the internship experience as an unknown quantity and quality. Consistency of the various field experiences is difficult to achieve and maintain. The academic advisor must work closely with the sponsor to ensure the quality of the experience.

Finally, the institution may not have the resources to support an effective internship program in terms of personnel to arrange and supervise internships and funds to pay the necessary faculty and graduate assistants. The institution should make every effort to provide sufficient funds to support internships in professional development. Inadequate resources, overworked faculty, and minimal field supervision can do more harm than good. The institution must decide whether or not to support a practical field experience as a capstone to its academic programs; to do so requires adequate funding.

Although the sponsoring agency appears to benefit financially from hosting interns, there are also several limitations to be considered. First, interns take a lot of time! They are not "free labor." They must be trained, guided, and advised. The agency sponsor must take time away from projects to assist the intern. Granted, interns do provide the sponsor with some production. That production, however, is not without cost; the training and supervisory time of the sponsor must be considered. Before accepting interns, an organization must have the necessary personnel to help with the training. The advisor and sponsor should realistically discuss the potential time costs to the sponsoring agency.

Second, interns may not initially be able to help with any of the organization's "real" work. Not only will this reduce the interns' productivity, it will also require the sponsor to assign and monitor alternate assignments as a training tool. This consumes more of the sponsor's time.

Finally, the sponsoring agency may experience lower staff morale while hosting interns. Some staff members may view interns as a threat; others resent the "special treatment" interns receive as "guests" of the organization. These and other potential problems need not be limitations to sponsoring internships. Through effective and continuous communication between management and staff, morale problems such as these can be reduced.

### LINES OF COMMUNICATION

Many of the limitations of internships can be minimized with adequate communication. As mentioned earlier, field experiences are only effective when the internship triad (the intern, the academic advisor, and the sponsor) continuously communicates goals, ideas, and expectations to the various participants. The academic advisor must establish the foundation for these communication patterns before the internship begins. In the early stages of selecting a sponsor organization, the advisor should outline the anticipated lines of communication to be used throughout the internship. At a minimum, these lines of communication must include the following steps.

1. Several planning meetings must be scheduled for the academic advisor and the agency sponsor to establish the ground rules, review the advisor's goals for the intern, select a supervisor for the intern, and determine the scope and nature of the work assignments.

2. A final planning meeting must be held prior to the beginning of the internship involving the intern, the advisor, the representative from the agency, and the intern's immediate work supervisor.

3. Periodic meetings should take place throughout the field experience for the advisor and supervisor to reassess the work assignment. Portions of these meetings should include the intern; this is an excellent time for formative evaluation and feedback.

4. Periodic meetings should be planned for the intern and advisor to discuss goals, expectations, performance, the work situation, and other issues. These discussions should take place before, during, and after the internship. Continuous dialogue between the intern and advisor is essential to the success of the field experience.

5. Continuous discussions between the intern and supervisor/mentor are needed to ensure the maximum benefits from the internship.

6. Periodic evaluation conferences are necessary to formally assess the intern's progress and the quality of the work experience.

Internships are rarely without difficulties. Continuous, honest, and articulate dialogue among the internship participants is vital to reducing the severity of these problems. Internship failures are often attributed to the lack of sufficient communication between the intern and the supervisor or advisor.

## RESPONSIBILITIES AND DUTIES

If effective communication is the foundation for a successful internship, then the duties and responsibilities of the participants form the supporting structure. No participant in the internship is more or less important than another; the internship is only effective if all participants understand their responsibilities and successfully execute their duties.

The interns have responsibilities to themselves, their advisors and academic institution, and to their employing agency. The interns' primary responsibility is to ensure that the internship is a meaningful academic experience (Stanton & Ali, 1987). They must take the initiative in bringing problems to the attention of the supervisor or advisor. The interns must actively suggest new projects and volunteer for work that would broaden their experience. Additionally, the interns have the responsibility to ask questions and get help when needed. Frequently, the supervisor/mentor may not fully appreciate the complexity of the assignment or understand an intern's present level of performance.

In addition to active participation in the internship process, students have many responsibilities to the academic institution. First, they must always remember that they are representatives of the institution. Appropriate dress, timeliness, and professionalism are minimum requirements. The interns must remember that future internships depend on the institution's positive experience with their internships. Second, the interns must not neglect their academic requirements. All other classwork must be completed on time. Attendance at internship seminars or conferences is mandatory. If the schedule becomes more than an intern can comfortably manage, that problem should be communicated to the advisor as soon as possible.

Finally, the interns have several important responsibilities and duties to the sponsoring agency. The interns must remember that they are guests of the organization. They must always conduct themselves in a professional manner. They owe the agency their loyalty and must always maintain strict confidentiality in all work. The interns should also make every effort to remain impartial about the agency and its work. Their duty is to complete the work assignments to the best of their abilities. They must be willing to work, learn, and take the initiative.

The sponsoring agency has many important responsibilities and duties in an internship program. First, the agency must provide a supervisor-mentor for the intern. Ideally, only one person should give the intern work assignments. This supervisor's duties include making staff introductions, orienting the intern, providing a dedicated work space, answering questions, and providing performance feedback. The supervisor ideally serves as the intern's mentor, acting as a resource, guide, and helper (Griswold, 1977).

The supervisor/mentor must also schedule blocks of time to meet with the advisor and intern to plan, evaluate, and redirect the internship assignments. The success of the field experience depends on continual dialogue among the internship participants. Such communication requires dedicated time periods; effective conferences cannot be rushed and will not happen spontaneously.

During these planning and assessment sessions, the supervisor provides the advisor and intern with a suggested job description for the position, modifying the job duties, if necessary. Throughout the internship and during the scheduled meetings, the supervisor provides performance feedback. It is also important to give the advisor feedback concerning the structure and function of the program as a whole.

Finally, the organization has the responsibility to provide the resources required to support the intern in the agency. The agency is responsible for the intern's salary, if any, the cost of assigning a supervisor to assist the intern, training costs, required work facilities, and supplies for the intern's projects.

The major duties and responsibilities often remain with the academic institution. The advisor must establish the internship program, find potential sponsor agencies, and match them with potential interns. The advisor has the responsibility to ensure the high academic standards of the institution are not compromised. The duties also include scheduling all meetings with the supervisor and intern, evaluating the intern's academic work related to the internship, evaluating the field experience, and revising the program as needed. Additionally, the advisor also coordinates the internship program with other programs on the campus and actively publicizes the program and the interns' achievements.

Last, and most importantly, the advisor must allow sufficient time to oversee each intern's field experience. Frequent visits to the work site, observations, and discussions with the intern, the coworkers, and the supervisor are important to an effective internship. The advisor has the added duty of providing each intern with periodic feedback about performance, both academic and work related. Often the advisor can offer suggestions or advice concerning a project. Many times this different point of view is helpful to the intern. Finally, at the end of the internship, the advisor is responsible for the follow-up conferences with all participants. The advisor evaluates any written assignments and determines the internship grade, if one is given. Additionally, the required grade reports and other institutional reports concerning the internship must be filed.

## EVALUATION

The final success of an internship is often difficult to judge. Each of the participants may have differing points of view. The assessments of these individuals are also quite subjective. The advisor and agency supervisor will often judge the intern based on their previous experiences with other interns. Since each internship is unique, such comparisons are inappropriate and inherently unfair; yet, there is no way to avoid them. To date there is no single systematic approach to internship evaluation; many fragmented approaches are used (Honon & Day, 1984). Internship advisors typically develop their own evaluation tools and methods.

Generally, internship evaluations cover two broad areas: the work experience and the program learning objectives. Both areas should be examined by all participants in the field experience. The actual evaluation can take one of several forms. Personal interviews, questionnaires, surveys, and daily journals or diaries are merely a few possible evaluation techniques (Stanton & Ali, 1987). Ideally, the advisor should use a combination of two, such as a personal interview and a questionnaire.

Although the content of the evaluation instruments should be tailored to the individual internship, two main areas of performance must be addressed. First, the intern's work experience is assessed. This area includes the student intern's work habits, general skills and abilities, attitudes toward work and the agency, and human relations skills (Honon & Day, 1984). In the area of "work experience" many questions must be answered:

- Is the intern an independent worker?

- Did the intern persist in assigned duties?

- Did the intern seek out help if needed?

- How well did this intern interact with coworkers?

- Would the intern "fit" into this organization?

- Did the intern successfully complete assignments?

Next, the intern's learning is evaluated. Remembering that the internship is also an academic experience, it is essential that the learning objectives for the program be evaluated. Particular attention should be paid to the intern's ability to integrate theory and practice during the internship. In this area, questions which may be asked include:

- Did the internship actually serve to bridge the gap between the academic world and the work environment?

- How well did the intern apply theory to practice?

- Were all learning objectives for the field experience met?

- What new ideas, concepts, or strategies did the intern develop as a result of the experience?

- What were the intern's feelings toward the field experience as a whole?

Results from these two areas of investigation should provide the advisor with the feedback needed to revise the institution's internship program and improve the field experience for future interns.

At the conclusion of the internship, the findings from the evaluation process should be shared with all participants—the intern, the supervisor, other agency representatives, and other campus officials or faculty members involved with internships. In bringing the experience to closure, the advisor is establishing the groundwork for future interns and potential internships.

## CONCLUSION

In spite of the numerous challenges in establishing, supervising, and evaluating internships, they are an effective method of teaching adults the many complex and interrelated tasks found in today's work place. Young adults completing academic programs, as well as older adults in graduate or professional schools, generally find this methodology relevant to their needs and compatable with their abilities. Internships offer adult learners an opportunity to learn while gaining needed work experience. Through these experiential learning programs, under the auspicies of an academic institution, the interns are able to make the vital transition from theory to practice.

## REFERENCES

Alperin, S. (1981). *Careers in nursing*. Cambridge: Ballinger.

Cross, K. (1981). *Adults as learners: Increasing participation and facilitating learning*. San Francisco: Jossey-Bass.

Davies, D. (1962). *The internship in educational administration*. Wasington, D.C.: The Center for Applied Research in Education, Inc.

Freidson, E. (1973). *The professions and their prospects*. Beverly Hills: Sage.

Griswold, D. (1977). Student internship. *The Personnel Administrator, 7,* 1-4.

Healy, C. (1982). *Career development: Counseling through the life stages.* Boston: Allyn and Bacon.

Honon, J., & Day, T. (Eds.). (1984). A planning and evaluation framework for internship academic programs. In A. Balutis & J. Honon (Eds.), *Public affairs internships: Theory and practice* (pp. 31-48). Cambridge: Schenkman.

Hoppack, R. (1976). *Occupational information* (4th ed.). New York: McGraw-Hill.

Krush, H. (1965). *Apprenticeship in America.* New York: W. W. Norton & Company.

Little, T. (Ed.). (1983). *Making sponsored experiential learning standard practice.* New Directions for Experiential Learning, no. 20. San Francisco: Jossey-Bass.

Macala, J. (1986). Sponsored experiential programs—learning by doing in the work place. In L. H. Lewis (Ed.), *Experiential simulation techniques for teaching adults* (pp. 15-22). New Directions for Continuing Education, no. 30. San Francisco: Jossey-Bass.

Ouchi, W. (1981). *Theory Z.* Reading: Addison-Wesley.

Profughi, V., & Warren, E. (1984). The internship triangle. In A. Baldutis & J. Honon (Eds.), *Public affairs internships: Theory and practice* (pp. 9-28). Cambridge: Schenkman.

Simmons, P., & Haggarty, R. (Eds.). (1980). *The student guide to fellowships and internships.* New York: E. P. Dutton.

Stanton, T., & Ali, K. (1987). *The experienced hand: A student manual for making the most of an internship.* Cranston: Carroll Press.

# Chapter 17

## Correspondence Study

MICHAEL G. MOORE

Correspondence study—its history, philosophy, techniques, and what it can tell us about the adult learner—is the essential basis for understanding a historic revolution in thinking about education that is occurring in our time. This is the discovery by a significant number of educators and educational institutions of something known to correspondence educators for more than a century: adult learners can study effectively, efficiently, happily, and with great self motivation, without being in the physical presence of an instructor. As this fact becomes readily, rather than reluctantly, accepted outside correspondence education, new freedoms are opened up not only for learners but for educators and administrators. Freedom for adult learners includes the opportunity to study wherever and whenever they want, drawing on instructional and other resources of their own choosing, wherever they happen to be located. For educators and their institutions, this revolution in thinking provides opportunity to offer instruction to a significantly enlarged student body over an almost universal catchment area in a curriculum that is nearly infinite.

The term *distance education* has been coined (or to be more exact it has been borrowed from the European terms *Fernunterricht*, *TeleEnseignement*, and *Educacion a distancia*) to describe all teaching-learning arrangements in which the learner and teacher are normally separated by space and/or by time, so that communication between them is through print and writing or by electronic media such as the computer, other interactive telecommunications, broadcasts, or as is increasingly common, combinations of these media.

The International Council for Correspondence Education

(ICCE) was founded in 1938 in Vancouver, Canada. The term *distance education* and the concept of distance as a dimension of teaching and learning was introduced at the quadrennial meeting of the council in Warrenton, Virginia, in 1972 (Moore, 1972). Ten years later, again in Vancouver, the council changed its name to International Council for Distance Education (ICDE). The concept of distance as an educational term with meanings far more significant than the merely geographic has helped to place the correspondence method in relationship to other, newer communications media being employed in education. Together with the gradual improvement in correspondence course design and instruction that occurred in the 1970s, this new concept of distance education led to a renaissance of interest in both the theory and the use of the correspondence method. Although the change of the name of ICCE to ICDE reflects the increasingly multimedia nature of the contemporary field, nevertheless the majority of the more than 150 members from about fifty different countries that make up the Council use print based correspondence study as the main educational method.

## DEFINITION OF CORRESPONDENCE STUDY

Distance education is defined as all deliberate and planned learning that is directed or facilitated in a structured manner by an instructor or instructors who are separated in space and/or in time from the learners so that communication between them is through print, or electronic media, or combinations of these. Correspondence study is that form of distance education in which the learning is directed or facilitated through communications in print and in writing, although these communications might be supplemented by other media.

## INSTITUTIONS AND AUDIENCES

In the United States, the history of correspondence education goes back more than a century. Today more than 250,000 people enroll annually in correspondence courses offered by over seventy member institutions of the National University Continuing Education Association (NUCEA). Once known as the Division of Correspondence Studies, since 1968 the correspondence educators of the NUCEA have called themselves the Division of Independent Study. The largest of these correspondence programs are at Brigham Young University, University of Missouri, University of Nebraska, Indiana University, and Pennsylvania State University. About 40 percent of the enrollments are in courses that are not for university credit, including courses offered to high schools. Noncredit courses provide much needed income since virtually all university correspondence study programs are required by their parent bodies to be wholly or largely self-supporting (Markowitz, 1983). According to Markowitz, the staff of an independent study program is usually quite small. A typical institution with 3,340 new enrollments in 1981-82 had a program staff consisting of two and one-half (one share time) professionals and five office workers. In 1983 in the United States, 519 persons administered the programs of 240,488 new registrants, a ratio of 1:463.

Outside the universities, correspondence education is regulated by the National Home Study Council (NHSC). Today there are as many as 500 private schools. About three of every four students take a course from one of the 110 schools accredited by the NHSC. These include the correspondence schools of each of the armed forces, the USAF Extension Courses Institute, the Marine Corps Institute, the U.S. Coast Guard Institute, and the Army Institute. The Air Force alone enrolls some 400,000 persons annually in its correspondence programs (Savarise, 1987). The majority of courses offered outside the university are in the areas of technical and vocational skills, especially in the business areas, although the NHSC is authorized by the federal government to accredit academic degree programs from the associate's through to the master's degree. The number of students enrolled in the nonuniversity sector is difficult to estimate. It is believed there are some two million active correspondence students in the United States, with 250,000 in universities and colleges, 600,000 in the armed forces, about 400,000 in courses provided by such government departments as the U.S. Office of Personnel Management and the Agriculture Department, and 600,000 in the accredited private schools. The remainder would be found in the nonaccredited private schools (Holbrook, 1982).

Perhaps the most significant development in distance education in the United States in recent years has been the establishment of the Annenberg/CPB Project. The Annenberg /CPB Project provides funds to enable institutions to develop innovative distance education course materials that will provide higher education to people and in places that conventional programs cannot reach. Most of these courses are used by colleges and universities and are taught in their correspondence divisions as well as on campus. While all courses produced with the support of Annenberg/CPB funds feature electronic communications media, usually broadcast or taped audio or video programs, the designers of most of these courses know the critical desirability of producing a study guide. Thus the Annenberg/CPB Project has led to new thinking about the role of print in distance teaching. An increasing number of academics involved in course design are focusing on the correspondence learner. Freed from the restraints of parsimonious budgets, correspondence course designers have the opportunity and challenge of designing courses to the standards of those produced in such pace-setting foreign institutions as the British Open University. Correspondence students and their instructors are able to work with high quality instructional materials, most for the first time, and the expectations about distance education in general, and correspondence study guides and instruction in particular are rising as a consequence.

## THE METHOD: HOW IT WORKS

In all teaching there are two phases, described by Jackson (1971) as "preactive" and "interactive", equivalent to what is more commonly referred to as program design and instruction. Thinking of the conventional classroom, he explains that in the preactive phase, the teacher selects objectives and plans the curriculum and the strategies for instruction. This is done at a time and place apart from the learner; as Jackson states it," these activities—occur when the teacher is alone" (Jackson, 1971, p.7). By contrast, in the interactive phase the classroom teacher and learners meet face to face in an environment in which "the teacher's behavior is more or less spontaneous. When students are in front of him, the teacher tends to do what he feels or knows is right rather than what he reasons is right" (Jackson, 1971, p.11). While preactive teaching is deliberative, a highly rational process, interactive teaching is more spontaneous and to some extent controlled by the students' questions, requests, and reactions. Jackson refers to the interactive as the "public" phase of teaching as contrasted with the preactive or "private" phase.

This distinction helps us to understand most basic characteristic of correspondence study and other forms of distance education. This is that both the preactive, and interactive phases of teaching are conducted when teacher and learners are apart. Correspondence study is always private. There is interaction, but it is delayed by the necessity for teacher and learner to communicate through the mail or other communications device. As a result, correspondence teaching is always more rational than emotional, more controlled, and more thorough. Correspondence instruction is however based on a relationship that is not only private but is between two individuals. As Jackson (1971, p.8) says, in classroom teaching "the teacher-student dialogue is usually public rather than private." When the classroom teacher is able to have a rare private session with a student there is "a much greater sense of physical and psychological intimacy between teacher and student—than when the teacher is responding to the class as a group" (p.9). In correspondence instruction, there is of course no physical intimacy but there may be less psychological distance than in face-to-face instruction.

In correspondence instruction the preactive or program design stage is especially important. Correspondence educators plan for larger numbers of learners, for learners not yet known as individuals, and for instruction that will occur over longer periods of time than in classroom teaching. The materials prepared by course designers might be the basis for study by thousands of learners for as long as four or five years in the future. One important implication of this is the careful structuring of materials required to appeal to and assist a large and potentially very diverse learner population. Of special importance is the study guide around which the rest of the teaching materials are organized and which the student in turn will use to organize individual study.

Because the scale of use of these course materials will be so much greater than that of the classroom teacher, the correspondence institution invests—or should invest—in many more hours of course design than can be economical in classroom education. For example at the British Open University the usual practice is to employ a team of between ten and twenty persons, some of whom divide their time among courses, but most of whom work full time, for a two year period, to design one course. A single course consists of up to thirty-six correspondence study guides, associated radio and television programs, and numerous supporting materials such as set books, offprints, written assignments, and experimental kits. Since the student is expected to devote between 360 and 450 hours over a year to studying this material, the ratio of design hours to study hours approaches 50:1. This compares well with the U.S. Office of Personnnel Management's estimates of between 50 and 100 hours of course production time for each hour of instruction that use materials that are "self-contained for handoff to other instructors" (Lee & Zemke, 1987, p.78.), the nearest description to what happens in correspondence instruction.

The team approach to designing courses is a recent innovation and differs from the traditional "author-editor" arrangement that is still the most common method of course development in American correspondence education. In the latter method, the authors, usually university professors employed in conventional teaching, are contracted to write the study guides for correspondence courses in their subjects, and these guides are edited by specialist editors in the correspondence school or the university Department of Independent Study. The academics usually have no training in correspondence course design, and it is left to the editors to supplement the material with suggestions about such matters as student workload, ambiguities in objectives, and pedantry in vocabulary, as well as give assistance with such mechanics as clearing copyright, locating relevant photographs, or ordering audio-tapes or other materials to support the study guides.

This is a low-cost, under-resourced approach to course design, and for this reason, as well as the lack of faculty expertise in correspondence study and the relatively weak authority of editors, the study guides are not always as good as they should be. The Australian distance educator, Kevin Smith, provides both a summary of what is found in the typical American study guide and also some criticism of it. He writes:

> The format is somewhat stereotyped consisting mainly of printed notes or study guides written around a central textbook. The guide consists only of assignments (up to 24 exercises per semester course), and these generally structure the course content. Each lesson contains an assignment, title, an introductory section stating objectives, a read-

ing assignment, study notes and other comments from the author, self-test questions and finally a written assignment to be submitted for correction. These courses are not supported by any face-to-face contact nor are television or radio broadcast programs incorporated to the extent that they are for non-credit courses where higher fees can be charged. (Smith, 1980, p.64)

Since Smith wrote, the idea of integrating electronic media, especially audio and video tapes, into correspondence courses has gained much ground under the influence of the Annenberg/CPB Project, but course study guides have not improved very much. To make matters worse, there have been in recent years numerous distance education projects and programs, offered through television, cable, and satellite, that have **no** study guides or have study guides slim in volume and pedagogically weak even by the standards of those that Smith criticizes.

There is a practice in other countries that colored Smith's view of American practice, although the United States is gradually incorporating it. This is to design correspondence instruction as one element—albeit in the opinion of many educators the most important element—in a multimedia package. In this package those parts of the instructional message best delivered by audio or video tape, live satellite audio or video broadcast, or computer conferencing, are fully integrated with the materials delivered by print. This, of course, demands the more expensive and more sophisticated team approach to the course design process. In what has been called "the industrial form of education," there is division of labor in course design. Different academics take responsibility for their special areas of content. Educational technologists guide the design and writing of the correspondence study guides and the evaluation materials and integrate the various parts of the course. Adult learning specialists advise the team on ways the material can best be used by the potential user. Some simpler course team models have evolved. At Athabasca in Canada, for example, the team consists of one academic, one educational technologist, an editor, a visual designer, and a media consultant. This arrangement gives only one academic's perception of the content being taught, and there is likely to be some loss of breadth and perhaps depth of analysis as a result, but of course it is a far less expensive system that that of the British Open University.

A very effective compromise between the costliness of the

British system and the undermanning of the American is found in the team method used by the University of Wisconsin Extension's project to produce audio/print packages in a range of undergraduate subjects, funded by the Annenberg/CPB Project. In both the Introduction to Music and the Nutrition courses, teams of about five academics were assembled from across the nation. They worked with specialist audio producers, correspondence study guide specialists, and educational design and evaluation consultants. Unlike the British Open University teams that consist mostly of full time Open University academics and other staff, the academics and most other personnel on the Wisconsin teams worked on the basis of part-time release from their own employing organizations. In this way the project obtained the assistance of some of the leading academics and best course designers and media producers in the country. In addition the cost was substantially lower than for other course teams of comparable size and academic distinction.


## THE STUDY GUIDE

As noted, correspondence education course design is a long process that results in one or more types of teaching materials. One is essential, however, and that is the printed study guide. The study guides vary according to the practices of different institutions and even within institutions, but there are some essential characteristics.

First, the study guide provides a body of knowledge . . . a body of information. Everything that an instructor would want to say in describing, explicating, analyzing, and discussing the topic is written out so that it can be presented to the learner in print rather than orally. The study guide should *not* resemble a textbook, nor should it try to replace a text. Just as the teacher in face-to-face teaching methods makes comments on the text, augments it, and develops a curriculum around it, so the study guide provides the academic's commentary on a text and perhaps on other resources also. The study guide must present the subject as the correspondence teacher or team sees it.

It is essential that the study guide do more than merely present subject matter. Although it must contain directions and guidance for the students, it may be fairly informal and quite personal. In it the instructors can state their goals and objectives, their general approach, and philosophy about the subject. They can give opinions and advice concerning pathways through the subject. As every teacher knows, the logical order or structure in the content area in any field is not necessarily the appropriate psychological order for its study. Textbooks are invariably designed to comply with the logic and structure of the discipline. The author of the study guide must break free from the structure of the content and text and construct devices and techniques to help the student master the content.

A common failure of much that claims to be distance education, including many correspondence study guides, is the failure to structure sufficient opportunity for learner activity. Just as nobody ever learned to play tennis from just watching the game on television, the correspondence student will not learn from simply reading the ideas of the course writers. Correspondence study is not more passive than any other form of learning. The learner must be given opportunity to apply and practice and must have chances to review, to reflect on, and to criticize, what is presented. This means the study guide must be packed with self-testing exercises, with projects, and with white space for the student to enter personal comments. Frequent self-tests provide the learner with a means of learning, with a form of self-pacing, and perhaps most important, with a self-motivating device.

The study guide serves not only as a vehicle for the learner's self-testing, giving feedback about the extent of understanding of the course, but also gives the instructor evidence of progress or difficulty. The latter is a major purpose of the written assignments. These might be contained in the study guide, but more likely will be revised frequently and therefore sent to students in an ancillary package.

The writers of the study guide need to look to other means of supporting the student's self-motivation. For example, long passages of prose that might be acceptable in a textbook should be broken to give the learner a sense of progress. The heaviness of print can be lightened by use of photographs and cartoons, and perhaps most usefully by the frequent opportunity to engage in some form of activity. "Reflect," "List," "Answer the following question," and "Write a few personal observations" are typical and essential phrases to help keep the student's interest and motivation. A style of writing that communicates the course team's concern for the student is important too. The writer's personality should be expressed where appropriate, and an understanding and encouraging tone should be evident. The style of writing one would expect of an academic text is *not* the style appropriate to teaching through print in distance education.

## INSTRUCTION: THE PHASE OF INTERACTION.

The skills required for course design and for instruction are very different, and since the numbers of students expected in a correspondence course can be very large, it is no longer common for courses to be both designed and taught by the same teacher. In correspondence instruction, *the preactive and interactive phases of instruction are usually the work of different people.*

While the responsibility of the academic in the course team is to be a resource for authoritative knowledge in the subject area, and the responsibility of the educational design specialists is to ensure the distance teaching package is the vehicle for providing the information together with guidance on its use, the correspondence instructor is the person who brings the course alive for particular individuals. The study guide and other materials are prepared for an anonymous, mass readership. In the hands of the instructor these materials become the medium of learning for each individual learner. It has even been argued that a course is *not* a course until it is engaged in by a student (Thorpe, 1979). A centrally produced package is not itself a course; the correspondence course can be considered the *process* of the learner's interaction with the materials through the instructor. Thus it will be seen, correspondence education has two equally important parts. To balance the course design and production process, the system must have an equally sophisticated process of instruction and learner support.

Distance education procedures vary among institutions, but the following chronology of events may be representative. First, the instructor is given a list of new registrants by the teaching institution and students are provided with the names of their instructors. Each instructor should have no more students than can be monitored and related to on a personal basis. Next, the students might receive a written or telephoned greeting from the instructor. When the students receive the study materials, the work will be divided into lessons or units. Each unit will be followed by the requirement to write a paper, essay, quiz, project, or some other assignment for submission to the instructor. In all correspondence courses the first assignment is the most critical. Among adult learners in particular there is an initial reluctance to expose one's feared ignorance to an unknown, equally feared judge. The student is likely not to understand at this early stage that the main purpose of the assignment is not evaluative, though to the teaching institution that might be an important secondary purpose. The main purpose of the written assignment should be to provide a basis for interaction between the instructor and the student. After studying the course materials, and after showing what is understood, the student is ready for the instructor's response. One of the main predictors of completion of a correspondence course is the completion of the first assignment. The student has to take the first step in order to have any chance of proceeding to the end of the course. Obviously, the instructor's response to the assignment—and to all assignments—-is crucially important. While there should be honest and solid criticism, it is vital that the instructor does nothing to deter or discourage the student at this stage. Style is all important. A criticism that can be communicated in a devastatingly destructive manner can also be transmitted in a friendly and encouraging manner by the use of such phrases as, "I see what you are trying to say here, but don't you think the following might be a better interpretation?" or "You haven't got this quite right, though you did much better with the exercise above it; here is the right answer." Some correspondence schools expect instructors to carry excessive student loads, and this is counterproductive. The instructor needs enough time to consider what each student writes, to make a comment on a substantial number of points in each assignment, and to do all this in a sensitive and friendly style. At major institutions, instructors receive training in their instructional techniques, and their written remarks to students are monitored to ensure that instructional standards are maintained. The instructor usually has to return a grade on each student's work and, as has been discussed, to use the student's writing as a trigger for further instruction. This might take the form of questions for the learner's further consideration, a correction of a misunderstanding, an alternative view, or suggestions for further reading or

other study. The instructor has to be thoroughly knowledgeable
about all aspects of the media package, but may also be critical and
independent of it. Specific references to particular passages in the
text are a valuable and economical way of expanding advice to the
student, but at the same time the student must be helped to develop
a critical view on the course material. It is particularly challenging
for the correspondence instructor to engage the student in debate,
controversy, and even disagreement for, as has been explained, comments need to be very carefully phrased since the opportunity for
added explanation is not available, and it is essential to do everything to prevent demoralization.

## CORRESPONDENCE LEARNERS AND STUDENT SUPPORT SERVICES

Correspondence learners are people for whom structured
learning is an important but nevertheless a secondary demand on
their time and energies. For them, study is usually subordinate to
family, work and perhaps community and social responsibilities.
Correspondence students study an almost infinite range of academic, vocational, professional and leisure subjects, but they have
a common need for their instruction and their learning to be integrated with work, family, and other concerns. They are invariable
people who are self-motivated and whose interest in learning is not
as a social event, but nearly always has a practical intent. They are
people who learn for their own purposes and who do not need close
personal relationships with an instructor or other learners to learn.
In other words the appropriate audience for the correspondence
method is the typical adult learner.

### Open Admissions and the Dropout Rate

By its very nature access to correspondence education is more
open than access to conventional education. In fact, 70 percent of
university level correspondence programs in the United States and
Canada have no educational prerequisites for admission (Hegel,
1981). Courses offered by nonmilitary NHSC institutions are open
to all.

A regrettable consequence of open admissions has been the

phenomenon of the dropout that has concerned correspondence educators for many years. One of the most alarming reports was the discovery in the 1950s that the dropout rate at the United States Armed Forces Institute, then the world's largest correspondence institution with 300,000 students, was about 90 percent. Several research programs have been established that are aimed at identifying the characteristics of these dropouts, learning their reasons for withdrawal, and recommending strategies for alleviating the problem. There emerged a consensus as long ago as the 1950s that dropout rates would be reduced by much enhanced learner support systems. Correspondence learners would receive counseling at the time of entry to instruction and throughout their student careers, but especially when they were faced with the requirement to submit written assignments.

Nearly thirty years later Woodley and Parlett (1983) reviewed the international research regarding dropouts. While allowances must be made for differences in the ways that institutions measure retention, they found that at Athabasca, 58 percent of persons who submitted the first assignment completed the entire course, and in Vancouver's Open Learning Institute 68 percent did so. In the United States, 60 percent of persons enrolling in courses of NUCEA member institutions completed. In Norway at the NKI School, which offers technical and vocational courses, between 65 percent and 80 percent of enrollees completed at least one course. At the British Open University, 71 percent of students who registered completed their yearlong course. While it would be dangerous to generalize without many reservations, there is some evidence that the majority of adult learners who commit themselves to the extent of completing one correspondence course assignment are likely to complete the course.

## Why do Students Drop Out?

In a study of Open University students, Murgatroyd (1982) found more than half experienced difficulties with planning and organizing their time. Also high on the list of student problems is the tension that exists between the demands of part-time study and those of family and friends. A third source of discouragement arises from students' unrealistic expectations of the work-related rewards that might follow study, leading them to drop out when hoped-for promotions, for example, do not materialize. Woodley and Parlett (1983) attribute dropout to a range of factors classified as course factors, study environment factors, motivational factors, and other factors. Students are likely to abandon a course that is badly designed. They give up in response to such environmental factors as illness, change in marital status, moving home, or changing jobs. Motivational factors include withdrawal when personal goals have been achieved, and other factors include such accidents as turning up for the wrong examination or registering for the wrong course.

## STUDENT SUPPORT

Dealing with the threat of dropout is the responsibility of the correspondence institution's student support service. This might be no more than an 800 number giving access by telephone to one or two full time counselors in the Independent Study Division of the university, or it might consist of the multimillion dollar subsystem at the Open University that employs more than 50 senior counselors and several thousand part-time counselors. The student support system provides the safety net that accounts for much of the success of so many otherwise educationally vulnerable adults. In the Open University system every student is on a counselor's case load of about fifty students. The counselors monitor their students' performance, telephone and write, and when necessary visit them in their homes. They maintain their association throughout the students' six or more years of study, and so develop a personal understanding that stands in good stead when crises that might otherwise lead to dropout occur. In most institutions instructors are expected to recognize symptoms of student problems and to treat them. They might have to respond on the basis of common sense or might be given special training in counseling distant learners. One of the better American organizational models of counseling adult part-time learners was the University of Wisconsin's Community Based Educational Counseling Service that maintained some twenty-three counselors in public libraries, courthouses, and extension offices in different parts of the state. In some Australian universities, graduates of the program are employed as itinerant counselors while in Canada's North Island College a mobile counseling team works out of a motor home.

## EVALUATION

The number and range of evaluation studies in correspondence study are enormous. At the most global level are attempts to gather data regarding to value, quality, or impact of whole systems. Correspondence and other distance education systems can be evaluated against criteria that are special just as their goals are special. These include the extent to which there is increased equality of opportunity for learning, the extent to which there is increased access for home-based learners, the quality of academic programs offered, the extent to which learners achieve their goals, whether these goals coincide with institutional goals or not, and the impact of distance education on the community in general and on other educational institutions (Gooler, 1979). Among the best documented evaluations of this kind are those of cost effectiveness. For example, evaluations of the Open Universities in Britain, Athabasca, and Costa Rica show that these systems are very cost efficient when compared with traditional higher education (Rumble, 1981).

Another macro-level evaluation topic—one with a long history—is that of student survival and dropout. As was indicated earlier in this chapter, research in various universities in this country and abroad has led to the conclusion that high dropout rates are a consequence of an extremely complex mixture of causes but can be substantially reduced by investment in student support systems. As a result of this and other measures, contemporary completion rates are in the range of 60 to 70 percent.

Evaluation of the internal operations of the correspondence based institution focuses on such subsystems as course design, production and distribution of course materials, admission of students, counseling, instruction, and assessment procedures. Reports of such evaluations are available from independent study divisions and from evaluation and research departments such as the Institute of Educational Technology at the British Open University.

In Australia and France it is common for students to take the same course from the same teacher through either correspondence based or face-to-face instruction. The experience of both the French National Centre for Teaching by Correspondence and the Australian universities is that there is no difference in the effectiveness of the two forms of teaching. One of the first attempts to compare the two approaches was reported in 1928. Although another study was done as recently as 1982, the issue seems to have been settled to the satisfaction of the correspondence educators nearly forty years ago when Childs (1949) reviewed the research on the relative achievement of students in classroom situations and students in correspondence and showed that there was no difference. Following on Dubin and Taveggia's landmark study that concluded that "no method of teaching is measurably to be preferred over another when evaluated by student performance" (Dubin and Taveggia, 1968), evaluation research has tended to concentrate more on identifying the characteristics of successful correspondence programs and also on the characteristics of successful learners as well as those that do less well in the method. The most recent of this type of study has been Coggins (1988) who investigated the effect of learning styles on completion in correspondence based external degree programs.

Perhaps there is need for replication of studies that demonstrate that the correspondence method is as effective as face-to-face education, but in the minds of the millions of people, including academics, that teach and learn in the method the question is irrelevant. Obviously the method works well for many and not as well for others. The important evaluation questions concern ways of making the method work better for everyone.

## ADVANTAGES OF THE METHOD

Correspondence study provides educational opportunity regardless of the student's geographic location or study schedule. Correspondence study permits learning to be integrated with work, family, social, and community responsibilities. Formal learning does not have to be crammed into specific years of schooling; correspondence education can be provided as learning needs arise in the course of personal development through the adult years. It is therefore an ideal method for continuing, lifelong education. Correspondence study gives students a greater degree of control of the study processes, so they can select approaches consistent with their own learning styles. By removing time pressures this method encourages reflective thinking. It stimulates creativity by removing the pressures of the peer group and the intimidating presence of the authority figure of the teacher that inhibits many from taking intellectual risks in the classroom. Correspondence study has the potential of providing instruction of higher quality than is available to adult learners generally. Apart from reasons already mentioned, this is because the expertise of the world's greatest authorities can be accessed by the correspondence student, who could never hope to study with such people face to face. In addition, the knowledge of these experts can be presented in a structure that makes the information more amenable for the learner than the expert is able to provide without the human, media, and other resources of the distance education institution. Since large student populations can be expected, large investments of time and money can be made, meaning that more expertise and more careful instruction is available to the correspondence learner than to any student enrolled with a single professor. In the instructional phase the correspondence student has the undivided attention of the instructor, and so correspondence study allows for individualization of instruction, especially when compared with other forms of distance education such as educational television or even teleconferencing. Being a medium of the printed and written word, correspondence study is particularly suited to the study of complex and abstract topics that the learner needs to process more thoughtfully and for longer than is possible when instruction is given by audio or video media or lecture. Since there are valid educational reasons for immediate, spontaneous, and emotional interactions as well as the more rational delayed interactions of the correspondence method, it is preferable for correspondence study to be integrated with methods that use other technologies to benefit for the special nature of each.

## LIMITATIONS OF THE METHOD.

The correspondence method has no more limitations than other methods of education, though it does have different limitations than those common to face-to-face instruction. On the side of the learner, it would seem that the ability to read and write would be an essential prerequisite. Still, successful correspondence pro-

grams for illiterate farmers in third world countries have been developed in which communication has been primarily through
drawings, reinforced by literate village leaders supplied with study
guides written at a very basic level. The limitation of language on
study by correspondence is that there should be *appropriate match-
ing* of the program's language and the reading and writing level of
the learners. If the language is at the correct level, most people, if
they have the motivation, can learn by correspondence. Motivation
is a more critical variable limiting the success of the method. The
power of the instructor to drive or cajole the learner into completion
and to success is more limited in this as in all forms of distance
education and, as has been seen, the adults who study by correspondence have many distracting claims on their time. However for
adult learners who have the appropriate level of literacy and who
are fully self-motivated, the main limitations of correspondence
study do not come from the method itself. The main limitation is
that there are too many inferior courses and too much mediocre
instruction. Study guides are often prepared too cheaply and too
quickly, and as a result are unattractive, uninteresting, and often
give only the minimum of guidance. Instructors have excessive numbers to teach or are paid too poorly for them to give enough time
to their correspondence teaching. Too many correspondence
courses are delivered by print alone with little or no integration
with teleconference, broadcast, or taped media. Training of course
designers and instructors as well as supervision and monitoring of
instructors is often minimal. So are the support services made available to students. These shortcomings are not limitations of the correspondence method, or of the personnel, usually underpaid,
overworked, and undervalued. These limitations derive from a
chronic underinvestment on the part of educational and other organizations. For the correspondence method to live up to its potential, it should be integrated into multimedia delivery systems.
The development of such systems will require educational institutions to change their policies regarding to distribution of teaching
resources between distance education and education based on the
classroom. The limitations of the correspondence method are the
result of the failure of policy makers to recognize the potential of
distance education, their failure to initiate policies that would empower their correspondence specialists to develop that potential,

and their failure to invest in the personnel and the technologies that could realize that potential.

## CONCLUSION

The situation is changing. The time has passed when distance education was an idea and practice of interest only to innovators. Now a substantial number of practitioners and decision makers in the educational mainstream are involved. For example, nearly half the Fortune 500 corporations use some form of distance education in their corporate training; the armed forces continue to plan and develop new delivery systems, especially using the microcomputer; there are visionaries who plan global universities. These trends indicate that in the future there will be few adult education administrators or practitioners who will not have to make curricular, instructional, or administrative decisions requiring an understanding of distance education. They will be wise to obtain a familiarity with correspondence study, not only because it is likely to remain a dominant method in distance education. Equally important, its hundred year history and universal experience provide a wealth of understanding about distance learners and about the techniques of teaching them, whether the particular communication medium employed is the latest electronic technology or more old-fashioned, and sometimes more reliable, print.

## REFERENCES

Childs, G. B. (1949). *Comparison of supervised correspondence pupils and classroom pupils in achievement*. Unpublish doctoral dissertation, University of Nebraska, Lincoln, NE.

Coggins, C. (1988). Preferred learning styles and their impact on completion of external degree programs. *The American Journal of Distance Education, 2* (1), 25-37.

Dubin, R., & Taveggia, T. (1969). *The teaching-learning paradox*. Eugene: University of Oregon Center for the Advanced Study of Educational Administration, p.33.

Gooler, D. D. (1979). Evaluating distance education programs. *Canadian Journal of University Continuing Education, 6* (1), 43-45.

Hegel, E. J. (1981). *Survey of policies in university level correspondence programs in Canada and the United States of America.* Mimeographed. Saskatoon, Saskatchewan: University of Saskatchewan. Quoted in Feasley, C. (1983). *Serving learners at a distance: a guide to program practices.* ASHE-ERIC Higher Education Research Report (no.5).

Holbrook, D. (1982). Accreditation, a workable option. In J. S. Daniel, M. A. Stroud, & J. R. Thompson (Eds.), *Learning at a distance* (pp. 204-206). Edmonton: Athabasca University.

Jackson, P. W. (1971). The way teaching is. In R. Hyman (Ed.), *Contemporary thought on teaching* (pp. 6-12). Englewood Cliffs: Prentice-Hall.

Ludlow, N. (1987). Speaking personally with Michael P. Lambert. *The American Journal of Distance Education, 1* (2), 67-71.

Lee, C., & Zemke, R. (1987). How long does it take? *Training,* (June), 75-80.

Markowitz, H., Jr. (1983). *Independent study in 1982: National University Continuing Education Association Independent Study Programs.* Gainsville, Fla.: Independent Study Program, University of Florida. (ERIC Document Reproduction Service No. ED 227 801).

Moore, M. G. (1972). Learner autonomy: The second dimension of independent study. *Convergence, 5* (2), 76-88.

Moore, M. G., Fiss, J., & Takemoto, P. (1988). *Nutrition today. A formative evaluation to determine the effectiveness of course materials.* Madison: University of Wisconsin Extension.

Murgatroyd, S. (1982). Student learning difficulties and the role of regional support services. *Teaching at a distance institutional research review* (Report No 1). Milton Keynes, U.K.: The Open University.

Rumble, G. (1981). Evaluation autonomous multi-media distance learning systems: A practical approach. *Distance Education,* 2(1), 64-90.

Savarise, P. (1987). Speaking personally with W. A. Wojciechowski. *The American Journal of Distance Education, 1* (3), 67-71.

Smith, K. C. (1980). Course development procedures. *Distance Education, 1,* 61-67.

Thompson, C., & Jensen, D. (1977). *Community based educational counseling for adults*. Madison: University of Wisconsin.

Thorpe, M. (1979). When is a course not a course? *Teaching at a Distance, 16,* 13-18.

Woodley, A., & Parlett, M. (1983). Student drop-out. *Teaching at a Distance, 24,* 2-23.

# CHAPTER 18

## Communications Technology in Adult Education and Learning

BARBARA M. FLORINI

Newer communications technology, which includes various forms of video, audio, telecommunications, and computer technologies, is transforming education. Dropping costs, improved ease of use, and growing recognition of its potential in education are accelerating the diffusion of the technology. Like other divisions of education, our field faces the challenge of understanding, responding to, and directing the changes that communications technology makes possible in adult education.

The challenge of communications technology is both personal and professional. Individually, we need to learn to use various forms of communications technology. Some skill in using the different forms fosters understanding of their strengths, limitations, and implications. As professionals, we are obliged to identify and interpret the social, economic, and political implications of communications technology as these implications have relevance for our field. By identifying and interpreting the implications of communications technology, we will be better able to respond to it and provide direction regarding its role in adult education.

At the same time that the technology challenges us, it also offers new opportunities. We can use communications technology to reach out to rural and homebound populations in new ways, to meet varied learning needs, to help manage our programs and agencies, and to invigorate our program offerings. The purpose here is to provide some perspective on the opportunities and challenges that today's communications technology presents to adult education. As the word *perspective* suggests, the chapter broadly surveys aspects of communications technology in relation to adult education and learning. This chapter has four objectives:

- To provide an overview of the newer communications technology relevant for use in adult education

- To discuss practical approaches for adopting the technology

- To identify some of the barriers to adopting the technology and to suggest ways for overcoming them

- To highlight some of the general applications of communications technology in adult education and learning

## OVERVIEW OF COMMUNICATIONS TECHNOLOGY

This section briefly reviews different forms of communications technology that are especially promising for use in adult education and learning. Following the review, the section illustrates some of the ways in which the separate technologies can be combined. These various combinations effectively produce new technologies whose capabilities exceed those of the individual components. The section concludes with a discussion of both the implications and the advantages and limitations of communications technologies in relation to adult education and learning.

### Computers

The award for the most startling of the technologies goes to computers. In less than a decade they have become essential and increasingly friendly tools in our daily environment. In 1979 most of us were asking, "What would I ever do with a computer?" In 1990 more of us are asking, "How do you expect me to do my job without a computer?" Although the biggest growth in computer use is work-related, a growing number of people are making personal use of computers. Activities range from tax preparation to entertainment to self-directed learning projects. Computers also have an expanded role at all levels of education. Various computer applications of special interest for adult education and learning are introduced later.

Along with computers, other forms of communications technology also have been evolving. Perhaps because of their greater familiarity, the dramatic advances in video, audio, telecommunications, and information storage technology have been greeted with less fanfare by the public and more readily accepted by people in general.

## Video Technology

As Donnelly (1986) points out, our video options have been proliferating in terms of choice of programs and viewing times. For example, not too long ago, video was available to us only through broadcast television. One-way signal transmission was the norm as far as the public was concerned. That is, a message originated from a broadcast site and was distributed to various receivers. Methods for transmitting video signals have expanded. Cable, satellite, and microwave relay transmissions have joined broadcast television as vehicles for sending video signals. As a result, competition has increased in the television arena, more people have a greater variety of viewing choices, and two-way signal transmission capabilities have added a new dimension to the role video can play in education.

Video tape offers viewers another new option. Until recently, we had to view video programs when others chose to make them available to us. Now we can use video tape to record and store information and to retrieve it when we wish. Many people also have ready access to video tape rentals and purchases.

In addition to having greater choices as to what we view and when we view video programs, we have opportunities to create video programs, too. Possibilities vary throughout the country. In some communities, people can use local cable TV facilities to originate programs. Elsewhere, different educational institutions have installed their own sophisticated video production and distribution systems that are available, under varying conditions, to faculty, students, and staffs. Also, institutions and individuals are purchasing easy-to-use video cameras and editors to purse community, educational, and personal activities.

## Audio Technology

Radio, one of the older of the "high tech" communications technologies, is readily available to us in our cars, as we jog, on the beach, at home, or virtually anywhere we choose to have it.

Unlike what has happened in some other countries, educators in the United States have made little formal use of radio. Perhaps we need to take a fresh look at the role this technology could play in adult education.

Audio tape, on the other hand, continues to be used widely for formal and informal educational purposes as well as for entertainment. We can purchase tapes covering diverse topics or make our own with easily used, inexpensive equipment. Like radios, cassette players readily go wherever we choose to take them: Nervous airline passengers listen to their relaxation tapes; commuters study foreign languages or effective management principles while driving to work; cross-country drivers listen to novels. One of the newer audio technologies, the compact disc, was promptly accepted by the public. But compact discs are not limited to storing sound. In the format known as CD-ROM (compact disc read-only memory), this new medium, along with videodiscs, extends our capabilities for storing various kinds of information.

## New Forms for Information Storage

Videodiscs and CD-ROMs, both of which are based on optical disc technology, are among the most exciting products accompanying the evolution of communications technology. CD-ROMs and videodiscs are capable of storing extensive amounts of information in various forms. Because information is encoded differently on the two types of discs, their capabilities somewhat vary at the present time.

CD-ROMs, for instance, can store printed text (up to 150,000 pages), sound, and images. Videodiscs, which also have audio capability, can contain 54,000 separate frames of text or graphic information. From another perspective, the videodisc contains up to thirty minutes of motion playing time. Information stored on either CD-ROMs or videodiscs can be retrieved within seconds. The storage and retrieval capabilities of these two formats, used in conjunction with different communications technologies, have implications for use in adult education and learning as we shall shortly see.

## Combinations of Technologies

Alone, each set of the technologies mentioned above provides powerful communications tools. The fact that they can be variously combined increases their potential exponentially. For example, yesterday's telecommunications for most of us meant talking to one other person on the telephone. Today's telecommunications options of special interest for education include computer networks, facsimile or fax machines (long distance versions of the office copy machine), and group conferencing opportunities. The following examples help illustrate how combining some of the technologies enhances their power.

Through various computer networks, people in many parts of the world are able to use their computers to exchange information with astonishing ease, convenience, and speed. This computer-mediated exchange is commonly called e-mail. With the use of telecommunications and fax machines, replicas of documents can be sent anywhere in the world. In this case, the copy simply appears many miles removed from the originating site. In addition, telecommunications, along with other technologies, provide conferencing options that allow people at different locations to communicate with each other almost as though they were at the same place.

Audio conferencing, for example, allows either individuals or groups of people at different locations to participate in the same telephone conversation. Similarly, computer conferencing lets people use their computers and telecommunication capabilities to join in group discussions or to communicate individually. Video conferencing facilitates group communication by providing visual as well as audio linkages among people at different sites.

Other combinations of technologies are equally exciting and powerful, especially those involving the use of optical discs. For instance, a personal computer plus a videodisc player and monitor plus some peripheral items adds up to a computer-assisted interactive video (CAIV) system. CD-ROMs can also be used in conjunction with computers. Compact disc drives that plug into some microcomputers are available today. A bit costly now, over the next few years the drives will become cheaper and the variety of material on discs will grow. The versatility of computers combined with the vast storage capacity of the optical discs has significance for a variety of applications, including instruction. The instructional potential of computer and optical disc technology will be discussed later.

## Implications of Communications Technology

Everything described thus far is here-and-now technology. In general, education has already experienced some of the effects of the dramatic emergence and convergence of communications technology (Hirschen 1987; Stahmer & Helm 1987). Continual growth in the use of communications technology in education is virtually guaranteed, the field of adult education not excepted. The newer forms of communications technology have already changed the ways we work, use our leisure time, communicate with others, view our society, and conduct our governance (Brand, 1987; Donnelly, 1986). Dropping costs and improved ease of use are accelerating the diffusion of the technology.

With this diffusion, adult learners have new options that are significant for adult learning programs. The following suggests just a few of the options. For example, in addition to providing home entertainment, the ubiquitous video tape offers home instruction ranging from physical exercise to home repair to effective sales techniques. What will be the effect of this on some informal and continuing education programs? To look at another home option, commercial services now provide electronic access to enormous quantities of data and bibliographic information. Users of the services can read the information on-line or order paper copies of the material. There also are often opportunities to seek information from other users of the services. With these alternatives, will self-directed learners become still more self-directed and begin by-passing traditional adult learning programs that have typically been their sources for information?

One final example illustrates another option learners can pursue from home. Communications technology makes distance learning more attractive because students can interact with each other as well as with the instructor. Students can participate from anywhere as long as they have the technological means to do so. Some institutions are already in the distance education market with degree programs and course offerings delivered through some form of advanced communications technology. By employing the technology, institutions can leapfrog local, state, or even national boundaries. What will be the effect of this new competition on more conventional adult learning programs?

In light of new learner options, one challenge adult education agencies face is that of reexamining what programs they offer and how they deliver them. Another challenge is to weigh the possible consequences to their programs of competition from new sources. A third challenge is to determine what role they want some of the newer technologies to play for them.

*Advantages and Limitations of Communications Technology*

Specific advantages and limitations of the various kinds of communications technology are particular to each type. In general, the technology can help us enrich the quality and variety of learning programs, reach out to people who have little or no other way of participating in adult learning experiences, provide alternative forms of instruction, and improve the operation of our own agencies. General limitations or barriers to using communications technology in adult education include lack of money, resistance to adopting the technology, lack of uniform availability of specific technologies, lack of skill and knowledge in using them, the continuing rapid changes taking place in communications technology, and the sheer variety of options. In light of the implications of communications technology and the opportunities it offers adult education, it is worth an effort to find ways to address these limitations. The following two sections suggest some approaches for doing so.

## PRACTICAL APPROACHES
## TO COMMUNICATIONS TECHNOLOGY

This section focuses on practical approaches for selecting among the many options offered by communications technology. Practitioners and scholars in the field of educational communications and technology have long been concerned with practical approaches in using communications technology, overcoming barriers to its adoption, and investigating its role in education. Much of the following discussion is drawn from the common knowledge that has grown out of these concerns.

Which of the myriad forms and combinations of communications technology is most relevant for adult education? For a particular agency? Neither question has a straightforward answer. No single agency has the resources to embrace all forms of communications technology in one fell swoop. Nor would doing so be a sensible expenditure of resources.

While acknowledging the potential of communications technology in adult learning, we must admit that we are not entirely sure how to make effective use of it. Effective use of communications technology implies that appropriate technology has been selected to solve a problem in a cost-effective and humanly sensitive manner. But what determines "appropriate technology"? Which factors relate to "cost-effectiveness"? How do you help ensure that communications technology is used in a "humanly sensitive manner"?

No one answer covers all situations, but planning is the common denominator for answering the questions in each situation. The important variables are 1) planning in the context of a specific problem, 2) selecting appropriate technology to solve the problem, 3) judging the cost-effectiveness of the solution, and 4) weighing the significant human issues in the situation.

*Planning in Context*

People involved with adult education know that planning makes good decision-making possible. We use planning to design, implement, and maintain programs as well as to establish and improve adult education agencies. Planning initially helps us clarify why we are doing something, what we will do, and how we will go about it. The result is clearly identified problems, accurate assessments of needs and of the situation, well-articulated goals and objectives, a sense of future direction, and thoughtful implementation of the solution to the immediate problem.

Planning is also the key to solving a problem with appropriate and effective technology. Without a planned role, technology becomes the often described "solution in search of a problem." Before selecting any technology, it is important to have a well-defined problem and clearly stated objectives. When we have reached the point in our planning process of asking, "How can we meet these objectives in this context?" we are ready to consider selecting appropriate technology.

*Selecting Appropriate Technology*

The appropriate technology to use in any situation is the simplest, most cost-effective technology that lets us reach our goal. Although this chapter focuses on the newer communications technologies, we need to remember that old standbys like print materials or audio tapes are still often the technology of choice. Three factors are important in selecting a suitable technology: its characteristics, the context in which it will be used, and its availability.

Considering the specific characteristics of media helps identify suitable technologies for use in a particular situation. For what we want to do now and in the foreseeable future are features like color, sound, rapid access to stored information, motion, interactive or real-time capabilities, large storage capacity, or graphics necessary? Are other characteristics needed? The answer to these questions often identifies several alternative forms of technology that could meet our needs.

In evaluating alternative forms for use in a given situation, we should ask ourselves some general questions:

1. Which technology would add the most value to what we want to do? For example, does it increase the numbers of learners who can be reached? Or, will it help our agency turn out higher-quality proposals more quickly?

2. Can the technology meet additional present or future needs?

3. Is expertise in using the technology readily available?

4. Which technology would make the best use of existing resources?

5. Which fits in best with what we are now doing?

6. Is the technology readily available to all who would need to use it?

Answering these questions will again reduce the number of technological alternatives.

A look at the technology at hand further narrows the range of alternatives. What is locally available? Will the technology meet current needs without imposing unreasonable compromises? A particular technology should not be chosen just because it is locally available, but there are several advantages to using it when it is suitable. Aside from saving new investment costs, using available technology saves the time and training costs associated with the introduction of new technology. Also, needed support systems are already in place, and the logistics of using the technology have been worked out.

Few of us have the knowledge to answer fully all the questions raised above. But by defining our desired outcomes and assessing our particular situation, we make it easier for others to help us answer the questions. The questioning process serves to narrow the range of technology appropriate for use in a particular situation.

The next step is to consider which of the remaining technological alternatives is the most cost-effective.

## Determining Cost-Effective Technology

Use of technology can be highly cost-effective if it improves productivity, reaches new populations, or increases available options. Determining cost-effectiveness is very dependent on situational variables. For example, in an instructional context variables of concern frequently include 1) numbers of students, 2) their location, 3) the significance of reaching the students, 4) the frequency of the offering, 5) student safety, 6) the value use of the technology adds to the learning opportunity, 7) availability and condition of equipment, 8) staffing requirements, 9) compatibility with existing equipment, and 10) the cost of acquiring, operating, maintaining, and replacing equipment. Other contexts have somewhat different variables. Identifying them is a first step in determining the cost-effectiveness of using a technology in a given situation.

## Weighing Human Concerns

Having reached defensible positions regarding cost-effectiveness and appropriateness through our planning activities, we still need to think about and respond to other issues. If electronic technology is to be used to deliver instruction, factors like learners' reactions to the introduction of technology, their access to the technology, and their ability to use it become important. If technology is to be introduced to help manage an adult education agency, then issues like staff training, physical comfort, and attitudes of personnel become important. Human issues will seldom impede the use of communications technology if they are addressed during the planning, adoption, and implementation processes.

## BARRIERS TO ADOPTING
## COMMUNICATIONS TECHNOLOGY

The preceding section presented some practical suggestions to help in choosing among the options offered by communications technology. This section discusses other limitations or barriers to the widespread adoption of communications technology in adult education. Promising though the use of communications technology is, its widespread adoption in our field faces powerful barriers. This is not to suggest that no use is made of the technology in educating adults. Both Zigerell (1984, 1986) and Stern (1986-1987) indicate otherwise. But current activity mostly reflects efforts of individuals and individual institutions. For the technology to play a significant role, the field of adult education needs to institutionalize the study of communications technology by including it in the academic programs designed for future educators and practitioners.

In general, lack of money, time, and staff; negative attitudes toward technology; poor institutional support; and lack of technological knowledge and skill limit the use of technology. What follows is based on the premise that the last of these, lack of knowledge and skill, is the most important to overcome. By becoming familiar with technology and skilled in its application, we will be in a stronger position to tackle the other barriers. As our knowledge and understanding grow, we will be able to envision more clearly uses for the technology in adult education. With a clearer vision, we can formulate effective proposals that will let us compete more vigorously for institutional and governmental funds. In turn, the funds will provide us with necessary communications equipment, personnel, and support materials. With adequate funding, we can provide staff development opportunities and develop attractive programs for adult learners.

How much do we need to know about technology? How skilled must we become in its use? Generally, we need to understand each technology at a conceptual level in order to grasp both its operating principles and its strengths and limitations. This knowledge helps in judging the value of a technology for a particular purpose. Other knowledge is important, too. Most educational uses of sophisticated technology require a team effort. As adult educators on a team, we have to communicate clearly with other team members. This usually requires learning the jargon associated with the technology. Finally, we need to envision the relationships among the various constituent components of the technology. For example, a course delivered by computer conferencing will have associated telecommunications charges. Who will pay them? Recognizing the need to ask this kind of question aids logistical planning and avoids unpleasant last minute surprises.

Finally, how can we learn what we need to know? As adult learners ourselves, we can take advantage of many possibilities to learn about communications technology. Opportunities are available through formal and informal courses, at the meetings of our professional associations, in our professional literature, at workshops, through informal communications with colleagues, and in relevant books and magazines. When we have become more knowledgeable about communications technology, we will be wiser in applying it in adult education.

## APPLICATIONS OF COMMUNICATIONS TECHNOLOGY IN ADULT EDUCATION AND LEARNING

There are three general uses for communications technology in adult education. One use is for instructional purposes. Through technology we can reach out to more adults with enriched and varied learning opportunities. Secondly, the domain of communications technology also suggests program planning ideas. For example, many adult learners need to develop skills in using the technology to compete in the job market. Equally important, adults need to be better informed about technology in order to exercise their rights and duties as citizens. Finally, we can also use technology to help us manage our agencies. The same types of tools used by business and industry to help people work more productively and intelligently are available to us. The following discusses these three applications in greater detail.

### Communications Technology and Agency Management

Successful adult learning programs depend in many ways on good management. In a well-managed agency, essential planning takes place, learners needs are recognized and met, available dollars are used effectively, personnel is well utilized, and goals are usually achieved. Technology can help meet management needs in agencies of various sizes.

Of the available forms of communications technology, computers are especially useful for managerial purposes. In less than a decade, computers have become attractive even for small agencies. Computer prices are lower; the machines are easier to use; they offer more features and capabilities. When chosen with care, the same computer can be used for word processing, to develop and manage budgets, to design and produce print and graphic materials, to layout and manage projects, to communicate with other computers, and to maintain personnel records. The following briefly addresses selecting a computer and its support material and then highlights some of the more popular uses for computers in agency management.

*Selecting Software and Hardware.* Most people are now familiar with several facts about computers:

1. They and their various peripheral devices are collectively termed hardware.

2. Programs, known as software, are needed in order for computers to perform a given task.

3. Due to lack of standardization, programs are not interchangeable among different types of computers.

4. A specific program typically works only on a specific type of computer or one of its compatibles.

It is critical that these points be kept in mind when selecting software and hardware.

A precise definition of present and future agency needs is fundamental to selecting the right hardware and software for accomplishing goals. Too many people begin by buying a computer and then wonder how to get it to do what they want it to do. Since it is the software that enables the computer to function, selecting software should come before chosing hardware. The more precise we can be in identifying what we want done, the better the chances we shall be satisfied with the hardware and software we choose. To help avoid outgrowing the software and hardware we select, we should consider both our present needs and those in the reasonably near future. Equally important, we should involve staff in the selection process and provide for their training in using the hardware and software chosen.

*Staff Training.* Even with the wisest selection of hardware and software, the introduction of computers into an agency will be a resounding failure if no provision is made for staff training. Training is especially effective when it begins with involving personnel in the decision-making process regarding the introduction of technology. Those who actually type correspondence and documents, maintain records, or monitor expenditures have unique insights regarding what a task requires. Their insights can foster more informed decision making. Early involvement also helps ensure that people await the technology eagerly rather than with dread.

The tutorials that are often packaged with hardware and software can help most people begin using the equipment or program. But the tutorials are seldom adequate even for moderately sophisticated use of machine and software. Sometimes intermediate and advanced training needs can be met by having one person struggle through reference manuals and then teach other staff members. Other times personnel may need to attend workshops and classes to receive the necessary training.

Absences and turnovers pose other staff training problems. If a single person has sole responsibility for, say, word processing, the agency faces paralysis if that person becomes ill or leaves. Other staff members need not attain the same level of proficiency working with a program as the primary user, but training plans should ensure that the work of the agency can continue regardless of personnel changes.

*Word Processing.* Very likely the first piece of software an agency will purchase is a word processing program. Word processing programs have facilitated the adoption of computers by nontechnical people. With the recognition that word processing meant the end of retyping, people were willing to invest time in learning to use word processing programs. Word processing also speeds editing, revising, and formatting written documents. The writing process itself becomes even easier with the addition of programs that check spelling and ones that examine grammar and style. Agencies can use word processing for internal and external correspondence, to prepare reports and proposals, to develop promotional materials, and to create instructional materials.

We usually associate word processing exclusively with computers. Many of today's typewriters, which are really limited computers in disguise, offer some restricted word processing capabilities. Although these typewriters do not support the same variety of applications that even small personal computers do, in some cases they might adequately meet an agency's needs.

*Desktop Publishing.* Many of the larger or more complex documents produced on a word processor are candidates for the closely allied process of desktop publishing. The necessary programs are available for different computers. As always, the programs vary in their features and sophistication. Basically they take the text generated in a word processing program and let the operator manipulate it much as a publisher would in laying out and formatting the text for publication as a book, journal article, or other document. Illustrated matter created in a graphics program can also be used by desktop publishing programs. Newsletters, promotional materials, and instructional materials are probably an agency's main candidates for desktop publishing.

*Communications.* Along with software, wiring, and communication devices, computers can also be used to facilitate agency communications, both internally and externally. Simple local area networks (LANs) unite in-house computers so that messages and information can be electronically exchanged and peripheral devices, like printers, shared. People can also use their in-house computers, together with devices called modems, to communicate over telephone lines with others in local, national, and international settings.

Electronically exchanging information between the same types of computers using the same software programs is straightforward. Often people need to send information to dissimilar types of machines using a variety of software. In the past, this was extremely difficult, but progress has been made in enabling different kinds of computers to exchange information electronically. As of this moment, information in plain text form (no underlining, boldfacing, varied type faces, fancy formatting) is most successfully transmitted electronically.

For example, assuming appropriate software and hardware, a report generated on one computer can be electronically transmitted to a different or same type of computer. Once there, another person can use the word processor available on that computer to edit the report. Then the edited report can be electronically retransmitted to the original sender or to someone at another computer for further editing.

*Other Applications.* The need to produce and disseminate text is common across adult education agencies. Other popular computer programs can help with different tasks. Graphics programs are useful for adding eye-catching visuals to flyers or informative visuals to instructional materials. Data bases can store personnel and student records in electronic folders inside electronic file cabinets. Budget planning can get an assist from spreadsheet programs that quickly illustrate the consequences of different financial decisions. Project management tools can help conceptualize resource needs, determine timelines, and track the progress of a project.

## Communications Technology and Instruction

Communications technology is as useful in instruction as in agency management. Along with the genesis of radio, broadcast television, and large institutional computers came predictions of how each would revolutionize education. No revolution occurred, although there are instances where these technologies have been successfully employed in education. Similar predictions have been made about desktop computers, telecommunications options, and other new technologies. The evidence suggests that this time a revolution really is taking place with implications for delivering instruction, enhancing it, and managing it (Hirschen 1987; Stahmer & Helm, 1987).

*Delivering Instruction.* We can use technology in instruction to reach out to our rural or homebound populations with more varied learning opportunities, to enhance certain learning experiences for all students, and to provide alternative forms of instruction. The more readily available delivery vehicles include stand-alone personal computers, computers electronically hooked together (networked), audio and video technology, various combinations of computers and video or audio technology, and computers with other technologies linked with telecommunications devices. Much of this technology can be used to deliver instruction both on-site and at a distance.

Use of communications technology can mean less distinction between on-site instruction and distance education. Instructors can be physically present in an on-site classroom and electronically present and available for interactive communication at remote sites. Students can interact both with the instructor and with each other. Learners at distant sites can actively participate in on-site class activities through a variety of technologies.

In one instance, students in eighteen rural schools are able to attend the same calculus class at the same time while remaining in their individual home schools. A combination of communications technology provides speech and interactive visual communication (Hirschen, 1987). The same technology can be used with adult learners in various classes. Sites might include libraries, homes, community centers, or other locations where adults could gather conveniently.

Through communications technology, learners also have more opportunities to tune into a learning situation at their own convenience. For example, the same on-site computer-assisted program can be made available to distance learners as long as the various locations are equipped with a phone line, a computer, a peripheral device called a modem, and an appropriate telecommunications program. Students can dial up at will. In another instance video technology can deliver an on-campus engineering course either simultaneously to practicing engineers at remote sites, or the course can be made available on video tape for viewing at the engineers' convenience.

Whether used for distance learning or for on-site instruction, technology clearly opens up learning experiences that more and more people can enjoy. No single technology is a panacea for all situations. Nor are all forms of technology affordable. In providing new opportunities for learners, adult education agencies can sometimes take advantage of local resources to help control costs. At other times agencies need to form new alliances with other educational agencies; local, state, and federal government; or with the private sector (Hirschen 1987).

The cost-effectiveness of using a particular technology for instructional delivery can vary widely among adult education agencies offering nearly identical programs. Some general cost-effectiveness variables were discussed earlier. What makes sense to use in a particular setting depends on variables such as: 1) the local availability and usage costs of any particular technology, 2) staff knowledge and skill in using it, 3) institutional support for its use in instruction, 4) the enrichment of the learning opportunity due to its use, 5) students' access to the technology, and 6) their attitude toward it.

*Enhancing Instruction.* The mere use of technology to deliver instruction does not imply that the instruction is high in quality. That is, it is not necessarily effective or efficient. Using technology to enhance instruction means that some value is added to the instruction due to taking advantage of the characteristics of the technology. A few examples suggest the variety of ways technology can enhance instruction.

We all recognize the value of interactive learning opportunities. Through technology, learners can interact with either a machine-based instructional program or with other people by means of telecommunications. Computers, singly or in combination with video technology, offer one form of interactive, machine-based instruction. A well-designed computer-assisted interactive video disc system can provide excellent simulated learning experiences. It is also possible to enhance instruction with the judicious use of sound, motion, and still graphics. Of equal importance, appreciable learner control can be built into the instruction. This includes determining the pace of instruction, selecting among an array of options, choosing to review particular sections, or electing to skip certain portions of the instruction.

Courses delivered by means of computer-mediated telecommunication enable distance learners to participate in electronic discussion groups, develop jointly written papers, exchange information, and socialize. In addition to enriching the learning environment, such additional communication opportunities may help individuals better cope with the isolation of distance learning. Finally, the most modest of computer-assisted instruction programs can contain lessons that branch to different options based on student responses. These same programs can also provide varied motivational and instructional feedback to learners.

Recognizing that technology offers many opportunities to enhance instruction, though, is not to suggest that most of the available features be used all the time. Too much "enhancement" might actually interfere with learning by obscuring the instructional message. Good design is critical for effective instruction.

The quality of the instructional design plays a major role in the successful use of electronic communication technology in instruction. Whether intended for electronic delivery or for more traditional means, efficient and effective instruction depends on good instructional design. Well-designed instruction intended for electronic delivery takes advantage of the strengths of a particular technology and compensates for its weaknesses. No amount of planning nor any particular technology can compensate for poorly designed instruction.

*Managing Instruction.* Computers and telecommunications are also useful in managing instruction. The following briefly suggests some of the more common uses. For one thing, class lists kept on computers are easily corrected and up-dated. Grades also can be calculated and stored on computers. Instructors can create handouts combining text and graphics for one class and revise the handout readily for uses with another. Computers also make it easier to create various assessment tools for testing and evaluations purposes. Analyzing assessment results is another computer option.

With the combination of computers and telecommunications, students can send class assignments to their instructors. After correcting the assignment, instructors can return it to the student electronically. Students and instructors can also use electronic messaging (e-mail) to communicate much as they would on the telephone. The advantage of e-mail is that a message is stored electronically until the intended receiver is free to accept it. Similarly, any response to the original message is also stored electronically until the recipient is free to get it.

*Issues in Technology and Instruction.* Whenever something new comes along, it introduces a new set of issues. Communications technology is no different. In adult education, issues like equity, fairness, and effects on people are of special concern. One major difficulty in addressing these particular issues at the present time is that the technology is not staying still. Its rapid evolution includes factors like growing variety, falling costs, increasing diffusion, and improving ease of use. Because of these factors, people who were excluded from using the technology in the recent past are included now. While we need to maintain our concern regarding these important human issues, the nature of the technological evolution seems to be our ally at the present time in our desire to include more and more people in adult education through using communications technology.

A special concern in using technology with adult learners is that the technology itself not hinder learning. For example, using communications technology frequently involves reading information on a TV or monitor screen. A common characteristic of adult learners is that they wear bifocals. Screens either need to be positioned for comfortable reading or adults need to invest in glasses that let them read the screen without straining their necks. As facilitators of adult learning, we need to be aware of the physical characteristics of adults and of the characteristics of the technology we select and to make accommodations where possible.

We also need to develop an awareness of copyright issues in relation to communications technology. A discussion of this murky area is beyond the scope of this chapter. Nonetheless, we should recognize that what is electronically possible is not necessarily legal. You could, for instance, use a computer with a peripheral device called a digitizer to copy a graphic from a publication into your computer. Once there, this same graphic can be incorporated into your own document, which you might then distribute free or sell. But the copyright holder of the graphic is very likely the publication from which it was copied. Failure to get written permission to use the graphic could result in a lawsuit.

Culture is another important issue in technology and instruction. People in adult education enjoy and are accustomed to interacting with others face to face. Even though electronic interaction is quite feasible, the nature of the interaction is somehow different. Not necessarily worse or better; just different. Consciously or not, the preference for face-to-face communication probably plays a role in making decisions regarding the use of technology in adult learning. We need to reminder ourselves of this preference and question its validity as we evaluate possible roles for technology in a given situation.

### Communications Technology and Program Planning

Communications technology offers program planners many opportunities to meet the varied needs of adult learners by addressing the economic, political, and social implications of the technology. Media attention tends to focus on the economic effects of communications technology. Concerns for the social and political effects of communications technology have accelerated with its growth. As Donnelly (1986) has stated, "Waiting for and accepting the impact of new technologies would be ethically indifferent were [it] not for the fact that communications technologies change our private lives and personalities, and consequently what we do to one another" (p. 172). Adult educators can help meet these economic, social, and political challenges through wise program planning.

Adult learners can also benefit from programs that help them 1) learn to use technology and 2) understand its strengths and limitations. Potential job and career benefits are widely recognized, but there are other benefits, too. Both skill and understanding enable people to identify significant issues and questions about the role of communications technology in a democratic society. Learning to use and understand technology may also enhance adult self-concept by helping people stay up-to-date in a changing world.

*Using Technology.* Most often when we think about helping adults learn to use communications technology, we think of helping them develop new job skills or improve existing ones. Computers especially should provide planners with additional program options for some time to come. As telecommunications opportunities grow, adults in a variety of jobs and professions will need to develop skills in searching and retrieving electronic information. With the continuing evolution of communications technology, people will need frequent opportunities to upgrade their skills and knowledge.

Important though they are, job-related factors are not the only reasons to help adults learn to use communications technology. Experiences in two different projects involving older people suggest that those involved enjoyed enhanced self-concept and increased prestige among family, friends, and associates (F. Middleton; N. Bellos, personal communications, April 5, 1988). One project, SeniorNet, is a multistate computer-based telecommunications network of older adults who use SeniorNet for various purposes. The second project, titled "Older Persons and Computers," was instituted by the Gerontology Center at Syracuse University. This project gave people an opportunity to learn basic computer operations and to try a variety of programs. Several participants are now using their computer skills to help out in public schools.

Individuals and groups of citizens can also use communications technology to help shape the kind of world they want. With a small computer and the appropriate hardware and software, citizens can retrieve, organize, and store the kind of information they need to contend with opposing interests. Computers can also be used to prepare materials like informational flyers, form letters, and newsletters for use in political and social activities.

Nor are computers the only communications technologies adults can use to shape their world. Through telecommunications, citizens can speedily share information with interested parties elsewhere. Panamanian exiles in the United States have been doing just this using a fax machine to get news into Panama ("Panamanians Use Technology," 1988).

Video is another potential tool for adults, who may require assistance in using it. Community access is often a provision in cable television licensing agreements. Although technical assistance may be available through the cable station, adults also need help learning to design and communicate their messages. Even where cable access is not available, adults can use video skills to maximize use of home equipment like video cameras and VCRs for personal pleasure, citizenship action, and community activities.

Stuart (1988) reports several uses of video by citizens of third world countries. In one instance, self-employed women in India effectively used video to resolve a quarrel with a municipal official. In another case, women in Mali used video to advance a literacy project. Stuart also describes the role video tapes made by Chinese farmers played in helping people in Guyana adopt biogas technology.

*Understanding Technology.* The ability to use communications technology effectively can benefit adults economically, socially, and politically. Even today, however, many more people need to acquire some understanding of the technology than need to use it. Legislators, managers, bureaucrats, judges, and others who may not actually use much advanced communications technology in their own work are called upon to make decisions about it. Their decisions often have significant implications that affect our lives. But the quality of their decisions is based in part on their having some understanding of the pertinent technology. Where and how are they to acquire the understanding they need? What constitutes "understanding"? Do people need to acquire some minimal skill in using technology in order to understand it? Is there not a role for adult education in addressing these questions?

Finally, in a society where information is increasingly a source of power, citizens in a democracy need to be literate about communications technology to maintain their independence and to avoid being manipulated by people who do understand the technology. Brand (1987) underscores this point in his discussion about the increasingly digital nature of the the various communications technologies: That is, they all deal with information as discrete bits. This common denominator means that, as long as information is digitized, it can be electronically altered or transmitted rather easily no matter what its original form. Pictures, sounds, and words can be sent as bits of data and recaptured as pictures, sounds, and words at the receiving site. This capability is both an asset and a threat. As Brand points out, the threat lies in the fact that no one can tell if the information has been changed in any way. Electronic editing leaves no evidence of alteration. To the extent that this is not understood, people are vulnerable to being manipulated by altered information.

## CONCLUSIONS AND RECOMMENDATIONS

Adult education can profit in several ways by involvement with communications technology. This technology can help us manage our agencies and reach more learners more effectively and with a greater variety of learning options and opportunities. In addition, the significance of communications technology in our era suggests new offerings to program planners.

Technology lets us do many things but does not ensure that they are the right things to do or that they are done well. Taking advantage of communications technology in adult education requires three things: 1) a realistic assessment of the limitations of a given technology, 2) a practical approach to its adoption, and 3) planned implementation of its use. Thus approached, the technology becomes an effective tool for use in a variety of situations.

Practitioners can make a major contribution to furthering our knowledge about and understanding of the role of communications technology in adult education by reporting their experiences and observations. Practice suggests valuable avenues for research, which in turn can facilitate better practice.

## REFERENCES

Brand, S. (1987). *The media lab: Inventing the future at MIT*. New York: Viking

Donnelly, W. J. (1986). *The confetti generation: How the new communications technology is fragmenting America*. New York: Henry Holt and Company.

Hirschen, W. (1987). *Video vision: A publication on instructional television, video production and distance learning*. Albany, New York: University of the State of New York, State Education Department, Center for Learning Technologies.

Panamanians use technology to balk censor. (February 14, 1988). *The New York Times*, p. 13.

Stahmer, A., & Helm, B. (1987). *Communications technology and distance learning in Canada: A survey of Canadian activities.* Ottawa: Social Policy Directorate, Department of Communications, Government of Canada.

Stern, C. (1986-1987). Teaching the distance learner using new technology. *Journal of Educational Technology Systems, 16*(4). 407-418.

Stuart, S. (1988). The village video: Video as a tool for local development and south-south exchange. *Convergence, 20*(2), 62-68.

Zigerell, J. (1984). *Distance education: An information age approach to adult education.* (ERIC Document Reproduction Service No. ED 246 311)

Zigerell, J. (Ed.) (1986). *Telelearning models: Expanding the community college community. Nine case studies showing how colleges, alone or in partnerships, creatively utilize new delivery systems to reach a variety of student clienteles.* (AACJC Issues Series No. 3). (ERIC Document Reproduction Service No. ED 271 182)

# PART THREE

# A Future Perspective

# CHAPTER 19

## Perspectives on the Future

SUSAN IMEL

*". . . . educators may be disabling learners by preparing them for a future that has already past." (Boshier, 1986, p. 16)*

Speculating about the future is more than just an idle pastime. Although we live and work in the present, thinking about the future as well as about how we can have a hand in creating or shaping it is an important activity. Rather than just responding to changes, adult educators need to take an active role in molding the future of the field. A proactive stance toward the future will help ensure that the field is prepared to serve adults appropriately when that future arrives (Deshler, 1987; Hiemstra, 1987).

Because our society is characterized by rapid and pervasive change, it is difficult to predict or forecast the future with any confidence, particularly for a field as diverse as adult education. However, there is information available that provides some perspectives on the future of adult education. In order to help adult educators anticipate and plan for the future, this chapter reviews some of this information. First, social, demographic, economic, and technological forces shaping adult education's future are discussed. Then, four critical issues for the future of adult education, which emerge from this context, are examined. Next, adult education methods related to these areas are highlighted. The chapter concludes with some possible scenarios for adult education in the future.

393

## THE CURRENT CONTEXT

Adult education operates within a broad context created by social, demographic, economic, and technological conditions. Because its future will emerge from this context, it is important for adult educators to be aware of current trends. This section highlights some of the social, demographic, economic, and technological factors shaping the future of adult education.

### Social and Demographic Trends

Changing demographics are a major force affecting adult education. The challenge for adult education will be to provide high-quality, accessible, and equitable education for an increasingly diverse adult clientele. Some of the social and demographic trends that will affect adult education in the future are the aging of the population, increases in minority populations, increases in nontraditional families, and increases in labor force participation by women. Each of these trends is discussed briefly below.

*Aging of the Population.* For the first time in U.S. history, there are more people over age sixty-five than there are teenagers. By the year 2000, the number of older adults is expected to exceed 32 million (Sanoff, 1984). Lower birth rates, increased life expectancy, and the aging of the "baby boom" generation are all factors that are likely to result in an increased demand for adult education.

*Increases in Minority Populations.* Currently, minority populations represent over one-third of new births in the United States each year, and by the year 2000, it is anticipated that 29 percent of the total U.S. population will be comprised of minority group members (Fay, McCune, & Begin, 1987; Thornton, 1984). Blacks now account for 12.1 percent of the population but by the year 2000, Hispanics are expected to become the largest minority group. The fastest growing minority group are Asian Americans (Thornton, 1984). Adult education programs will need to seek ways to serve these emerging population groups. For example, since high school dropout rates for black and Hispanic students are about twice that of the national average (General Accounting Office, 1986), in the future, high school completion programs may serve a disproportionate number of minority adults.

*Increases in Nontraditional Families.* Only 9 percent of Americans now live in families with a working husband, homemaker wife, and two children. Single-parent families have become so common that approximately one-third of all children will spend some of their childhood in a single parent household (Rossman, 1985). There has also been a significant increase in the birthrate among teenage women with more than half of the births occurring out of wedlock (Wallis, 1985). Single mothers will continue to have a critical need for adult education programs if they are to enter and progress in the work force.

*Increases in Labor Force Participation by Women.* A trend related to increases in nontraditional families is the increasing numbers of women in the labor force. Approximately 55 percent of women are currently employed, and that figure is expected to increase to about 61 percent by the year 2000 because women will continue to comprise most of the new entrants into the labor force. Furthermore, women will be working for longer periods of time, averaging over twenty-six years of gainful employment (Johnston & Packer, 1987; Miller, 1987). Because many of these women are displaced homemaker and single parents, they have income levels below the poverty level. They will need training opportunities to improve their economic security (Miller, 1987).

## Economic and Technological Trends

Economic and technological changes are also affecting the need for adult education and where and how it is delivered. Two areas of particular importance are changes in the workplace and the emergence of an information society.

*Changes in the Workplace.* The nature of work and the workplace is changing. Some of these changes are due to technological and economic factors while others are the result of changing expectations about work.

Although most jobs won't become "high tech," technology will alter how jobs are performed. Also, jobs will change dramatically every five to ten years, and increasingly, they will require higher level skills to perform. Basic academic skills, problem-solving and decision-making abilities, and interpersonal skills are becoming more important in the workplace. Advanced education and training will be a prerequisite for many jobs. By 1990, three out of four jobs will require some education or technical training beyond high school, and by 1995, approximately 20 percent (compared to 16 percent in 1987) of all workers will be college graduates (Fay,

McCune, & Begin, 1987; Institute for the Future, 1987; National Alliance of Business, 1986).

The ways Americans work and their expectations about work will continue to evolve. Because the educational attainment of the work force will continue to increase, workers will place additional demands on their employers for career planning, midcareer occupational training, and personal enhancement courses (Institute for the Future, 1987). More and more, work will be structured around the work group or the work team. The emergence of the small group will result from both the increasing educational levels of employees as well as the increase in numbers of service and information jobs (Edmondson, 1987; Institute for the Future, 1987).

*Emergence of an Information Society.* Breakthroughs in science and technology—particularly in the area of microelectronics— are creating an information society. Society is being transformed "from a civilization based on raw materials, capital and production to one based on human resources and knowledge" (Elmandjra, 1986, p. 732). In an information society there is a dramatic increase in the power of individuals to think and organize because information is the critical resource (Marchello, 1987).

One of the characteristics of the era is a rapid increase in the growth of available information. Currently, the amount of knowledge doubles every seven or eight years, but a study conducted by the Massachusetts Institute of Technology predicts that due to the escalation of the information revolution, by the year 2000, the world's knowledge base will double every eleven hours (Elmandjra, 1986; Hornung, 1987).

Another characteristic of the information age is rapid change. Increases in available information and knowledge result in new ideas and new discoveries. These in turn fuel the cycle of change. Change is occurring so rapidly that much of what people know is in danger of becoming obsolete (Marchello, 1987; McMahon, 1983). This growing obsolescence affects all aspects of the lives of individuals.

The emergence of an information society has implications for learning and the educational system. Education will be increasingly important because information, rather than raw materials, will be the basis of the economy. Knowledge will be treated as an article of commerce (Elmandjra, 1986; Marchello, 1987).

According to Marchello, the role of education in an information society is critical. He describes this role as follows:

> The growing dominance of information resources points to the fact that our quality of life depends on how relevant, broad, demanding and continuous the learning process is. Education is the primary force of the information society. (p. 556)

## Summary

This section has briefly highlighted some current demographic, social, technological, and economic trends. Although many factors constitute the context in which adult education operates, the ones discussed here are expected to influence it significantly in the future. The next section examines four critical issues for the future of adult education that emerge from the current context.

## CRITICAL ISSUES FOR ADULT EDUCATION'S FUTURE

Four critical issues for adult education's future emerge from the current context. These issues are (1) providing accessible and equitable learning opportunities, (2) adjusting to the demands of an information society, (3) making effective use of technology, and (4) developing learning management skills. Like the demographic, social, technological, and economic conditions described earlier, these issues are interrelated, and they emerge from trends affiliated with the current context. Because these issues are important in planning for the future, adult educators need to be aware of them.

### Providing Accessible and Equitable Adult Education Programs

The issue of access and equity is concerned with the accessibility of adult education opportunities as well as how equitably all groups within the adult population are served. Many adult educators are already concerned about this issue. That relatively few adults engage in educational activities has negative consequences for both the individuals and society. Changing socioeconomic, cultural, and demographic forces as well as the democratic idea of equal opportunity make educational nonparticipation among adults an important social issue (Scanlon, 1986).

Current evidence reveals that those most in need of adult education programs and services are among the least served. The inequities of the existing adult education system were noted in *The Forgotten Half* (William T. Grant Foundation, 1988), which observed that "most lifelong learning efforts are geared to adults who have met with success in traditional education. . . . [while] those [individuals] who make up the 'forgotten half' are largely ignored" (p. 67).

Demographic and social trends indicate that the adult population of the future will be even more diverse than that of today. To serve this clientele, an adult education system that is comprehensive, accessible, and equitable will be necessary for the following reasons: "to train and retrain workers, to develop human potential, and to reduce some of the inequities associated with race and class" (William T. Grant Foundation, 1988, p. 69).

To help overcome future problems of access and equity, Garrison (1987) proposes an open learning system. Such a system would be flexible, permitting individuals to learn how, when, and where they desired. It would provide access to education and also, support the learning process. In this learner-centered system, learning would take place in both traditional and nontraditional settings and be delivered through a variety of methods.

## Adjusting to the Demands of an Information Society

A society based on knowledge or information places a number of demands on its citizens. Because of the so-called information explosion, lifelong or recurrent education must become a way of life. If it does not, Harlan Cleveland of the University of Minnesota foresees negative implications for both the individual and society. He predicts that "people who do not educate and continue to re-educate themselves to participate in the new knowledge environment will become the peasants of the information society" while those societies that do not provide relevant and adequate educational opportunities for their citizens "will be left in the jetstream of history by those who do" (cited in Marchello, 1987, p. 559).

Accessing, evaluating, and using information are critical processes in an information society. Individuals who know how to access information sources such as electronic databases have a distinct advantage over those who do not. However, unless they also know how to select the most appropriate resources, they, too, will be at a disadvantage. Dealing with information overload requires an awareness of a wide range of possible resources as well as the ability to sort through and evaluate their relevance (Barrows, 1987; Birkey, 1984). The gap between those who know how to access and use information and those who do not will widen in the future unless all individuals are equipped with the appropriate skills.

In a society in which knowledge is a commodity, individuals need to understand the importance of being involved in its creation. Power will accrue to those who create and control knowledge. According to Tobin (1987), by becoming involved in knowledge creation, "individuals [will] learn about themselves and about the structure and power in the socio-economic political world around them" (p. 185). In the future, adult educators should strive to emphasize the knowledge-creation, rather than the rote-banking, approach to education (Tobin, 1987).

## Making Effective Use of Technology

Technological changes are affecting virtually all aspects of our lives. Advances in technology have brought about the information era and have radically altered the workplace. Technological change is also influencing the field of adult education (see Chapter 18). Although technology has been used to deliver or support adult education for many years, due to continuing advancements in its development, its use will undoubtedly become more widespread in the future. Depending on how it is used, technology may have the power to transform education.

Although neither good nor bad in itself, technology has capacities that can be used for expanding learning experiences and for achieving many of the generally accepted goals of adult education (Gerver, 1987; Tobin, 1987). However, in order to realize the full potential of technology in the educational process, adult educators need to be aware of some of the issues related to its use.

One of the obvious benefits of using technology is that it makes education more accessible. It eliminates many barriers associated with time and distance because it permits individuals to learn at times and places of their own choosing. However, the access and equity issue is frequently raised in conjunction with technology. There are concerns that because of factors such as cost, not all groups of learners have equal access to technology. Also, for one reason or another, some groups of learners may not find technology particularly attractive. Tobin (1987) makes this point when she says, "technology has the potential to alienate and marginalize portions of the population who are seen as passive receivers rather than actors in an educational structure" (p. 176).

Garrison (1987) suggests that in order to use technology appropriately in the future, adult educators will need to go beyond simply providing access to knowledge. They will need to concentrate on providing a personalized, learner-centered approach that permits individuals to have more control over the how, when, and where of learning.

As technology is used more frequently, adult educators will need to make it compatible with adult education principles. An obvious benefit of technology arises from its power to individualize instruction. However, this feature should not be emphasized at the expense of group learning experiences. Adult educators must assume the responsibility for using technology in a more collaborative mode. Although interactions via technology will never "truly approximate the richness of live interaction . . . educators can still involve themselves in an exchange that values all participants" (Tobin, 1987, p. 179).

Technology must be a part of a total learning system that is designed to meet individual and societal needs. Adult educators will need to become informed about what can be achieved through technology and then seek to use it in creative and imaginative ways. Technology should never be employed as an afterthought or as an add-on; instead it should be integrated into a total educational system designed to address constituent needs and curriculum requirements (Garrison, 1987).

*Developing Learning Management Skills*

In a constantly changing society, those educators concerned with developing competent lifelong learners will need to assist adults become more aware of their learning processes in order to facilitate greater self-direction in learning (Cheren, 1987). The ability to understand and manage one's own learning will enable an adult to learn new things quickly, to adjust to rapidly changing societal conditions, and to accommodate job and career changes (Birkey, 1984).

More commonly referred to as learning how to learn, learning management has received increasing attention as the need for lifelong or recurrent education has become more acute. Through a review of literature, Birkey (1984) discovered that most individuals writing about the future agreed that the goal of education should be "to develop self-directed people with knowledge, skills, and attitudes to assist them in dealing with a continuously changing society" (p. 25). Learning management is a strategy that can be used to achieve this goal. When individuals are involved in managing their own learning, they become more knowledgeable about how they learn and thus are able to learn more efficiently and effectively.

An essential element of learning management is problem solving, and the ability to solve problems will be a critical skill in the future. While it is impossible to predict what will occur in the future, it is relatively safe to assume that it will contain problems that will need solutions. Therefore, people must be prepared to define problems; to create, process, and develop ideas related to them; to evaluate solutions; and to develop and implement action plans for carrying out the solutions (Birkey, 1987). The steps involved in problem solving require the ability to think critically and reflectively, so these skills must also be fostered in learners (Smith, 1987).

Although some attention has been given to helping adults manage their own learning, this area will become more essential. Due to rapidly changing job requirements, learning management has frequently been affiliated with workplace learning. However, since change will continue to touch all areas of their lives, adults need these skills for all their learning endeavors.

*Summary*

This section has discussed four critical issues that will be significant in adult education's future. An awareness of these issues can help adult educators anticipate and plan. The next section relates adult education methods to these issues by suggesting some implications for the future.


METHODS FOR THE FUTURE

Forecasting what methods will be used to deliver adult education in the future is a difficult task. Limited knowledge exists about the relationship between adult learning and the effectiveness of various instructional methods (Garrison, 1987). Research on information technologies used to deliver education is still in its infancy. The nature of the relationship between how technologies present and organize knowledge and cognitive learning processes is unclear (Bates, 1985). It is likely that current and future research findings will influence how adult education will be delivered. Nevertheless, the four critical issues described in the previous section contain some implications for adult education methods in the future. These implications include the following:

1. Adult educators will need to employ a wide variety of methods. In order to address the broad spectrum of learning needs of an increasingly diverse adult clientele, it will be imperative to deliver instruction in many different formats. Furthermore, methods that emphasize collaborative learning as well as those that individualize instruction will be equally important.

2. Advances in artificial intelligence will provide greater individualization of instruction through information technologies. However, unless future research findings provide more information about how to match the appropriate technology and method with individual learner characteristics, learners will have to assume more of the responsibility for their own learning by selecting those methods that best fit their characteristics (Garrison, 1987; Tobin, 1987).

3. Methods that stress collaborative learning, problem solving, and critical and reflective thinking will increase in importance. Brookfield (1985; 1986) has identified the discussion method as an ideal way to facilitate critical thinking as long as certain conditions are met. Marsick and Watkins (1986) suggest that critical reflectivity can best be taught through methods that provide simulation experiences including case studies and role play.

4. The group will become an important vehicle for collaborative learning due to changes in the workplace. Adult educators will be able to help individuals become better group members by assisting them to develop group process skills (e.g., teamwork, leadership, participation) and group member skills (e.g., active listening, staying on task, giving and receiving feedback). Smith (1987) recommends that these skills be developed using simulation experiences that include facilitator-led critiques and exercises focusing on a specific process or skill.

5. Because microcomputers are expected to become widely available, computer-assisted instruction (CAI) will increase in importance. Although CAI will be used to individualize instruction, adult educators will also develop ways of making it more collab-

orative. A broad range of cognitive skills can be developed through CAI; therefore, it will be used in many different learning situations. Some common CAI modes of the future will include tutorial, drill and practice, problem solving, gaming, simulation, inquiry, and dialogue (Ayers, 1980).

6. Adult educators will develop methods designed to help adults evaluate available information sources. The use of exercises or discussions in which individuals critique a resource they have actually used; reflect on its accuracy, reliability, and contemporaneousness; and evaluate its overall usefulness will be one way to achieve this goal (Barrows, 1987).

7. Adult educators will also concentrate more on helping adults become better managers of their own learning. Smith (1987) suggests that the following methods can be used to help people learn more effectively: (a) diagnosing their learning style and providing feedback about it, (b) keeping logs and journals as they learn, (c) assigning retrospective reports following learning episodes, (d) providing exercises to help people reflect on the purpose of the learning strategies they employ, (e) conducting critiques to analyze the process dimensions of such activities as group discussion, and (f) providing relevant theoretical information through lecture and assigned readings.

8. The development of learning management skills will be supported by computer software that will help adults learn while simultaneously making them aware of their own learning processes (Tobin, 1987). This software will help adults become more independent in their learning and assist them in selecting methods that suit their preferred ways of learning.

No single method is likely to dominate in the future. Instead, if the open learning system described by Garrison (1987) is to become a reality, diversity will be its hallmark. Adult education will be delivered in many different formats and in many different locations. Print, media, and human resources will all have important roles to play in this system.

## FUTURE SCENARIOS

What will adult education be like in the future? Although this question cannot be answered with complete confidence, existing information can be used to develop some possible scenarios. Which of these, if any, might actually occur will depend to a great extent upon adult educators themselves. Current social, demographic, economic, and technological trends are creating the context for adult education's future. By acting upon information emerging from this context, adult educators can work to bring about the future they desire.

In the first scenario, adult education in the year 2010 looks much like it did in 1990. Adult education programs are serving only a limited portion of the adult population; those adults who participate tend to be well educated already. Most programs are held in traditional educational institutions. The lecture is the preferred method although some classes use collaborative learning methods such as discussion, but only under the guidance of the teacher. Information technologies are used to deliver some instruction, but in many classrooms the microcomputers are never "booted up." There has been little increase in public or private support for adult education programs even through educational expenditures for traditional age students have decreased due to the continuing decline in the birth rate.

In the second scenario, also in the year 2010, there are few individuals who even claim to be adult educators. Instead the functions previously performed by adult educators have been assumed by human resource technologists (HRTs). In 1995, when America's competitiveness was at a low ebb, a presidential commission was created to examine ways to develop the country's human resource capacity. At the commission's recommendation, all resources for adult learning were directed to economic development, and special programs were developed to train HRTs. The work groups that emerged in the early 1980s have died out, and most learning is individualized under the direction of HRTs. In the year 2000, there were still a few adult education programs that focused on personal and social development, but by 2010, most of those had folded. Groups of adults still meet in homes and community centers to learn about social issues through collaborative learning methods such as discussion. Also, many adults pursue individual learning projects to enhance their personal development. But, there is no support for these activities from trained adult educators.

In the third scenario, adult education is flourishing in the year 2010. Adult educators are among the most respected of professionals because they support the important activity of lifelong learning. Nearly 95 percent of the adult population participate in learning activities each year, choosing from a wide variety of programs and formats. After it was used as a vehicle for public education during the AIDS crisis of the 1990s, the public forum became an important discussion method for helping adults deal with a rapidly changing society. Now public forums are held regularly in nearly every part of the country. Information technologies are an integral component in the adult learning system, but they do not dominate it as some had once feared. Most adult pursue learning for both work-related and personal reasons.

None of these scenarios accurately predicts the future of adult education. What they do, though, is suggest directions the field might take in the future. Adult educators of the 1990s can be involved in determining adult education of the year 2010, but in order to do this, they must be proactive in guiding the field toward the future they desire.

## REFERENCES

Ayers, G. (1980). *The learner and the computer.* Paper presented at the National Conference on Computer Based Education, Bloomington, Minnesota. (ERIC Document Reproduction Service No. ED 201 305)

Barrows, H. S. (1987). Learning management in the context of small group problem-based learning. In M. E. Cheren (Ed.), *Learning management: Emerging directions for learning to learn in the workplace* (pp. 17-20). Information series no. 320. Columbus: ERIC Clearinghouse on Adult, Career, and Vocational Education, The National Center for Research in Vocational Education, The Ohio State University.

Bates, A. W. (1985). *Research into the use of advanced technology in education: Future requirements.* Paper on information technology, no. 244. Bucks, United Kingdom: Open University, Institute of Educational Technology. (ERIC Document Reproduction Service No. ED 274 324)

Birkey, C. J. M. (1984). Future directions for adult education and adult educators. *Journal of Teacher Education, 35* (30), 25-29.

Boshier, R. (1986). Proaction for a change: Some guidelines for the future. *International Journal of Lifelong Education, 5* (1), 15-31.

Brookfield, S. (1985). Discussion as an effective educational method. In S. H. Rosenblum, (Ed.), *Involving adults in the educational process* (pp. 55-67). New Directions for Continuing Education, no. 26. San Francisco: Jossey-Bass.

Brookfield, S. D. (1986). *Understanding and facilitating adult learning.* San Francisco: Jossey-Bass.

Cheren, M. (Ed.). (1987). *Learning management: Emerging directions for learning to learn in the workplace.* Information series no. 320. Columbus: ERIC Clearinghouse on Adult, Career, and Vocational Education, The National Center for Research in Vocational Education, The Ohio State University.

Deshler, D. (1987). Techniques for generating future perspectives. In R. E. Brockett (Ed.), *Continuing education in the year 2000* (pp. 79-92). New Directions for Continuing Education, no. 36. San Francisco: Jossey-Bass.

Edmondson, B. (1987, October). *The demographics of adult education.* Paper presented at the Fifteenth Annual Conference of the Learning Resources Network.

Elmandjra, M. (1986). Learning needs in a changing world: The role of human resources in a civilization of knowledge. *Futures, 18,* 731-737.

Fay, C. H., McCune, J. T., & Begin, J. P. (1987). The setting for continuing education in the year 2000. In R.G. Brockett (Ed.), *Continuing education in the year 2000* (pp. 15-27). New Directions for Continuing Education, no. 36. San Francisco: Jossey-Bass.

Garrison, D. R. (1987). The role of technology in continuing education. In R. G. Brockett (Ed.), *Continuing education in the year 2000* (pp. 41-53). New Directions for Continuing Education, no. 36. San Francisco: Jossey-Bass.

General Accounting Office. (1986). *School dropouts. The extent and nature of the problem.* Washington, DC: Division of Human Resources, GAO. (ERIC Document Reproduction Service No. ED 274 756)

Gerver, E. (1987). Issues in computers and adult learning. In W. M. Rivera & S. M. Walker, *Lifelong Learning Research Conference Proceedings* (pp. 18-22). College Park: University of

Maryland. (ERIC Document Reproduction Service No. ED 278 786)

Hiemstra, R. (1987). Creating the future. In R. G. Brockett (Ed.), *Continuing education in the year 2000* (pp. 3-13). New Directions for Continuing Education, no. 36. San Francisco: Jossey-Bass.

Hornung, B. (1987, February). Paychecks will shrink, MIT study predicts. *AVA Update*, p. 3.

Institute for the Future. (1987). Training for strategic advantage. (Supporting data). An excerpt from the 1987 *Ten-year forecast*. Menlo Park, CA: IFF.

Johnston, W. B., & Packer, A. H. (1987). *Workforce 2000: Work and workers for the 21st century*. Indianapolis: Hudson Institute.

McMahon, E. M. (1983). *The national issues forum: Bridging the human gap through innovative learning*. Paper presented at the Annual Meeting of the Speech Communication Association, Washington, DC. (ERIC Document Reproduction Service No. ED 240 635)

Marchello, J. M. (1987). Education for a technological age. *Futures*, 19, 555-565.

Marsick, V., & Watkins, K. (1986). *Learning and development in the workplace*. Paper presented to the American Society for Training and Development Conference, St. Louis, Missouri.

Miller, J. (1987). *At-risk study group report*. Unpublished manuscript, The Ohio State University, The National Center for Research in Vocational Education.

National Alliance of Business. (1986). *Employment policies: Looking to the year 2000*. Washington, DC: NAB.

Rossman, P. (1985). The network family: Support systems for times of crisis and contentment. *The Futurist*, 19 (6), 19-21.

Sanoff, A. P. (1984, March 19). 10 forces reshaping America: Force one, a maturing society. *U.S. News and World Report*, pp. 40-41.

Scanlon, C. L. (1986). *Deterrents to participation: An adult education dilemma*. Information series no. 308. Columbus: ERIC Clearinghouse on Adult, Career, and Vocational Education, The National Center for Research in Vocational Education, The Ohio State University. (ERIC Document Reproduction Service No. ED 272 768)

Smith, R. M. (1987). Learning to learn in the workplace. In M. E. Cheren (Ed.), *Learning management: Emerging directions for learning to learn in the workplace* (pp. 39-50). Information series no. 320. Columbus: ERIC Clearinghouse on Adult, Career, and Vocational Education, The National Center for Research in Vocational Education, The Ohio State University.

Thornton, J. (1984, March 19). 10 forces reshaping America: Force six, rise of minorities. *U.S. News and World Report*, p. 48.

Tobin, J. (1987). Technology's promises are ours to keep: Adult educators and technology. In F. Cassidy & R. Faris (Eds.), *Choosing our future: Adult education and public policy in Canada* (pp. 176-186). Toronto: The Ontario Institute for Studies in Education.

Wallis, C. (1985, December 9). Children having children. *Time*, pp. 78-90.

William T. Grant Foundation. (1988). *The forgotten half: Non-college youth in America*. Washington, DC: Youth and America's Future, The William T. Grant Foundation's Commission on Work, Family, and Citizenship.

# INDEX

Acronym alienation
related to computer instruction,
305
Administrative applications of
computers (AAC), 305
Adult education
the future of, 393–408
Adult educator
attributes and skills of, 3–22
interpersonal skills of, 4–8
labels for the, 3
personality characteristics of, 4–
8
program planning skills of the,
8–16
transaction skills of the, 16–20
Adult learners
enhance motivation to learn for,
97–117
physiological variables of, 28–
30
psychological variables of, 30–
35
understanding, 23–37
variability of, 25–26
Adult learning methods
case study, 225–246
communication technology,
367–390
computer-enriched instruction,
303–328

correspondence study, 345–366
demonstration and simulation,
261–282
discussion, 187–204
forum, panel, and symposium,
283–302
internship, 329–344
learning contracts, 133–160
lecture, 161–186
mentorship, 205–224
nominal group technique, 247–
260
Assumptions
identifying, 214–215
Audio technology, 369–370

Behavior modeling, 263–264
Benefits
discussion cognitive and affective, 188–190
Brainstorming, 257

Case analysis, 227–228
Case discussion, 228–229
Case report, 226–227
Case study
advantages and disadvantages
of, 239–240
components of, 226–229
defining, 225

Case study (*Continued*)
  designing, 230–239
  evaluating, 238
  variations of, 241–244
CD-ROM (compact disc read-only
  memory), 370
Cognitive levels of questioning,
  125–128
Collegial assessment
  methods of, 222
Communications technology, 367–
  390
  advantages and limitations of,
  373
  application to adult education
  and learning, 378–389
  barriers to adopting, 376–378
  implications of, 371–372
  overview of, 368–371
  practical approaches to, 373–
  376
Computer-assisted instruction
  (CAI), 304–305
Computer-assisted interactive
  video (CAIV), 371
Computer-based education (CBE),
  305
Computer-based testing (CBT),
  305
Computer-enriched instruction,
  303–328
  advantages of, 307–309
  definition of, 306
  developing an agenda, 325–327
  facilitating learning through,
  310–316
  limitations of, 309–310
  strategies and methods for,
  322–325
Computer-managed instruction
  (CMI), 305
Computer-managed learning
  (CML), 306

Computer-supported instruction
  (CSI), 305
Computer use
  as resource, 315
  dialogue and programming,
  314–315
  drill and practice, 311–312
  facilitating learning through,
  310–316
  simulations and games, 313–
  314
  tutorials, 312–313
  vehicles for instruction, 311–
  315
Consensual rules
  evolving of, 193
Context analysis, 10–11
Cooperative education, 330
Correspondence study, 345–365
  advantages and limitations of,
  360–363
  definition of, 345
  evaluation of, 359–360
  institutions and audiences for,
  346–348
  instruction in, 354–356
  learners in, 356–358
  methods for, 348–352
  student support, 358–359
  study guide for, 352–354
  support services in, 356–358
Critical thinking
  activities associated with, 19–20
  purpose of, 192
  strategies for, 19

Delivery
  of effective lectures, 176–182
Delphi technique, 258
Demonstration, 261–281
  advantages of, 265–266
  appropriateness of, 264–265

Demonstration (*Continued*)
communication patterns of,
269–270
disadvantages of, 266–267
evaluation of, 270
purpose of, 262–263
responsibilities of adult learners
in, 269
room and facilities layout for,
270
types of, 263
Demonstrator
responsibilities of, 267–269
Developing an agenda
for computer-enriched instruction, 325–327
Differences between forum, panel,
and symposium, 285–287
Discussion
cognitive and affective benefits
of, 188–192
emotional dimensions of, 197–
199
evaluation of, 200–201
facilitating, 195–199
method of, 187–204
preparing for, 192–195
Distance education, 345–346

Educational climate
physical environment of the,
16–17
psychological aspects of the,
17–18
Evaluation
of demonstrations, 270
of a discussion, 200–201
of a forum, 291
of internship, 341–343
of learning contracts, 157–158
of a lecture, 184–185
of mentorship, 221–222
of a panel, 296

of a symposium, 300
of the teaching and learning
transaction, 16
Expectations
positive expression of, 211

Facilitation
art of, 3–20
of computer-enriched instruction, 307–309
of discussions, 195–199
of simulations, 275–277
Formulating questions
for nominal group technique,
248
Forum
advantages of, 288–289
audience in a, 291
definition of, 284–285
evaluating a, 291
limitations of, 289
lines of communication, 289
moderator in, 289
resource persons in, 290
roles and responsibilities of involved personnel, 288–291
room and facilities layout, 291–
293
when used, 288
Future of adult education, 393–
408
critical issues concerning, 397–
401
forecasting the, 401–403
scenarios for, 403–405
social and demographic trends,
394–397

Generation of ideas
for nominal group technique,
248
Group dynamics
process of, 194–195

Group leader
   of nominal group technique pro-
      cess, 255
Guided group process
   in case studies, 243–244

Hypothetical thinking
   encouraging, 215

Implementing program plans, 8–16
Instructional applications of com-
      puters (IAC), 305
Instructional design and com-
      puters, 316–322
   computer laboratories, 320–321
   computers in the classroom,
      319–320
   organization of computer re-
      sources, 319
   resource centers, 321–322
Interns
   responsibilities and duties of,
      339–341
Internship, 329–344
   advantages of, 332–335
   audience for, 331–332
   definition of, 330–331
   evaluation of, 341–343
   limitations of, 335–338
   lines of communication, 338–
      339
   sponsoring agencies for, 331,
      333–335

Learning
   motives for, 26–28
Learning contracts
   advantages of, 138–148
   assumptions of, 137
   audience for, 137–138
   definition of, 134–137
   evaluation of, 157–158
   roles and duties of contract par-
      ties, 149–157

Lecture
   advantages and limitations of,
      164–166
   anatomy of, 182–184
   determining the use of, 162–
      164
   evaluating, 184–185
   patterns of communication,
      171–173
   responsibilities of teacher and
      learner, 169–171
   room size and seating arrange-
      ments, 173–176
   teacher qualifications, 166–169

Mentor
   challenges by the, 212–216
   gifts of the, 220–221
   keeping tradition, 217
   offering a map, 216
   providing a mirror, 218–219
   providing vision, 216
   suggesting new language, 218
   support of the, 209–212
Mentorship, 205–224
   aim of, 206–208
   evaluating the, 221–222
   limitations and problems of,
      219–220
Methodologies (see Adult learning
      methods)
Moderator of a forum, 289–290
Motivation
   levels of, 99–101
   planning, 101–107
   strategies to enhance, 107–117

Needs assessment, 8–10
Nominal group technique, 247–
      259
   adaptations of, 249–254
   advantages and limitations of,
      254–255
   application of, 258–259

Nominal group technique
(*Continued*)
defining, 247
development of, 248–249
discussing ideas in, 249
evaluation of, 256–257
group leader and learner responsibilities in, 255
satisfaction measures, 255–256

Organizing learning activities, 13–
14
Open admissions
for correspondence study, 356–
357

Panel
advantages of, 293
definition of, 285
duties of personnel, 294–295
evaluation of, 296
limitations of, 293
lines of communication for a,
293–294
personnel involved in a, 292–
293
room and facilities layout, 295–
296
when used, 292
Participatory learning
encouragement of, 18–20, 190–
192
Personalizing discussion topics,
193–194
Philosophy
benefits of, 44–48
identifying a, 39–77
matrix of adult education, 76–
77
personal values as related to,
42–43
relationship to education, 40–
42

Philosophy of Adult Education Inventory (PAEI), 59–77
instructions for scoring, 72
interpreting results, 53
practical application of the, 54–
55
scoring sheet for, 73
Practice
principles of effective, 5–7:
Practicum, 330
Principles of Adult Learning Scale
(PALS), 91–96
explanation of, 82–86
factors associated with, 84–86
Program planning
communication technology and,
386–389
components of, 8–16
context analysis of, 10–11
evaluation process in, 15–16
needs assessment of, 8–10
organizing learning activities,
13–14
setting educational objectives in,
11–13

Qualifications
for teachers using lecture, 166–
169
Questioning
art of, 119–128
characteristics of, 120–121
to foster enhanced learning,
279–280
levels of, 122–125
procedure in, 121–122
purpose of, 119–120

Responsibilities
learners in simulations, 277–
278
participants in a forum, 289–
291

Responsibilities (*Continued*)
  participants in a panel, 294–295
  participants in a symposium, 298–299
  teacher and learner in lecture method, 169–171
Round robin listing
  in nominal group technique, 248

Self-assessment, 222
Setting discussion themes, 192
Setting learning objectives, 11–13
Simulation, 272–280
  advantages of, 274
  appropriateness of, 272–274
  communication patterns in, 278
  disadvantages of, 274–275
  evaluation of, 278–280
  responsibilities of the facilitator in, 275–277
  room and facilities layout for, 278
Student assessment, 221
Supervisor
  for intern, 339–341
Symposium
  advantages of, 297
  definition of, 285
  duties of personnel, 298–299
  evaluation of, 300
  limitations of, 298
  lines of communication, 298
  personnel involved in a, 297

room and facilities layout, 299–300
  when used, 296–297
Synetics, 257–258

Teaching and learning
  providing challenges in, 18–20
  transaction skills of, 16–20
Teaching style
  collaborative, 80–82
  evaluation of, 86–89
  identification of, 79–96
  teacher-centered, 80–82
Theory-in-use, 195
Time Continuum Model of Motivation, 104–107

Variations of case studies, 241–244
Video technology, 369
Vision
  mentors provide, 216
Voice
  alternative, 213–214
  of mentoring relationship, 210
Voting on individual ideas
  in the nominal group technique, 249
  tabulating process, 249

Weighing human concerns
  in communication technology, 376
Work-study, 330

Please remember that this is a library book,
and that it belongs only temporarily to each
person who uses it. Be considerate. Do
not write in this, or any, library book.